Michael Murphy has produced a deeply researched and highly revealing history of the political career of one the most fascinating political figures in recent Northern Irish politics … Intelligent, critical and well written it will be essential reading of all those interested in the history of Northern Ireland and the Troubles.

– Henry Patterson, Professor of Politics, University of Ulster

Well written and well researched, *Gerry Fitt: A Political Chameleon* traces the lonely rise of Fitt from his humble beginnings, to his stormy period as founding leader of the SDLP, and his brave stand against the violence that racked Northern Ireland … He was prepared to stand alone, even as the ultimate republican contradiction in the House of Lords.

– T. Ryle Dwyer, author of *The Squad* and *Forty Years of Controversy*

Michael Murphy believes that Gerry Fitt's acceptance of a British peerage betrayed his proclaimed commitments to James Connolly, socialism and Irish nationalism. However, he pays tribute to Fitt's charisma, courage in confronting enemies, bringing Northern Ireland realities to the attention of British MPs, and participation in the struggle for Catholic civil liberties … *Gerry Fitt: a Political Chameleon* is an impressive portrait of a complicated man, one of the most important Irish figures in the second half of the twentieth-century. Based upon extensive research and thoughtful, perceptive analysis, Murphy's well-written book is a highly significant addition to Irish historiography.

– Lawrence J. McCaffrey
Professor of Irish History (Emeritus), Loyola University of Chicago

A carefully-researched book. Murphy throws fascinating new light on the enigma that was Gerry Fitt.

– Paul Bew Professor of Irish History, Queens University, Belfast

GERRY FITT

A POLITICAL CHAMELEON

MICHAEL A. MURPHY

MERCIER PRESS
WHAT YOU NEED TO READ

Mercier Press
Douglas Village, Cork
www.mercierpress.ie

Trade enquiries to CMD Distribution
55A Spruce Avenue, Stillorgan Industrial Park, Blackrock County Dublin

© Michael A. Murphy, 2007

ISBN 978 1 85635 531 5

10 9 8 7 6 5 4 3 2 1

A CIP record for this title is available from the British Library

Mercier Press receives financial assistance from the Arts Council/
An Chomhairle Ealaíon

Printed and bound by J.H Haynes & Co. Ltd, Sparkford

CONTENTS

For Linda and Ellen

PREFACE

Since the resumption of the Irish 'Troubles' at the end of the 1960s, historians, sociologists and political scientists have predictably been attracted to the Northern Ireland problem. As a consequence there has been a plethora of books, articles and other works produced on the subject. Nevertheless, although Gerry Fitt is often mentioned in general texts he has only recently been the subject of a biography. This is surprising in view of the extremely high profile he held in Irish politics for over twenty-five years. It would be no exaggeration to say that he was a major protagonist in this turbulent phase in the history of Anglo-Irish relations. The primary purpose of this book is to provide a comprehensive analysis of the political career of Gerry Fitt.

If the breaking of new ground was all, this work would be of sufficient interest. It is my contention, however, that Fitt's political career constitutes a seemingly remarkable *volte face* from republican socialist to peer of the realm; so the second purpose of this book is to analyse this intriguing paradox.

Given this work's biographical nature the approach adopted is largely chronological. It consists of eleven sections: an introduction, eight chapters, a conclusion and an epilogue. The introduction comprises, for the benefit of those unfamiliar with the historical background, a sketch of modern Irish history from the late eighteenth century until partition in 1920. In addition, it attempts to ascertain Fitt's political orientation, if not philosophy, by identifying important factors in his early life that helped shape his subsequent career.

Chapter 1 discusses the transformation in Catholic politics from the late 1950s to the mid-1960s, and Chapter 2 traces Fitt's political development during the same period. Fitt's activities during, and his relationship with, the Civil Rights Movement of the late 1960s form the substance of Chapter 3.

Chapter 4 investigates the formation of the Social Democratic and

Labour Party (SDLP), of which Fitt was a founder member and first leader. The basis of Chapter 5 is an analysis of the role played by Fitt and the SDLP in the attempts to find a solution to the political breakdown that took place in the mid-1970s. Fitt's increasing isolation in the SDLP and his subsequent disenchantment in the late 1970s provide the framework for Chapter 6. Chapter 7 traces the events that led to the loss of Fitt's Westminster seat (after seventeen years) to Gerry Adams, head of Sinn Féin, the political wing of the Provisional Irish Republican Army (PIRA) and Fitt's subsequent elevation to the House of Lords. The final chapter deals with Fitt's time in the Upper House. The conclusion and an epilogue follow.

Michael A. Murphy

ACKNOWLEDGEMENTS

This work has been a long time in the making, so long in fact that I would like to thank my father for his interest in the politics of Northern Ireland and his insistence that I watched the news when I was a child.

I should like to thank the following people at the Loyola University of Chicago: my main supervisor Professor Larry McCaffrey for supervising my doctoral thesis and identifying the political career of Gerry Fitt as an area absent from current research; Dr Janet Nolan and Dr Jo Hays for acting as readers. I would also like to acknowledge the support of Dr Joseph Gagliano during my time in Chicago.

I must also thank Paul Bew, Gordon Gillespie, Briege McGuckin, Brian O'Rourke, Brian Griffin and Michael O'Mahoney for reading my PhD manuscript and providing helpful and insightful comments.

My thanks to the staff of the many libraries and repositories that facilitated my research. In particular, I would like to thank Mike Maulstaid, formally of the Central Newspaper Library Belfast, where much of the research for this study took place.

Irish journalists, both past and present, deserve my thanks. Their dedication to their profession ensured I had a wealth of primary material on which to base my findings.

My mother deserves great credit for typing the original manuscript, a task made more arduous by my dreadful handwriting. I am sincerely grateful for this and all the support that she and my father lent during my long years as an 'eternal student'.

The conversion of the original manuscript into a book has been an enjoyable task made more so by the generosity of friends and family. I would like to thank Pat Walsh for his keen eye and keener intelligence. A special note of thanks goes to Ken Dawson for his scholarship, unstinting help and remarkable patience. Thanks also to Philip Orr who read the completed manuscript and offered valuable insight. I would also like to thank Caoimhe McErlane for retyping the text.

I am thankful to Anthony Coughlan, for permission to quote from the Greaves Diaries, and to Dr Roy Johnston for access to the hypertext selection from the Diaries which is referenced from his book *Century of Endeavour* (Tyndall/Lilliput 2006). My grateful thanks to Tim Pat Coogan for providing the foreword to this book and for his conviction that I had something valuable to say. The staff of Mercier Press must also be thanked for their affability as much as their professionalism.

Finally, and most importantly, I must express my gratitude to my wife and daughter for putting up with my idiosyncratic behaviour in the last few months of writing. I will always be grateful for their constant encouragement, patience and support. Linda and Ellen; thank you.

ABBREVIATIONS

CEA	Catholic Ex-Servicemen's Association
CDU	Campaign for Democracy in Ulster
CSJ	Campaign for Social Justice
CRF	Catholic Reaction Force
DUP	Democratic Unionist Party
EEC	European Economic Community
IIP	Irish Independence Party
INLA	Irish National Liberation Army
IRA	Irish Republican Army
IRB	Irish Republican Brotherhood
ITGWU	Irish Transport and General Workers Union
MP	Member of Parliament
NDP	National Democratic Party
NI	Northern Ireland
NICRA	Northern Ireland Civil Rights Association
NILP	Northern Ireland Labour Party
NIO	Northern Ireland Office
NPF	National Political Front
OIRA	Official Irish Republican Army
PD	People's Democracy
PIRA	Provisional Irish Republican Army
PR	Proportional Representation
PSNI	Police Service Northern Ireland
RTÉ	Radio Telefís Éireann
RUC	Royal Ulster Constabulary
SDLP	Social Democratic and Labour Party
TD	Member of the Dáil
UAC	Ulster Army Council
UDA	Ulster Defence Association
UDR	Ulster Defence Regiment

UFF	Ulster Freedom Fighters
UN	United Nations
UPA	Ulster Protestant Action
UPNI	Unionist Party of Northern Ireland
UUP	Ulster Unionist Party
UUUC	United Ulster Unionist Coalition
UVF	Ulster Volunteer Force
UWC	Ulster Workers' Council
VPP	Volunteer Political Party

FOREWORD

In Cardiff on the day that in 1973 Phil Bennett was jinking his way through the All Blacks for the Barbarians, in Belfast, Gerry Fitt was talking to me about barbarians of another sort as he showed me his revolver: 'It may not save my life, but it means that they won't get me into that car. They won't get me into that car.'

Beside him, his election agent, Paddy Wilson, a thin, pale faced, little man who somehow exuded an air of poverty, nodded approvingly: 'Aye, surely. Once they get you into that car, you're done.'

He then excused himself and went to answer a call of nature. Gerry smiled after him and commented: 'Paddy's having a hard time, they're after cutting off his phone.' More deadly cuts were to follow.

A few months later, on June 26th, they got Paddy into a car. He, and a female companion, Irene Andrews, had been kidnapped after leaving the Windsor Hotel. They were driven to an old quarry where Paddy was slowly stabbed to death. The woman was forced to lie face upwards so that she could see each incision, before she too was ritualistically murdered. The attackers were loyalist paramilitaries. Members of the tribe Gerry Fitt had armed himself against. But, by an irony of fate, he was to draw the gun, not against a loyalist death squad, but against an IRA-inspired mob of his own Catholic constituents, in what ultimately proved to be a vain attempt to prevent his house being set on fire.

By that time his need to be protected against his own people was such that he needed a police bodyguard going to mass. The 26,000 plus votes he had received in the 1966 election had dwindled to around a third of that in June 1983. Even Joe Hendron of the SDLP came in ahead of him. Another Gerry (Adams), took the seat and Margaret Thatcher had come to admire the fallen Fitt so much that a month later, on 21 July, she made him a life peer.

How did such a political metamorphosis befall a friendly, decent man who was once attacked in Paisley's *Protestant Telegraph* (April, 1967) as

'Fenian Fitt'? A man who in his time was a courageous campaigner for civil rights, a founder and leader of the SDLP, of whom, as Michael Murphy reminds us, it was once said: 'There was a crack in the Tory edifice when, like a breath of fresh air, Gerry Fitt came as a true Irish representative to Westminster.'

Murphy's important, critical, but fair minded biography explains in fascinating detail how the transformation occurred. Part of the reason was given to me by Fitt himself that day in Belfast back in 1973. He said: 'I came into politics to do things like getting a house for the little woman, get "the brew" (the dole) for someone out of work, you know, socialist things. I'm a socialist. There's terrible unemployment in my constituency. People appreciated what I done. They were coming up to me in the street thanking me. Now this ghost from the past's after turning up – Rep. Lab.'

Beside him Paddy Wilson again nodded approvingly in agreement. After Fitt had taken the West Belfast Westminister seat as a Republican Labour candidate in 1966, the troubles had broken out and the political pendulum had indeed swung from the Labour component of Fitt's support to that of the Republicans. Fitt was finding it hard to get his head around the changes.

Apart from being inclined towards socialism rather than nationalism there were other disturbing resonances from the past in his mind. A good deal of his early conditioning had occurred during his time as a seaman in the British merchant navy. During the Second World War he served on the Atlantic convoy route to Russia along which U-Boats took a deadly toll. A brother had been killed on active service with the British Army. Now, in his own back yard, rebels were attacking that army.

Such a background made him susceptible to that siren call which traditionally seduced Irish MPs – the tone of the House, the effect of the trappings and traditions of the House of Commons. There was also the effect of the traditional rivalry between Belfast and Derry which contributed to Fitt's antipathy towards John Hume, whom he described as: '… an inflexible fanatic' who saw everything in terms of Derry and could not take a wider view.

Both men had formidable egos. Neither troubled themselves unduly with party organisation. But, if asked in confidence, for an evaluation of the SDLP which they co-founded, either could well have replied: 'The Party – c'est moi!'

The difference was that John Hume was a figure of international calibre, a genuine statesman. A fact calculated to increase rather than diminish Fitt's envy.

There were sporadic Republican attacks on Hume's home also, but respect for him was so widespread that there was never the slightest possibility of his being driven out of Ireland.

However the bitterness surrounding Fitt's later political life has tended to air brush from the record the fact that Fitt did achieve something which Hume never did. He brought down a British government. Appalled at Callaghan's increasing of the Unionist representation at Westminster in a vain attempt to stay in power, Fitt withheld his crucial casting vote in the censure motion which de-throned Labour in 1979 and so brought Margaret Thatcher to power.

But two years later, during a debate on the hunger strike he made an infamous speech, worthy of Thatcher herself, in which he urged that no concessions should be made to the hunger strikers. In a very real sense that speech helped to give Gerry Adams his seat. Only his Protestant constituents voted for Fitt

The rejected man's rage and chagrin at all shades of opinion within his constituency was reflected subsequently in the monumentally infelicitous comment he made to the Protestant *Belfast News Letter*. He said he felt 'like a nigger in Alabama who had been voted in by the Klu Klux Klan.'

And so fate decreed that Gerry Fitt, from West Belfast, ended his days signing the attendance book in the House of Lords, like those former Belfast constituents for whom he once secured the dole. It is a tale for whose telling we are indebted to Michael Murphy.

Tim Pat Coogan

INTRODUCTION

HISTORICAL BACKGROUND

In the early part of his political career Gerry Fitt claimed to be a republican. But defining the concept of republicanism is not straightforward in the Irish context. It can mean militant nationalism, often of the kind that espouses physical force. It can more generally mean an opposition to monarchy – in this case the British crown. It has usually been associated with the politics of Irish Catholics, although it is generally agreed that it originated with the largely Ulster Presbyterian United Irishmen of the late eighteenth century.

In 1791, a radical organisation called the Society of United Irishmen was founded in Belfast and Dublin. Led by Anglicans and Presbyterians and inspired by events in America and France, the United Irishmen evolved into a secretive revolutionary group intent on establishing an Irish Republic.[1]

Alarmed by revolutionary ideology in Ireland and the apparent threat of an armed uprising, the authorities in Ireland (the lord lieutenant, his chief secretary and a largely compliant ascendancy parliament in Dublin) imposed martial law and brought in severe anti-insurgency measures across the Irish countryside. Despite this repressive policy, or perhaps because of it, in May 1798 the United Irishmen attempted an insurrection, in conjunction with revolutionary France. This rebellion was designed to subvert British rule in Ireland and to assert Irish national independence. However, French assistance was minimal and marginal, failing to live up to its billing because of the priorities of its military command in other parts of Europe.

By 1798 the epicentre of United Irish organisation had clearly moved from the Presbyterian north, where a campaign of military repression had been waged during 1797. As a consequence the rising was fragmented, consisting of three somewhat disparate and largely unconnected events in different places. In Wexford, a largely Catholic peasant rising was initially successful but was ultimately crushed at Vinegar Hill on 21 June. In Ulster the rebels, who were mainly if not exclusively Presbyterian, were also defeated at the battles of Antrim and Ballynahinch, both also in June. In August a French invasion force under the command of Jean Joseph Humbert landed in the west and gathered support from the Gaelic Irish before being defeated by British forces and Irish loyalists at the Battle of Ballinamuck.

Ironically, the most significant result of the rebellion was the Act of Union of 1800, which directly linked Ireland to the British parliament at Westminster. Britain and Ireland became a single kingdom. The old Irish parliament of the ascendancy class was abolished and all laws for Ireland were to be made by Westminster. Ireland was to be represented in the United Kingdom by 100 MPs, and free trade, that is, the ability to exercise autonomy over commercial affairs, was also affirmed more tangibly than had been the case in 1779.

The amalgamation, which was largely achieved by bribery, provoked hostility and led to opposition movements, including Robert Emmet's attempted rebellion in 1803, which was a poor sequel to the 1798 rising. The hope that the capture of Dublin would result in spontaneous uprisings throughout the country was wildly optimistic, even if the first objective had been achieved. Emmet and other leading figures were arrested and later executed.

The most significant result of the Act of Union was its political effect on the two main communities in Ireland. The Ulster Protestants, the very people who had produced the first republicans, became attached to the union and saw their interests as being bound up with it. They became largely unionist and monarchist in their political orientation. Irish Catholics, who had been cautious and conservative during much of the eighteenth century, adopted a Catholic nationalist outlook associated with the politics and campaigns of Daniel O'Connell.

Nineteenth-century opposition to the union came in two forms, both arising from Catholic nationalism. The political revolutionaries, such as the Young Irelanders of 1848 and the Fenians of the 1860s, championed the use of physical force to overthrow British rule in Ireland. The parliamentary constitutionalists sought repeal of the Act of Union and Home Rule for Ireland through non-violent methods. Foremost among these were Daniel O'Connell in the 1830s and 1840s, Isaac Butt in the 1870s and Charles Stewart Parnell in the 1880s.

The Young Irelanders were intellectuals who were influenced by the men of 1798 and fired by the revolutions in France, Italy and Germany in 1848. They inspired later nationalists by providing a rich literature of story and song in their newspaper the *Nation*. They were led by William Smith O'Brien. Without weapons and with few followers their rising was an unmitigated disaster, contemptuously referred to as 'the cabbage patch rebellion'. Death sentences against the leaders were commuted and instead they were transported to penal colonies in Australia.

The Fenians fared no better in 1867. Despite being strong in Irish America (primarily as a consequence of the famine diaspora), the Fenian rebellion in Ireland was little more than a series of isolated incidents and had little short-term impact.

Constitutional nationalism was marginally more successful in the nineteenth century. O'Connell won a victory for Irish nationalism by forcing the government to pass the Catholic Emancipation Act in 1829, but failed in his ultimate aim of the repeal of the Act of Union. In 1873 Isaac Butt founded the Irish Home Rule League, which later spawned the Irish Parliamentary Party. The party proposed that Ireland should have its own parliament for domestic matters while remaining an integral part of the United Kingdom of Britain and Ireland. It was not the case that many constitutionalists desired Irish government any less than militant nationalists. It was more that they lowered their sights, and became more realistic in their aspirations, as British power in the world grew and Irish independence appeared less and less likely to happen. As the century came to an end, those who favoured physical force turned to agitational campaigns, based on land reform, waged by men like Michael Davitt and O'Brien.

Towards the end of the nineteenth century, constitutional nationalism grew in strength and gained the support of most of the Liberal Party and its Prime Minister Gladstone, primarily because of the leadership of Charles Stewart Parnell. The increasingly urgent demand for the re-establishment of an Irish parliament to control Irish affairs became difficult for the British to ignore because of the success of the 'New Departure', a policy that linked the land and national questions. The first Home Rule Bill in 1886 was defeated by a combination of Unionist and Conservative Party opposition and indeed some Liberal Unionists.

In 1893 Gladstone introduced the Second Home Rule Bill. Although he succeeded in winning a majority for the measure in the House of

Commons it was overwhelmingly defeated in the Conservative-dominated House of Lords.

The 'Irish Question' was complicated by the attitude of the descendants of Protestant settlers concentrated in the north-east of the province of Ulster. Although relieved by the protection they were given by the House of Lords, they viewed the development of the Home Rule movement anxiously. Unlike the rest of Ireland, Ulster had benefited from the union with Britain. This was because in economic terms eastern Ulster was largely industrial whereas the rest of Ireland was predominantly agricultural. The six counties of Antrim, Armagh, Derry, Down, Fermanagh and Tyrone contained almost half the total industrial workers in Ireland. Shipbuilding, engineering and the linen industry brought prosperity and led the north-east of Ireland to develop differently, politically and socially, from the rest of the island.

In an effort to maintain their relative prosperity, Ulster's Protestant unionists were determined to resist any move towards Home Rule. They also believed that the Irish Catholic majority was incapable of producing good government and they equated Home Rule with Rome Rule. Most significantly, the Conservative Party supported the Irish Unionists in their opposition to Home Rule.

The Liberal Party had been in opposition for almost the entire two decades before 1905. During this period the Tories had attempted to 'kill Home Rule with kindness', enacting some of the most important reforms in Ireland during this time, including the Land Act of 1903. But the demand for Home Rule remained. The Irish Parliamentary Party had suffered a disastrous split at the time of Parnell's scandalous relationship with Katharine O'Shea, but John Redmond had reunited it during Irish opposition to the Boer War in 1900.

When the Liberals won a landslide victory in 1906 things looked promising. But the Liberal Party was now lukewarm on Home Rule and some party members in leading positions were hostile to the old Gladstonian pledges to Ireland. In 1907 the Liberals introduced an Irish Councils Bill – a kind of local government bill. The Irish rejected this and demanded the whole Home Rule Bill or nothing. But during the first Liberal government of 1905–10 no such legislation was forthcoming.

Redmond's fortunes changed when the House of Lords obstructed Lloyd George's budget of 1909. Asquith needed Redmond's support to reform the Lords and pass the budget. Redmond's price was a Home Rule Bill, something that appeared likely given the unprecedented parliamentary arithmetic of December 1910. A Third Home Rule Bill emerged when John Redmond's Irish Party held the balance of power at Westminster: the second general election of that year left the Liberal Party needing the support of the Irish Parliamentary Party to form a government. The Parliament Act of 1911 ensured that the House of Lords could only delay by two years bills passed in the House of Commons. In short, any future Home Rule bill for Ireland would ultimately become law, if parliamentary procedure was allowed to take its course. The Third Home Rule Bill was introduced into the Commons in April 1912. At last, it seemed, the Dublin parliament would be restored. However, the unionists had two years to resist the bill's implementation. Bolstered by Bonar Law and the Conservative Party, as well as mutinous British army officers stationed at the Curragh, they used the time to organise a resistance campaign against the government.

In September 1912, 400,000 Ulster Protestants, under Edward Carson, signed the Solemn League and Covenant, pledging to use all means necessary to defeat Home Rule. In 1913 the Ulster Volunteer Force (UVF) was formed and 100,000 volunteers threatened to revolt against the Home Rule proposal and to establish a provisional government in 'Protestant Ulster' if Ireland were given its own legislature.

In 1914 the UVF landed 25,000 rifles and two and a half million rounds of ammunition at Larne in County Antrim. Asquith, paralysed by the party conflict over Home Rule in Britain, did little to prevent this and adopted the policy of 'wait and see', as the situation drifted towards civil conflict.

In contrast to unionist cohesion, nationalists were divided in their response. Occasionally the constitutional and revolutionary strands had come together, but they were more often separate and antagonistic. The new leader of the Irish Parliamentary Party, John Redmond, had witnessed the formation of a large army of Irish Volunteers (inspired, ironically, by the creation of the UVF) pledged to defend a Home Rule Act, and he feared that widespread violence might result from the existence of two private armies. To prevent such an outcome Redmond took command of the Irish Volunteers. When Asquith proposed that the Ulster counties be allowed to opt out of the Irish parliament for six years, Redmond agreed, but he insisted on plebiscites in each of the counties and in Derry. Carson, however, rejected the compromise. As an Irish Unionist, he wanted all of Ireland to remain under Westminster's control.

By 1914 confrontation seemed inevitable and was only averted by British participation in the European war that broke out in August 1914. This changed the situation utterly. Redmond had great faith in the British parliament. He was convinced that if Irishmen helped Britain's war effort the Liberal government would honour its commitment to Home Rule. Asquith put the bill on the statute book but suspended its operation until after the war. In this way he ensured both nationalist and unionist recruitment to the British army. Redmond responded in a speech in his Woodenbridge constituency by urging Irish Volunteers to join the British army. Eighty thousand heeded his call and, at first, proportionately more Belfast Catholics than Protestants joined up. But his appeal led to a split in the Irish Volunteers: those who supported Redmond became known as the National Volunteers; those who opposed any involvement in the war kept the name Irish Volunteers.

By this time Redmond saw British imperialism and Irish nationalism as complementary. An early British victory in the war, armed Irish Nationalists in the empire's military forces and a grateful Liberal government would all enhance the prospects for Home Rule. But the war was not over by Christmas, nor even by 1915, as the Redmondites had calculated, and things began to unravel.

Revolutionary republicans took a very different view of events in Europe. Inspired by the Gaelic Revival, and taking a different view from Redmond's of Henry Grattan's statement during the American War of Independence in the eighteenth century – 'England's difficulty is Ireland's opportunity' – they believed the time for action had arrived.

In April 1916 the socialist leader James Connolly allied himself and his Irish Citizen Army with the revolutionary nationalists led by Patrick Pearse. Together they organised the Easter rebellion and signed the proclamation establishing an Irish republic. The rising was poorly planned and collapsed after six days. At 2.30 p.m. on Saturday 29 April, Pearse and Connolly signed an unconditional surrender. The Irish people were mainly apathetic and many in Dublin were hostile towards the rebels, but attitudes changed radically when Britain decided to execute the leaders. Their deaths marked a watershed in Irish history and changed the political situation dramatically.

Redmond's brand of parliamentary gradualism had been damaged beyond repair by a chain of events that began with the failure to secure Home Rule, the seeming acceptance of partition by the party, and the unionist rise to power in the unelected coalition government of 1915. As Home Rule looked a 'beaten docket', the rising and the subsequent executions impacted on the litany of failure with spectacular results during 1917–18.

Another significant factor was British war propaganda, which called for volunteers in Ireland on the basis of a 'war for the rights of small nations'. How could Britain fight for the small nations of Europe when ignoring the rights of the small nation nearest to it and under its own control?

Sinn Féin, founded in 1905, came to be seen as the party of the rebels, even though it had had little to do with the rising (which had been organised by the Irish Republican Brotherhood (IRB)). The party became the voice of mass republicanism in the years following the rising and was successful in all four by-elections held in 1917.

Limited self-government was no longer enough for the radicalised majority in Irish society, and they began to support candidates who demanded an independent republic. When John Redmond died in March 1918 the constitutional nationalism of the previous few years quickly followed him to the grave.

After a spectacular victory in the general election of 1918 (outside Ulster), Sinn Féin decided to ignore the British parliament and set up a national assembly in Ireland. Sinn Féin formed Dáil Éireann in January 1919 and declared itself the legitimate governing body of Ireland. This declaration of secession from the United Kingdom resulted in the Anglo-Irish War. The Westminster government decided to ignore the democratic verdict of 1918 and moved to close down Dáil Éireann using military force.

The Sinn Féin government used its own volunteer army, now called the Irish Republican Army (IRA), in a guerrilla campaign to make imperial rule impossible and ultimately to force the British authorities out of Ireland. The War of Independence had begun.

Despite British military power and the use of a quasi-military force, the Black and Tans, Britain could not destroy the Republican will to continue fighting. As the war went on, Britain suffered internationally more and more, which undermined its attempts to take the moral high ground in post-war Europe. Britain was also in debt to America for large war loans, and the Irish lobby obstructed a naval treaty that Britain badly needed to save money.

In an attempt to end the conflict, Britain proposed the Government of Ireland Act (1920). This offered limited Home Rule for Ireland with two separate parliaments in Belfast and Dublin. The unionists of the north-east now reluctantly agreed to division but opted for only six of the nine Ulster counties, believing this would be the largest area they could control without fear of Catholics becoming a majority.

The Ulster Unionists under James Craig were persuaded, against Carson's judgement, that their own devolved administration would act as a bulwark to any further attempt by the British government to seek to re-unite the island of Ireland. Partition, coupled with the relationship of the new state with the United Kingdom, was totally unacceptable to Sinn Féin, and the Anglo-Irish war continued.

In 1921 elections took place for both the new Home Rule parliaments. In the south, Sinn Féin used the election as a referendum on national independence and won 124 of the 128 seats, while in the north-east the Unionists won forty of the fifty-two seats. After the elections, the British again tried to end the conflict. They offered a new treaty, which would give the south a kind of dominion status within the empire and a larger degree of self-government than Home Rule. However, partition was still a thorny problem. Britain declared that the 1920 Act was non-negotiable, but offered a boundary commission to determine the final borders between north and south.

The southern Irish delegation to the talks with the British government reluctantly accepted the treaty on behalf of the new state. Michael Collins knew he had signed at the point of a gun when Lloyd George threatened 'immediate and terrible war' if their signatures were not forthcoming, but he reasoned that the treaty provided the 'freedom to achieve freedom' in time. On the delegation's return, however, a bloody civil war broke out ostensibly because of the failure to secure an independent Irish republic. Those in favour of the treaty eventually won in 1923.

Partition had become a reality. In the north the unionists took control, knowing that within their border was a substantial and resentful Catholic minority deprived of their right to be part of an overall majority in a larger state. The south, on the other hand, developed into a largely homogeneous Catholic state that finally achieved the substance of a republic during the period 1937–45 and the status of a republic in 1948.

GERRY FITT: FORMATIVE INFLUENCES

Gerry Fitt was a Catholic raised in the working-class Dock area of Belfast. That seemingly innocuous sentence condenses information that is extremely significant and that needs to be appreciated in order to gain a full understanding of Fitt's political career. I will deal with each element in turn.

First, as a Catholic Fitt was a member of a permanent minority in Northern Ireland, which was governed by the unionist majority. (Fitt was born in 1926, six years after partition.) Because northern Catholics wanted to be part of the developing Irish nation in a new state comprising the whole island, Catholics were regarded by many unionists as subversive, a 'fifth column' intent on undermining the link with Britain. This suspicion was regularly quoted to justify discriminatory practices in places of work (and other social areas) that were, by and large, staffed and owned by members of the Protestant community. In other words, major areas of employment such as heavy industry (shipbuilding, for example) and administration were closed to Catholics, who were therefore largely limited to unskilled or temporary work. As a result Catholic emigration levels were higher than those of the Protestant community.

Second, coming from the working-class would not enhance a Catholic's life choices. Before the creation of the UK welfare state in the late 1940s, which was to prove so influential in the development of nationalist politics (and will be considered in later chapters), access to the normal means of self-improvement – education – was limited to the better off. The cost of secondary education, the vehicle of social mobility, would have been too great a burden for most families.

Finally, Belfast was a predominantly Protestant city. The Protestant community outnumbered the Catholic by about three to one. The Marquis of Donegall, the landowner who created Belfast, had built on land where no earlier settlement existed, in contrast to the province's second city of Londonderry. The Protestant inhabitants initially tolerated, even welcomed Catholics, even making donations of land and money to build the first Catholic churches. However, successive waves of Catholic migrants to the city in search of employment, together with the revival of both the Catholic and Protestant churches from the mid-nineteenth century, led to worsening relations between the two communities. Conflict often led to sectarian riots, which increased in savagery and frequency throughout the rest of the century.[2]

Crucially, from about 1860, Protestant migration to the city to take up jobs in its growing industrial base began to overtake Catholic migration. Belfast was secured as a Protestant city, built and largely owned by Protestants, run by unionists, with Catholics in the position of an economic migrant community – despite its location in a Catholic-dominated island. As a result, Catholics in Belfast suffered from feelings of insecurity and a sense that they did not belong. In contrast, Catholics in Derry, by virtue of their growing numerical superiority and history, were relatively confident of their position.

This situation has, however, changed in recent years, and the growing confidence within the Catholic community is symbolised by the election of nationalist and republican mayors in Belfast. The reasons for this include: demographic changes favouring Catholic population growth; educational success; the removal of discriminatory practices in commerce and the public sector brought about by direct rule; the decline of the powerful and traditionally Protestant heavy industries and the withdrawal of the Protestant middle-classes from politics and civil society.

As we shall see, Fitt's early years were by no means untypical of his class, generation and community, but his interest in politics ensured that Fitt's life would be somewhat more distinctive than most.

Fitt was the adopted son of George and Mary Ann Fitt who resided in the Dock area of north Belfast.[3] His stepfather died when he was eight years old, leaving his adoptive mother with six children. His was not the only working-class household in Belfast to endure poverty, but the death of a breadwinner could only have made life more difficult at a time when there was no welfare state to fall back on. Fitt left St Patrick's Christian Brothers School in 1940 at the age of fourteen. Although it was felt that he had the ability to continue his schooling, education was considered a luxury rather than a right and he, like most working-class males, sought paid employment.

He worked at various jobs between the ages of fourteen and fifteen, including messenger boy, and soap boy in a barber's shop in Donegall Street. At the age of fifteen, two years earlier than legally permissible, he joined the merchant navy as a stoker. When his deception was detected he was given the position of cabin boy. He remained at sea until 1952, and during the war saw service in the North and Baltic Seas in ships conveying goods to Russia. This was not work for the faint-hearted.

The involvement of the Fitt family in the British military (his brother George died in the uniform of the Irish Guards in Normandy in 1944) is not as incongruous as it may initially appear.

Republicanism has not always flourished in West Belfast. Republicans, in the interests of maintaining the IRA campaign over three decades, have been keen to stress the republican history of West Belfast to the exclusion of its other history. In the first part of the century it was dominated by Joe Devlin, chief lieutenant to John Redmond, who held on to his West Belfast seat when republicans swept all before them in 1918. Devlin combined social agitation with Redmondite 'constitutional' nationalism. West Belfast retained this character (although ironically the Nationalist Party became an irrelevance in the city) and this is reflected in the fact that many West Belfast families, even those inclined to republicanism, had relations serving in the British army and navy. (Danny Morrison, a former editor of *An Phoblacht/Republican News*, had a granduncle in the British army, for example.) Further evidence of this trend was the existence of the Catholic Ex-Servicemen's Association (CEA), an organisation set up in 1971 following the introduction of internment, which had the stated aim of 'protecting' Catholic areas. Former members of the British army had been prominent in defending nationalist areas during 1969–70 and some had gone on to join the IRA. CEA claimed a membership of 8,000 in 1972.

The Fitt family was not from the west of the city – the hub of Belfast Catholic politics is West Belfast – but it is reasonable to assume that they were influenced by the same tradition and had the same values, and that they did not, like the Redmondites before them, see membership of the British armed forces as incompatible with nationalist ideals.

Fitt met his wife Ann, a native of Castlederg, County Tyrone, at Hyde Park tube station during a visit to London, where she was working as a telephone operator at a Conservative club. In 1947 the Fitts moved to Belfast.

Having left the merchant navy in 1952 Fitt held a series of jobs. He worked in the gasworks and the labour exchange, and as an insurance agent, encyclopaedia salesman and clerk. However, much of his time was taken up with politics. In view of his subsequent political career, it seems Fitt was imbued with the same resentment against the unionist state as his co-religionists. While at sea, Fitt had become a disciple of the Irish

Marxist James Connolly, who had been so instrumental in organising the 1916 rebellion. Connolly argued that the subjection of the Irish working-classes was a result of the unresolved national question. He saw British domination of Ireland as a continuation of neo-colonialism and an obstruction to the establishment of politics based on class loyalties. Fitt maintained that the writings of Connolly were his political inspiration. His own poverty and the poverty he witnessed when he was at sea prompted his initial interest in socialism.[4] Fitt never put his political thoughts on paper and it would be reasonable to assume that his allegiance was more emotional than intellectual.

While on leave from the merchant navy in 1951, Fitt took part in his first election campaign. His goal, like Connolly's, was to unite the Catholic and Protestant working-classes. He supported Jack Beattie, a Presbyterian, who stood on an Irish Labour ticket and was thus a socialist and opposed to partition. Beattie won the Westminster West Belfast seat from the unionists by twenty-five votes after five recounts.

The drama of the close Beattie victory ensured that Fitt's concern with politics became a commitment rather than an interest. Politics became his obsession. In 1956 he stood as an Independent Irish Labour candidate in a Belfast Corporation (the local government) by-election for the Falls Ward but was defeated by Paddy Devlin, a future political colleague but then a member of the Irish Labour Party. Two years later he ran unsuccessfully for the Northern Ireland parliament. Despite these reverses Fitt's political profile was high enough for him to be elected in his second attempt to Belfast Corporation in 1958. So began his uninterrupted twenty-five years of electoral success.

Catholic Politics in Transition

> It is often argued that we never accepted the state. That is true for most
> of us. But we had little choice. We were the unfortunate baggage of a par-
> titionist arrangement. We were the human flotsam floating about in the
> political limbo of an unfinished struggle.[1]

This is Sinn Féin president Gerry Adams' summary of the plight of the
Catholic/nationalist population after partition in 1920. The historians
Lord Longford and Ann McHardy believed that the workings of the
Northern Ireland state contained 'serious genetic defects', the worst
being that a substantial Catholic/nationalist minority was deprived of its
declared right to be part of an overall majority in a larger state.[2]

Ironically, as a result of their opposition to Home Rule and the British
desire (after the Home Rule conflict between Tories and Liberals) to
distance Northern Ireland affairs from Westminster, unionists found
themselves with their own Home Rule of sorts. The first years of the
new state were extremely violent. Between July 1920 and July 1922, 257
Catholics and 157 Protestants were killed in Belfast. It is hardly surprising
that divisions widened.

In order to defend the northern state from what unionists saw as the
enemy within, there was discrimination in housing, the allocation of votes,
policing, employment and local government. There were two main results
of this discrimination. First, Protestants of all denominations and classes
came together in a pan-class alliance; second, the Catholic population
– who were already unwilling to accept the legitimacy of the state and its
institutions – became more alienated.

The northern parliament, lodged after 1932 at the newly built Parliament Buildings, was totally dominated by the Unionist Party. Nationalist resentment was further fuelled by security measures designed to protect the state: the establishment of an exclusively Protestant Ulster Special Constabulary (the B Specials), drawn largely from Carson's UVF; and the Special Powers Act, which allowed for civil liberties to be suspended in so-called emergency situations. Although discrimination was often intentional, the unco-operative attitude of the subdued Catholic minority made it even worse. Michael Farrell, in his Marxist critique of the history of Northern Ireland, *The Orange State*, describes the consequences as he saw them:

> [Nationalists] were treated with contempt and forced into abstentionism, and the frustration of the minority eventually erupted into an abortive campaign by the IRA. This was the first of several cycles of parliamentary agitation followed by rebuff and abstentionism, then by a military campaign. All the strategies proving equally unsuccessful and only confirming the total alienation of the minority from the state.[3]

This pattern continued until the late 1950s, when there was evidence of a change of attitude. Catholic politics was in transition on both sides of the border. There were signs that Catholics were willing to participate in the workings of the Northern Ireland state: they had evidently recognised the futility of armed struggle.

The failure of the IRA border campaign of 1956–62 had revealed the pointlessness of physical force nationalism. This campaign was a largely southern effort in which northern Catholics did not become involved – partly because of the better material conditions of the northern population, with its attachment to Westminster and its welfare state; and partly because of improvements in education (including more grammar school places for children from both communities).

These developments helped to thaw the relations between north and south, and the softening of attitudes became evident by the mid-1960s. Perhaps the most positive sign was the fact that in 1965 Seán Lemass, prime minister of the Republic, and his northern counterpart Terence O'Neill enjoyed a convivial summit in Belfast.

There were other constructive developments. Goaded into a co-operative and conciliatory position by Lemass, the Nationalist Party accepted the role of official opposition at Stormont. The emergence of new groups such as National Unity, the National Democratic Party (NDP) and the Campaign for Social Justice (CSJ) reflected an aspiration to improve the lot of northern Catholics with minimal reference to the border.

In Britain, the newly established Campaign for Democracy in Ulster (CDU) reflected a growing awareness of and sympathy for the plight of Catholics in Northern Ireland. In short, in the mid-1960s the future appeared to offer less emphasis on partition and more on social reform in Northern Ireland. The Dublin-based current affairs publication *Hibernia* said in November 1965:

> The little, bitter, closed in world of Ulster is everywhere being penetrated by the greater problems of human progress and human survival. The people are less satisfied in seeing themselves as either outposts of the British Empire or defenders of the ideal world. They desire for their children prosperity, peace and progress. They want an ending to the tyranny of upholding ancient old quarrels.[4]

As Paul Bew and Henry Patterson noted, events '… seemed to indicate that the Irish question as traditionally posed was no longer pertinent'.[5]

Against this backdrop Gerry Fitt, the Catholic republican socialist, was elected to Westminster. To put his election into context and to gain a greater understanding of Catholic politics in the period, the rest of the chapter will be devoted to analysing the developments touched on above.

THE IRA BORDER CAMPAIGN 1956 – 62

Irish nationalism has never accepted the partition arrangement of 1920. The difference between constitutional nationalism and militant republicanism has been their different responses to this problem. Even before partition republicans saw it as the right, indeed duty, of Irish people to resist British rule in Ireland, by force if necessary. From the time of the Act of Union of 1800 Irish history has been punctuated by military insurrections designed to break this union and to establish an independent state. After the creation of Northern Ireland, the political history of the state was also characterised by modestly supported, sporadic military campaigns. J. Bowyer Bell explains why this physical force reaction has endured:

For a few, generation after generation, what Pearse and Connolly began in the name of Tone on April 24, 1916, is an unfinished legacy – but a clearly defined responsibility. As long as the British border cuts across the Republic of 1916, as long as Ireland and its people are neither free of exploitation nor Gaelic in tongue and heart, then men will turn to the task as defined by Tone, no matter how bleak the prospects: to do less would be to betray the past and deny the future.[6]

One commitment to this 'clearly defined responsibility' began with the IRA's adoption of Seán Cronin's 'Operation Harvest'. Cronin's plan to bring the six-county state to an end was implemented in December 1956.[7] The strategy involved a guerrilla campaign that would bring about the wholesale destruction of political, administrative and economic centres. This would paralyse the infrastructure of the state and destroy it. The strategy contained one major contradiction: Belfast, which was the political, administrative and economic centre, was not attacked because of the fear of reprisals against the unprotected nationalist enclaves in the city.[8] This incongruity was one of the major inadequacies of the campaign, which ultimately led to its failure in 1962.

Nevertheless, the taking up of arms once again aroused republican sentiment in the Irish Republic. In the elections to the Dáil in 1957, Sinn Féin candidates polled 66,000 votes and four of them gained parliamentary seats.[9] Seán South's funeral was one of the biggest ever seen in Ireland. (He was the leader of an IRA military column who was fatally wounded during an attempt to storm an RUC barracks in Fermanagh on New Year's Day 1957.) This republicanism, however, was short-lived. Ineffective military strategy was compounded by a general lack of discipline in the IRA.

However, there were a number of fatalities in border areas and the campaign was significant enough for the governments of both Belfast and Dublin to take harsh security measures. The Republic re-introduced internment, a policy that had always been a major element of Stormont's weaponry, in 1957. There were some spectacular exploits at the beginning of 1958, but internment severely weakened the IRA. Towards the end of 1958, when 187 men were interned south of the border, the IRA did not have enough personnel to be effective, and the command structure lost any cohesion it had established.[10]

The performance of the political wing reflected the decline of IRA fortunes. In the 1959 Northern Ireland Westminster elections the Nationalist

Party, in what had become standard policy, stood aside so as not to split the Catholic vote. Sinn Féin contested all twelve seats but managed to poll only 73,415 votes.[11] This was less than half the number they had received in the 1955 election; clear evidence of their declining support.

The pattern of Sinn Féin decline was repeated in the Republic. In the 1961 Dáil election the number of votes cast were also less than half received previously and no republicans were elected. On both sides of the border popular support for the campaign had been greatly reduced. Tim Pat Coogan, in his sympathetic history of the IRA, explains the attitudes to which that fall could be attributed:

> In the North the nationalists refer to the campaign today as 'the incidents' because this is in fact what it was, a series of incidents along the border, impinging very little on Belfast and annoying rather than terrifying the Northern administration ... But once it became obvious that the campaign could have no effect on the permanency of the Northern regime public interest diminished.

As regards the sentiment in the south, Coogan concludes:

> At no time did this interest ever betoken any hostility to England or indeed towards the North. Most people in the Republic were rather puzzled by the whole thing and were inclined to write the whole thing off as the 'IRA at it again', without any clear appreciation of why it should have been at it again.[12]

The IRA had become increasingly isolated. The organisation finally ended the struggle in February 1962. Its statement read:

> The decision to end the resistance campaign had been taken in view of the general situation. Foremost among the factors motivating this course of action has been the attitude of the general public whose minds have been deliberately distracted from the supreme issue facing the Irish people – the unity and freedom of Ireland.[13]

The declaration contained no self-criticism, no recognition of inadequte strategy. Instead, the IRA blamed the people. The campaign had resulted in fifteen deaths, damage estimated at a million pounds, and increased security in the six counties at an estimated cost of ten million pounds.[14]

In retrospect, it is clear that the IRA in the late 1950s and early 1960s did not really reflect the material desires of nationalists. In the north, the *Irish News* (a daily newspaper read mostly by Catholics) said the physical force tradition was no longer enough: 'Unionists in commenting on the IRA decision to abandon their campaign of violence against the north describe it as an admission of defeat. It is forgotten that the IRA were from the start doomed to defeat without the support of the Irish people and that they did not receive'.[15]

Elsewhere, the physical force tradition was seen as no more than a historical relic. In the United States the *New York Times* argued:

> Partition is resented but the present generation knows that if partition is ever to be ended it must be by peaceful arrangements. The few young thugs who make up the tiny remnant that now lays down its arms used a grand and famous name for their organisation, but the Irish Republican Army belongs to history, and it belongs to better men in times that are gone. So does the Sinn Féin. Let us put a wreath of roses on their grave and move on.[16]

Above all, the failure of the border campaign showed that political and social conditions in Northern Ireland would not be conducive to creating a mass movement that would strive for a united Ireland through physical force. The collapse of this campaign represented a crisis for militant physical force republicanism and led to the re-emergence of social republicanism. A more grass-roots movement replaced the elitism of revolutionary republicanism. Policy was transformed from refusing to recognise the *status quo* to an involvement in left-wing politics, combined with a resolve to bring down the system from within. Quintessential physical force republicanism was apparently a thing of the past. *New Nation* magazine argued in 1964:

> As nationalists our first concern is with all those who wished to see the ultimate unity of Ireland brought about by peaceful means. In this statement we do not wish to deny that there have been times when Irishmen were justified in using other means and that such times may come again, but we do maintain that at the present time there is no justification whatever for violence.[17]

Apart from the odd symbolic gesture of defiance, the most spectacular being the destruction of Nelson's Pillar in Dublin on 7 March 1966, revolutionary republicanism in the mid-1960s kept a very low profile. In the words of J. Bowyer Bell:

> Physical force as a means to break the connection with Britain had never seemed more irrelevant. Ireland in the sixties seemed more concerned with the fruits of the good life than the bootless ambitions of the romantic past. All the wild dreams were dead and gone; the roads were clogged with traffic and the pubs with whiskey drinkers.[18]

The border campaign was the last throw of the dice by doctrinaire republicans south of the border against the north. These hard-line republicans would reappear in 1969 as guiding hands for the new republicanism of the Provisional Irish Republican Army (PIRA). But this new republicanism's roots would come from the conditions of life of the northern Catholic working-class rather than the Second Dáil. And this fact would have great implications for the course of events during which Gerry Fitt made his mark.

THE NATIONALIST PARTY

The only difference between Sinn Féin and constitutional Irish nationalism as represented by the Nationalist Party – the direct descendant of John Redmond's party – was what method should be used to gain a united Ireland. Both were essentially Catholic conservative organisations, with anti-partition and abstention policies. The word 'party' to describe the constitutional nationalists of the north was something of a misnomer: they did not resemble a modern political party in structure or organisation. In short, there was no structured or cohesive Nationalist Party.

From the inception of the state, the nationalists denied its legitimacy. It was only after 1945 that they regularly attended the northern parliament. Before then their refusal to acknowledge the existence of Northern Ireland was shown in their frequent abstentions. Ian McAllister explains the dilemma of the nationalists and their response to it:

> They had no incentive to participate in the normal political activity of the state because they could never hope to influence, let alone become, the

government, yet they were committed to parliamentary politics.

In the event, the nationalists overcame the dilemma by a half-hearted commitment to constitutional politics. They failed to organise and restricted their activities to enclaves where they possessed a numerical majority, moreover they frequently abstained from parliament and continued to emphasise partition to the exclusion of other social issues affecting the welfare of their supporters.[19]

These social issues included housing, employment and welfare spending. To the Nationalist Party, all social problems were summed up in the word 'discrimination', and they maintained this attitude from 1921 to the 1960s. To the constitutional nationalist, a united Ireland was the solution to all social and economic grievances.

Nationalists, then, made no real attempts to work within the system and they failed to look after the social and economic interests of their constituents. Any efforts to do so would probably have failed, but the fact that they did not even suggest measures for reform (outside the national question) that might have helped the people they represented led to disillusionment and general apathy in the community.

The Nationalist Party, apart from its stance on the partition issue, was highly conservative, and its clerical links strengthened its conservatism. The only legislation it saw through Stormont was the politically unimportant Wild Birds Act of 1931.[20] Little wonder that Bernadette Devlin (now McAliskey), expressing the radical fervour of the times, referred to the party as the 'Green Tories of Ireland'.[21] Eddie McAteer, a Derry Catholic and the 1960s leader of the Nationalist Party, underlined its passivity: 'Our policy is a realistic one. Broadly speaking we realise that partition is a matter between Dublin and London. On that issue ours must be a passive role. We oppose partition as a great evil, but we ourselves cannot change the partition situation'.[22]

There were, as we shall see, groups on both sides of the border who were no longer convinced that this 'passive role' was a valid one. They challenged what they saw as the futility of isolation and non-co-operation. During the 1960s, the Nationalist Party came under increasing pressure to improve its performance and profile. One of the party's loudest critics south of the border was the Dublin-based current affairs review *Hibernia*. It was particularly critical of the party's lack of structure. In 1961 *Hibernia* complained: 'The nationalists of course have no organisation whatsoever.

The party is not a party in any political sense but rather in an Alice in Wonderland sense'.[23] In 1963 it argued:

> In order to hold and improve its standing in the 'Province' to the point where it can be considered as an alternative to the Unionist government, the Nationalist Party must become a more purposeful, vigorous and progressive looking organisation.
>
> It must organise in every constituency in Northern Ireland and not as heretofore in safe constituencies only.
>
> It must plan and produce for the electorate vigorous progressive policies covering all aspects of economic and social endeavours in Northern Ireland, policies which could become a real and dangerous challenge to the unionists' policy of step by step with Britain.
>
> Most important of all: the future policies of the Nationalist Party, even allowing for the ideal of a united country, must appeal to all sections of the community and not at present, to one section only.[24]

Throughout the early 1960s *Hibernia* was consistently critical of the Nationalist Party's weakness, which it saw as not merely obstructing reunification but helping partition to continue.

North of the border, criticism of the 'Green Tories' was equally strong. The leader of the Ulster Liberal Association, Albert McElroy, when asked in 1962 what he thought of the Nationalist Party in Stormont, replied: 'Politically speaking, it is the other side of the unionist penny. Most of its members, had they been born Protestants instead of Catholics, would find themselves quite at home on a Twelfth of July Platform'.[25]

However, the nationalists would have been most sensitive to the criticism that came from their own community. In 1964, John Hume, a Derry schoolteacher who later became a civil rights activist and leader of the SDLP, chastised the Nationalist Party in an *Irish Times* article. While rebuking the unionist administration for the plight of northern nationalists, Hume also blamed the Nationalist Party:

> Good government depends as much on the opposition as on the party in power. Weak opposition leads to corrupt government. Nationalists in opposition have been in no way constructive. They have quite rightly been loud in their demands for rights, but they have remained silent and inactive about their duties. In forty years of opposition they have not

produced one constructive contribution on either the social or economic plane to the development of Northern Ireland which is, after all, a substantial part of the united Ireland for which they strive. Leadership has been the comfortable leadership of flags and slogans. Easy no doubt but irresponsible.

With regard to the Nationalist Party's ambiguous attitude toward the Westminster parliament, Hume expressed an opinion that only a few years earlier would have been seen as virtual heresy. He argued that accepting the constitutional position could be reconciled with aspiring to a united Ireland:

> There is nothing inconsistent with such acceptance and a belief that a thirty-two county republic is best for Ireland. In fact, if we are to pursue a policy of non-recognition, the only logical policy is that of Sinn Féin. If one wishes to create a united Ireland by constitutional means, then one must accept the constitutional position.[26]

The Nationalist Party could not ignore such criticism, which was becoming more and more vocal. In November 1964, under pressure from converging forces, it published a thirty-nine-point policy statement in which it pledged to work within the system. The party declared it was committed to becoming a modern political organisation. The statement also demanded an end to discrimination and gerrymandering, and made reference to economic considerations.[27]

In January 1965, Taoiseach Seán Lemass, visited his counterpart in the north, Terence O'Neill. This meeting, the first of its kind, was a major watershed in the relationship between the two states. One immediate tangible result of the summit was that the Nationalist Party, prompted by Lemass, decided for the first time in its history to form the official opposition. Eddie McAteer made the following statement:

> The Nationalist Party has reviewed the whole political landscape and has reached the following conclusions. Stormont must be seen as a federated regional Irish parliament to continue in existence until fears of an all Ireland parliament are finally resolved. There must be co-operation to ensure that the Stormont parliament makes good or better laws for the benefit of all the people thus promoting better harmony.[28]

The Nationalists had ended a negative policy that had endured for over forty years and had finally accepted the status of Northern Ireland. They had committed themselves to co-operate within the system whenever their principles would permit, and, superficially at least, Northern Ireland appeared to be entering a period of conciliation.

NATIONAL UNITY AND THE
NATIONAL DEMOCRATIC PARTY

The questioning of traditional beliefs and the criticism of the Nationalist Party stemmed from a new generation of northern Catholics, who were more concerned with social and economic conditions than with the ideal of a united Ireland. John Hume's *Irish Times* article was indicative of a growing change in attitude. Now there really was a Catholic nationalist desire to pursue a reasonable political dialogue on the constitution and government of Ireland. Hume and others were prompted by a sense of frustration with their position in public life and weariness with the never-ending cycles of violence. There was a growing feeling that they could and should have a stake in Northern Ireland. Catholic resentment of discrimination continued, but there was a willingness to adopt a fresh approach to old grievances. Much of the impetus for improving the status of Catholics in the existing political framework sprang from a new middle-class, which was no longer prepared to tolerate discrimination.

In November 1959, the Catholic organisation National Unity was formed. It was composed largely of university graduates who had bene-fited from the higher education opportunities resulting from the 1947 Education Acts. Initially, members of National Unity saw it as an integral part of the Nationalist Party, as a reform body that would push the party towards more progressive socio-economic positions.[29] The concept of National Unity suggested that a united opposition to unionism was now an attainable goal. *Hibernia* commented in 1961: 'At the moment, there is no Nationalist Party to join, a circumstance which has brought into existence a group, Nationalist Unity, which aims to unite the nationalist people with a solid blow'.[30]

Middle-class National Unity saw itself as providing (for the north-ern nationalist community) an intellectual and moral leadership that had been lacking in the Nationalist Party. Its aim was to instil confidence in members of the minority community, to encourage them to get involved in political life so that they could influence the course of nationalist politics. In short, National Unity hoped to provide a rallying point for a new brand of nationalism.

Towards the end of 1963 it had become apparent to National Unity that the Nationalist Party was incapable of reform – it had remained stagnant for so long that any change in policy verged on the revolutionary. The party's conservative nature would not allow it to adapt to the changing times.

In January 1964 National Unity published the first issue of an independent quarterly journal of social, cultural and political comment on Irish affairs. This magazine was *New Nation*. As Ian McAllister points out, its title was intended to 'invoke parallels'[31] with the newspaper of the Young Irelanders founded in 1843.[32] The growing rift between the group and the Nationalist Party was made clear in the April 1964 edition:

> It was one of the minor ironies of history that the Parnellite line of succession from the first Irish Party should be maintained to this day in the persons of the Nationalist parliamentary representatives in Stormont. The irony is contained in the fact that the Irish Party was the first example of an organised political party in these islands while the present nationalist representation is the very antithesis of party organisation.
>
> For the academic historian such a reversal provides a lengthy footnote to a political history of Ireland. For the nationalist electorate on the other hand it implies a state of confusion, frustration and bewilderment.[33]

National Unity made a major effort to establish some uniformity in nationalist policy by calling a convention of anti-partition groups in Maghery, County Armagh in April 1964. This convention was attended by nationalist elected representatives. Other delegates included Republican, Labour and independent senators and MPs, many members of the professions – doctors, teachers, solicitors – and a number of university students. They discussed a previously circulated motion calling for the creation of a united democratic political party to represent all sections of the nationalist movement and to fulfil its aspiration for a united Ireland. The meeting led to the formation of a new political unit – the National Political Front (NPF). Afterwards McAteer said, 'The keynote was unity of national forces and the end of weakening divisions.' The resolution contained the following statement: 'In conjunction with the Nationalist parliamentary representatives and with other MPs, who support the national ideal to take immediate steps to create such a national political front with all the machinery of a normal political party in such areas where these do not already exist'.[34]

An *Irish News* editorial welcomed this outcome.

Any political movement … that works for the unity of national groups deserves encouragement and support. Wise counsel and single-hearted purpose can repair past errors and mend broken friendships. Force has proved a failure. But there should be no other failure in fresh and deter-mined efforts to heal the wound that has weakened the country and to end the friction that has kept so many unity workers in rival camps.[35]

It seemed that the creation of a united political party had begun. The political domination of the Nationalist Party was certainly drawing to a close.[36] However, it still retained enough prestige to ensure the fragmentation of the nascent National Political Front.

In September 1964, the NPF condemned the Nationalist Party in a resolution censuring its decision not to contest the Fermanagh–South Tyrone seat at the forthcoming Westminster election. This decision was consistent with the party's policy of standing aside at imperial elections and allowing Sinn Féin a straight fight with the unionists. The resolution also declared: 'the present situation has developed due to the failure of the Nationalist Parliamentary Party to co-operate within the National Political Front in the creation of a normal democratic political party'. Commenting on the resolution, McAteer said:

This has placed the future of the front in grave jeopardy. In my opinion it has crumbled and will require rebuilding from the foundation …

I am disappointed that it has not been found possible to build a new organisation. In my judgment the materials were incompatible. Certainly the high hopes of the Maghery Convention are a long way from fulfilment but I am hopeful that a new phoenix may arise from the ashes.[37]

Unfortunately for McAteer and his fellow Nationalist MPs, what did emerge from the ashes was a new political party that would further frag-ment Catholic politics. The Nationalist Party's thirty-nine-point plan in November 1964 was too little, too late. Finally, in 1965 National Unity created the National Democratic Party (NDP). The party was content to participate in the social, economic and political life of Northern Ireland and to end partition democratically. Its open membership was designed to attract the best talent from the whole nationalist community. Despite its secular and progressive profile, the NDP made little impression on the electorate and had little success in uniting the anti-partition forces. McAllister explains the failure of the party strategy:

> The overall aim of the strategy was to form a radical and viable alternative to unionism and to appear as a responsible and constructive opposition in the British tradition. In a province with a permanent opposition and an equally permanent one-party government this was a forlorn hope. The failure to achieve a credible parliamentary representation had lasting consequences in shortening the life of the NDP.[38]

In the mid-1960s, unionism seemed as secure as ever and nationalists had decided it was necessary to work within the system – yet their ability to do just that was hindered by continued fragmentation and disunity.

THE CAMPAIGN FOR DEMOCRACY IN ULSTER AND THE CAMPAIGN FOR SOCIAL JUSTICE

National Unity and the NDP were not the only organisations to evolve from Catholic frustration in the 1960s. Two other groups, which were to make a great political impact on both unionism and the history of Ireland, also emerged: the Campaign for Democracy in Ulster (CDU); and the Campaign for Social Justice (CSJ).

In their biography of Ian Paisley, Ed Moloney and Andy Pollack correctly consider July 1960 as a watershed in northern nationalist politics.[39] In that month, Orangemen were given permission by the home affairs ministry to march through the Catholic village of Dungiven: 'Paisley's pressure had established the right of Loyalists to parade their truimphalism through Catholic districts'.[40]

Frustration with Stormont's attitude led nationalists to seek a meeting with a British home office minister to vent their anger, and Dennis Vosper, a parliamentary secretary, agreed to see them. The meeting did little to pacify the nationalists; Vosper refused to stray from unionist policy. The meeting was important, however, because it was the first time a British minister had listened to Catholic grievances and it therefore encouraged a significant change in nationalist tactics. Thereafter, nationalists would begin to strive for justice in Northern Ireland through Westminster.[41]

This change in strategy came to fruition in June 1965, when a group of backbench Labour MPs set up the Campaign for Democracy in Ulster. Their aim was to set up an enquiry into the affairs of Northern Ireland. The group had been founded as a response to the House of Commons' refusal to change the convention that Northern Ireland's affairs could not be discussed at Westminster. The CDU based its demand on Section 75 of the 1920 Government of Ireland Act, which stated that supreme authority over Northern Ireland remained at Westminster. One of the most prominent members of the reform group was Paul Rose, the MP for Blakeley, Manchester. He argued, 'What riles us above all is that when we question injustices in the six counties we are accused of interfering, yet there is no question of any Constitutional limit on the voting powers of the Unionist members in the House.' He insisted that the border was not a concern of the new group: 'It is not for us to raise the issue of the border in this campaign. We are intent on drawing attention to injustices over which the House of Commons has direct or indirect control. The Irish people themselves will solve the border problem in time.'[42]

As we shall see, the CDU gained considerable impetus when Gerry Fitt was elected MP for West Belfast in March 1966.

The struggle against discrimination in Northern Ireland took another step forward in January 1964 when the Campaign for Social Justice was inaugurated in Belfast. This non-political body had sprung from the Homeless Citizens League, a pressure group established on 24 May 1963 in Dungannon, County Tyrone, by Dr Conn McCluskey and his wife Patricia to campaign for better housing in the county. Reflecting the new civil rights consciousness in the Catholic community, the league evolved into the CSJ. This movement, like National Unity and, later, the NDP, was composed largely of middle-class professional Catholics. Its immediate aims were as follows:

The first objective was a fact finding investigation of injustices against people of all creeds and political opinions ...

The government of Northern Ireland's policies of apartheid and discrimination have continued to be implemented at all levels with such zeal that we have banded ourselves together to oppose them.[43]

The campaign aimed to rise above party politics by striving to end injustice for any group or individual Protestant or Catholic: the question of the border was incidental. The CSJ began what was to become the civil rights movement.

THE WELFARE STATE

Why in the 1960s did a significant number of Catholics stop being passive and demand first-class citizenship in Northern Ireland? The establishment of the British welfare state may provide an answer.

The 'welfare state' was the government plan to set up a system of care and benefits for everyone who needed them 'from the cradle to the grave'. Considerable improvements were made in public transport, health and social services, housing and education. The Labour government also nationalised key industries, bringing them under state ownership and control. The Unionist government was innately conservative but it was prepared (albeit reluctantly) to reproduce Westminster legislation, even of a socialist nature, to ensure parity with the rest of the UK. It also helped that the British government agreed to foot the bill.

Social policy in Northern Ireland therefore underwent radical changes in the 1940s.[44] These measures compared favourably with the static situation south of the border. The social provisions of the British state in Northern Ireland appeared to be much more progressive than the Republic's Poor Law provision.

Perhaps the most significant of all the welfare state advances to the northern Catholic was the 1947 Education Act. Based on the 1944 British Education Act, it introduced free post-primary education, which enabled children of working-class parents to continue at school until the age of fifteen. Improvements in the university grants system also created greater opportunities in further education. Michael Farrell believed that in the late 1950s and early 1960s, 'The first generation to go through University on scholarships under the post-war education scheme emerged. They had no experience of the previous defeats and were not demoralised. They chafed at their own second-class status and began to articulate the grievances of their community.'[45]

National Unity and the CSJ were examples of the changing social structure. A northern Irish Catholic middle-class emerged. It started to become involved in the public life of Northern Ireland without abandoning the aspiration to a united Ireland. In fact, since the Republic seemed to compare so poorly with the northern state, the people of Northern Ireland were in no particular rush to achieve unity – which again contributed to their willingness to participate in the existing political framework. To borrow Professor J. A. Murphy's phrase, 'the Education Act of 1947 sowed Dragons' Teeth'.[46] The American journalist and historian Kevin Kelley suggests:

> Seemingly tangential events like the election of President John F. Kennedy and the installation of Pope John XXIII were in fact key morale boosters for nationalists in the North. A dashing young U.S. President of Irish Catholic descent and a Pope committed to social justice and ecumenism had their effect on the Northern minority's self esteem and its own sense of potential.[47]

In retrospect, then, there are grounds to suggest that the emergence of a new minority attitude in the 1960s resulted directly from the establishment of the welfare state and international changes in the status and focus of Catholicism. A new Catholic intelligentsia became dissatisfied with the moribund nationalist politics of the previous forty years. It reacted with hostility to the futile IRA border campaign and initiated a new, less militant brand of nationalism prompted in part by the liberalising tendencies of the Second Vatican Council on Catholic politics (which started to have an effect throughout Catholic society by 1967).

The problem was that these changes began to raise expectations in the Catholic community, but unionism was unable to satisfy these expectations within the confines of its six-county domain. Meanwhile the British state, which had provoked these heightened aspirations, was unwilling to do the necessary to satisfy them because of its desire to keep Northern Ireland at arm's length.

THE O'NEILL/LEMASS SUMMIT

Another important factor in the transformation of Catholic politics in Northern Ireland was the significant change in the politics of the Republic that occurred around this time. Northern nationalists had traditionally looked south for the impetus to end partition. However, in the late 1950s and early 1960s politicians in the Republic began to realise that partition would be ended not by dramatic gestures, but rather by a slow process of reconciliation. This change of perception, combined with a change in the mentality of some unionist elements, would, it was believed, lead to the end of the political atrophy that had characterised the history of Northern Ireland.

In the mid-1950s, the Republic was experiencing an economic depression. Unemployment and inflation were rising, resulting in poor living standards and large-scale emigration; and the economic indicators did not point to any improvement in the foreseeable future. A new breed of politicians and economists argued that the traditional policy of protectionism had become redundant by the late 1950s. They maintained that economic expansion required the establishment of free trade relations with the rest of the world.

In 1958, the new Fianna Fáil government accepted this argument. It abandoned the old Sinn Féin economics of high tariff barriers to develop Irish industry and agricultural self-sufficiency. Instead it put in place an economic expansion programme designed to inject foreign capital into the country through tax and plant incentives. As part of this programme, in 1961 the Republic's government announced its intention to join the European Economic Community (EEC) and to participate in free trade with Britain and the rest of Europe. Bew and Patterson point to the significance for the Republic of the twenty-year period after the Second World War and, in particular, the watershed of the late 1950s and early 1960s:

… the significance of the period analysed in the study (1945–65) lies in the fact that we can see the emergence of a quite novel attitude. We are no longer dealing with a formal programme of agrarian radicalism and a nationalist industrialisation drive which only a few really believe in but which is also never rejected outright. In this epoch – by the late 1950s and early 1960s at any rate – the dominance of grassland production, foreign capital and economic liberalisation is openly recognised and avowed.[48]

Much of the impetus for this policy change can be attributed to Seán Lemass, who replaced de Valera as Taoiseach (Prime Minister) in 1959.

On becoming leader of Fianna Fáil, his rhetoric, without threatening the aspiration of Irish unity, suggested that co-operation between north and south made economic sense. In July 1959 he said, 'The fact that we have that hope of eventual unity is not a reason why people in the north should refuse to consider even now possibilities of converting activities for the practical economic advantages that may result.'[49] The following November he claimed, 'We desire to see our people and country reunited. Our method is, and we are making clear – to try to abolish memory of past dissensions and to strengthen contacts and promote co-operation between the two areas into which the country is now divided.'[50]

These overtures were ignored by the northern Prime Minister, Lord Brookeborough. Nevertheless, Lemass' nationalism became diluted enough eventually to undermine the traditional antagonisms between Britain and Ireland that had perpetuated partition. The new political philosophy dramatically improved the living standards of those south of the border, thus reducing the importance of partition.

This modernising trend in the Republic was paralleled in the north. It also featured a new-style politician, in this instance one intent on regenerating unionism. When Captain Terence O'Neill succeeded Brookeborough in March 1963, strategies that for over forty years had preserved unionist cohesion were dropped in favour of a policy that attempted to encourage Catholic participation in the state.

O'Neill was more moderate than his predecessors, at least in tone, and he seemed to offer the prospect of change and progress. He also realised that if Northern Ireland was to prosper it had to modernise politically and socially as well as economically. O'Neill was the first Prime Minister of Northern Ireland to visit a Catholic school and to be photographed with members of the Catholic clergy. In June 1963 he even offered official condolences to the Catholic Church on the death of Pope John XXIII.

O'Neill's seemingly non-sectarian style was part of his strategy to modernise the northern economy. Like the government in the Republic, he realised that Northern Ireland needed foreign capital to stimulate expansion. O'Neill intended to attract potential investors by selling Northern Ireland as a state of religious peace. Major economic initiatives were put in place. A total of £900 million was invested in the economy and a Ministry of Development was created to drive economic revival. Future Northern Ireland premier Brian Faulkner led an economic council. A new city was established, modelled on Lurgan and Portadown, which was to be called Craigavon; and Coleraine was selected as the site for a new university. These policies were partly successful and a number of multinational firms opened factories in Northern Ireland.

The extent to which O'Neill had distanced himself from the traditional tenets of unionism was no more clearly shown than in his 1965 invitation to Lemass to meet in Belfast.

This meeting was perhaps the most sensational event in Irish politics since the establishment of the border some forty-five years earlier, and was a direct result of both states' adoption of free trade policies. They could now expect considerable profits through increased trade and other forms of economic co-operation. The politics of pragmatism had, it seemed, triumphed.

Lemass had not gone so far as to recognise Stormont, yet it looked as if the traditional antagonisms between unionism and republicanism had begun to thaw. Both premiers feared the militants' response to the summit, but these fears proved groundless.[51]

On the unionist side, O'Neill went to the electorate in October 1965 to seek endorsement for co-operation between north and south. He swept the country and then asked, 'where was the backlash against my invitation to Mr Lemass? It did not exist except in the minds of the extremists ...'[52]

In the Republic, *Hibernia* commented:

A reassessment of Captain Terence O'Neill is necessary. His meeting with Mr Lemass was not only an act of courage, the whole manoeuvre was carried off with greater political skill than his past record would have promised. The northern premier begins to fulfil the hopes of those who welcomed his accession as the beginning of a new era in the six counties.[53]

The response from northern Catholics was also favourable. The *New Nation* reported:

Men and women of every political allegiance, of every denomination, and all classes welcomed the meeting between Captain O'Neill and Mr Lemass, and in their almost universal welcome revealed the fanatics for what they were – a divided and meaningless rabble of inconsequential men whose apparent power was founded only upon the silence of the majority, a silence that was too often taken as approval.[54]

The *Irish News* editorial also endorsed the historic meeting:

> If this and further meetings are fruitful it is the whole people, and especi-
> ally the working population in Ireland who will benefit from this co-
> operation and harmony in high political quarters. The two Premiers need
> have no misgivings. They and the majority of the Irish people know that
> they are doing the right thing.[55]

The healthier atmosphere in relations between north and south seemed
to bode well for the future, and there was a feeling that perhaps at last the
old Orange and Green shibboleths were losing their strength. Optimism
that national and religious antagonisms were abating grew in Belfast,
Dublin and London. Few could have foreseen that within five years
Ireland would be on the verge of civil war.

2

FROM DOCK TO WESTMINSTER: GERRY FITT 1958 – 66

From the late 1950s to the mid-1960s Catholic politics changed from boycott to tentative involvement in the system. In the same period, Gerry Fitt built the foundations of his own political career. Electoral success in Northern Ireland was followed in April 1966 by election to Westminster as MP for West Belfast. *Hibernia* commented on his greatest triumph so far:

> The most melodramatic event was, of course, Gerry Fitt's elevation to the Palace of Westminster as the simultaneous holder of the offices of city councillor, Stormont MP and Member of Parliament in London. This is quite some attainment for a working-class boy who left to become a seaman and entered political life while being an unemployed man on the dole. He has become something of a myth in Belfast. He has already made his mark in Irish history. It is bound to deepen with time.[1]

This chapter will describe Fitt's politics in this period, demonstrating that his republicanism was essentially idealistic and based largely on sentiment – though it also had a practical dimension. The chapter will also show that Fitt was very much a nationalist who held strong views on the reunification of Ireland. It is true that he consistently used socialist rhetoric, but this could not be divorced from his nationalist views. The two strands were inextricably linked and it was their fusion that made him such a formidable electoral commodity.

We shall also see that his socialism was not driven by any theoretical understanding. It is more accurate to conclude that it was based on bread-

and-butter issues rather than any adherence to Marxism or any other leftist philosophy. Although he used the language of James Connolly, the evidence suggests that the two men were very different. Fitt could be described as a 'Connolly socialist' only in terms of the way he tried to combine some aspects of social agitation with nationalism. But in this he was much more in the tradition of Joe Devlin, the West Belfast Irish Parliamentary Party MP, who combined Hibernianism with the social policies of Lloyd George's Liberalism.[2] And, of course, Connolly had little time for the member for West Belfast.

It is also clear that Fitt had to cope with the sectarian complexion of life in Northern Ireland, which meant he had to expend much of his undoubted energy attacking discrimination at both local and provincial government levels.

This chapter makes two further assertions. First, it will prove that Fitt's 1966 election victory was not symptomatic of the change in Catholic politics outlined in Chapter 1. Although Fitt may have been helped by the growing demands for representation and attendance, he was essentially a 'lone operator' uninterested in large parties and fundamental reorganisation. This contrast would be significant in Fitt's later political career.

Second, it will show that there is some substance to Fitt's claim that he obtained Protestant support in his early career, which enabled him to win West Belfast in 1966.[3] Given that political analysts at the time claimed the religious divide in the constituency was about equal, his contention had important implications.[4] Considering the sectarian nature of northern Irish politics, this was a considerable achievement. Fitt not only had to cope with sectarian politics, he also had to compete with the new aggressive Catholic middle class that wanted to lead nationalist politics.

Middle-class strength should not be over-estimated, though: the rank and file of the nationalist community was overwhelmingly working-class; and the dichotomy between classes was not the only division in nationalist politics. E. Rumpf and A. C. Hepburn see a geographic factor: 'One of the clearest characteristics of anti-partitionist politics between 1945 and 1969 was the total rift between Belfast and the rest of the province'.[5] The strained relationship between rural and city nationalists was a product of the conflicting interests of the societies they represented. In 1970 Fitt tried to explain the discord:

A natural suspicion exists between the town and city on one hand and rural areas on the other. The rural areas are very suspicious; they don't like the word 'Labour' and they don't like the word 'socialist'. They feel that they are going to have their small farms and holdings taken from them. In the cities you have the reverse. There is the industrial complex; trade union affiliation and Labour ideology.[6]

There were antagonisms within the Unionist Party for the same reasons. The two blocs had conservative and socialist tendencies that were connected to the conditions of life in rural and urban Northern Ireland, but there were also tensions within these blocs, which had to be reconciled with a suitably popular brand of nationalism or unionism.

In Belfast, nationalists like Fitt used socialist rhetoric, which alarmed their conservative colleagues in the countryside, particularly west of the River Bann, where rural constituencies predominated. The conservative characteristics of nationalist politics in these areas were reinforced, if not produced, through clerical influence.

This feature of nationalist politics was a feature of the Irish Parliamentary Party of the late nineteenth century. In many ways it was also a continuation of Joe Devlin's Hibernian political organisation, which he had used from 1905 to 1914 to spread his own and his party's influence outward from Belfast to the country areas. Outside Belfast, the Catholic Church paid for the services of a full-time registration agent whose function was to compile a register of eligible Catholic voters. The agent was the Nationalist Party's only constituency organisation and therefore quantified the Catholic rural community vote. That vote was used to support the Church's opinion on how society should be run, as directed from the pulpit. Furthermore, the local parish priest was usually chairman of the convention called to select a candidate. As Eamon McCann says, 'Nationalist candidates were not elected, they were anointed'.[7]

Rural politics contrasted with the slightly more secular inclinations of Belfast anti-partition politics. The attitudes found in rural areas were not as common in the industrial urban setting: for example, Catholic doctrine on family planning and mixed marriages was less rigidly followed. In Belfast, therefore, nationalist politics became somewhat more complex and ambiguous in its social characteristics, particularly given the influence of the British welfare state. By 1952 the Nationalist Party was no longer an electoral force in the capital: a more adaptable politics was necessary to secure political influence.

Belfast anti-partition politics did have internal factions. Schism and fragmentation were common and perhaps inevitable, given the necessity of juggling the correct combinations of political character. This can be illustrated by the failure of local Belfast nationalists to agree on a united political party to replace the discredited Nationalist Party and the Northern Ireland Labour Party (NILP), which in 1949 formally acknowledged that it was pro-partition.

Belfast working-class Catholics, no longer content to listen to traditional nationalist and Catholic rhetoric, became more and more concerned with the basic necessities of life – the problems of social deprivation, unsatisfactory housing and high unemployment. They could choose between a multiplicity of Labour interests – one was pro-border, more were anti-border, and some were based on individual personalities. Of the anti-border groups Rumpf and Hepburn note:

> The various groups all had in common a radical stance on social questions and an ability to bring the socialist republican arguments of James Connolly into play when necessary, but they relied far more for support on their own efforts and individual popularity than on any formal Trade Union backing, while their socialism, unlike Connolly's would scarcely have alarmed the most moderate member of the British Labour Party.[8]

The Belfast working-class cared little for socialist theory, yet it did receive the benefits of post-war parity policies implemented by the British Labour government. Despite clerical hostility to socialism, the creation of the welfare state gave the term 'Labour' positive connotations, particularly where socialist policies had eased the worst symptoms of deprivation.

At this stage, Gerry Fitt's position matched the profile of Belfast nationalists discussed by Rumpf and Hepburn. He was consistent in his condemnation of partition: in fact it could be argued that he was fundamentally an anti-partitionist. However, he had a genuine empathy with the working-class and he was also astute enough to realise that if he wanted to achieve electoral success the term 'Labour' was a very handy addition to his ticket.

Although Belfast was predominantly Protestant and unionist, there were three Stormont seats in the city that were potentially nationalist – Falls, Central and Dock. Dock was unique because it had never successively elected the same party or politician, always alternating between unionist and some form of Labour. Unlike Falls and Central, which had large Catholic majorities, Dock had a small Protestant majority and was open to capture by a Catholic with a Labour following.

Gerry Fitt became a member of the Dock Irish Labour Party, itself a product of the innate factionalism in northern Labour politics. The party was partly financed by Catholic publicans and bookies – the mainstay professions of the Catholic petty bourgeoisie, who made their money alleviating the deprivations of the Catholic working man: at least until the hangovers came and winnings from the last race ran out. Dock Irish Labour's stated intention was to unite the working-class and break down unionism. Fitt became one of the group's most prominent operators in the 1950s; so much so that in March 1958 he was chosen to contest the Stormont election for Dock Labour in a straight fight with the unionists.

From its establishment in 1920, the Unionist Party dominated Stormont. Under Craigavon, Andrews and Brookeborough the northern parliament operated largely as a rubber stamp for Westminster legislation. Electoral activity in the north had nothing to do with governing the state, since state power was at Westminster; elections were invariably fought on the question of partition rather than on social and economic issues. Focus on the border ensured that voting would be conducted on factional lines: Protestants turned out in favour of maintaining the border; the majority of Catholics for restoring the territorial unity of Ireland. The 1958 election was no exception.

In Dock, like every other constituency, orange and green arguments were more significant than social and economic problems. The *Belfast News Letter* (the daily newspaper read mainly by Protestants) sketched the character of electioneering in the area with particular reference to Fitt. It also deliberately misnamed his party to emphasise its nationalist credentials:

The Unionist Party in Dock has no difficulty persuading the electorate of the paramount importance of the constitutional position. It is placed there, priority number 1, by the Eire Labour candidate [*sic*] who is opposing Alderman William Oliver with the aid of a van flying the flag by O'Casey in *The Plough and the Stars*.[9]

At the time of the election, Fitt was employed as a clerk. His opponent, William Oliver, a shopkeeper, was also a member of Belfast Corporation, working as chairman of the Housing and Redevelopment Committee. The see-saw nature of the seat meant it was closely observed by the press.

In 1949 Alderman T. L. Cole had won this Dock seat for the Unionists by 284 votes, but lost it to Murtagh Morgan (Eire Labour) by 179 votes in 1953 – the smallest majority in that election. Given the margin of success and failure in the past, party workers felt that whichever candidate came closest to a 100 per cent turnout would win the day.

Oliver's appeal to his supporters lay primarily in stressing the benefits of social services in Northern Ireland compared with those available outside the United Kingdom.[10]

On the other hand, while Fitt and the Dock Irish Labour Party employed non-sectarian rhetoric, their instincts were always in line with Irish republicanism and nationalism. Fitt proclaimed, 'James Connolly came into this historic division forty-five years ago to ask for your vote and we come to you under his flag.'[11] Michael Ferran, chairman of the party, rather grandiosely declared that it was 'fighting the same enemies, under the same banner and for the same ideals for which Connolly fought and died'.[12]

To supporters of the union Connolly's name was synonymous with the idea of Irish separatism and independence. Although Fitt's words were couched in terms of Labourite solidarity, it was quite clear to which section of the community he was directing his appeal. He argued: 'There was no fear of losing the contest if the people rallied to the cause of Labour. It was the duty of the nationalist minded electors to cast their vote as he was not only fighting a unionist opponent but the full weight of Glengall Street.'[13]

Conforming to the nationalist ideal that reunification would solve the country's economic problems, Fitt made no attempt to hide his hope to see a united Ireland: 'Ulster's economic problems will never be solved by the Unionist Party. The only way it could be would be through a 32 county republic.'[14]

Fitt was clearly anti-unionist and hence anti-Stormont. Yet he also made an appeal to Protestant workers. Jack Brady of the Irish Transport and General Workers Union (ITGWU) assured the people of Dock 'that if elected Gerry Fitt would prove a worthy representative and serve the people of all classes, irrespective of religion'.[15] This aspect of Fitt's political philosophy would later become very important when he did take public office, but in this election he tended to seek redress for the traditional Catholic grievance of discrimination in the face of Protestant privilege.

In an attempt to swing the election in favour of the unionists, Prime Minister Brookeborough announced he would visit the constituency. Fitt fulminated that he would 'personally conduct the provincial Lord on a tour of the working-class area. Perhaps he would see the misery which had resulted from the Unionist Party policy and their mismanagement of affairs for the past 40 years.'[16] At this point in his political career Fitt could never have conceived that he too would become a 'provincial Lord', albeit as a reward for political service rather than as a member of the landed gentry.

Fitt endeavoured to focus attention on the rich – poor divide regardless of religion. These 'Parliamentary Marionettes ... had no interest whatsoever in the well being of the common people.'[17]

He also said: 'I am determined to fight the Unionist Party and if elected will show unrelenting opposition to the vicious policy of discrimination being practised by our opponents.'[18]

Nationalist politicians had always asserted that discrimination in housing was one of the mechanisms that kept the unionist bloc together. The argument was that Protestants were granted advantages in housing allocation in order to ensure their loyalty to the state. Another reason for the charge of discrimination in housing was that the restricted local government franchise (a person could only vote in the local government elections if he or she owned property) meant that the allocation of local authority houses also meant, in effect, the allocation of votes; so constituencies and wards could be gerrymandered. The lack of home ownership was also a feature of the Protestant community and some Protestants were similarly disenfranchised.

Fitt's 1958 campaign was very much concerned with housing. He claimed the housing and redevelopment committee of Belfast Corporation had shown a consistent policy of discrimination in siting new estates. As for his own area he declared: 'This division has already been cruelly gerrymandered and with the erection of flats in Victoria Barracks which would be handed to unionist supporters the nationally minded majority would be wiped out.'[19] Oliver contemptuously dismissed Fitt's charges of discrimination:

'Mr what-do-you-call-him, this man talks about discrimination. Roman

Catholics know what treatment they are getting from the Ulster Government. Instead of the 50% grants they get towards their schools in Great Britain, here they get 80 or 90%. Yet this man talks about discrimination.'[20]

As polling day drew closer, the unionists became confident of victory – it was, after all, their turn. Brian Faulkner, then chief whip of the Unionist Party, speculated: 'We have a really good chance of winning this seat because our candidate has been active in housing and social work and is well known in the constituency. Dock is always a see-saw seat but our chances were never better.'[21]

Faulkner's conjecture proved correct. On 20 March 1958, it was the Protestant community that turned out in greater numbers. Oliver polled 3,156 votes to Fitt's 2,900. The unionists had established a majority of 256 with a swing of 500 votes. However, Oliver's poll was below that of Cole, who lost the seat in 1953, and in the not so distant future, Oliver would recall the name of his opponent a little more readily.

In May 1958 elections for the Belfast local government took place.[22] The Dock Irish Labour Party forwarded two candidates: Fitt and James O'Kane, a publican.

In the Dock ward, Fitt and O'Kane campaigned against three unionists and one independent unionist, and although this was an election for local government, the issues were essentially the same as they had been in the Stormont election two months earlier. Fitt again focused on what he considered a sustained policy of discrimination in the allocation of houses. He alleged that unionists''ultimate aim was to denude Dock ward entirely of the nationally minded voters'.[23]

On the eve of the poll, Fitt again used socialist rhetoric but he made no attempt to hide his nationalist sentiment and brought the issue of partition to the forefront. He claimed:

The Unionist Party would throw everything into this fight and only the good will of the working-class people of the area could prevent Dock from once again being handed over to the unionist reactionaries. If he was successful in this election his policy would be based on the ideals of the Labour movement in Ireland – a policy that will lead the working-class people of not only the six counties but all Ireland to an Irish socialist working-class republic.[24]

In an interview with me, Fitt claimed he was always more of a socialist than a nationalist:

> In the context of Ireland I am a socialist. Unhesitatingly socialist. I would like to see Ireland united in the belief that in a united Ireland you would have Protestant Labour supporters and Catholic Labour supporters; you would have the class division that you would have say in London and elsewhere. But put to the crunch I would say I was many more miles a socialist than a nationalist.[25]

There can be no doubt about Fitt's innate altruism, but it could be argued that in this period the relationship between Fitt's nationalism and socialism, while a constant feature of his political discourse, was an adaptable blend presented to achieve maximum political advantage by appearing to have something for everyone.

Dock Irish Labour was very successful in the election. Its two representatives ousted the unionists, with Fitt leading the poll after a particularly ingenious (or devious) electoral strategy.

In early 1969, Fitt told the RTÉ television programme *Seven Days* that he had 'persuaded' a politically disgruntled Protestant, Hugh Hawks, to stand as an independent unionist calculating that this would split the unionist vote. Fitt claimed that once the campaign began he proceeded to denounce his stooge to ensure that some unionists, angered by his comments, would support the 'maligned' independent. Fitt's strategy worked well. Hawks managed to secure 403 votes which enabled Fitt to be elected with a majority of 24.

Fitt's success can also be partly attributed to the fact that it was a local government election. Although the constitutional issue was again used as an election tool, the electorate would have considered it secondary to community politics. Fitt's election was all the more satisfying because of the franchise restrictions that existed in local government polls.

If the non-sectarian socialist rhetoric of Fitt and O'Kane somewhat blurred the sectarian nature of elections in Dock, their party's victory parade clearly showed the divide in the district as well as Fitt's mixture of socialism and nationalism. The *Irish News* reported:

> The parade which was headed by the Wolfe Tone Pipe Band was large and a number of people carried green flags, the tricolour having been banned

by a police order. The two successful Dock Irish Labour Councillors travelled in a brake on which the Plough and the Stars, flag of the Labour movement, was carried in addition to a number of green flags.

During the parade, unionist supporters – a number of them teenagers – assembled around bonfires on blitz ground adjacent to Earl Street waving Union Jacks and singing Orange songs. Police had to patrol the area to keep the parties apart.

In the aftermath of his victory, Fitt showed that he was quite capable of playing the nationalist card. He commented that on polling day the electors had dealt the Unionist Party one of the most telling defeats in the whole history of the municipal battles in the 'six counties'. During the election campaign he claimed that they had been faced with all sorts of handicaps and were not permitted to fly the national flag in the ward.[26]

Other indications of the sectarian characteristic of Dock were two questions tabled for answer at Stormont after the election. Having defeated Fitt in March, Oliver, the unionist member for Dock, asked the Minister for Home Affairs, W. Topping: 'Whether his attention has been drawn to the fact that on the declaration of the result of the municipal elections in Dock Ward a Union Jack was snatched from a person and trampled on the ground, and whether the police have made an arrest?'

Topping was aware of this incident but answered that no arrests had been made. Oliver then suggested that there could have been a riot if the police had not intervened. Cahal Healey, the Nationalist Party member for South Fermanagh, then asked:

Does the Right Hon. and Learned Gentlemen not think that the time has come when the party opposite (Unionist) should cease carrying the Union Jack as a party flag in order to incite their opponents? Does the Minister not know that Councillor Fitt was assaulted in Belfast City Hall in the presence of the police by a lady carrying the Union Jack with a very robust stick attached to it? He merely threw the stick back and it fell to the ground.[27]

Notwithstanding the 'very robust stick', it is clear that religious and political allegiances in Dock were evident at all elections. Although Fitt mostly used non-sectarian rhetoric, it was obvious that the vast bulk of his supporters came from what he himself termed the 'nationally minded' population – Catholics. Fitt had achieved public office and it was as a Belfast city councillor that he would try to make Dock a non-polarised constituency.

Fitt maintained that the three most important years in his political career were between 1958 and 1961: it was during this period that he established himself as a working-class representative who helped both Protestants and Catholics in a very underprivileged area.[28] He did indeed make himself available to all sections of the community, both at home and at the window ledges of Belfast City Hall. His hard work and warm personality quickly overcame the reservations of many Protestants. It was also at this time that Fitt began a campaign against unionist discrimination in housing, votes and jobs. His maiden speech at the Belfast Corporation indicated the dual purpose of his politics – to represent the working-class and to focus attention on Catholic inequality.

Fitt claimed that in the council he would keep an open mind, and that any criticism he had to offer would be made with honesty and sincerity. He also asserted that if he saw something taking place in the council that was worthy of commendation or beneficial to the working-class he would not hesitate to commend it.[29]

In August 1958, the Dock Labour Party held its quarterly meeting. Ferran referred to the work of both Fitt and O'Kane in local government. He said, 'in the three months they had been members of the Council they have interviewed over 300 people of all creeds and classes concerning houses and other matters'. Many of these other matters pertained to unemployment benefit, then called National Assistance. At the time entitlements to National Assistance were somewhat vague, and more often than not people were not receiving their full allowance. Fitt familiarised himself with the features of the National Insurance Acts and represented both Protestants and Catholics who had been previously been rejected at local tribunals. His efforts on his constituents' behalf earned him the nickname Perry Mason, after the aggressive American television lawyer. If Fitt secured Protestant support, much of it stemmed from his concern for their interests. Nevertheless, Ferran also drew attention to the main composition of the party of which Fitt was now vice-chairman: 'The membership at present was a record, and it proved that the nationally minded people of the area were behind the party.'[30]

Fitt was never one for socialist theory, distrusting anything that smacked of 'education'. (An attitude perhaps born from an understandable resentment that his personal circumstances had denied him the opportunity to extend his schooling.) He was content with short-term practical remedies based on welfare improvements designed to assist the working-class. Connolly would have bracketed him with the 'gas and water' socialism of Belfast socialist William Walker. Housing – resisting evictions and safeguarding working-class interests – was one of Fitt's primary concerns.

In August 1959, Fitt made one of his strongest attacks on discrimination against Catholics in housing. Belfast Corporation allocated houses on a points system, under which no points were given to families with more than three children. As Catholics tended to have larger families than Protestants, this policy worked against them. Fitt also argued that the estates superintendent should not be allowed the discretionary powers that enabled him to accept or reject a family's suitability to be rehoused, regardless of how many points they had. Fitt argued that this denial of justice to Catholics was a violation of the Government of Ireland Act, which explicitly said there should be no discrimination against the minority. While Catholic families of nine and ten were being refused houses, Protestant married couples with only one child were being given three-bedroomed houses. He claimed this was an outrageous state of affairs that cried out for amendment. He knew a Catholic family whose father had to sleep in the armchair at night because there was too little room, and although registered for years this family was refused a house.[31]

Fitt's motion describing the system as unsatisfactory and calling for a review and appropriate amendments was defeated by twenty-eight votes to eight. Setbacks such as this prompted indignation and action in Catholic circles.

As discussed in Chapter 1, National Unity was formed in November 1959 to press the Nationalist Party to organise and thus be better equipped to contest such discrimination. Fitt's reaction to it at the time is not on record but he said later that it was completely sectarian: 'National Unity was a misnomer. National Unity meant Catholic nationalist against Protestant unionist.' If Fitt's opinion at the time was similar it further demonstrates that he was not part of the transformation in Catholic politics inspired by the new middle-class.

As for the Nationalist Party, he said: 'They got the Catholic vote. A Catholic Registration Office meant that they got Catholic votes and the Protestants had to look after themselves. It was totally tribal. I would have agreed with the nationalists in their opposition to the unionist treatment of Catholics but that was about all.'[32]

In 1960, Fitt continued to champion causes affecting the working-class, challenging proposed increases in local government rates, objecting to salary increases for the heads of major departments and their deputies in the corporation, and exhibiting a tendency to push for Belfast jobs for Belfast people.[33]

In December 1960, Fitt began a campaign to highlight discrimination in voting. He lodged an objection to two limited companies holding local government votes in the Dock Ward and considered them test cases.[34] In the event, Fitt's case was rejected; but before long the principle of 'one man one vote' in local government elections would become a basic demand from the Catholic community.

In 1961, Fitt had to defend his local government seat. The election tested his ability to attract the Protestant working-class vote. As the election drew near the division in the ward was further highlighted by Fitt's objection to the re-siting of a polling station in what he called a 'hostile area'. He maintained that positioning the new station in the heart of a unionist area would reduce the anti-unionist vote considerably.[35] The complaint was rejected, but the fact that it was made at all further confirms the polarisation in Dock at election times.

The election was in May. Fitt said the coming months would be very trying for the ordinary people of Belfast. He claimed the city was entering a period of recession comparable with the 'hungry' 1930s, arguing that the working-class needed a strong representative to speak on their behalf.[36] Harry Diamond, the Stormont MP for Falls, who would later form the Republican Labour Party with Fitt, spoke in support of his future party colleague. He said he had known Fitt for many years, especially as a member of the city council, and he felt that during the last three years Fitt had proved a capable and authentic representative of the interests of the working-class people of Dock. In fact, as a constant attendee at the City Hall, Councillor Fitt had made himself available to everyone who needed his help, regardless of creed, politics or where they resided.[37]

Fitt was confident of victory. Again referring to the moving of the polling station to a 'hostile area', he declared, 'knowing the people of this area where I have been born and reared, I feel that they would travel to Sandy Row [a staunchly loyalist area in Belfast] to record their vote for me in this election'.[38] He was evidently still aware that his main support base lay within the Catholic community, and his optimism proved accurate when he again topped the poll.

At the enthusiastic Dock victory parade, Fitt declared:

> I attribute my magnificent majority to the fact that I received support from all sections of the community in Dock Ward, irrespective of creed, in this election. This indeed has been a vindication of the policy which I have carried out during the past three years and I solemnly pledge to the electors that I will continue with that policy, should any man or woman in Dock Ward be in need of a friend at any time, I will be at their service.[39]

It would not be unreasonable to conclude that Fitt's growing reputation for hard work as a public representative of the working-class allowed him, to a degree, to cross the religious divide.

Fitt's commitment to working-class politics was further illustrated in October 1961. In the previous August, he had opposed rent increases in the ward. At that time the lord mayor warned that since Fitt himself was a tenant, he would be open to the accusation of self-interest. Fitt decided to disregard the advice and face the consequences.[40] The consequences turned out to be a corporation enquiry in which Fitt was named for an alleged breach of the statute in 'voting or taking part on a matter in which he had a pecuniary interest'. He represented himself, did not deny the facts, but questioned their interpretation, saying that when he decided to speak it was not on his own behalf. Arguing that he was not a rich man and was in a similar financial position to other tenants, he concluded: 'I regard myself as a working-class representative, and I will fight tooth and nail against anyone who attempts to take away my right to usurp [sic] my functions'.[41] The corporation enquiry found that Fitt took his stance from conscientious motives.

The year 1962 saw elections for the northern parliament and in March Fitt was unanimously selected as the Dock Irish Labour Party's candidate. This nomination came as no surprise. He had been narrowly defeated by Oliver in 1958, and since then had topped the poll at two successive corporation elections. Ferran declared: 'I feel there can be no doubt about the outcome of this election as the working-class people in the area of all creeds have found Councillor Fitt a sincere friend and a valuable representative.' In accepting the nomination, Fitt again conveyed his blend of republicanism and working-class solidarity, saying he 'felt proud and honoured to be asked once again to carry the banner of Connolly into the contest against the traditional enemy of the working-class in the Dock'.[42]

Whatever rhetoric Fitt may have used, and however he was perceived by the Protestant electorate in Dock itself, Moloney and Pollack note that Ulster Protestant Action (UPA), an association formed by Paisley in 1959 – ostensibly to encourage the employment of Protestants in industry – was aware of 'a Republican Labour Councillor called Gerry Fitt, who was making his mark as an aggressive exponent of the nationalist cause'.[43] Evidently not all strands of Protestant opinion were impressed with Fitt's non-sectarian oratory.

As usual, the 1962 election was characterised by accusations of sectarianism. Fitt challenged Oliver to an open debate on the economic situation in the six counties: 'But I know it will be a challenge which will not be accepted. My information is that my unionist opponents, far from meeting me on the economic issue, are endeavouring to make the forthcoming election a sectarian wrangle.'[44]

Fitt would have been content to appear to be an advocate of the nationalist cause to gain Catholic votes, but he was aware of how he was perceived by many Protestants, so as a 'socialist' he tried to focus on economic and social issues. He challenged Oliver to deny 'that the constituency has suffered a greater degree of unemployment and poor housing than any other in Belfast'.[45] He also argued that Lord Brookeborough was afraid to enter Dock to put his record to the working-class people.[46] He castigated the record of the Unionist Party in the ward:

They are a party that has shown no conception of the industrial problems as they affect the working-class in 1962. It has always been the unionist boast that the constitutional position has safeguarded the employment in the shipyards. What is their answer now, when the slips are lying empty and thousands of workers are walking the streets of the city?[47]

Fitt's election address was also overwhelmingly concerned with social and economic issues:

When I contested the last parliamentary election a slogan was written on the wall in North Queen Street drawing attention to the fact that there were 40,000 people unemployed. Today that slogan has faded a little but the terrible scourge and heartbreak of unemployment is still with us, more poignant than ever.

He emphasised his connection to the ward:

Unlike my opponent I was born and reared, and I still reside, in the area which I seek to represent at Stormont. I am married with a family of four little girls of school age and it is my humble opinion that I am more in touch with the everyday needs of the working-classes than any representative of the reactionary Tory Unionist Party.

The reference to the 'reactionary Tory Unionist Party' was characteristic of nationalist abuse of unionism during this period. This kind of language is seldom heard today. Of course it was mainly a propagandist device aimed at gaining favour on the left (when socialism enjoyed a better press), and getting some left-wing Protestant votes by characterising unionism as anti-working class and implying those who voted for it were deluded. It would be true to say that the Tories formed an alliance with the Unionists at the time of the Liberal Home Rule bills, and some right-wing Tories have been among the most vociferous supporters of Ulster unionism. But the Unionist Party, like the Nationalist Party and its successor, the SDLP, had always been a pan-class alliance and not at all 'Tory'. Of course, this does not mean that unionists did not use political manipulation to persuade working-class people to vote for them.

Fitt was certainly no 'Tory' and he presented himself to his electorate as a man of the people regardless of their religious faith. He quoted his record as a councillor: 'I have now represented this area on the City Council for over four years and during this time I have endeavoured at all times to give of my utmost for the poor and underprivileged, irrespective of creed. My home has been my Advice Centre and no one seeking my help has done so in vain.' The only public hint of republicanism was his conclusion: 'Under the banner of Connolly I go forward with confidence.'[48]

In contrast to Fitt's astute concentration on social and economic concerns during his campaign, Oliver emphasised the partition issue. 'I intend to keep unionism in Dock, the only way to prosperity.'[49] In 1958 Oliver's majority was only 256 in a seat that regularly changed hands. Fitt predicted a 'working-class revolt with an Irish Labour victory'.[50] Even the *Belfast News Letter* suggested, 'It is Eire Labour's [sic] turn to win. They have a 256 majority to upset, not a Herculean task'.[51] This prophecy proved correct. Fitt polled 3,288 votes to Oliver's 2,781.

Fitt's victory was the only Unionist defeat in the city, and the swing to Dock Irish Labour was an impressive 6.4 per cent After the results were in, Fitt declared in what was fast becoming a hackneyed, though necessary, sentiment, 'I regard it as a signal honour. I now feel I am the spokesman for the working-class and I will continue to serve the working-class in Dock irrespective of their creed.'[52]

Fitt told me that he won both the 1961 local government election and the 1962 Stormont election with the help of the Protestant community. 'I was breaking through to the Protestant unionist where no nationalist had.'[53] The election figures support his claim, although this remark also reveals that Fitt did indeed consider himself a nationalist.

Paddy Devlin, very much involved in Belfast Labourite politics at this time, made the interesting observation that Fitt's victories were due in part to Oliver's unionist patronage working against him, making the Dock Irish Labour Party's success more pronounced. As we have noted, Oliver was chairman of the housing and redevelopment committee of Belfast Corporation. Devlin told me that by rehousing his own supporters for services rendered in elections, Oliver effectively transported his political machine out of Dock. Devlin did, however, acknowledge that Protestants voted for Fitt because of his work on the corporation and the tribunals.[54] Devlin's account reinforces the image of Belfast politicians' dependence on brokerage.

It seems that despite the sectarian nature of the Dock seat, Fitt's victory was to some extent a tribute to his popularity in the area, and an appreciation of the service he had given since entering local government. The Protestant vote is hard to quantify, yet it seems the triumphs could not have been won without some cross-community support. Charles Stewart, MP for Queen's University at Stormont, commented on Fitt's greatest victory to date: 'In the see-saw constituency of Dock, Mr Fitt won a comfortable victory. The result was not exactly a surprise and was due to the great work done by him in the corporation and to a well planned campaign.'[55]

The alliance of the Protestant and Catholic working class under Gerry Fitt should not be exaggerated. After the election result it was the Unionist losers who received the ovation outside the Ulster Hall, and Fitt deemed it judicious to leave by the side door following the announcement that he was the victor.[56] Furthermore, the police presence at the victory parade is evidence that the authorities had expected communal strife. The *Irish News* reported:

> Belfast's Dock Ward showed its support for Councillor Gerry Fitt last night when 2,000 people turned out for a victory parade. The parade started in the New Lodge and wound its way around the entire constituency. At times the victory wagon carrying Councillor Fitt and his supporters was almost stopped by the enthusiastic constituents. Throughout the parade, the entire constituency was circled by a water tight contingent of police. At every strategic point the police were noticeably in force with vans, Land Rovers, walkie-talkies and man force.[57]

Fitt now had a larger platform on which to express his views. His maiden speech at Stormont contained the same components of the oratory that put him there. He began by explicitly attacking the entity of Northern Ireland. He described the queen's speech as an 'innocuous and insignificant document' relating to a manipulatively composed artifice that could not exist if it had to rely on its own resources. Fitt argued that the situation would remain the same until Ireland was reunited:

> This Government, this puppet Government in Northern Ireland, this artificial Government has been bolstered up and subsidised by the Lancashire lassies and the boys from the Chiltern Hills. They may be ignorant of that fact, but it remains that it is purely and simply from the subsidies of the English working-classes that this Government exists at all. The Government could never exist on their own economic foundations and will never exist until the industrial north is joined to the agricultural south and Ireland is once more united.

Housing was again one of Fitt's main topics of concern. Again, he did not quote doctrinaire socialist theory but reacted against injustice.[58]

As noted in the first chapter, the IRA border campaign was called off at the end of February 1962. During that campaign Fitt had represented the Dock Irish Party at the annual 1916 Easter Rising commemoration ceremony held at the republican plot in Milltown Cemetery, Belfast.[59] In an interview with me, Fitt maintained that he saw the IRA offensive 'as a completely sectarian fight'. Evidence suggests that his attitude at the time was very different. In his maiden Stormont speech he had made a strong appeal for the release of over twenty men who were still in prison as a result of the campaign. Fitt argued for compassion, claiming the prisoners were only guilty of being idealists in a situation that was intolerable:

> After all, these men had a principle and they had the courage to go out and try to put that principle into practice. They may have acted wrongly. Perhaps they did act wrongly, but in the state of affairs that exists in our community the Minister would be doing nothing wrong in releasing those men.

Fitt's sympathy for the plight of the republican prisoners could be attributed to the notion that the physical force tradition had been made redundant by the contemporary political situation. He did not envisage a resumption of political violence and made it clear that he was committed to constitutional reunification. 'Ireland within my lifetime will be united constitutionally and it is my ideal to see Ireland united under the terms of Connolly who founded my party and that it will eventually finish as an Irish workers' republic.'[60]

This, however, was the public face of Gerry Fitt's republicanism. Belfast republican John Kelly revealed that in the mid-1950s, 'Fitt sanctioned and allowed republicans to use the Dock Irish Labour Party premises for IRA gun lectures.' This was, according to Kelly, a 'very courageous and dangerous thing to do as the penalty if detected would have been prison'.[61] Kelly himself, while still a teenager, had been sentenced to seven years for the possession of arms in 1956. Perhaps it is not surprising that Fitt pleaded for leniency for republican prisoners, when young men like Kelly were locked up for weapons offences: after all, their introduction to these weapons had come courtesy of the Dock Irish Labour Party. Interestingly, these detainees included the brother of James O'Kane, Fitt's former party colleague.[62]

The wrangle over the republican prisoners continued throughout the year. In October 1962 Fitt, Diamond and Independent Labour MP Frank Hanna tabled a motion calling for the release of all those imprisoned for actions arising from political activity during 1956 and 1961. In December the debate on this motion began in Stormont. Brian Faulkner, by now Minister of Home Affairs, refused to accept the motion, insisting that the government could not assume the IRA was finished. Fitt was again dismayed by what he felt was a lack of compassion from the administration.

In arguing for the motion he gave the IRA a measure of political credibility. 'If the government had one spark of humanity or Christian charity they would have relented over the past months. But they were still activated by an implacable hatred towards their political opponents.'[63]

The debate was concluded on 18 December when a government amendment asking for approval of the *status quo* was passed. Fitt said of the prisoners' condition: 'If he was incarcerated he would not get down on his bended knees and ask for forgiveness and seek the prerogative of mercy from the Minister. As these young men did not recognise the court he could not see how they could be expected to ask for the prerogative of mercy.'[64]

Fitt's attitude to the IRA at this point in his career was at least sympathetic and indeed in many respects supportive. He probably felt genuine compassion for the plight of the individuals concerned, but he was shrewd enough to realise that concern for the predicament of the prisoners would strike a chord with those supporters with republican leanings. In short, he used the situation to his own political advantage. As we shall see, Fitt's relationship with the reconstituted IRA in the 1970s (when it had become a power in his own back yard) was not so accommodating.

In March 1963, Terence O'Neill became leader of the Unionist Party and Prime Minister, heralding, many hoped, the beginning of a new era. In hindsight, Fitt said that he believed O'Neill did try to reform the Unionist Party:

> But he was like Botha trying to reform South Africa and they have exactly the same mentality, the unionists in Northern Ireland and the whites in South Africa. It was an impossible task. Consequently, he fell between two stools; the unionists regarded him as some sort of traitor and the Catholics as some sort of liar that could not deliver.[65]

Throughout the rest of 1963 at Stormont, Fitt continued in his capacity as a representative of the working-class, attacking the Unionist Party's handling of the economy, highlighting discrimination in housing and employment, and frequently denouncing the machinations of the Orange Order.[66]

Towards the end of the year his political profile was apparently altered when, with Harry Diamond, he formed the Republican Labour Party. The coalition was anti-partitionist and comprised former members of the Dublin-based Labour Party. Thus there was now an Irish Labour Party with local leaders, which despite its republican label was committed to participation in the system. Fergus Pyle of the *Irish Times* asked Fitt about the formation of the party and reported:

> Looking back on nearly 40 years in local and national politics, Fitt says that he was never interested in nationalism and that the Republican Labour tag that he took to form a two-man party with the veteran MP for Falls, Harry Diamond in the 1960s was purely tactical. A journalist launched the idea and he found himself swept along.[67]

Fitt's recollection that he was never interested in nationalism is not reflected in his political rhetoric at the time. On the other hand, the term 'republican' is misleading: it conjures up different images for different people. In the recent sequence of violence it has taken on pejorative connotations, particularly in some Dublin media and academic circles – largely as a reaction against the methods of the IRA. In the 1950s and 1960s, a republican in Northern Ireland was simply someone who wanted to see the restoration of the territorial unity of Ireland in the form of a republic. The term and ideology was respected throughout the nationalist community, at least in an idealistic fashion. Nevertheless, Fitt, working in a marginal constituency, was taking more of a gamble than Diamond, who was from the predominantly Catholic Falls area. When asked 'How republican was Republican Labour?' Fitt replied:

> It was not republican as such. Harry Diamond had the term Republican Labour before I had it. He could afford to have it in the Falls Road where the Protestant vote did not count. In Dock it was totally different, so I took a calculated chance in bringing Republican Labour into Dock and succeeded in winning elections after election even with that term. I won them not because they were voting Republican Labour; I won them because they were voting for Gerry Fitt.[68]

Paddy Devlin concurred that 'Republican Labour was only a label'.[69] Fitt made the decision on the name without consulting his colleagues in the Dock Irish Labour Party. Although he managed to persuade them to come with him, the episode reflects an individualistic and opportunist streak, a trait that can be seen throughout his political career. The amalgamation was well received in nationalist circles. *New Nation* commented:

The recent news of the formation of the Republican Labour Party following the merger of the Dock and Falls groups is heartening news, especially in view of the forthcoming Westminster elections, in which the party will be contesting West Belfast. By their action this group has given a lead to all other political groupings on the National Front throughout the six counties, and one would hope that there would be further mergers before the election comes round.[70]

Hibernia remarked:

The coming together of Mr Harry Diamond and Mr G Fitt to form the Irish Republican Labour Party could be of real significance if they can create a genuine Irish socialist group which would take up where James Connolly left off and bring some passion and intelligence to the solution of economic problems, especially in relation to the unemployment crisis.[71]

The two politicians frequently proposed motions aimed at government reform. For example, at Stormont in April 1964 they called for reform in parliamentary and local government elections, urging that legislation be introduced to provide the right for everyone over eighteen to vote in such elections and asking for the removal of the 'one man one vote' restrictions in the local government franchise.[72] This motion was predictably defeated by twenty votes to fourteen and a major Catholic grievance remained.

The local elections with which Diamond and Fitt were concerned were held in May 1964. They would give the first indication of whether or not the 'republican' tag had adversely affected Fitt's non-sectarian credibility. He argued that these would be the most crucial elections ever to have taken place in Dock and suggested that the result would decide if the ward was to exist as a residential district or be developed as a commercial centre.[73]

Fitt insisted that his record since being elected as a public representative would defy all comers: he had consistently served the interests of all sections of the Dock area and would continue to do so.[74] He ran with two more prospective councillors from the Republican Labour Party – Tom Fitzpatrick, a docker and James McMenamin, a publican.

The Unionists, hoping to counter the reverses they had been suffering, selected candidates with strong connections in Dock: Seán McMaster, chairman of the local Unionist Association and a crane man by occupation; Charles Maginnis, a labourer, also a native of the area; and Billy McDowell, a shop owner who had lived there for twenty years. Paddy Wilson, who ran on a straight Labour ticket, and who would become Fitt's closest political ally, was a native of Dock, working in an aircraft factory. Fitt's opponents could not be considered as opulent outsiders.

The *Belfast News Letter* conveyed something of the carnival atmosphere of electioneering in the locality:

> The other Wards had nothing on Dock, where pacemaker Gerry Fitt set a swinging pattern for his Republican colleagues Messrs Fitzpatrick and McMenamin. Youngsters and adults alike turned out in their hundreds to add something of the 'Lagan beat' to the proceedings and to add that final touch. St Peter's Brass and Reed Band provided the music and accompaniment.
>
> But wait, Gerry Fitt and his boys didn't quite have it all their own way in Belfast's dockland. For although his party set a cracking pace and the band struck up to the music of the 'Minstrel Boy' a few yards around the corner was none other than a party of unionists singing and dancing to the music of 'Derry Walls'.[75]

The results of the election were impressive for Republican Labour – all three candidates were returned, with Fitt again topping the poll. Gerry Fitt and the Republican Labour Party had achieved dominance in Dock.

The next opportunity for the party to test their electoral strength was the October 1964 United Kingdom general election.

Diamond was chosen by Republican Labour to contest the West Belfast seat. (It should be noted that the Dock Ward, although geographically in the north of the city, was within the East Belfast constituency – which always returned a unionist.) The unionist candidate was Jim Kilfedder, a Donegal-born barrister. The NILP selected Billy Boyd, whose platform was pro-border yet non-sectarian; and the republican candidate was Liam McMillan. Gerry Fitt was Diamond's election agent.

The election became particularly noteworthy for the rioting that broke out on Divis Street at the foot of the Catholic Falls Road. At his Divis Street headquarters, McMillan displayed traditional republican regalia – pictures of James Connolly and Patrick Pearse and the Irish tricolour. This was in direct violation of the 1954 Flags and Emblems Act, under which it was illegal to display any symbol that would cause provocation and lead to the disruption of public order. In such a situation the Royal Ulster Constabulary (RUC) was empowered to remove the 'objectionable' material.

Loyalists, led by a publicity-hungry Ian Paisley, made it known that they were offended by the republican display and threatened to remove it if the RUC did not. The Minister for Home Affairs, Brian McConnell, capitulated under this pressure and ordered the RUC into Divis Street. The police presence caused a riot, with local Catholics emerging to defend the republican symbols. It was the worst disturbance in Northern Ireland since the 1930s, lasting for three days and ending with twenty-one policemen and fifty civilians injured.

Fitt tried to end the fray by asking Belfast Corporation to pass an emergency resolution calling on all sections of the community 'to desist from any action which could lead to a further exacerbation of relations'.[76] While Fitt made some effort to end the episode he was not convinced that all politicians shared his attitude.

After the riots, Fitt was very critical of the unionist administration. He spoke at Stormont and alleged that the whole affair was an intrigue and further maintained that the government announcements to have the flags taken down were designed to bring out the largest possible crowd to witness their removal. In short, the riot was a 'political stunt' to swing votes away from Diamond.[77]

It was in these abnormal conditions that the election in West Belfast took place. The stunt worked and the unionists won, but on a minority vote. Kilfedder polled 21,337 votes, Diamond 14,678, Boyd 12,571 and McMillan 3,256.

It is unlikely that Diamond secured any Protestant support: as MP for Catholic Falls at Stormont he had no need to do so. The republican Labour support in Dock was inaccessible; and much of the Protestant vote would have been of a personal kind for Fitt. It is also possible that Boyd made some inroads on the Catholic vote; certainly the republican element was not formidable. McMillan lost his deposit, as did his three colleagues in the other constituencies. He would perhaps have got fewer votes but for the unrest in Divis Street, which no doubt made some of the electorate more militant. Even with this motivation the republican vote, as expressed by McMillan, was still only 6 per cent.

The *New Nation*, still voicing a demand for greater method in nationalist politics, commented on the defeat of Diamond: 'The failure of the Republican Labour candidate in West Belfast clearly indicates that a large number of enthusiastic helpers is no substitute for a good machine.'[78]

In the Republic, *Hibernia* was disillusioned:

The Anglophiles, intent on guarding their dominant position, behaved as though they were the injured party, the opposition pathetically divided made feeble attempts to find a united banner, aired their grievances without hope of redress, and lost their deposits. The result was the same as before. Twelve true men and blue[79] represent us in the mother of Parliaments.[80]

Diamond and Boyd both polled reasonable figures (28.3 per cent and 24.3 per cent respectively), which if combined would have defeated the unionists. As it was, both gained enough support to allow the common enemy to win, to the detriment of Labourite politics. The next time, with Fitt as the candidate, the results of the West Belfast election for the United Kingdom parliament would be different.

The 1964 election had one wider implication for Northern Ireland politics. In Britain, the Labour Party under Harold Wilson was elected. Some Labour politicians were concerned about and sympathetic to Catholic complaints of discrimination in Northern Ireland and were opposed to the cross-party consensus in Britain to keep Northern Ireland affairs at arm's length under the tutelage of the Unionist Party. This group was a potential support base for Fitt, which he would not have encountered from a Conservative administration.

In the same month as the 1964 election, McAteer, under increasing pressure to form a vigorous nationalist coalition, invited the Belfast 'Labour-orientated anti-partitionist' MPs to join a new organisation, and the Republican Labour Party agreed to enter into talks. Any optimism about a merger between nationalists of the rural areas and the Republican Labourites was soon dashed, for on 6 December the party decided to postpone consideration of a possible link-up. Commenting on this decision, Fitt told the *Irish News* that he had been disenchanted by the failure of past attempts at unity. Fitt added that while he was very pleased to see the nationally minded moving in the direction of unity, there would have to be definite guarantees that all sections of the working-class were represented in any such united front.[81]

The voting of the party's Executive was very close. The Dock branch was totally opposed to the prospect of a merger. On the other hand, Seán McGivern of the Andersonstown branch, and party secretary, resigned because of what he saw as the leadership's reluctance to create a unified national movement.[82] It is possible that Fitt and his Dock colleagues felt that freely entering an openly nationalist structure would have alienated Protestant support in the area. However, it is also probable that careerist concerns militated against unity – a point noted by the *New Nation*:

> We regret that breakdown in the negotiations between the leaders of the Nationalist Party and the Belfast anti-partitionist groups especially as the reason given seems to amount to little more than distrust arising over past experiences. In such an attitude there is evidence of a pathetic lack of vision and a miserable concern with merely personal prestige, which creates divisions and prevents any real progress.[83]

The episode illustrates that at this stage Fitt felt unable to reconcile his nationalist and socialist sentiments in a fixed relationship. Fitt was very much part of the nationalist tradition of disaffection and had frequently posed as a champion of Irish unity. But when his affiliation to a coalition geared to fulfil that aspiration was proposed, he fell back on his working-class socialist credentials. Fitt was a political acrobat who continually juggled the rhetoric of socialism and nationalism to advance his political fortunes. Yet perhaps his inclination to decline signing up to a team was prudent – as his spell with the SDLP was later to prove.

Fitt's political activity was temporarily interrupted on 9 December, when he suddenly collapsed while speaking at Stormont. He was admitted to the Royal Victoria Hospital and required a blood transfusion for a gastric haemorrhage. This was not the only time that the rigours of political life would hospitalise Fitt, but on this occasion he was well enough to return to the House on 19 January 1965, and was personally welcomed back by O'Neill.[84]

Five days earlier, and just three months after the riots in Divis Street, O'Neill and Lemass met in Belfast. Although Fitt would have considered his politics substantially different from those of the two premiers, he considered the meeting a welcome gesture and articulated his feelings at Stormont. In the same speech he also voiced his approval of the Nationalist Party becoming the official opposition; a step he felt had brought about 'a more realistic political atmosphere in Northern Ireland'. In keeping with the conciliatory spirit of his speech and indeed with the apparent normalising of northern politics at the time, Fitt re-affirmed his own brand of constitutional nationalism and showed he was not a socialist republican of the Connolly type:

> In my constituency there are many people who believe in the ultimate ideal in which I believe, the eventual reunification of this country. The way to bring this about is to recognise that Stormont exists, to use this House and all its institutions to further the interests and well being of all constituents, irrespective of their political beliefs. If we can bring peace and harmony to this community it will be only a little step before we can eventually bring about a unity of mind in the whole island.[85]

Two days after these words, the divisions within the Republican Labour Party were becoming apparent. On 5 February 1965, the *Irish News* reported that the Andersonstown Branch of West Belfast had unanimously voted to disaffiliate from the party.[86] Evidently there were elements in the party who were more concerned with the republican than the labour tag, and the fact that Andersonstown was a predominantly Catholic middle-class area may well have accounted for this emphasis.

The Unionist administration was remarkably adept at taking decisions that lacked political sensitivity and brought traditional attitudes to the forefront. Maybe this was because O'Neillism had not percolated down through the party, or perhaps it was symptomatic of the increasing political incompetence that was about to bring down the Stormont regime. Or maybe it was simply part of the routine of communal politics.

One such decision was made by the minister of development, William Craig, to name the new city in County Armagh, Craigavon, after the first Prime Minister of Northern Ireland, James Craig. Craig was considered, perhaps unfairly, an arch bigot by the Catholic community. The *Irish News* reported Fitt's reaction:

> The name could only be accepted as a calculated insult to the minority in Northern Ireland. It was the final insult at this time when there was so much talk about building bridges between different sections of the community.
>
> The minority had often been charged with having long memories but

it was within the memory of many members that Lord Craigavon said this was a Protestant parliament for a Protestant people.

The minority could never forget this statement and the naming of the city seemed to show that the policy of the Northern Ireland Government was to maintain a Protestant parliament for a Protestant people.[87]

This statement was an emotional response from an emotional politician. Much of Fitt's fluent rhetoric stemmed from fervent reaction to perceived prejudice: he had a strong sense of grievance that made him a formidable and tenacious debater. The following day he argued that if the inhabitants of the new city were going to be faced with sectarian strife, any advantages would be negated. He fulminated: 'Why not go the whole hog and call it Paisleyville? This would be accepted just as well by the people who are now congratulating the minister on the name selected.'[88]

Despite tension generated by Craigavon and other matters (such as the siting of the new university in largely Protestant Coleraine rather than largely Catholic and depressed Derry, and the controversy over the naming of a bridge over the river Lagan), there was optimism about a thaw in community relations.[89] This was noted by *Hibernia*, which re-published two editorials: one from the staunchly pro-unionist *Belfast News Letter*, the other from the more moderate pro-unionist *Belfast Telegraph*, both confirming new attitudes:

Senator Lennon[90] is entitled to call for more from the Government than expressions of greater goodwill – deeds must follow words if bridges are to be built between the two sections of the population but he should appreciate that progress towards a new order must be slow if it is to be sure, and that too precipitate action could wipe out the advances already made.[91]

As for the Unionist Party, the curiosity, some would say the tragedy of the situation is that despite the knowledge of the way rising living standards have dulled anti-partition protest, it will not make a direct move to enlist support for the constitution from members of the steadily growing Catholic population.

If a policy of co-operation is to mean anything more than window dressing it must have this end in view. But what unionist will brave the Protestant flank and say so? When in fact will the attempt be made to diminish the influence of religion in politics?[92]

In the midst of this seemingly cordial era, Fitt had to defend his Stormont seat: O'Neill called an election for 25 November 1965. Dock constituency had never been retained, so Fitt was to some extent fighting against history. The communal divisions of the ward would again be put to the test. The Unionist Party again put forward William Oliver to contest the Dock seat.

In an attempt to swing the election, O'Neill decided to visit the constituency himself. The *Irish News* reported Fitt's reaction to this attempt to 'cadge votes': 'No Arab tribesman or African pearl diver could be more foreign to the people of Dock or more ignorant of their needs and problems than the Eton-bred schoolboy who proposed to descend on the place with scarf flying on election eve.'[93]

Also worthy of mention in this issue of the *Irish News* was the publication of a telegram to Fitt from James Connolly's daughter Ina: 'I wish you every success and return once more to parliament for this historic division which my father contested in 1913. I sincerely pray that the electorate of Dock will, to his memory, give you an overwhelming majority.'[94] There can be little doubt that Fitt had an acute sensitivity to what was required on the ground, and was well aware that a fusion of nationalism, republicanism and socialism would unite the various strands of potential voters.

Fitt's prediction of the result was assured. 'There can be no doubt about the outcome. I, as one of the people, have faith in the peoples' verdict.'[95] His optimism was well founded: he was again successful.

The result was the only substantial unionist reverse in the Stormont election. Fitt more than doubled his majority, despite a lower poll, and the *Belfast News Letter* acknowledged:

> Dodgy Dock turned up trumps for Republican Labour man, Mr Gerry Fitt, who withstood the unionist challenge, from Mr William Oliver, whom Mr Fitt beat by 507 votes in 1962. He built on this vote this time, adding nearly 1,000 votes. The result represents a substantial swing to the anti-partition candidate.[96]

The *News Letter* clearly considered Fitt to be a nationalist and now no longer had to adjust the name of his political party. Fitt, on the other hand, claimed that his victory was one for the working-class and socialism. Yet although this election had been less crudely sectarian, it was still, as ever, Protestant unionist versus Catholic nationalist. *Hibernia* reported Oliver's reaction to his defeat: 'Alderman Oliver explaining on television why he had lost in Dock to Republican Labour said some of his people had stayed at home. Asked why they had done this he said that it was because they favoured Labour or Liberal or other parties. His people presumably include all Protestants.'[97]

At the end of the year, Harold Wilson called another UK general election for 31 March 1966, and the newly formed NDP stated its intent to contest West Belfast.[98] In the following week Fitt announced his candidacy for the same seat. He again combined his nationalist, republican and socialist credentials:

> I believe that this division can only be won by someone adhering to the principles of James Connolly and fighting tenaciously for the ultimate reunification of this country. I realise that many of the electorate in this area are of a different religious persuasion to my own, but I also am aware that these people know me as a Labour representative who has taken an unequivocal stand where the needs of the working-classes have been concerned. I will be fighting this election on my record as a Labour representative, and as such, I feel confident that the working-class in West Belfast will ensure my return to Westminster.[99]

Fitt's intervention clearly threatened to split the 'nationally minded vote' and leave it open for the unionists to retain the seat. When I asked Fitt why he decided to stand and perhaps split the Catholic vote, he replied:

> The new party was totally anathema to me. They were Catholic middle-class schoolteachers and called themselves the National Democratic Party. They were people I had nothing in common with. They were Catholic middle-class who believed they had been educated and there was a God-given right for them to represent the Catholic working-class ... People who had no idea how Catholic people live in Dock or Falls or Ballymurphy. They appointed themselves as such and totally infuriated me.[100]

Fitt had a certain distrust of people with a formal education. I met him on two occasions and although warm and generous he was absolutely insistent on his version of events. I had the temerity to challenge him on some issues and on occasion tried to move the conversation in a different direction only to be left feeling that Fitt viewed with some suspicion anyone who had not gained their political intelligence in the university of life.

This sense of Fitt's resentful attitude is corroborated by a recollection of Austin Currie, which shows that although he may not have had much time for academia he could certainly learn a lesson:

> … I was insensitive enough to criticise his grammar during a TV appearance, particularly his misuse of 'seen' and 'done'. I tried to explain that the use of such expressions went largely unnoticed in ordinary speech but came across badly on television. Gerry didn't like my advice and called me 'a fucking snob' and slammed the door behind him and stormed out. The next day he sought me out, did not apologise, but asked me to repeat what I had said to him. I never again heard him, on TV or radio, use those words in the wrong context.[101]

Evidently the middle-class professional image of the NDP caused friction with the other nationalist elements.[102] There was some debate within the Republican Labour Party about whether or not they should contest the election. Fitt was in favour of participation regardless of the result, because he felt that if the NDP established their presence the political influence of the Republican Labour Party would be greatly diminished. Harry Diamond, on the other hand, was against splitting the Catholic vote, arguing that West Belfast was a sectarian constituency. Without consulting his party colleagues, Fitt leaked to the press Republican Labour's 'unanimous' decision to participate, with him as the candidate – another indication of the individualistic and impulsive nature of his politics. He later admitted: 'I am very much of an individualist. I make my own mind up on something and think that I am right and other people have their point of view but it is not going to change my opinion – so I was never the ideal party leader.'[103] On this occasion, Fitt's assertive attitude won the day. He subsequently confirmed the 'unanimous' decision with his party and was indeed selected to contest the election, although Diamond was recorded as dissenting.[104]

On 2 March 1966, the NDP announced their candidate – a thirty-six-year-old primary school teacher, Joseph Lavery, who claimed: 'The time has now come when elections in Northern Ireland must not be fought on shibboleths and slogans, but rather on intelligent and rational argument about the issues involved.'[105]

Fitt went on record as regretting the NDP decision, which he believed would lead to unionist retention of the seat:

> The NDP entered the political arena last year with the intention of unify-ing the nationally minded forces against the Unionist Party ... and since then they have adopted the attitude that they are the only spokesman for the nationally minded electorate. In effect they are one more splinter party in opposition to the unionists.[106]

The dispute between the two parties precipitated bitter recrimination in the following week. On 6 March, Fitt declared: 'Not one single vote has so far been cast for the National Democratic Party in the City of Belfast and I am certain that the electors of the Falls area will show in no uncertain manner their distaste for the tactics being employed by the National Democratic Party.'[107] Answering suggestions that the NDP withdraw from the contest to avoid a split vote, a party spokesman argued with an undisguised jibe at Fitt:

> The Northern Ireland electorate is sick to death of the lone operator and the opportunist in politics. We want to help build a proper political party because this is the only way to get rid of the unionists. We believe that the electorate recognises this and will continue to support us accordingly.[108]

Fitt retorted that the NDP was campaigning on a purely sectional ap-peal.[109] On the following day, 10 March, the rift between the two parties widened as both indicated that they intended to remain in contention. An NDP spokesman declared that they would not be stampeded by the 'Tammany Hall tactics that are being used in the West'.[110]

Meanwhile, Fitt acquired the backing of eight nationalist MPs, in-cluding McAteer and Austin Currie.[111] This mounting support for Fitt from the Nationalist Party forced the NDP to seek a compromise, and they suggested that he could win the nomination from a united party – a merger between the two. Diamond strongly opposed this suggestion, his comment reflecting the temper of the argument:

> A proposal of a shotgun wedding or merger with a faction outside of this

unity (the unity of support for Fitt) on the eve of the election cannot be taken seriously when accompanied by taunts and sneers and statements dripping with hatred and abuse of a popular hard-working representative.[112]

The threat of a three-cornered challenge for West Belfast was finally ended on 13 March when the NDP capitulated to the increased pressure and withdrew Lavery. The statement announcing the withdrawal followed an appeal from McAteer to the party's central council. Fitt's intractable attitude had won the day. His determination had ensured that he would be the only nationalist in the contest against the unionists. Nevertheless, the severity of the clash revealed a great deal of enmity between the 'working-class nationalists' and the 'middle-class nationalists'. This dissonance would have important implications for Fitt in the 1970s.

The episode points to a significant characteristic of Fitt – he was not a team player. He seemed to enjoy being a maverick and was not predisposed to party discipline. He needed to be leader or to be able to do his own thing; to further his ambitions free from constraint. In essence he was anti-organisation and anti-organisations.

Lavery, for his part, has no regrets about the outcome. He told me that he did not have 'the temperament and experience' for the job and 'was pushed into it' by his NDP colleagues. He thinks 'Fitt was the right man in the right place'. Lavery was also keen to stress Fitt's 'amiable' nature. There is no doubt that Fitt was good company and possessed a vibrant, humorous and engaging personality. He was very likeable. Lavery also suggested that the publicity generated by the episode did assist Fitt in the Westminster election.[113]

If Fitt was to overcome the Unionist Party incumbent Kilfedder, he had to gain at least 5,000 of the voters who had previously plumped for the NILP. However, many of the people who would have voted for Boyd would have been appalled at Fitt's republican tag and nationalist aspirations. Kilfedder predictably laid great emphasis on his opponent's republicanism and the question of the constitution: 'Why doesn't Mr Fitt talk about his policies – his republicanism which will put us in with the south?'[114] He told a *Belfast Telegraph* reporter: 'No amount of pretence at being the Labour candidate by my Republican opponent can hide the fact that the contest is a simple referendum – a vote for or against the Ulster constitutional position.'[115]

Fitt, however, was typically ambiguous in his election speeches, managing to emphasise both his socialist credentials and his nationalism.[116] This approach did not fool all Protestant electors, as the following appraisal from the *Belfast Telegraph* indicated: 'Mr Fitt, for all his engaging personality and his avoidance of an exclusively religious appeal, is primarily an anti-partitionist, and it will be an elastic conscience which is able to support both him and the constitution at the same time.'[117]

Fitt was no innocent when it came to electioneering. He told me how he employed his Protestant campaign workers:

A few Protestant workers came to work for me. Some of them I was wary about because it was going to be a dirty election and I was going to be as dirty as them. These Protestants asked 'how they could help me' and I said 'how can I be sure you won't sink me?' I said 'if you want to help go down to Unionist Party Headquarters on Glengall Street and sign on as workers for Kilfedder and tell me everything that was happening in the unionist camp'. This they did and I was able to take counter-measures.

He also had the wit to 'tip off' Ulster Television and the *Belfast Telegraph* of 'possible trouble' at a polling station in a unionist area having previously arranged to transport thirty nuns there to vote for him. As he expected the local unionists hurled abuse at the sisters and the cameras and reporters were there to witness it.[118] One can only imagine what his Protestant campaign workers must have thought. Not only were they helping an outspoken Catholic win an election, they were also driving a car full of nuns to a polling station to help do it.

Fitt was undoubtedly a tough and resourceful political competitor and no account of his political career would be complete without at least a mention of voter impersonation. Fitt and his 'markers' maximised the 'graveyard' vote, 'pluggers' were instructed to vote early and often. Myth suggests that Fitt was particularly adept at such subterfuge, but to what extent such vote theft proved crucial to election results is obviously difficult to quantify.

In a letter to the *Belfast Telegraph*, Michael Farrell, then chairman of the Queen's University Labour group, and later to become an important member of People's Democracy (PD), wrote that he recognised the dilemma facing Labour voters in West Belfast due to the importance of the constitutional issue. Farrell appealed to the people who had voted for

Boyd in 1964 to vote for Fitt in 1966, citing three inducements:

> Because the border is not an issue in this election and Mr Fitt has made it clear he does not intend to make it one.
>
> Because the issue in the election is whether there should be a Labour or Conservative government at Westminster, and Mr Fitt has made it abundantly clear that he will support a Labour government.
>
> Because we believe that Mr Fitt has shown, since his election to the Stormont parliament, that he is prepared to work extremely hard for all his constituents and indeed for many outside his constituency. By this he has proved his claim to be a working-class and Labour representative.[119]

Fitt's victory and majority of over 2,000 was presumably a product of these factors. Fitt polled 26,292 votes to Kilfedder's 24,281.

Fitt had become the first candidate since 1955 to wrest West Belfast from the unionists, achieving this despite one of the most concentrated campaigns ever mounted by the Unionist Party machine. His victory was sensational, but unionist support in the other three Belfast constituencies was also severely reduced. After his victory, Fitt again made no secret of where he stood on the constitutional position while simultaneously emphasising his socialist fervour:

> West Belfast has shown its repulsion of unionism, and while the majority of the support which I received came from those people who believe in the national unity of this country, I also received the working-class support on my record as a public representative.
>
> I have been elected on the Republican Labour ticket which to me consists of the twin ideals of the unity of the island and the betterment of all the people. In Westminster I will support the Labour government on its initiation of social and progressive legislation. I will maintain my stand to propagate the unity of Ireland and I have no doubt that I will receive the support of many progressive British Labour MPs in this connection. This is the happiest day of my life. It is a victory for sanity in Northern Ireland politics. I have received the confidence of the working-class. Now I will carry all my efforts to bring the workers under the Labour umbrella.[120]

Reaction to the outcome of the election in West Belfast predictably corresponded to political and religious affiliation. Nationalist sentiment was obviously delighted. Diamond described the result as a 'sensational breakthrough. It is a tribute to the people who disregard the sectarian appeal of unionism'. McAteer sent Fitt a congratulatory telegram which read 'and then there was [*sic*] eleven'. Nationalists clearly regarded Fitt as one of their own, and, despite his non-sectarian and Labourite rhetoric, he was. Unionist reaction reinforced this perception. Captain Willy Orr, leader of the Unionist Party at Westminster, said, 'It is a sad thing for Ulster, when the famous constituency of West Belfast has chosen to go republican.'[121]

To what extent, then, did Protestants vote for Fitt? A degree of elucidation can be provided by looking at past elections for the constituency.

The 1964 election was a four-cornered contest, with the opposition split three ways. The Unionist Party was victorious but it was out-polled by 9,000 votes. In that contest, Kilfedder received 21,337 votes while the anti-border candidates representing the Republican Labour Party and republicans achieved a combined total of 17,934 votes. The socialist NILP polled 12,571 votes.

In 1966, therefore, the unknown quantity was the voters who had previously supported the NILP. It was these votes that would decide the election. Fitt's task was to gain Protestant votes from Kilfedder, without alienating his nucleus of nationally minded supporters. The last straight unionist versus anti-unionist Labour contest was Jack Beattie's triumph. Beattie won by twenty-five votes. This would reinforce the claim that the religious divide in the constituency was about equal. If this is the case, it seems Fitt did succeed in his mission (although it is worth noting that Fitt's vote was 3,113 below the total opposition vote in 1964, and that Kilfedder polled 2,844 more than he had done in 1964 – suggesting that many who had previously voted NILP were merely dissatisfied unionists). One factor that would have persuaded this element was Fitt's commitment to support the Labour Party at Westminster on social issues. In addition he had already proved his ability in local government elections to win a proportion of Protestant working-class votes. It is also likely that he won the votes of a high proportion of those who had previously voted republican. It was, as Budge and O'Leary concluded, an 'odd combination of religious and political loyalties' that saw Fitt elected to Westminster.[122]

A juggling act was required to secure short-term electoral gain in Northern Ireland, but would Gerry Fitt's demonstrable juggling ability be enough to change the political landscape in the longer term? And would the same act be adequate when new political forces appeared on the scene and began changing that very landscape?

3

CIVIL RIGHTS
OR NATIONAL RIGHTS

What had seemed to be positive political developments in Northern Ireland during the mid-1960s turned out to be illusory; and these developments, beginning with the Lemass/O'Neill détente, had negative rather than positive consequences for the stability of Northern Ireland.

The Nationalist Party, with prompting from Lemass, reluctantly became an official opposition at Stormont on 23 January 1965. But in doing so it entered into a charade that brought home to it and the Catholic community the futility of being a permanent opposition in a parliament that was mainly a rubber stamp for the real business of politics – the governing of the state – which was done at Westminster. In most parliaments the opposition exerts a moderating influence on the government, and since the government is always aware that the present opposition might be in power in the future, it acts with restraint. But in Stormont, where the Unionist government was always going to be the government, there was no such restraining influence, and the opposition were permanent patsies. Such a position did not help maintain the modicum of self-respect that at least abstention had provided. All the Lemass/O'Neill initiative did was to expose the predicament of the representatives of the northern Catholic community and the true nature of the Stormont system. And by doing so Lemass and O'Neill destabilised the very thing O'Neill had aimed to protect.

Lemass' visit signalled an end to de Valera's policy on the north. The traditional policy amounted to drawing attention to the injustice of partition while largely leaving the north alone, and exploiting the Irish Republic's political, social and political independence from Britain to the maximum. Lemass began to move away from this policy by meddling in the north, with the intention of improving relations between the two. But this was to lead to catastrophe.

Terence O'Neill later pinpointed 1966 – the same year Fitt was elected to Westminster – as the year of deterioration.[1] Fitt promised to ensure that the discrimination that existed in Northern Ireland would be vigorously exposed. At Westminster, his attempts to highlight the iniquities of Stormont were met with an almost total ignorance of the reality, brought about by the quarantining of Northern Ireland from the party conflict at Westminster.

However, four years later the unionist government was fighting for survival. Fitt had fulfilled his promise and must take some credit for destabilising the state – if indeed, that was his objective. This is not to say that the Labour government of the time was instrumental in helping him, since the last thing they wanted was the destabilisation of Northern Ireland. But for the Civil Rights movement, that government would have adopted the arm's length policy of its predecessors towards Northern Ireland and done nothing.

Although O'Neill could claim to have made some effort to win over the minority to unionism, his liberalism was essentially a façade, and a very dangerous one at that. However, his style of government was far enough removed from traditional tenets to ensure the fragmentation of unionism. He had no greater critic than Ian Paisley, who judged the new politics a betrayal of both Protestantism and unionism. Bew and Patterson comment: 'The effect of O'Neill's policies was therefore to create tensions between his government and some of the most backward elements of the Unionist Party, and this allowed him to represent himself as a progressive force whilst in fact no actual strategy of reforming sectarian relations existed.'[2]

On 18 April 1966 the fiftieth anniversary of the Easter Rebellion was celebrated with colourful parades in Dublin and Belfast. John Kelly later stated how important the Dublin celebrations were for the morale of Belfast republicans: 'It meant that the Republican movement was still alive, that the sacrifice of 1916 had not been forgotten, that it was being commemorated 50 years later, not only by Republicans but by the state. It meant a reaffirmation of the whole Republican ethos.'[3]

In the north O'Neill had exhibited the typical unionist fear of nationalist expression by banning trains from Dublin to Belfast – an action that exacerbated rather than reduced tension. In the Belfast parade, Fitt walked with the ITGWU and was loudly applauded by the crowds, reflecting his tremendous popularity.[4] He had actually not intended to march, but O'Neill's move prompted him to break a prior engagement in London to take part.[5] The march was, like its southern counterpart, a tribute to the republican rising and an avowal of republican philosophy. Fitt's attendance presumably meant that he endorsed the ideal behind the Easter Rebellion, albeit perhaps in a sentimental way. His view was to change: 'I believe Connolly may have made a mistake by getting involved in 1916 because he was a Labour man, a socialist, an internationalist but he was caught up in the whole nationalist upheaval of the time. Patrick Pearse and James Connolly were like chalk and cheese.'[6]

In Fitt's view, Pearse and Connolly were fighting for different Irelands. Pearse was an Irish cultural nationalist who had been a Home Ruler up until the Northern Ireland rebellion. He put social issues in a secondary position. In Pearse's view the Easter rebellion would be a blood sacrifice to rejuvenate the Irish people's desire to assert their independence; an independence which history had shown him they had continually striven to achieve. Connolly, on the other hand, wanted an independent workers' republic of Ireland.

Connolly's behaviour in 1916 has been rendered incomprehensible by attempts to fit him into the Leninist mould – particularly influenced by the writings of the communist Desmond Greaves. Connolly had considered Pearse to be something of a fool in his idea of blood sacrifice. Fitt had got Connolly badly wrong in believing that he went with Pearse's rising. Connolly had, in fact, been the main advocate of a rising in 1915–1916 be-cause he was a great admirer of Germany, which he believed to be a virtual socialist state. Connolly's logic in propounding a rising with the advanced nationalists rested on the calculation he shared with Sir Roger Casement that Ireland could develop as a progressive state under the sponsorship of a victorious Germany, and that the opportunity would be lost if they did not act quickly.[7]

What is of more contemporary importance, however, is that the on-lookers of the 1966 parade would not have made much of a distinction between Pearse and Connolly and Fitt was astute enough to know that his identification with such a parade would have secured him some support. To be fair, there was then no perception that such physical force would ever be used again as a political weapon. In 1966 the IRA was practically defunct in the north. Danny Morrison, then education officer of Sinn Féin, remarked, 'As far as we were concerned there was absolutely no chance of the IRA appearing again. They were something in the history books.'[8] Kelly also confirmed that 'There were very few republicans in the Belfast area at that time', and retrospectively explained the situation:[9]

> The IRA was in a state of reorganisation. It had been in disarray after the campaign having been defeated. The only thing that had been achieved was that the Republican movement had struck a blow as they had done in every generation, and so that was the only achievement, the only thing that had been achieved … there was a process of rethinking within the movement, that perhaps the arms struggle was not the way forward on its own. That an arms struggle, on its own, was getting nowhere unless you had the political support of the population. That is why, basically, the 1956 campaign failed, because there was no political foundation for sustaining an armed struggle.[10]

Bowyer Bell talks of the relationship between Fitt and republicans in the mid – 1960s:

> In Belfast relations with Gerry Fitt who as good as owned and operated the new Republican Labour Party, were good if not intimate. His tactic of using his seats in Stormont and Westminster to harass the unionist machine was analysed if not emulated.[11]

But the display of mutual respect between Fitt and republican elements in the 1960s would not continue in the 1970s.

Fitt made it clear that he wished to retain his individuality at Westminster by discounting rumours that he would apply for the Labour Party Whip. He told the *Irish News*:

> I am contemplating no such move but as I have already indicated I will support the government on its initiation of social and progressive legislation. As a socialist I have admired Mr Wilson's government in the last session and I have no doubt that in the next session we will have a great deal in common in our approach to present day problems.[12]

Fitt actually could not have taken the Whip unless he joined the Labour Party; which raises the important issue of why he did not try to do this. Fitt's failure to exploit his influential relationship with the Labour Party was arguably a missed opportunity. He seemed to think so. Years later he said, 'Over the years, I have said to many of my colleagues that it is a tragedy that there is no Labour Party in Northern Ireland.'[13] He became a signatory of the Democracy Now campaign in the 1990s to 'build a non-sectarian political presence that could begin to attract the support and participation of thousands of Catholics, Protestants and people of no religion.'[14] But by then it was too late, and the campaign was viewed very much as an anti-nationalist manoeuvre by Labour MPs of a unionist disposition rather than an honest grass-roots campaign by ordinary Protestants and Catholics in Northern Ireland for the development of real labour politics. And by that time Fitt's influence was negligible and confined to the House of Lords.

But between 1967 and 1970 Fitt was at the height of his political influence vis-à-vis the British Labour Party. In those days the British labour movement and trade unions were far more powerful than they are today, and the labour movement had largely determined the political, economic and social agenda in the UK until at least 1970. If Fitt had put the case to it that it should end its abrogation of responsibility for the state and organise there, with himself as its local leader, he would certainly have provoked thought on the matter high up in the Labour leadership of the time. Labour was as bereft as any party of a policy for Northern Ireland. And it is possible he could have changed the course of events.

But Fitt was never likely to use his influence on Labour in this way, and the Labour Party preferred to remain aloof from Northern Ireland.

What is important to consider regarding Fitt's 'missed opportunity' was the predicament faced by his own community in the years 1970–2. The northern Catholic community had effectively been abandoned by the Dublin government, under British pressure, from early 1970. The British state had shown little inclination to address its needs in any politically meaningful way and had condemned that community to another period of Protestant Unionist rule under the Stormont system, backed up by British forces. It effectively set Catholics against the Stormont regime, placing them in a political void and effectively handing them over to the emerging Provisional IRA. Since there was no alternative to the repressive regime at Stormont it was little wonder the Provisional IRA grew as it did.

Fitt described his relationship with the British labour movement in the following way: 'I am on the friendliest terms with at least 60 members of the new Labour government. They regard my victory in West Belfast as a signal breakthrough and I feel I can now propagate the cause they have been advocating.'

Fitt was indeed the most substantial Labourite Northern Ireland ever produced. He had more influence on the Labour Party than any Ulster politician. And yet he was not disposed to take the Labour Whip, let alone convert his socialist politics into something more substantial, something that had the power truly to transform the position and destiny of his constituents. Did Fitt prefer to remain a big fish in the small pond of local politics rather than putting himself under the discipline of a labour movement? Did he feel that such a move would alienate his Catholic support? Did he even construe his position as pivotal? It is difficult to say, but one thing is certain. Fitt did not have a long-term vision. Instead he continued trying to ride the two horses of nationalism and socialism, as they grew further apart: 'Never at any time will I renounce either. I realise that there are many members in the British Labour Movement who agree with the eventual reuniting of the country.'[15] So what, one might ask, was the problem in joining it? The answer is simple. Fitt was a nationalist and at this point would not countenance doing anything that suggested otherwise. If he had become linked with the British Labour Party he would have been condemned as a West Briton and his political career would have been over.

Considering this commitment to a united Ireland, in addition to other statements throughout the late 1950s and 1960s, one might have expected his maiden speech at Westminster to have been heavily spiced with nationalist sentiment. It did not happen. The contradiction between what Fitt told the *Irish News* and what he asked for in his speech at Westminster is revealing. It is evident that Fitt had one voice for London and another for Belfast.

The fact that there was little or no nationalist bluster in Fitt's maiden speech is not to say that the speech was not dramatic. Fitt was a skilful orator, and, although he was mindful of the Westminster convention that the imperial government would not interfere in Ulster's affairs, he used the opportunity to make a decided impact on the House. The speech is worth looking at in some detail as it shows that Fitt presented himself as a democratic socialist. He began with an elucidation of his personal brand of republicanism:

Since the election I have read in sections of the British press that I have been classified as an Irish Republican. I should take this opportunity to classify my political allegiance. To classify me as an Irish Republican is not strictly correct. The Irish Republican Party in Ireland does not recognise the authority of this House in any part of Ireland and its members would indeed refuse to take their seats in this House.

He then reveals a trust in the British parliament and the British people, a trust that he would never relinquish:

I have not given up hope, and I have not yet determined to follow the line of the Irish Republican Party, because I believe that during my term as the representative of West Belfast in this House I will be able to appeal to every reasonable member in this chamber, and, through them, to every reasonable member of the British public. I feel certain that at the end of this parliament dramatic changes will have taken place in the north of Ireland.

Fitt was intent on presenting himself as a parliamentarian intent on achieving equal rights for British citizens. His intuition that British measures would solve the Irish problem remained a dictum of Fitt's political philosophy and would eventually lead him into confrontation with more radical elements.

In the next section of his maiden speech Fitt demonstrated a distinct proclivity towards the class-based politics of the UK state. Rather than using nationalist rhetoric to lament the existence of the border, he explained the differences between elections in Great Britain and Northern Ireland, showing that the latter were devoid of economic and social content:

In Northern Ireland, at every succeeding election there are no economic issues involved. In this island of Britain, the recent election was fought on the different policies and philosophies of the Conservative Party, the Liberal Party and the Labour Party, and the Labour Party were victorious. In Northern Ireland, no such issues entered the contest.

Fitt's demand for assimilation focused on the 1920 Government of Ireland Act, which implemented devolved administration in Northern Ireland. He asked for the act to be modified to deprive Stormont of control over the electoral process. 'The changing social conditions over the past 50 years make the Government of Ireland Act completely unworkable. When we realise how every concept of British democracy is being flouted in Northern Ireland we conclude, that now, immediately, is the time to amend that Act.'

The logic of Fitt's argument was that Westminster should resume direct control over the area in which it had devolved powers so that citizens might enjoy the full rights of the state in which they lived and that class-based politics should be encouraged to replace the communal politics of the state.

A further demand for equity between the United Kingdom and Northern Ireland was voiced through a request for the extension to the state of the British Representation of the Peoples Act of 1949. Fitt claimed that the fundamental basis of democracy – 'one man, one vote' – was abused there:

> We have an anti-democratic electoral system. This would not be tolerated in any other freedom-loving country. In Northern Ireland the same people are elected to administer the different Acts – the one applicable to Northern Ireland and the one applicable for Imperial elections. Can we expect these same people to administer their own electoral laws, on the one hand, and then to wear a different hat and administer the 1949 Representation of the People Act? The first aim of the Northern Ireland Unionist Party is to perpetuate its own existence there. Let there be no mistake about that.

Fitt was determined to inform the House that Northern Irish elections revolved around whether one was a Catholic or a Protestant.

Although Fitt went on to declare his socialist values, he did not propose a socialist hypothesis to resolve the political anachronism that was Northern Ireland.[16] As had been his habit, he resorted to highlighting discrimination through anecdotes reinforced by facts compiled by the McCluskeys of the CSJ.

Although Fitt's nationalist sentiment was conspicuous by its absence, the address provoked a medley of responses. Willie Orr, leader of the Unionist Party in the Commons, described it: 'As quite the most controversial maiden speech I have listened to in my 16 years in the House. It contained, I regret to say, some of the wildest and most irresponsible assertions in any speech at the House of Commons.'[17]

The *Belfast Telegraph* suggested:

By delivering the most discussed maiden speech of the new parliament, Mr Gerry Fitt ... succeeded in putting himself on the Westminster map at a single stroke. It was not just that the speech defied convention by being strongly controversial: it was delivered fluently and with confidence, and a wealth of gesture added to its impact. From now onwards, Mr Fitt can be assured of considerable attention in the Commons.[18]

In the Republic, *Hibernia* talked of 'Fitt's fireworks ... eleven to one and none (to date) capable of a coherent reply'.[19] By the end of April 1966 he had undeniably made his mark and enjoyed one of his finest moments. Conversely, media coverage in Britain was virtually non-existent: which was indicative of British ignorance of, and lack of interest in, Northern Ireland.

Fitt endeavoured to consolidate the impact his maiden speech had produced in parliament. His gregarious personality and the issues he identified with gave him a distinct advantage in this task and made him very popular with Labour ministers and backbenchers alike. At the end of May, he managed to secure Wilson's commitment to talk about the 'goings on' in Northern Ireland. In the Commons, he asked the Prime Minister:

Would my right hon. friend agree that under section 75 of the Government of Ireland Act 1920, the ultimate responsibility for everything which happens and good government in Northern Ireland is with the United Kingdom government? Would he further agree that in the 46 years which have elapsed since this Act was put on the Statute Book it has been made increasingly obvious that democracy does not exist in Northern Ireland?

Wilson's reply indicates both the jurisdictional dilemma Fitt's question posed and a distinct underplaying of the gravity of the situation.

This question raises some very difficult issues because of the division of functions between the United Kingdom parliament and government and the Northern Ireland parliament and government. We are all aware the hon. members in more than one part of the House are very disturbed about certain things which go on. I am not taking sides in this because there are allegations and counter allegations by one side or another within Northern Ireland.

I do not believe that this is a matter to be dealt with in the manner suggested [setting up a Royal Commission to investigate the workings of the Government of Ireland Act]. I think that the right thing to do would be for my hon. friend the Home Secretary and myself to have informal talks with the Prime Minister of Northern Ireland to see whether some of the difficulties which all of us recognise exist might be overcome in an informal way.[20]

It was a minor victory for Fitt, but a victory nonetheless. Wilson had at least acknowledged that all was not well in Northern Ireland. The CDU had tried unsuccessfully to gain a comparable recognition since 1964.

Fitt quickly followed this up with twenty amendments to the soon-to-be-debated British finance bill. These amendments were grievances he had been articulating, and he insisted that clause 48 should not come into operation until they had been redressed. Clause 48 of the bill provided for payment from the British treasury to Northern Ireland.[21] He said:

I have taken this action because I believe that the electoral laws here are completely unfair and react against working-class people and are loaded in favour of the business vote. I contend that while we are British subjects, allegedly members of the UK we are entitled to the same electoral laws. Several of the amendments refer to discrimination in Northern Ireland, and I believe that it is only right that I should highlight this state of affairs in the British Parliament, since entry into political life I have always opposed discrimination or sectarianism in any way. This is not applicable to one religion only, because if anyone not of my own religion was a victim of discrimination, I would be the first to fight on his behalf.[22]

Fitt was comfortable in the role of the constitutional nationalist.

In June, speaking at the Irish Club in London, Fitt discounted force as an instrument to unite Ireland, arguing that to love Ireland did not mean it was necessary to hate England:

Ireland cannot be united by the use of force. Today, the world is contracting. The advent of the EEC and economic factors will lead to the abolition of the border. It is because Sinn Féin advocates a Republic immediately that they win no seats and lose their deposits. Their slogan is: 'Give us a Republic now' whether everybody will starve or not is no concern of ours.[23]

This declaration from the most well-known nationalist politician was the only bright spot in a damaging month for the unionist regime. Fitt's activities had prompted the British media to probe into Northern Ireland affairs a little more than they had been accustomed to, which had resulted in some derogatory conclusions.[24]

Events in Northern Ireland did not help. There were two days of sectarian riots at Cromac Square in Belfast, and at the end of June there were fatalities. The Ulster Volunteer Force (UVF), a Protestant paramilitary force completely opposed to what they perceived as the liberal unionist regime, ambushed four Catholics at Malvern Street in Belfast on 26 June 1966, killing Peter Ward and seriously wounding two others. The following day, a Protestant pensioner, Martha Gould, died from burns received seven weeks earlier when loyalists had mistakenly set fire to her home while attempting to firebomb the Catholic-owned bar next door. Although crisis point had not yet been reached, these were arguably the first deaths of the 'Troubles'.

In the immediate aftermath of the murders, Fitt and Labour MP Paul Rose called an emergency meeting of MPs at Westminster and decided to form a deputation to see the Prime Minister, Harold Wilson, and the home secretary, Roy Jenkins. Meanwhile, O'Neill announced at Stormont that the UVF was to be declared illegal; he equated them with the IRA. At Westminster, Wilson labelled the UVF a 'quasi-Fascist organisation masquerading behind a clerical cloak'. Mere denunciation from Wilson was not enough for Fitt and he again called on Britain to fulfil its responsibility. 'It is for the government to take action and not the government of Northern Ireland.'[25]

In August, 'the informal' meeting between O'Neill and Wilson took place, brought about by Fitt's persistence at Westminster. Fitt made sure that Wilson knew the facts about Northern Ireland. The agenda included discussion on electoral practices, and discrimination in housing and jobs – the details that Fitt had highlighted at Westminster. Evidently Wilson was more conscious of minority charges than any of his predecessors had been. Fitt, for his part, was optimistic about the meeting's results.[26]

O'Neill's autobiography reveals that the encounter between the two Prime Ministers was very cordial. The exchanges were along general lines, and Wilson exhibited sympathy for the circumstances in which O'Neill had to operate.[27] Three days later, Fitt launched yet another attack on what he considered Britain's dereliction of duty in not conforming to the dictates of the Government of Ireland Act:

> I say, Sir, that this Act gives ultimate and over-riding responsibility to the parliament of the United Kingdom, and as the representative of Belfast West, as the representative of 26,000 people, I stand here to demand of the British government that they accept the responsibility which they themselves have written into this Act of 1920.

He then launched a scathing attack on unionist policy in the north, claiming that unemployment figures in places like Strabane, Newcastle, Dungannon, Enniskillen and Derry had never been brought to the attention of the London parliament. He argued that it was because every one of these areas had an anti-unionist majority that money dispensed by Westminster was denied them:

> These areas are denied any industrial development on the ground that they are not worth it, that they are anti-unionist and worthy of no consideration … As a socialist I do not want to see any unemployed man in Northern Ireland, irrespective of his religious or political beliefs. This is not so with my unionist colleagues, who deliberately deny employment to areas in the country because they do not support the Unionist Party.

Fitt finished this parliamentary offensive with a plea to be relieved of the restrictions of the Westminster Convention, a plea which the deputy speaker rejected.[28]

In the following week the *Irish News* contained an editorial that summed up the nationalist perception of what Fitt had accomplished so far at Westminster. It also revealed the respect he had gained. Entitled 'Voice from West Belfast', it read:

> In his direct and unaffected fashion, Mr Gerry Fitt is making a habit of disturbing that august and leisurely institution at Westminster to which he was elected earlier this year. Making no genuflections to convention, he wants the House to remember that there are other voices in this area than those of the cohort of Unionist MPs who sit so complacently on the Tory benches; silent in their subservience to the Tory Whip, and trudging dutifully into the division lobby against the government. Mr Fitt's hard hitting speech on Tuesday night was another example of his efforts to

bring six county affairs to the attention of the British government. Whilst he provides much needed illumination, he is also adding considerably to the education of the new MPs who are less informed about this area than they are about Bangkok or Bechuanaland.[29]

After the summer, pressure on Wilson from Labour backbenchers slackened somewhat. The lull can be attributed to the crisis that had arisen in Rhodesia, which occupied much of the Prime Minister's attention. Fitt had nevertheless made a mark on the Westminster scene. Although tangible reforms were negligible, he had succeeded in isolating the unionist MPs, and with the help of Paisley's actions had focused attention on the undemocratic set-up in Northern Ireland. It seemed as if the unionist administration at Stormont would not be permitted to press on regardless, as in the old days of Conservative government.

During 1967, Fitt continued to push the Northern Ireland unionist administration into a defensive position. In February, an *Irish Democrat* conference on the Irish question was held in London and attended by delegates from the British trade union and Labour movement. This conference was organised by Desmond Greaves and the Connolly Association, a front organisation for the Communist Party of Great Britain.

In sharp contrast to his maiden speech at Westminster, Fitt's address to the conference was much more 'nationalist'. It retained some of the rhetoric of his Commons speech, but, judging his audience well, Fitt placed his democratic pretensions within a more nationalist framework. Although again calling for parity between Northern Ireland and Britain, Fitt also addressed the problem of partition. He warned that if matters in Northern Ireland did not improve, 'men of principle' would take matters into their own hands:

Many people in Northern Ireland have a Sinn Féin outlook, and indeed in years gone by I have disagreed with them on the question of violence. As an Irish socialist I do not want to see one Irishman shooting another Irishman. I do not believe that they will solve the Irish question. But these people have a principle 'they say that the partition of Ireland has existed now for forty-seven years, that it is useless to try to talk to a British government, that they will not listen, that they themselves created the problem and they are unwilling to take any steps to solve it, and I have been told time and time again that the only answer to the partition of Ireland, lies in the hands of Irishmen themselves and it can only be reunited by force. I would sincerely hope that the day will never come when we, once again, have to take to the gun in Ireland. But I do say this, that at the end of the lifetime of the present parliament, if I have to go back to N.Ireland and say that I have spent four, four and a half or five years talking to the British government … if I feel in all honesty I have achieved nothing, I will be the first man to say I have achieved nothing and I am unwilling to go back to Westminster again. I am neither intimidated by, nor enamoured of, Westminster.

I am there to try and do a job, to try to highlight the injustices which exist in Northern Ireland, the injustices yes… which beset not only Catholics in Northern Ireland, but many hard working decent Protestants.

Ireland, for over seven hundred years, has had a very long and troubled relationship with the island of Great Britain.

It is born in every Irishman, as it is born in many other nationalities of the world, to seek the right to govern his own country. [Applause.] Many nations of the world, and indeed, the larger nations of the world, have gone to war for exactly this principle. Britain went to war allegedly for the defence of Belgium in the First World War and for the defence of Poland in the Second World War. If that is right, then I must ask for my country the same rights as Britain went to war for in Belgium and Poland. [Applause.][30]

In his recent affectionate biography of Fitt, Chris Ryder cites Fitt's speech to the Connolly Association. However, his quotation omits a number of sentences – lines that change the whole complexion of what Fitt actually told his audience. Part of Ryder's extract reads:

As an Irish socialist, I do not want to see one Irishman shooting another Irishman. I do not believe that will solve the Irish question. But some say that the partition of Ireland has existed now for forty-seven years, that it is useless to try to talk to a British government, that they will not listen, that they themselves created the problem and they are unwilling to take any steps to solve it, and I have been told time and time again that the only answer to the partition of Ireland lies in the hands of Irishmen themselves and it can only be reunited by force. I would sincerely hope that the day will never come when we, once again, have to take the gun in Ireland… [31]

Ryder suggested that Fitt chose his words with care due to the sensitivity of the situation then prevalent in the north. But the section of the speech where Fitt declares that many people in Northern Ireland had a 'Sinn Fein' outlook (something that was not true, at least in an electoral sense, in 1967), and that these 'people have a principle', a concession Fitt would have been more than reluctant to make in the 1970s and beyond, is omitted. This is all the more curious in the light of his biographer's attack on Fitt's 'detractors' for using 'remarks taken selectively out of context'.[32]

Another section of Fitt's speech that is omitted by Ryder is interesting for its Hibernian perspective on Northern Ireland:

> … the trouble in Ireland really began in the sixteenth century, when Britain drove the Irish natives from their own lands, particularly in the North-East corner of Ulster. They then began a plantation. English aristocracy was planted in the parts of North-Eastern Ireland. They have been there quite a long time now. They have not been assimilated in a long time now. They have not been assimilated in to the Irish race, though they do not call themselves English either. They call themselves 'Ulster – Scots'.

Fitt's Hibernian racial analysis of the Ulster problem seems very out of place with socialist rhetoric. It is the type of thing that has seldom been heard on political platforms in recent times.

As if to balance things up Fitt reverted to a somewhat superficial discussion of the 1913 Dublin lockout, stating, 'I view the partition of Ireland from a socialist angle.'[33] He then, as at Westminster, recounted the various Catholic grievances and re-emphasised his clear warning that the minority would not wait forever for civil justice:

> There is no time for delay in facing up to the problem which exists in Northern Ireland. Those people in Northern Ireland who are at the moment British subjects and citizens of the United Kingdom are not being treated as such, and are looking to the British parliament for reforms. If reforms are not forthcoming who could blame them for taking whatever action they see fit in the circumstances? I for one … would certainly not blame them.[34]

In the 1970s, Fitt did what once he claimed he would not do. When the Provos emerged and embarked on a military campaign to oust the British from Ireland, he continually denounced them. He was not, of course, the first Irish politician to capitalise on the perceived threat of unconstitutional methods of political agitation to gain constitutional reform – both O'Connell and Parnell employed such methods to punch above their political weight. In 1967 sabre-rattling would not have been taken seriously – at least not as seriously as it would a few years later – and Fitt, like all constitutional politicians, was totally unprepared for the revival of the IRA in 1969 and the brutality of its subsequent campaign. Yet, despite all this, there is a fundamental inconsistency in Fitt's politics, possibly born of a desire to be all things to all men.

Fitt's closing statement also contained his usual mix of nationalist and socialist rhetoric with the emphasis on this occasion resting on nationalism. He made it very clear that this was an Irish problem:

> I am a member of the Republican Labour Party. I am not a member of the British Labour Party … Therefore I have no say in its Party Conference. Now I realise that although I have made many friends in the House of Commons, in the final analysis I could be left standing completely alone, as an Irishman fighting for a solution to the Irish question.

The rhetorical juggling ended with the declaration, 'I am only a nationalist because I am a socialist.'[35]

The contrast between the democratic character of Fitt's maiden speech in the Commons and his more anti-partitionist emphasis in his address to the *Irish Democrat* can be explained in Fitt's developing political relationship with Desmond Greaves and the Connolly Association during this period.

Charles Desmond Greaves (1913–88) was a member of the Communist Party of Great Britain. Throughout his political life he interested himself primarily in issues of nationality and anti-imperialism, particularly with regard to Ireland. He was the guiding influence in the Connolly Association in Britain, which sought to organise and influence Irish immigrants toward trade unionism and socialism. He was editor of the Connolly Association's monthly newspaper, the *Irish Democrat*, for a great part of its existence.

In Irish affairs Greaves advanced the view that the way to end partition was to discredit Ulster unionism in Britain by exposing the discriminatory practices of the Stormont regime and by winning support for the cause of Irish reunification within the British labour movement. With this in mind Greaves conducted a long campaign of political propaganda in the Labour Party and in trade union circles that did much to win over British Labour opinion to the nationalist cause by the time of the civil rights campaign.

Greaves pioneered the idea of a civil rights campaign as the way to undermine Ulster unionism, and he had considerable personal influence on leading figures of that campaign. In this endeavour he came into contact with Gerry Fitt, who, with his position as MP and his contacts within the British labour movement, was obviously useful in Greaves' overall scheme.

Associates of Greaves, including Roy Johnston and Anthony Coughlan, were influential in winning the republican leadership over to social agitation during the mid-1960s, using the iconography surrounding Connolly to achieve greater acceptance of socialism in anti-communist Catholic Ireland. Greaves' principal contribution in this respect was his work, *The Life and Times of James Connolly,* written in 1961. It was through Connolly that Greaves hoped to gain a foothold for Marxist–Leninism in Ireland.

There can be little doubt that Greaves had an influence on Fitt. In an edition of the *Irish Democrat* in September 2005, Barney Morgan, a long-term colleague and friend of Greaves in the Connolly Association, stated:

> He (Greaves) was responsible for many things that people have long since forgotten. For example, Gerry Fitt, the northern MP, died on Friday last. Now Desmond invited Gerry Fitt to Liverpool when he first became an MP, and I drove him and Fitt up to Manchester for other meetings, for Fitt was the only person in the north of Ireland speaking out at that time about the dire situation there.
>
> At that time in the 1960s, whenever Connolly Association people in Britain tried to raise the situation in Northern Ireland, the standard answer was that people in this country had nothing to do with it. As I said this morning, the face of the clock was over in Belfast, but the machinery was here in Britain. Desmond Greaves went to see the lawyer D. N. Pritt QC, and asked him about this, and Pritt brought down the Government of Ireland Act 1920 and pointed out Section 75, which indicated that anything to do with the Northern Ireland government was the ultimate responsibility of the British parliament in London. So when this came out, people began to ask questions in parliament.
>
> I am not saying that this achieved very much, but at least it began to put things on the table. Those were the days when in the north you could have up to eight votes for certain people in local elections and other people had no votes. And this was accompanied by gerrymandering, discrimination against Catholics in allocating jobs and houses and so on. When people

nowadays give out about the IRA and its activities, they need to look back and appreciate how bad things were for the nationalist minority in those days before the IRA came on the scene. Desmond helped Fitt to bring about this change.[36]

Anthony Coughlan confirmed to me how important the alliance was:

There was a close political connection between the Connolly Association, Desmond Greaves and Fitt from 1961 – 2 onward, and possibly earlier. Certainly from when Fitt was elected for Dock Ward, for he was the first breakthrough as regards a civil rights-oriented critic of Unionism in the Six Counties. The Connolly Association had been seeking to expose Unionism in Britain since 1958, and indeed earlier, and yet there was very little support for or response to that from the Six Counties itself until Fitt's advent in Britain following his election as an MP. His arrival in Britain from the 'belly of the beast' in the Six Counties was of great practical and symbolic importance at the time. The Connolly Association campaigning since the mid-1950s had led to the emergence of a significant anti-Unionist element among British Labour MPs at Westminster by the mid-1960s, but the Six Counties themselves seemed to be virtually somnolent so far as civil rights issues were concerned. So when Fitt was elected to Westminster he found himself in the congenial company of quite a number of Labour MPs who knew what he was talking about and were sympathetic to his anti-Unionist message. But it had taken a decade of hard work in Britain, overwhelmingly by the Connolly Association and the bodies it was affiliated to and influenced – the NCCL (National Council for Civil Liberties) and MCF (Movement for Colonial Freedom) – to bring that situation about. It contrasted fundamentally of course with Labour's wholesale endorsement of the Unionist position by means of the Ireland Act 1949, when the Labour Party had been overwhelmingly pro Unionist.[37]

There is no evidence that Greaves helped draft Fitt's maiden speech to the Commons, but it bears his hallmark. It was certainly vital for the success of the Greaves project that Fitt presented his case differently to the Commons than he did elsewhere, to more nationalistically inclined audiences. And so, in the Commons, Fitt declared the issue to be equal rights for equal citizens; and outside, to different constituencies, to be rooted in partition. The only logical way of squaring this circle is to assume that what Fitt really wanted was British rights, not from any democratic inclination, but more to disrupt the unionist regime that in some way would be advantageous to anti-partitionism – the thinking prevalent in the Greaves-inspired Connolly Association. Fitt, a shrewd political operator himself and no mean juggler, internalised it and became its willing instrument. It was a vote-winner for him and he was, after all, an Irish nationalist.

So a case can be made that Fitt believed that in working up nationalist resentment over the democratic shortcomings of the Stormont system, and in the disturbances that would occur within unionism (and between unionism and the British state) with their rectification, a situation would be produced that would be exploitable for anti-partitionist purposes. If so he was helped in his purpose by the Northern Ireland Prime Minister.

As already stated, the principal contradiction in O'Neill's liberalism was that it raised Catholic expectations but avoided authentic reform. Northern Ireland remained a Protestant state for a Protestant people, but it was a state with a softer underbelly.

An indication of how Fitt was viewed by the more extreme elements in the Protestant community was revealed in April 1967. In that month, the *Protestant Telegraph* (a sectarian newspaper that had been launched by Paisley) demanded 'ARREST FENIAN FITT'.[38] Fitt complained at Westminster, arguing that it was an attack on his integrity as an MP. The speaker ruled that in publishing the demand, the newspaper was guilty of a *prima facie* breach of privilege, and referred the grievance to the committee of privileges. The committee declared that the publication was in contempt for using such statements, but it resolved to take no further action as this would only highlight the abusive statement.[39] The incident shows that Fitt was considered a fundamental nationalist and detested by certain elements of the unionist population. (I asked Fitt in 1989 what he thought of Paisley and he replied in his inimitable way; 'Paisley – twenty per cent mad'! The outspoken loyalist was not the only one that Fitt considered so afflicted. Tony Benn,[40] Keith Joseph,[41] Arthur Scargill[42] and Enoch Powell[43] were, according to Fitt, 'all fucking mad'. And how could Fitt make this diagnosis? 'Look at their eyes; they all have Rasputin-like eyes').[44] Undeterred, Fitt continued to attack the unionist administration.

Also in April, Fitt brought three Labour MPs – Paul Rose, Maurice Miller and Stan Orme – over to Northern Ireland, intending to show them the north's 'ugliest spots' in an effort to verify the allegations he had been making at Westminster.[45] The four toured the towns west of the Bann, including Coalisland, Dungannon and Strabane. Austin Currie remarked that Fitt delivered the most 'powerful oratorical performance' he had ever witnessed at the last stop.[46] Unionist MPs were outraged at the intrusion, and not impressed by the report submitted to the home secretary, Roy Jenkins, severely critcising the unionist administration. Miller maintained that, despite all its problems and difficulties, India had more democratic rights than Northern Ireland. Orme told the *Irish News*:

> There was a crack in the Tory edifice when like a breath of fresh air Gerry Fitt came as a true Irish representative to Westminster. The Unionist Party at that time decided that Gerry Fitt would not have much influence on his own, but Mr Fitt had brought the Irish question fully and fairly before the British MPs. He had been able to refute the quasi liberalism of the unionists who were sweet reasonableness in Westminster.[47]

Fitt promised that this fact-finding mission was only the first. In 1968 this policy would pay handsome dividends.

In May, the local government elections took place. This was another opportunity to see if Fitt's behaviour at Westminster would cause his Protestant support to diminish. The conflict between the Republican Labour Party and the NDP continued during the election. Initially the two parties formed a pact designed to prevent them competing against each other for Catholic votes in the same wards. The NDP claimed that the concord collapsed because Fitt failed to carry out an undertaking not to put Republican Labour candidates into the Falls Ward. Fitt, on the other hand, claimed there was a faction in the West Belfast branch of the NDP that was bitterly opposed to him and the Republican Labour Party. He felt, therefore, that the only honourable course was to fight for as many seats as possible.[48] The clash between Fitt and the NDP is a clear indication that the antagonisms of the previous year had not abated. It also shows that Fitt was capable of reneging on an agreement if he felt it politically expedient.

During the election Fitt was opposed for the aldermanship in Dock, but, as was becoming customary, he was successful, as were his three colleagues who were elected as councillors. The results meant that the Republican Labour Party had gained complete control of the Dock Ward.

Fitt polled 2,499 votes and won with the highest majority ever in local government in the history of Dock, presumably with the help of non-Catholic support. He now also had the backing of seven party colleagues at the City Hall: the three councillors elected in Dock and two each from Smithfield and the Falls. Republican Labour was firmly established in Belfast. After his triumph he reasserted his republican socialist attitude:

> For far too long the opposition forces in the North have been divided against themselves to the advantage of our unionist masters. I think that the results of this election prove that the only alternative to unionism is a progressive Labour and socialist movement embodying the principles of the eventual reunification of this country into a 32 county republic.[49]

Fitt remained very much the darling of the *Irish News*. In the wake of his victory its editorial stated:

> Only Mr Fitt, it seems, has the sort of influence that can diminish prejudices, even among those not normally his supporters, to carry his standard to victory at the polls. His rousing victory in Dock, with three colleagues riding in on the tide, was no inconsiderable achievement, and the overwhelming defeat of his avowedly sectarian opponent set the pattern for a general rejection of Protestant unionists in other Wards.[50]

At the end of the month, Glasgow Celtic became the first British soccer club to win the European Cup. That success produced utterances from Fitt that have taken on a mythical dimension, and since the episode is often cited as an example of the 'real' Gerry Fitt it deserves some attention. Glasgow Celtic was and is traditionally supported by Scottish Catholics; Glasgow Rangers by Scottish Protestants. This support extends to Northern Ireland, which exhibits the same religious split. A crowd of 15,000 took part in one of the largest parades ever seen in the Falls Road district to celebrate Celtic's victory. Fitt was invited to the celebrations and addressed the crowd on 29 May:

> As I stand on this platform and witness such a vast concourse, I am more than ever convinced that the ordinary people of West Belfast are prepared to take a stand in defence of all the ideals which have been their way of life for so long. 1966 has indeed proved to be a year of great significance to

Falls, Central, Dock and many other areas. We have beaten our opponents in politics, sports and in every other field they dare to confront us and I have no doubt that this will be the continuing trend in the years to come.[51]

In certain circles in Belfast today it is commonly assumed that Fitt's remarks were a direct reference to a Celtic victory over Rangers, a Catholic victory over Protestantism. The irony is that in order to win the cup Celtic had to defeat Inter Milan of Catholic Italy in the final. The misconception may have occurred due to the fact that on 31 May Rangers were defeated in the second major European soccer competition final, the European Cup Winners' Cup, two days after Fitt's bravado.

Nevertheless, Fitt was at the time severely criticised for his bluster. An editorial in the *Belfast Telegraph* disparaged him.[52] A resolution passed by the Belfast Young Unionist Association read: 'The remarks were deliberately intended to incite bad community relations and this would appear to be another illustration of Mr Fitt's hypocrisy.'[53]

Fitt was reported to be amused at the sectarian allegations:

When I said we had beaten our opponents I was referring to the ordinary working-class people who supported the Glasgow Celtic football team and to those around who were listening to my remarks – many of whom were supporters of mine in the West Belfast election. I insist I was not bringing religion into sport and I repeat that at no time have I regarded myself as a representative solely of Catholic people as opposed to Protestants.[54]

For all his back-pedalling and prevarication it is clear that Fitt was, for an instant at least, taken up with the spirit of the moment. In this celebrated instant he again displayed a propensity for impulsive, emotional outbursts. There seems little doubt that in this case he classified the opponents of republican socialism as non-Catholics and as people who did not support Glasgow Celtic. He was not the first northern Irish politician to tell the crowd what it wanted to hear, yet this was the most blatant example of his playing the sectarian card. He was clearly at ease in the role of the 'Green politician'. Other incidents confirm this.

In June, Fitt spoke at a Connolly Association rally in Trafalgar Square that was attended by some British Labour MPs. This meeting was another occasion when there was controversy over what Fitt did or did not say. The accuser this time was Prime Minister O'Neill who, at an Orange

Order function in Cloughmills, alleged that Fitt had advocated a return to violence in Ulster politics. He quoted Fitt as saying: 'If constitutional methods fail, the people of Northern Ireland who are at present victims of this oppression are quite entitled to take what means they can to end it.'

In his defence Fitt claimed that O'Neill had distorted his words:

What I said was, if the Northern Ireland government continues its present policies of discrimination, gerrymandering and social injustice, some members of the minority might in desperation resort to extreme methods. I believe that this is a risk which exists in the unhealthy atmosphere of Northern Ireland and which persists in the absence of any tangible evidence of bridge building activities by the prime minister, about which he talks so much and does so little.[55]

It seems the only certain conclusion that can be drawn from the episode is that Fitt's rhetoric was not always totally unambiguous. The indeterminate nature of Fitt's politics left him open to accusations of indulging in political intrigue. The ill-feeling between unionists and nationalists continued. In November, O'Neill said that both Fitt and Austin Currie were playing with fire. Fitt took the opportunity to declare, 'I have never at any time in my political career in Northern Ireland incited or will incite anyone to violence.'[56] There is no evidence to suggest that Fitt goaded people to violence. He, like constitutional politicians before him, used a perceived threat of violence to force constitutional change. However, it cannot be denied that he must have been aware of the encouragement such speeches would have given to more extreme nationalists. A dispassionate assessment might conclude that there was a contrast between the voice of moderation at Westminster and his speeches outside the House.

Nevertheless Eamon Phoenix has pointed out that by April 1967 Fitt's activities were being monitored by the unionist government. Referring to files released under the thirty years rule, Phoenix reported that on 9 June Stratton Mills, Unionist MP for North Belfast, told Harold Black of the Northern Ireland Cabinet Office:

...in relation to the forthcoming debate on Northern Ireland (at Westminster) I am very anxious to use the opportunity to present Mr Fitt in his true light in the nicest possible way. I am wondering if you have any useful quotations showing him allied with those sections of the community who wish to keep relations at boiling point. Incidentally, has he ever condemned the IRA?

Replying to Mills, Black observed:

> I have gone through such cuttings as we have of GFs utterances and can find little that would support criticism of his actions that would appeal to the Labour backbench. It may be that I have not got enough cuttings. I think he has been fairly assiduous in attending regularly the Easter Rising parade to Milltown Cemetery which, as you know, is sponsored by the IRA and Sinn Féin.[57]

The episode highlights three things. First, Fitt was not up to much intrigue – if any. Second, unionists were anxious about the scheduled Westminster debate; and third, dirty tricks campaigns in Northern Ireland in the mid-1960s, although sinister, were quaint and almost gentlemanly in their execution.

Two other events in the summer of 1967 exposed the political dilemma of Gerry Fitt. Fitt again paid deference to the republican dead of 1916 when he spoke at the annual tribute to the memory of Roger Casement at Murlough in County Antrim, arguing that the British government had gone out of its way to defame Casement's character.[58] In the previous July Fitt had been rebuked for not paying due deference to the men of the 36th Ulster Division who lost their lives at the Somme, also in 1916. Eileen Paisley, wife of Ian, criticised the fact that Fitt and other Republican Labour members of the Belfast City Council were not present to join in passing the annual resolution paying tribute. Paisley considered it an insult to 'those who fought and died for freedom'. Fitt retorted, 'I did my bit in the war as a merchant seaman and I had a brother killed serving in the Irish Guards – unlike Mrs Paisley's husband, who had he wished, could have served the cause his wife is now upholding.'[59]

Fitt's comments are revealing of the sense of betrayal felt by northern nationalists at the non-recognition of their war service to the British state. In recent years a big issue has been made of how the southern state largely ignored the 35,000 Irish men who died fighting for Britain against Germany in the First World War – and the 250, 000 who served in the British army. But at least that is understandable: the Irish Republic was born in opposition to the British state during the war and its ideology was fundamentally anti-imperialist. Given that Remembrance Day was viewed as an extravagant exhibition of British imperial militarism and has, at least locally, been embraced by the Orange tradition, it is hardly surprising that it has repelled nationalist Ireland (until now).

But under the prompting of Joe Devlin, many northern nationalists joined up in the first year of the First World War. In that first year (before Carson joined the government) Catholic recruitment actually proportionately surpassed Protestant recruitment in Belfast.[60] When Catholic servicemen returned they found their sacrifice meant nothing: Home Rule had been suspended indefinitely; small nations were forgotten; and Catholic areas were under attack from the UVF. Despite this West Belfast continued to supply substantial numbers to the British forces in the Second World War and after. So Fitt was echoing a kind of lost Redmondism – something that continued much longer in the north than the south.

Paradoxically, Fitt was eager to present himself as a disciple of Connolly and an admirer of Casement (two republicans who supported Germany's case in the First World War) while at the same time emphasising his own contribution to Britain's war effort in dismissing criticism directed at him by unionists.

The long-awaited Northern Ireland debate at Westminster finally came in October. Fitt's contribution showed how little the Labour government had changed conditions in Northern Ireland. It had been fourteen months since the region's problems had last been debated by parliament and Fitt had hoped there would have been dramatic changes in the state. It was with deep disappointment he told the House that no changes in Northern Ireland had taken place.

The British parties are geared towards – more than anything else – the business of gaining governmental power through winning elections. This was the real problem in expecting a party that had no votes to gain or lose in Northern Ireland to concern itself with its problems. Northern Ireland did not figure on the British political agenda because it was an issue that both parties had agreed to leave aside from the political conflict in the state. So the tendency was to ignore Northern Ireland until something really serious occurred.

Fitt pressed for the Race Relations Act to be implemented in Northern Ireland. He argued that the same protection afforded to Pakistanis, Indians and other immigrants in Britain should be applied to all United Kingdom citizens, including the Catholics of Northern Ireland.

Fitt again made a plea for parity between Northern Ireland and Britain and made it explicit that he did not require anything else. 'That is all we ask. We do not ask for more.' He again forecast future disorder, claiming, 'As a pacifist, I do not want to see violence, but I do not want to see the people trampled under by the jackboot Unionist Party.'[61]

Replying to Fitt's speech, Roy Jenkins acknowledged that the Labour government was 'deeply concerned' about the situation in Northern Ireland. He cautioned Stormont that Westminster would not interfere in Ulster 'provided' it was satisfied things were moving in the right direction. Despite the home secretary's salutary warning, it is evident from Fitt's utterances that the situation in Northern Ireland remained unchanged. Fitt's goal to speed up the liberalisation of the Stormont regime had not materialised. He had secured a hearing among Labour MPs, ministers and backbenchers alike, and had proved himself an able orator and an astute political operator, but although his presence at Westminster had put the unionists on the defensive, the parliamentary convention of non-interference relating to Northern Ireland remained intact. In his book *A House Divided*, James Callaghan stressed how little public attention was paid to Northern Ireland.[62] If the truth be told, the Labour government stood 'idly by'.

Nevertheless, Fitt remained optimistic about the prospects for the nationalist vision and in his political review of 1967 written for the *Irish News* he concluded:

It is my sincere hope that on the next occasion when the people of these constituencies have an opportunity to elect representatives they will ensure that the nationalist ideal will be given expression in the corridors of power at Westminster.

On entering into the year 1968, I can only pledge myself to carry on as I have been doing in the past and I am confident that the New Year will bring further defeats for unionism in Northern Ireland.[63]

Although much of Fitt's wrath was directed at the unionist administration he was not averse to criticising the government in the south. In these instances, his rhetoric was often set in a framework of nationalist resentment, a component missing from his Westminster addresses.

In January 1968 he spoke at University College Galway's Literary and Debating Society. He reiterated his wish for the integration of the Labour movement in the north and the south and likened the Republic's Fianna Fáil Party to the Unionist Party, calling them 'Siamese Twins'.[64]

In October 1968, in a speech calling for stronger action to end partition, he attacked the Fianna Fáil government's attitude to the issue of the border. Fitt told the United Ireland Association in Manchester: 'I wonder sometimes if the southern government is prepared to accept the responsibility of the reunification of Ireland. If they are, they have not taken any very dramatic steps to achieve this. They could be much more forceful in demanding their right to the six county territory.'[65]

Evidently Fitt believed the southern administration had a catalytic role to play in the ending of partition. In his address to the Galway students, he argued that there were hundred of thousands of northern Irish holding an uncompromising allegiance to the ideal of a united Ireland who had looked in vain for support from successive southern governments.[66] Fitt's nationalism was undeniably more evident in the Republic than at Westminster.

In the same month, Fitt tabled an emergency resolution, which was adopted, at a CDU conference in the Irish Club in London. This resolution called on those MPs at Westminster who were sponsors of the CDU to take 'all possible action in the House of Commons to question the legality of the existing convention'. In his speech he argued, 'Northern Ireland seemed to be the forgotten child of British politics and the British Prime Minister is not prepared to risk a constitutional crisis over it.'[67] The resolution was further evidence of the lack of vigour from Fitt's fellow socialists in government.

Fitt's continued attacks on the unionists brought him into inevitable conflict with O'Neill. In a speech in Strabane, O'Neill described Fitt as a political opportunist who could not go on being a republican in Belfast and a socialist in London. He said:

Mr Fitt is like that remarkable animal, the chameleon which changes its colour to suit its background. [He] did not recall much use of the term British subject when Mr Fitt marched behind the Tricolour in Belfast to celebrate the 1916 Rebellion.

... I believe that the political opportunists, although they may win short term successes, generally fail in the long run, because in due course people find them out. One cannot forever be a republican in Belfast and a socialist in London – a nationalist at Stormont and a British subject at

Westminster. Nor can one build an enduring political career upon a great heap of irresponsible criticism and denigration.

O'Neill's speech typifies the allegations that were made against Fitt in this period. Fitt retorted: 'This speech will be recognised for what it is – the sordid attempt by a puny politician who is fighting for his political life. As I have said before if the day ever dawns when the prime minister congratulates me, I shall hastily re-examine my conscience to see what I have done wrong.' Fitt then went on to reaffirm his allegiance to the Connolly ideal:

He (O'Neill) recognises that during my political career I have sought to unite and serve the working-class people of this area, irrespective of religion or political adherence, and so hasten the day when all people of the six counties will find their true place in the establishment of an Irish Socialist Republic for the 32 counties of this island.[68]

In June, Fitt had another opportunity to express his fealty to the Connolly doctrine at a ceremony on the Falls Road honouring the hundredth birthday of his hero. Fitt addressed the crowd, saying they 'had gathered to commemorate the birth and death of one of Ireland's greatest sons who bound himself to the cause of the working-class'. He argued that when Connolly died by firing squad the oppressors of the people thought they had seen the end of him and his ideals, but they were wrong. They did not foresee that young men would take up the banner that he laid down. Fitt, declared that, like Connolly, he believed there could be no peace in Ireland until it was a socialist republic. All present at the ceremony would also have been aware and were celebrating the fact that Connolly was a physical force republican.

The most revealing aspect of Fitt's address was the time span envisaged for the transformation of Ireland. Fitt hoped that 'as a result of this week of remembrance they would dedicate themselves to the task of establishing an Irish socialist republic within the lifetime of the oldest member of the platform party'.[69]

The dissimilarity between the content of this speech and Fitt's speeches at Westminster is very apparent. There is certainly evidence to suggest that although in London Fitt may have demanded only civil rights, he was in Belfast equally vociferous in his demand for a united Ireland.

It is an odd fact of history that while unionism dealt easily with the direct anti-partitionist efforts to which it was subjected, it began to fall apart when the democratic pretensions of its statelet were acted upon. The Northern Irish Civil Rights Association (NICRA), formed in February 1967 to combat religious inequalities, sprang from the amalgamation of the CSJ and the Northern Wolfe Tone Society (the Irish version of the British based Connolly Association).[70] It is wrong to suggest that the movement was an entirely Catholic one. However, throughout its life, unionists claimed that it was a front for the IRA. In reality it was a broad coalition of socialists, nationalists, communists, liberals and even the leader of the Young Unionists at Queen's University.

The important thing to remember about the civil rights movement was that all sorts of people were involved for all sorts of reasons: there were people whose objectives were purely democratic, who simply wanted the Stormont regime reformed into something more suited to modern times; there were people who wanted to make the lot of the Catholic community better, to make it possible for Catholics to end their marginalisation and play a fuller part in the life of Northern Ireland; there were people who simply wanted 'British rights for British citizens'; others thought civil rights could be used to destabilise the unionist regime to promote anti-partitionist possibilities; and there were Trotskyites who saw it as the start of some kind of socialist revolution in which green and orange Tories could be thrown out through popular protest.

In short, the civil rights movement could have taken a number of paths: at various times the different and often contradictory elements assumed temporary leadership and determined its direction. But the most important factor in deciding what the civil rights movement would be was the attitude of the British state. If the state remained aloof it meant that the Stormont regime itself would decide, by its response to the movement, what it would turn out to be. And in 1968–9 it was clear that the Stormont regime saw the civil rights movement as, in essence, another anti-partitionist manoeuvre – as war by other means conducted by those who had failed in 1956–62. What occurred thereafter was something of a self-fulfilling prophecy.

The Campaign for Democracy in Ulster's sympathy for the plight of the British Catholics in Northern Ireland developed into demands for the liberalisation and democratisation of the Stormont regime – electoral reform and the abolition of discrimination. Most important, the

Campaign for Social Justice evolved into a civil rights movement that would achieve more reforms than any armed struggle had managed.

NICRA's formal aims were: 'one man, one vote' in local elections; the ending of gerrymandered electoral boundaries; apparatus to eliminate discrimination by public authorities; the fair allocation of public housing; the disbandment of the B Specials; and the repeal of the Special Powers Act. The campaign was not designed to end partition and it eschewed the historic tradition of violence and bloodshed. Like Fitt, it was intent on seeking 'British' rights for all the people in Northern Ireland. Nevertheless, unionist opinion was convinced that this was just another bout of nationalist agitation, albeit in a somewhat unconventional form. NICRA, it was thought, was simply a vehicle to subvert the constitution. Although it was Derry rather than Belfast that provided the inspiration for the movement, it was not long before its strengths and Fitt's began to complement each other.

In retrospect, Fitt maintained that the legitimate civil rights campaign began on 29 June when Austin Currie began a squat in Dungannon to highlight the discrimination in housing.[71] At the time Fitt fully supported Currie. He said he regretted that the situation had escalated so far, but argued that Currie had used every parliamentary vehicle to right the wrongs in the area. He believed responsibility for the situation rested with the Unionist Party.[72]

Three days later a protest meeting was held in the town. Fitt argued that the Unionist Party had undergone a recent right-wing fascist attempt to take over the administration:

We have been told that Captain O'Neill is a great Liberal – he is a great Liberal but he certainly does not act as a great Liberal. We have been told that he is the best of a bad bunch, that the minority of Northern Ireland should not do anything to upset Terence's plans. I say this. A lot of people try to impress upon you that Paisley would walk over you with hobnail boots and Captain O'Neill would walk over you with bedroom slippers. So far as I am concerned nobody is going to walk over me whether they are in their bare feet or not.[73]

The civil rights movement had begun and Fitt was determined to be a part of it. At Westminster, he continued to raise the Northern Ireland question through the only vehicle available to him: Question Time.

Fitt continually demanded that the British government take responsibility for the problems of Northern Ireland. Although Wilson acknowledged that Fitt had been very active in raising the issues of human rights and discrimination since he had entered the Commons, he was as steadfast in his reliance on Stormont putting its own house in order as Fitt was in his appeal to the imperial parliament. He told Fitt: 'I think these matters must be left for discussion with the government of Northern Ireland. The Prime Minister of Northern Ireland and his colleagues know we cannot continue indefinitely with the present situation. Something has to be done.'[74]

Yet nothing was done in Northern Ireland to appease minority leaders. Fitt responded with undisguised sabre-rattling. At a James Connolly commemoration meeting in Derry in July, he announced his intention to establish the Republican Labour Party in that city.

> I am prepared to take my ideals and my philosophies out of Belfast because by staying in the city I am only denigrating every principle for which Connolly ever stood. When I come to Derry I promise you I will change the system … The day for talking has gone, the day for action has arrived. If every individual here today goes home and re-dedicates himself to change the system as it operates in Derry, then we will change the system as it operates in the six counties and in the whole island of Ireland. If constitutional methods do not bring social justice, if they do not bring democracy to Northern Ireland, then I am quite prepared to go outside constitutional methods …[75]

What did Fitt mean by 'The day for talking has gone, the day for action has arrived' and 'I am quite prepared to go outside constitutional methods'? It is difficult to say. What is certain is the disparity between Fitt's remarks in Derry and his moderate tone in London. McAteer predictably disapproved of Fitt's move into Derry, correctly feeling that it would damage his own party's prominence in the city. He remarked: 'It is a rather poor way to seek the unity which is preached to us on all sides.[76] It is enough to make James Connolly turn in his grave.'[77]

Fitt was unrepentant, and although he was unwilling to attack the integrity of the Nationalist Party he argued that the Derry people had not been given the leadership to fight unionism to which they were entitled. He did not want his party to remain confined to Belfast:

In the past we have been roundly attacked just for this. I am sure on reflection Mr McAteer will realise that his gimmicky reply to my Derry speech will be no answer to the problems which beset that city ... The decision was taken in line with the party's policy to extend its sphere of influence and to propagate the ideals and philosophy of James Connolly.[78]

This episode was indicative of the ever-present divide in nationalist politics. It also shows that Fitt did, at least on this occasion, advocate 'unconstitutional' methods of political agitation. Politicians do tend to excuse themselves of any accountability for their verbal excesses in front of a crowd, and it is not clear what he meant by 'unconstitutional methods', but some members of the gathering may have considered it a vindication of the use of violence to achieve political aims.

This incident adds further weight to Kelly's claim that Fitt gave at least tacit approval to republicans attending 'gun lectures' at Dock Irish Labour Party premises in the mid-1950s.

On 24 August 1968, the CSJ, backed by NICRA organised the first big civil rights march, from Coalisland to Dungannon in County Tyrone. The protest arose from discontent about discrimination in housing, rather than specifically political issues. Nevertheless, it offended Paisley's brand of loyalism and he announced a counter-demonstration. This led to the civil rights march being banned from entering the town centre – an attempt to restrict it to Catholic areas. Fitt called for support, exhibiting yet again a shift in emphasis from his moderate Westminster stance: 'Ireland's history teaches us that unless the ordinary citizens are prepared to fight on their own behalf victory will not be achieved. I now ask all those who have supported this campaign to let our unionist opponents and the whole world see that the time has arrived.'[79]

The march attracted 2,500 people and passed off without any major trouble. Fitt was one of the speakers. The *Irish News* reported him as saying: 'A fire has been lit tonight which will not go out until Civil Rights have been established.'[80]

Bernadette Devlin, who was also elected to Westminster in this period, recalls a far more colourful account of Fitt's contribution to the march. It was her first encounter with him and her account gives a valuable insight to Gerry Fitt at street level. 'It was the first time in my life that I ever heard a politician in public use foul language. That is my first memory of Gerry Fitt; he was blackguarding the police and just kept referring to them as those black bastards.'[81] Devlin also referred to the incident in her autobiography, recalling Fitt saying, 'If one of those black bastards of the Northern Ireland Gestapo puts a hand on any man here I'll lead you through.'[82] Fitt clearly had little faith in the impartiality of the RUC at this point in his career. (Interestingly, Fitt told me that he vividly remembered his first encounter with Devlin at Stormont on 10 October 1968 for similar reasons. With absolutely no hint of irony, he recalled; 'I will never forget it – she cursed like a fucking trooper.')[83]

The demonstration had minimal repercussions at Westminster. Fitt had a ten-minute meeting with Wilson and he put down a motion objecting to the banning of the march. By the evening of 28 August, he had acquired fifty-nine signatures.[84] Despite the meeting with the Prime Minister and the tabled motion, the August march had not inspired alarm at Westminster. The situation would change in October.

The date when politics in Northern Ireland became 'fashionable' was 5 October 1968, the day of the seminal civil rights march. Two days earlier, in a speech in Blackpool (the venue of the Labour Party Conference), Fitt addressed a large gathering of the CDU. He repeated the requests he had been making for two and a half years:

> I do not consider I am making any outlandish requests. All I am asking for is that the same rights and privileges which are enjoyed by the people of Doncaster should be afforded to the people of Dungannon and Derry.
>
> If you consider this is too much to ask then I must say in return that the six counties should no longer be considered an integral part of the UK.

In a reference to the forthcoming civil rights march, he predicted there would be trouble from the RUC: 'I have no doubt that once again we will be subjected to police intervention and I am now in the process of inviting six of my Westminster colleagues to attend this march in what is allegedly an integral part of the UK.' He again did a little sabre-rattling: 'I have said before and I repeat now that the inaction of the British government has brought about a situation where the oppressed minority in Northern Ireland are now prepared to take steps to remedy the situation. The British government cannot say they have not been warned …'[85]

Derry was the obvious venue for the demonstration. It was there that discrimination was at its most institutionalised and efficient, where two-thirds of the people were denied basic civil rights and placed in the position

of a persecuted majority. In the autumn of 1968, a collective realisation of
the predicament of Catholics, altered the pattern of events.

After the Apprentice Boys of Derry announced an annual parade to be
held on 5 October along the same route as the civil rights march, William
Craig, Minister of Home Affairs, banned all parades, except in Catholic
areas, on that date.[86] Fitt considered this a stupid act by the minister. 'It is
a deliberate attempt to provoke a peaceful demonstration. This is the only
interpretation that can be put on it.'[87]

It seems that by banning the march the unionists had again blundered:
it is likely that more people attended because it was prohibited than
would have had the government ignored it. To avoid characterisation as
a nationalist parade, no Irish tricolours were permitted by NICRA. For
the march, Fitt brought over from Blackpool three Labour backbenchers
who had a brief to report back to Wilson and his home secretary, James
Callaghan. An alliance had developed between Fitt and young radicals in
Northern Ireland. This was to prove a short-lived but potent combination.

Despite NICRA efforts, the authorities perceived the protest as a
nationalist conspiracy, a smokescreen for the IRA. The marchers were
prevented from entering the city by a barrier of constables. Fitt was at
the front of the march and as it tried to breach the RUC cordon he was
batoned. There followed a vicious baton charge on the demonstrators,
during which over seventy people were injured.

The events in Derry were reported in newspapers and on television, not
only in Ireland and Britain, but throughout the world. Fitt had previously
established a close contact with Mary Holland, a journalist with the *Observer*. A photograph of him showing the injury he had sustained – a head
wound – appeared on the front page of the following day's edition. The
picture of a British MP being attacked for protesting against abuses of
democracy was a forceful image. The fact that television had captured
the moment meant that any official whitewashing was impossible, and
in the aftermath of the march all the media began to carry features on
the problems of Northern Ireland. It was not unreasonable to infer that
had Fitt not been beaten this publicity would never have materialised. He
described the moment to the *Irish News*:

As I approached the police cordon at the top of Duke Street, a crowd of
police ran over and attacked me. They didn't seem to be attacking anyone
else and this is proved conclusively by the film. While I was completely

surrounded by police one of them hit me on the head with his baton. I fell to the ground and tried to put my hand up to protect myself. I was hit again. I was then dragged away and thrown into the police van.[88]

Bernadette Devlin, also on the march, took a slightly different view of the incident:

> This was the Gerry Fitt I came to know. Gerry stuck his head under a police baton. There was never any doubt about that. He never denied it. It was a measure of the man. I'm not saying that to criticise him. The police attack was devastating. Gerry Fitt made a very astute political decision that if the press were going to be interested in it, there would have to be an interesting head, so Gerry stuck his in the way and got sliced – proceeded to bandage it up very ostentatiously and give interviews outside the City Hall. In between interviews he would come into the bar and take the bandage off and have a few drinks and go out again when he was called upon.[89]

In retrospect, Fitt himself did not deny that he used the political opportunity that presented itself: 'I knew long before that they were going to beat me up. I wasn't going to retaliate. I wasn't going to throw stones. I got pins and needles and I felt the blood running down. I thought to myself, I'm going to let that blood run because the cameras are there.'[90]

The most significant repercussions of the Derry march were at Westminster, where the Labour government was greatly embarrassed by the damaging international publicity. Paul Rose quizzed Wilson as to what he now intended to do about the RUC. Willie Orr resented this and asked the Prime Minister if he was aware that the RUC was being disparaged. Wilson was curt in his reply: 'Up to now we have had perhaps to rely on the statement of himself and others on these matters. Since then we have had British television.'[91]

Although parliamentary procedure had not been his vehicle, Fitt's message to the government had finally been received. In November, he clarified his position, or at least his Westminster position, when he told the Commons, 'I say that the present situation is in no way aimed at the achievement of an Irish Republic. The question of partition does not enter into the demand of Civil Rights.'[92]

In November, Fitt was again criticised for the duality of his politics. He had criticised Fianna Fáil for its attempt to replace proportional representation with a new electoral system via a referendum. Neil Blaney, the TD for Donegal, accused Fitt of being a chameleon:

> He is something of a chameleon who rings his colours up and down as it suits his purpose. He criticises the Taoiseach for referring to partition and says this has strengthened the Unionist case and could be very injurious to the Civil Rights movement. I question Mr Fitt's motives in regard to the nationalist population of Derry city for he no sooner got himself batoned in Derry than he was off over the border to use this incident in a most despicable and dishonest way in relation to the referendum.[93]

The contradiction in Fitt's politics is reflected in his reply:

> Over a great number of years I have been appalled at the deafening silence that has emanated from Fianna Fáil sources in relation to the situation in Northern Ireland. I do know from quite authentic sources in the Republic that Fianna Fáil supporters had been advised not to associate themselves with the Civil Rights movement in Northern Ireland. And now at this rather late stage, after the overwhelming defeat in the referendum, Fianna Fáil now proclaim themselves as the great Republican Party of Ireland. I think their past inactivity in this matter is sufficient to condemn them out of hand.[94]

Fitt therefore criticised Taoiseach Lynch for associating civil rights with anti-partitionism, yet also criticised Lynch's Fianna Fáil Party for not being republican enough and for not involving itself in the civil rights struggle.

Whatever the contradictions and inconsistencies in Fitt's politics, there can be no doubt that after the Derry rally he was hugely popular with the minority community. His direct and dramatic involvement was arguably his finest moment in politics. Yet the episode also marked the point at which events began to subsume the individual. The batoning of Gerry Fitt had at last convinced the Labour government to take notice. Fitt was an important mouthpiece of a minority that was becoming increasingly conscious of their position.

When Fitt was elected to Westminster in 1966, the Catholic community had low expectations of Stormont and was locked into the routine of the Nationalist Party's form of politics. The events of 5 October 1968 radically altered the political climate. The formation of a new student group at Queen's University, People's Democracy (PD) (a radical leftist group that by and large adhered to Connollyite republicanism), was the most important manifestation. The Connollyite republicanism espoused by the PD was very different from the brand enunciated by Fitt.

The ruthless rout of the marchers by the RUC in Derry meant that civil rights became increasingly concerned with the security machinery of the Northern Ireland state. Derry also altered Protestant understanding of the issues involved.[95] NICRA could not be discredited as republican, and the RUC had been unable to intimidate it off the streets. O'Neill tried to mollify it, but once the organisation began to press for reforms the contradictions in the state began to surface: this led to his demise. The civil rights movement exposed the discrimination and sectarianism inherent in the infrastructure of the state; and Stormont's opposition to demands for equality led to the emergence of the IRA in the summer of 1969. Fitt, like all constitutional nationalists, was unprepared for the sequence of events sparked by the Derry march.

In November 1968, O'Neill announced a reform package that conceded to some of the civil rights demands. However, the principle of 'one man, one vote' was not among them and the movement would not be placated without it.

On 9 December, O'Neill made another attempt to defuse the growing tension by making a television appeal for support. He maintained that Northern Ireland stood 'on the brink of chaos' and called for an end to the increasing civil disorder. O'Neill told civil rights organisers, 'Your voice has been heard, and clearly heard. Your duty now is to play your part in taking the heat out of the situation before blood is shed.'[96] While the speech was generally welcomed, there was disappointment that an auspicious statement on 'one man, one vote' was not forthcoming. This, it was thought, would have cleared the streets of civil rights protesters. O'Neill was hindered by opposition within his party to the extension of universal franchise to local government elections – a point not lost on Fitt:

> Mr O'Neill has appealed to the Civil Rights marchers to desist from further activity on the streets, and yet he had it within his power to en-sure that this would take place by granting the elementary principle of One Man One Vote. I think this proves that Mr O'Neill is shackled to a reactionary Unionist Party and while this situation remains the Civil

Rights association must remain in existence and continue their demands for concrete reforms.[97]

Although O'Neill's appeal was somewhat melodramatic, NICRA responded to it with a one-month *moratorium* on demonstrations. Fitt followed suit when he announced a 'Christmas truce' with the government. He said he would be the 'quiet man' of northern Irish politics, and had decided to cease his attack on both the government and O'Neill, to allow them the opportunity to implement O'Neill's programme of reforms.[98]

The PD, however, was unimpressed by O'Neill's television address and the lack of substantial reform. In an effort to break the truce and relaunch the civil rights movement, a march from Belfast to Derry was announced for 1 January 1969. The organisers were well aware that they would be harassed. Leaders of NICRA opposed the march, fearing that a strategy designed to provoke a predictable reaction would itself be construed as provocation. In the event, about eighty marchers left Belfast and were duly molested at various locations, the most serious incident occurring at Burntollet Bridge. It was there that an ambush had been planned, and the marchers were brutally attacked by loyalists, including off-duty members of the B Specials. The marchers eventually made their way to Derry city and were welcomed by a large crowd. That night rioting broke out, culminating in an unprecedented police attack on the Catholic Bogside district. Barricades were built and the RUC kept out of the area for a week. 'Free Derry' was born.

O'Neill predictably accused the PD of provocation. Fitt, in an interview with Fergus Pyle in 1988, also maintained that the legitimate civil rights campaign ended with the PD march. 'The march was intended to show how rotten the Northern Ireland state was, but everyone knew how rotten it was … That whole episode introduced sectarian thinking into the campaign. Burntollet was a sectarian offer and a Protestant take up. It was no way to demand Civil Rights.'[99]

The march was also a watershed in other respects. After it, many Catholics believed that peaceful reform of the state was hopeless: the march had, after all, been completely legal. It also marked the point where Catholic areas rather than civil rights marches became the focus of attack. As violence escalated throughout the year, the leaders of NICRA and conventional nationalist leaders like Fitt began to lose what control they had of the situation.

Fitt's attitude to the march and its aftermath seems to have been some-what more equivocal at the time. After the police attack in Derry, Eamonn McCann recalls Fitt declaring, at an open air meeting called to discuss the question of community defence, 'it's time to get the guns out'.[100] The meeting led to the setting up of the Derry Citizens' Defence Association. McCann says that the 'impromptu gathering' was 'of its time' and that Fitt 'was given to rhetoric that would please his audience'. I asked McCann if he thought Fitt meant what he said and he replied 'I don't know, but there were people there that assumed that he meant it and would have under-stood that he meant it and took it literally.' Was this meeting and Fitt's aggression then partly responsible for the origins of what later became the Provisional IRA? Not according to McCann: 'To suggest that they went off and eventually joined the Provos is stretching it too far. Fitt was not an important influence on those people.' However, to the charge that Fitt was one of those responsible for 'stirring the pot of dissension until it boiled over' and 'fanning the flames' of violence, McCann claims 'Fitt took no re-sponsibility about what inevitably followed. He washed his hands and was not alone in doing so.' (McCann acknowledged that the same charge has been levelled at him.)[101]

After the Bogside attack Fitt told the *Irish News* that he was prepared to lead a deputation of the PD to meet Harold Wilson.[102] On 8 January the same paper reported Fitt saying that he knew many of the young members of the Peoples' Democracy, including Catholics, Protestants and people of no religion. He admired their idealism and sense of justice and believed they epitomised a new generation who were not prepared to live under the shackles that bound their forebears.[103]

Fitt was highly critical of the activities of the RUC in the Bogside after the march, calling it a 'three hour reign of terror'.[104] When it was announced that the enquiry was to be undertaken within the RUC, Fitt was again highly critical, claiming it was a 'charade and a white-washing exercise designed to protect those members of the RUC who violently abused innocent people in Derry city'.[105]

Any gains O'Neill had made from his television address were lost after his attack on the marchers and the mildness of his rebuke to the assailants. The demand for universal suffrage in local government elections gained renewed impetus.

On 11 January 1969, there was another march, this time in the border town of Newry. Violence occurred after the government banned a section of the route through the largely Catholic town. Fitt told Chris Ryder that he considered the perpetrators 'rioters' that 'had no justification for attacking the police'.[106] His recollection was clearly wrong. Fitt had in fact claimed that the violence was justified. The *Irish Press* reported his address to the Labour Party conference in Dublin: 'Some people had criticised violence in the Civil Rights movement in the North, but the young people who had thrown stones and burned police tenders in Newry were justified in doing so because they had been walked on and oppressed for many years of frustration.'[107] It is perhaps significant that these utterances were made south of the border.

The episode is another example of Fitt endorsing 'unconstitutional methods' of political agitation. It also shows the wavering that characterised his political thinking and rhetoric as the situation changed, Fitt the 'chameleon' altering his colours to suit the prevailing environment.

Under further pressure from within his party, O'Neill called an election for 24 February. He was gambling on obtaining a mandate by mustering up moderate Protestant and Catholic support. Fitt again defended Dock. In his manifesto he alleged that there was collusion between extremists and the 'so called Liberal unionists'. He argued that the Dock Unionist Association was a Paisleyite cell:

> Who selected my opponents? First, the Dock Unionist Association which everyone knows is now a Paisleyite cell. And who was Chairman at the selection meeting? None other than the very same Paisleyite who opposed me for the Aldermanship of Dock in 1967 and was overwhelmingly de-feated by the combined votes of both the Catholic and Protestant socially conscious working people in this area.

True to form, Fitt's manifesto steered well clear from overt republicanism. Instead it claimed that the unionist's new tactic was pretence of being progressive:

> No matter what my unionist opponent may claim to be, electors of Dock knew that he is a unionist who therefore will be a Paisleyite if the company suits him, or an O'Neill man if he is looking for money from the 'Moderate Ulster' businessmen. But he can be no friend of the people of Dock.[108]

As the election drew near, Fitt maintained that the people of Dock had not been fooled by the O'Neill euphoria, and would not be prepared to sell their heritage: 'Let our answer ring out loud and clear so that the people of Northern Ireland will be in no doubt that whatever happens elsewhere, the working-class of this area steadfastly cling to the Connolly idealism.'[109]

The *Belfast News Letter* forecast a victory for Fitt, but with a reduced majority.[110] This prediction was logical: it might have been expected that Fitt's Protestant support would have diminished as a result of his activities at Westminster and his political rhetoric in Belfast. But the reverse happened: Fitt won the election with an increased margin – the largest in the history of the division. Fitt had built up a high degree of trust with the Protestant community, a worthy achievement.

The results of the Stormont election on the nationalist side were to have important repercussions. In Derry, Eddie McAteer was defeated by John Hume, one of the civil rights leaders. The Nationalist Party, which had by now given up its role as official opposition, was also defeated by opponents who stood on civil rights tickets in South Armagh and mid-Derry. It had been slow in its response to the new militancy and suffered the consequences: by the 1970s it would cease to be a political force. The PD won nine per cent of the vote.

Fitt's long-time party colleague Harry Diamond was defeated in the Falls district by Paddy Devlin, chairman of the NILP and active participant in the civil rights movement. Fitt told me that Diamond's defeat was a consequence of his conducting a campaign that was essentially inert. Devlin's triumph had grave consequences for the Republican Labour Party, and Diamond's failure would be instrumental in influencing Fitt's later decisions.[111]

On the same day as the Burntollet march, it was announced that Fitt and Roddy Connolly, James Connolly's son, were to undertake an extensive United States lecture tour, at the invitation of the American Irish Heritage Society. The lectures were designed to 'enlighten' Americans about the situation in Northern Ireland and civil rights. Fitt claimed that it would not be his intention to disparage Northern Ireland. Although he intended to castigate the unionist administration for a lack of social justice, he maintained he was keen to clear up American misconceptions. 'I will be telling them the truth, that there are many decent Protestant and Catholic people living in harmony.'[112] The tour was to take in several US cities including New York, Chicago, San Francisco, Boston and Los Angeles.

In March, Fitt travelled to Dublin to obtain an Irish passport for his trip. 'I'm a 32 county Irishman and this the one way of proving it.'[113] His symbolic gesture would later cause some controversy.

Just as the tone and content of the speeches he delivered at Westminster contrasted with those made elsewhere, Fitt's US tour proved somewhat different from what he had told the press it would be. Despite his insistence that he would not smear Northern Ireland, Fitt made headlines in the Irish media for some unequivocal statements. The *Belfast Telegraph* reported him speaking at Los Angeles comparing the Unionist Party with governments in South Africa and the American Deep South confederacy. He told US newsmen that Catholics in Northern Ireland were treated worse than negroes in America.[114] Fitt's behaviour in America provoked hostile reaction from unionists. Basil McIvor, Unionist Party member for Larkfield, described Fitt as a 'pantomime performer': 'The world is his stage. He performs in Stormont, Westminster, America, or wherever he happens to be. He is in the nature of an entertainer whose act has recently been wearing very thin – so thin he had to think up something really startling for his American audience.'[115]

Fitt was not finished. The *Irish Times* reported him chastising the 'sectarian RUC' and it noted his desire to see 'the total elimination of British control in any part of Ireland'. The paper also reported Fitt's claim that he was 'as much opposed to the reactionary Government in Dublin as to the sectarian junta in Belfast'.[116]

It was only after the violence of the summer of 1969 that American interest in Northern Ireland became fully stimulated. Nevertheless, Fitt made an impression. He was met by three mayors, was given a standing ovation when he addressed the Massachusetts House of Representatives and was made an honorary citizen of Los Angeles. He attended a banquet in his honour, at which he was one of the principal speakers, together with Hubert Humphrey, the Democratic candidate in the 1968 American presidential election. Fitt also met Edward Kennedy. In all, he made forty-seven speeches and appeared on seventeen radio programmes.

Fitt later denied that he made the sweeping statement that Catholics were treated worse in Northern Ireland than negroes in the US. He explained:

I said that many Catholics in Derry are living in worse conditions than many coloured people in the US. That cannot be contradicted. I was talking specifically about housing and the failure of the Unionist government to provide homes. I have told American people the truth about the Civil Rights struggle in Northern Ireland and I have said nothing in America that I have not said at Westminster and Stormont.[117]

On 9 April, the *Belfast News Letter* reported attempts by Robin Chichester Clark, Westminster Unionist MP for Derry, to raise questions with James Callaghan about Fitt's use of an Irish passport. In a letter to the home secretary he asked whether this was 'within the obligation imposed by the Oath of Allegiance and with the letter and spirit of the Oath'. He told the *News Letter*, 'It seems a little odd that someone who is constantly asking for British standards of behaviour at home should acquire an un-British passport to travel abroad.'[118] Two days later he went further, telling the *Belfast Telegraph* that Fitt 'now provides proof of what I have always said, that he believes in the dismemberment of the UK'.[119]

For his part, Fitt claimed to be delighted that his tour was receiving so much publicity: 'But I make no apology for having an Irish passport.'[120] Evidently Fitt's nationalism was more fervent than he recalled and, to use a colloquialism, he was 'winding up' the unionists. In a more functionalist sense, Ryder oberves that Fitt's acquisition of an Irish passport was attributable as much to the need to avoid awkward bureaucracy. The complexity surrounding Fitt's birth and adoption made it necessary to apply to the less particular Irish Republic for a passport.[121] Nevertheless, Fitt seemed to relish the chance to antagonise his political opponents and the decision to secure travel documentation from what many perceived to be a 'foreign state' would seem to have given him immense pleasure. During a press conference in America Fitt was asked about his attitude to the PD. He maintained that he was extremely pleased about the spirit of justice that motivated these young adults and the most encouraging outlook for Northern Ireland politics was the community spirit that had been engendered between the Catholic and Protestant students at Queen's.[122]

On 17 April, there was a by-election for the Westminster seat in Mid-Ulster. Bernadette Devlin was then a young student member of the PD, whose rhetoric was militant and anti-sectarian. On his return from America Fitt endorsed her: 'Bernadette Devlin symbolises the young generation in Northern Ireland who are not prepared to tolerate the conditions under which their parents lived. I am absolutely delighted that we have found a single candidate to oppose the Unionist Party.'[123]

Fitt told me that he really wanted Austin Currie to be selected and that Devlin merely 'sneered' at those who endorsed her candidacy.[124]

Devlin won the crucial by-election, defeating the Unionist Party candidate Anna Forrest with the largest majority (4,211) since the seat was created in 1950. The turnout for the poll was 91.7 per cent, indicating that almost the entire nationalist community had mobilised behind the civil rights campaign. Devlin had tried to fight the election on non-sectarian, radical socialist policies, but the reality was that she was a pan-Catholic candidate and her election marked the pinnacle of Catholic unity. Thereafter, this cohesion would fragment and eventually disintegrate.

James Callaghan considered Fitt the 'guiding spirit' of the civil rights movement.[125] Fitt did indeed use his personal qualities and high profile to highlight the condition of the northern Catholic and he clearly enjoyed the freedom that his individual style of politics allowed. But by 1969 there was emerging a new group of articulate, talented and pragmatic political operators – Paddy Devlin, John Hume, Bernadette Devlin, Ivan Cooper, Paddy O'Hanlon and Austin Currie – who, though they never obscured Fitt, did make him slightly less distinct. This circumstance also created the impression that Fitt was a kind of elder statesman of nationalist politics. The contacts with senior members of the Labour Party, further reinforced this image. By 1970, therefore, Fitt would increasingly be regarded as the voice of moderation, which was bound to lead him into disagreement with radicals like Bernadette Devlin who was also taking her seat at Westminster. Fitt said of their time at parliament:

> There was no relationship. I was quite happy when Bernadette came here to show her around. She was after all an anti-unionist representative but Bernadette always had a crowd ... all round her, including Michael Farrell, Louden Seth[126] and Eamon McCann.[127]

Fitt was convinced that Labour MP Paul Rose, who had done so much to help publicise discrimination in Northern Ireland, terminated his interest in provincial affairs in the aftermath of Devlin's 'brilliant' maiden speech in 1969. Devlin was surrounded in the Members' Lobby (which normally does not admit strangers) by what Fitt alliteratively termed 'lefties and loonies from London'. Lord Longford asked Fitt if 'we could take Miss

Devlin to my house for dinner this evening'. Fitt was not sure, so Rose
tried to make the invitation, a difficult task considering the excitement
and the crowd of admirers. According to Fitt one of Devlin's associates
shouted at Rose, 'Who the fuck are you, trying to jump on Bernadette's
bandwagon? Fuck away off.' Evidently there was no space left on the
bandwagon and Rose returned to Fitt as 'white as a sheet' and said 'that's
me finished'. He was true to his word.

I asked Fitt if he would expand his views on the 'nutters' – Michael
Farrell and the radical socialist from Derry, Eamon McCann. And he did
in a fashion. He regarded them and particularly McCann, as 'head cases,
intellectual head cases but fucking head cases nonetheless'. He felt they
had a detrimental effect on Devlin 'who had everything going for her'. The
pair he said 'were totally leftie and talked like Trots'.[128]

Talk of the young generation in Northern Ireland, who were 'not
prepared to tolerate the conditions under which their parents lived', was a
distant memory for Fitt.

In sharp contrast to the socialism of Farrell and McCann, Fitt's socialism in this period retained its less radical and intuitive characteristics but
his nationalism was not unvarying. On occasion between 1966 and 1970,
Fitt presented himself as a militant, though it must be remembered that
much of this militancy was voiced against a background of stability within Northern Ireland. Fitt would not have been the first Irish politician
to promote constitutional change through the threat of revolution.
Furthermore, there is evidence that Fitt's nationalism was more discernible
in Northern Ireland and the Republic than it was in London; he had different voices for different venues. This wavering suggests that Fitt had no
clear political ideology beyond an instinctive labourism. It also left him
open to the unionist charge that although he said he did not want the
border removed by force, his actions showed the reverse.

Devlin's entry to Westminster as the youngest MP since Pitt also marked
a watershed in Fitt's career. I asked Devlin if she felt she had somewhat
eroded Fitt's authority and stature by her arrival in London. She answered:
'I never had much to do with him at Westminster simply because I was too
young to be sensitive to the fact that Gerry Fitt had ploughed that furrow
and I had bounced in as some kind of new invention that had stolen his
thunder ... It affected Gerry. His nose was knocked out of joint.'[129]

Devlin was correct in her analysis. There was little affection from Fitt
in his recollections of his fellow anti-unionist. He claimed that he could

'write a book on Bernadette Devlin'. He went as far as to suggest that she was something of a 'head case' and he knew she 'would come to a bad end and make a fool of herself'. For Fitt that time came on Monday 31 January 1972, the day after Bloody Sunday,[130] when Devlin punched Reginald Maudling, the Conservative secretary of state for home affairs when he made a statement to Parliament supporting the British army line that it had fired only in self-defence.[131]

Despite Fitt's retrospective comments, he was instrumental in ensuring that Devlin's maiden speech was such a stunning success. Loyalists had exploded a number of bombs in March and April and Paul Rose had cited the bombings in making use of a procedural device (Standing Order No. 9 of the House rules) to persuade the speaker to allow an adjournment debate. It was unusual for new members to make their maiden speech on taking their seat. Fitt and Rose agreed to sponsor her. Fitt told me that he had terrible trouble locating Devlin to inform her of the debate: 'I rang the whole country.' He finally located her at the bar of the Stormont Hotel, Belfast. He said:

> She came to the phone pissed. I said 'Look, Bernadette, we have just been successful here in getting an adjournment debate and if you come over, everything is in your favour. I will sponsor you and so will Paul Rose.' Never was a maiden speech so arranged to be in anyone's favour. She said 'I'm not too sure if I want to go there and anyway I haven't any fucking money.' I pleaded with her and said, 'I'll pay your fare' and the next morning she came over.

Fitt got hold of the hotel manageress and arranged that she would lend Devlin £50, for which he would be responsible.[132] Devlin corroborated that Fitt had indeed contacted her and lent her the money.[133]

Bernadette Devlin was ultimately a disappointment to Catholic nationalism: an unfair appraisal, as she had never sought to represent it. Nevertheless, there can be no doubt that she stimulated the public imagination, particularly in Britain, and one indication of this is an editorial in the *Irish News* that stated: 'Westminster's MPs have learned a lot about Northern Ireland from Mr Gerry Fitt, they are going to learn a lot more and more vividly from Miss Devlin.'[134]

On 16 April 1969, with a general election in the Republic looming large, the *Belfast News Letter* reported that approaches had been made to Fitt to stand as a Labour candidate in Louth. Fitt claimed it would be a 'physical impossibility' for him to hold seats in three parliaments and he had not taken the offers 'too seriously'. His allegiance was to his constituents in Dock and West Belfast. He would enter the Dáil only as a 'symbolic gesture' and had not discussed the possibility of standing in Louth, despite the 'friendly relations' he had with some of its members.[135]

This episode perhaps could be construed as another missed opportunity. Surely this was an opening for Fitt to develop an all-Ireland approach to Labour politics, in the absence of the British Labour Party organising in the north. In fact, it would have been more consistent for Fitt, considering his 'socialist republican' standpoint, to gravitate towards the Irish labour movement established by his great hero Connolly.

The truth of the matter was that Fitt understood socialism in a British framework and he was much more comfortable at Westminster and Stormont than he was with southern politics. His attitude to the south, was in stark contrast to the attitude of some of his colleagues in the SDLP. In some respects or, more to the point, at certain times Fitt appeared to be a British socialist with a kind of socialist republican froth.

Towards the end of April the situation in Northern Ireland was becoming increasingly fraught. There were serious riots in both Derry and Belfast. Members of the minority community, who had earlier been responsive to O'Neill's overtures, began to relinquish hopes of peaceful reform. In a further attempt to pacify them, O'Neill finally accepted the principle of 'one man, one vote'. The following day – 23 April – James Chichester-Clark, the Minister for Agriculture and O'Neill's cousin, resigned from the government, complaining about the timing of O'Neill's statement. It is more likely that the real reason for his departure was speculation that he might become Prime Minister if the premier were forced to resign.

On 24 and 25 April, bombs destroyed Belfast's water supply pipes. The blasts were attributed to the IRA and turned members of the Unionist Party against O'Neill and his policy of conciliation. Rather than attend a meeting of the Unionist Party's standing committee, which would have seen O'Neill lose a vote of confidence, he resigned. (It was later shown that the UVF was responsible for planting the explosives, a tactic designed both to incriminate the IRA and bring about the fall of O'Neill.)

After O'Neill's departure, Fitt issued the following warning: 'The new Prime Minister must realise urgently that steps must be taken to introduce reforms, otherwise the same fate would befall him. Repression was not an answer.'[136]

The selection of Chichester-Clark as the new Prime Minister changed nothing. He was essentially in the same mould as O'Neill, and was similarly susceptible to the more extreme elements in his party – a point not lost on Fitt, who claimed: 'It is extremely obvious that Mr Chichester-Clark will be a prisoner within the ranks of his own party as was his predecessor and that his actions will be dictated by his reactionaries in the party.'[137]

Despite the truth of Fitt's statement, Chichester-Clark did make some effort to reduce tension. He re-affirmed the government's newly acquired pledge of 'one man, one vote' and ordered an amnesty for those convicted of or charged with political offences. The timing of these directives – just before the summer marching season – was unfortunate.

In an attempt to reduce confrontation on the streets, Chichester-Clark's administration introduced a public order bill to prevent inflammatory counter-demonstrations. This move was construed as repressive legislation by the opposition. Fitt, who had recently left hospital having been admitted suffering from exhaustion, was at Stormont to voice his disapproval and make a prophetic prediction. He argued that the new legislation 'will make violent revolution inevitable'.[138] Despite its intent, the public order bill did nothing to prevent a series of riots and sectarian clashes throughout the month of July.

On 25 July, Fitt gave evidence to the Cameron Commission in Belfast. This commission was instructed to trace the causes of the violence of 5 October 1968 and to analyse the forces involved. In a two-and-a-half-hour interview, Fitt gave his version of why the people had taken to the streets.

The disturbances of July 1969 were paltry compared with the incidents in August. On 2 August an Orange march passed the Catholic Unity flats in Belfast, and led to three days of rioting. As a result, families began to move away from areas – Protestant and Catholic – where they were in a minority. Fitt urged the police to stop this happening: 'These evictions could snowball with disastrous results. The government and the police will have to take strong action to protect threatened families. The court should impose the severest penalties on people convicted of threatening families – Protestant and Roman Catholic.'

Fitt also announced that a housing action committee would be set up in his Dock constituency to protect families and their homes.[139] Fitt was unable to prevent the population shifts, however, and many families were forced to move. It is estimated that ultimately around 40,000 people were forced to flee their homes.

On 3 August, as Stormont seemed to be losing control, Chichester-Clark met with Callaghan. Fitt predicted that the forthcoming week would be a testing time for Northern Ireland. He recommended that Britain should assert its authority and take full power under the Government of Ireland Act to maintain law and order.[140] Fitt's intervention was conducted against the backdrop of Irish government warnings to Britain, through its ambassador, that the situation in the north was becoming extremely dangerous, and that a catastrophe was looming if matters were left to the Stormont regime to handle. But the British government rebuffed the Irish ambassador and insisted that the internal affairs of the north were a matter for the unionist government alone, and no one else – not even itself! This, of course, was a total misrepresentation: sovereign authority rested at Westminster, as subsequent events would demonstrate. The result of this dereliction of governmental duty in 1969 was to be twenty-five years of warfare.

The critical moment came on 12 August, the date marking the end of the 1689 siege of the city by the Catholic Jacobite army, which was commemorated annually by the Apprentice Boys of Derry. At the end of July, Fitt had drawn attention to what he had termed the 'invasion' of Derry by the Apprentice Boys and he warned of a series of confrontations, yet again placing all responsibility for any eventualities on the British government. 'We have now done all we can to make the British government fully aware of the present situation. The rest is up to them.'[141] The government disregarded all pleas to ban the march, and stone-throwing quickly escalated into a full-scale riot in the Bogside area of Derry. Encouraged by Bernadette Devlin, the Derry Defence Association had constructed barricades, which were manned by petrol bombers.

The attack continued for twenty-four hours before the RUC fell back having failed to penetrate the Catholic area. In an effort to re-establish authority the unionists ordered the mobilisation of the B Specials, and what became known as the Battle of the Bogside ensued. By 14 August, the prospect of civil war was looming, and was given brief stimulus by the provocative rhetoric from Jack Lynch, Taoiseach of the Irish Republic:

> It is also evident that the Stormont government is no longer in control of the situation. Indeed the present situation is the inevitable outcome of the policies pursued for decades by successive Stormont governments. It is clear that the Irish government can no longer stand by and see innocent people injured and perhaps worse.[142]

The violence in Derry ended only with the intervention of British troops. On 14 August the army entered the city centre and undertook negotiations with the Derry Defence Association. The authorities agreed to withdraw the RUC and the B Specials and not to infringe on the Bogside. Meanwhile, violence had erupted again in Belfast.

Catholic crowds had gathered at the interface between the Lower Falls and Shankill in an attempt to 'keep the heat off Derry'. This had led to disturbances, which provoked a powerful attack on the Catholic houses in the mixed streets that connected the two districts. But most serious of all was the appearance of the armed state security forces mingling with the Protestant crowds; then armoured cars firing heavy machine guns at Divis flats.

Parts of the Falls Road and other Catholic streets were burnt out. There were six fatalities – five Catholics and one Protestant. Barricades were erected in Catholic areas. As in Derry, James Callaghan introduced troops, which succeeded in defusing the situation. Callaghan confirmed that Fitt was strongly instrumental in this decision. He recalled:

> Gerry Fitt telephoned again and said that only British troops could restore calm in Belfast. There was no doubt that his apprehensions were genuine but I could not forebear to remind him that Lynch had said that British troops would be unwelcome. What was his opinion? Fitt was emphatic that the Catholic minority in Belfast would not take that view. Only British troops could save them from the wrath of the Protestants and he urged that they should be brought in at once.[143]

On 18 August, opposition politicians called a press conference to give their account of what was happening in Northern Ireland. Fitt alleged that the unionist version of what had occurred in Belfast was a 'verbal avalanche of misrepresentation and downright lies'. He categorically denied that the IRA had inspired the rioting: 'The IRA had no part to play in the campaign, and any republicans evident in the course of the confrontation were armed only with sticks, stones and perhaps petrol bombs. They had to take a stand to defend their lives and the lives of their wives and children.'

On the contrary, he maintained, it was the B Specials who fired the first shot, supported by the UVF and extreme unionists. He made a candid appeal for direct rule from Westminster 'so that we may all have a chance of social justice for the rest of our lives'.[144] Two days later, Wilson set up a commission under Lord Hunt to enquire into the structure of the RUC and B Specials. Fitt welcomed the move, feeling that such an enquiry would 'clear the air'.[145]

On the same day (22 August) Desmond Greaves was in Belfast. Roy Johnston, who edited Greave's journal, related:

> Later he [Greaves] sees Gerry Fitt, who describes the desperation on the Falls Road and the demand for arms. He had rung up Callaghan and got a secretary; finally he got through to the man himself, and soon afterwards the troops came in. Presumably Callaghan had consulted Wilson. Subsequently Callaghan promised to disarm the B-men, and assured Fitt that the reason he was not doing it at one blow was that the arms would then mysteriously disappear. Fitt was on top of the world, and quite convinced that what had happened was a result of a 'plan' that CDG [Greaves] and he had hatched in the car on the road between Liverpool and Manchester. The next step was to get the B-Specials to fire on the British troops. '... Between you and me that's being fixed up now ...'[146]

The possibilities for nationalist mischief-making seemed to have gone to Fitt's head in the excitement of the moment.

Johnston checked Greaves' journal for the meeting of the two recalled by Fitt. It took place on 26 May 1968. He reports, 'I can see no evidence of a 'plan' as such, but some evidence that Fitt was in a position to influence Wilson to be critical of the RUC and B-Special situation.'[147]

Johnston told me that the strategy was justified, and this suggests that on this occasion Fitt was adopting a republican-socialist persona:

> Fitt was dead right, as was Greaves; the key issue was to disarm the Specials, who triggered the Provisionals and gave the latter credibility; the gun was re-introduced by the Orangemen, as they had done in Larne in 1914. Our objective was to take the gun out, and develop a political environment in which common interests of working people could be identified.[148]

One week later, Callaghan came to Belfast and outlined his plans for a prescription of social and government reform that he felt would normalise the situation. Fitt accompanied him on a tour of the riot areas in Belfast, where the home secretary received a genial welcome from the residents.

It is uniformly acknowledged that in the summer of 1969 the IRA as a military force was almost non-existent in Northern Ireland. The organisation was rural rather than urban, and any activists they had were submerged into the civil rights movement. Nevertheless, at the time the IRA claimed that twenty of its men were involved in defending the Catholic enclaves.[149] This claim was resented by more moderate leaders as it added weight to the unionist myth that the riots had been sparked off by the IRA.

As events developed the IRA was reborn from a small traditionalist republican cadre, first by the abandonment of West Belfast and Derry to republicans and then by insensitive British security measures that characterised the attempts to reoccupy these areas. In December the republican movement split, with the traditional republican 'Provisional' IRA breaking away from the left-leaning 'Officials'. It was the 'Provisionals' who would embark on the most sustained military campaign in the history of Northern Ireland.

The events of August 1969 had some significant consequences. For example, the violent confrontation of that month instilled a greater political consciousness among the working-class Catholics in urban areas. It also proved conclusively that the unionist administration was unable to govern or resist the new social forces that had emerged. The intervention of the army had opened up the constitutional position, and, most importantly in connection with Fitt, the diminishing role of leading individuals was further reduced, particularly in Belfast.

Despite Callaghan's efforts, the barricades that had been set up by street defence committees remained intact. Paddy Devlin argued later that Fitt kept his distance from the committees, an astute move, according to Devlin, as 'the business usually concerned relationships with the security forces, both army and police, who were pressurising us to remove the barricades and restore, as they saw it, normal law and order'.[150]

As loyalists demanded an end to the 'no-go' Catholic areas, Fitt issued a peace appeal: 'I have no hesitation in supporting the prime minister's call for peace particularly over the weekend. I call on all those who support me politically to do nothing, by word or action, which could possibly inflame the already very dangerous situation.'[151] There was no indication now that Fitt wished to flirt with 'unconstitutional methods'.

Despite the pleas of Fitt and others, rioting continued. On 11 September Fitt, Paddy Devlin and Paddy Kennedy, the Republican Labour Stormont MP for Belfast Central, together with members of the Belfast Citizens' Defence Committee, went to London for talks with Callaghan and agreed to take the barricades down. In a joint statement Fitt said:

> We have been given guarantees which we have accepted as strong enough to give adequate protection to all those behind the barricades. We recognise the dangerous situation which exists and we fully recognise the distress and tragedy, particularly to many innocent people, over the last few weeks.[152]

On the same day Fitt and other local politicians were apparently re-asserting their influence as elected representatives, the Cameron Commission reported its findings. These clearly indicated the injustices of the Northern Ireland governmental system and, in so doing, provided some endorsement of the demands of the civil rights movement. The behaviour of the RUC and the B Specials also attracted severe criticism, as did Fitt, although it was admitted that the police assault he suffered was unjustified. The report concluded:

> Mr Fitt sought publicity for himself and his political views, and must clearly have envisaged the possibility of a violent clash with the police as providing the publicity he so ardently sought. His conduct in our judgement was reckless and wholly irresponsible in a person occupying his public position.[153]

Fitt was unrepentant: 'I make no apology for my action on that day. On the contrary, I am glad I have lived to see the day when the oppressed people of Northern Ireland finally got off their knees to throw off the yoke of unionist oppression.'[154]

The nationalist community felt little apprehension about the Cameron charge. Paul Rose, however, felt it necessary to defend Fitt:

> I have known Mr Fitt for five years and while like all politicians he may seek publicity, this can hardly be a criticism. There are times when his speeches may have been emotive, but I know of no occasion on which

he has ever been inflammatory and it was not his fault that the police set upon him as a target in full view of millions of television viewers at the beginning of the current disturbances.[155]

Despite the irrelevance of the charge to the nationalist community and the remonstrations of Rose, the Cameron verdict might arguably have damaged Fitt's standing at Westminster.

Two days after the publication of Cameron's findings, Captain James Kelly met Fitt and Belfast republicans John and Billy Kelly (no relation to the captain) at Fitt's home on the Antrim Road. This was the same John Kelly who had gone to 'gun lectures' in the Dock Ward in the 1950s. Captain Kelly was an Irish army intelligence officer under orders to concentrate on Northern Ireland affairs by developing contacts in Derry and Belfast. The Dublin government, while worried about the situation in the north, was also concerned to preserve the stability of the southern state or, as Justin O'Brien put it, 'to avoid the threat of anarchy infecting the Southern body politic'.[156] (Kelly had met Paddy Devlin and Paddy Kennedy in Dublin the month before, and both men were keen to procure arms for defence purposes. Kelly had urged them to make contact with members of the Irish government.) Captain Kelly's remit may have been to try to establish control over the direction of Catholic politics in the north and to take the northern nationalists in hand. This objective was entirely understandable in the light of the political vacuum that existed in nationalist areas, which the British government was effectively ignoring, and which could only encourage the growth of forces that might exacerbate the situation – with dire consequences for all. Dublin understandably feared the emergence of radical forces and hoped to use constitutional politicians like Fitt to stymie any such developments. (This, it should be noted, is quite different from the conspiracy theory presented by Official Republicans after the event – that Fianna Fail created the Provisionals to divert republicanism away from social revolution.)

Paddy Wilson had urged Kelly to meet Fitt, and Paddy Kennedy had made arrangements for the meeting. Kelly later recalled what happened:

A meeting was arranged for Fitt's house on the night of Saturday September 13. An initial get-together was arranged between Fitt, Billy Kelly, his brother, John, and others. This took place in the Fitt sitting room, overlooking the Antrim Road. Mr Fitt had returned from London that day and told me that the Kellys escorted him in from the airport, as he no longer trusted the Royal Ulster Constabulary (RUC).He shoved a gin and tonic into my hand and I sat in the armchair, as he stood at the mantelpiece, a drink in his hand, expounding on Republicanism and quoting Pearse and Connolly. When I got a chance, I told him that all the people I had met right across from Derry to Belfast asked for arms to defend themselves and their communities. I suggested that at that stage, there might be a period of calm in which to organise and put a case to the Irish Government, saying something to the effect that governments are slow to move. Mr Fitt responded with passion:

'You're wrong. You say we have time to work out something. I tell you we haven't. We're sitting on a tinder-box here. Violence could break out at any time, today or tomorrow, tonight, even tonight; it's not too late yet. It could happen any minute.'

At that moment, the room door burst open and Mrs Fitt stood there.

'It's on, Gerry. It's on, Gerry,' in a half-whispered shout.

'Where?'

'Round the corner, the New Lodge.'

'What did I tell you? It's not next month we need arms. It's now, now in the next five minutes maybe.'[157]

John Kelly confirmed this recollection:

We were having this discussion about the necessity for weapons and Gerry was arguing the case, and just at that his wife Ann came bursting into the room and she shouted: Gerry, Gerry they're coming, they're coming and we could hear the noise out on the street as if a mob was coming. Gerry stood up and shouted: I told you, I fucking told you, there it is. Do you need any more proof?[158]

According to this analysis, Fitt was making the urgency of the situation clear, and it was manifest that he wanted weaponry. This was not his only appeal. John Kelly revealed: 'Fitt came to Dublin with me to get guns. We went to Leinster House. He advocated very strongly that it was the responsibility of the Irish government to supply guns to defend the nationalist population. There was absolutely no equivocation.'[159]

John Kelly had acted as Fitt's bodyguard and supplied others to perform this service for the MP. Alongside other republicans he wrested control from the existing IRA leadership in Belfast. Concerned by the official leadership's reluctance to utilise the opportunities presented by the post-August situation, this group of disaffected traditionalists formed the Provisional IRA. The question must be asked: did Fitt help to facilitate the rise of the Provisionals?

In September 1969 the Provisional IRA did not exist, so it could be argued on Fitt's behalf that he could not be held responsible for knowingly facilitating its creation. But, according to John Kelly: 'The Provisionals were not there in a formal sense but they were in an embryonic sense. The people who were going to be in charge of the guns were going to be the IRA and I have no doubt that Fitt was fully aware and fully appreciative of who would have control of the weapons.'[160]

While some may question John Kelly's impartiality, his recollection is probably true: this was a period of flux in which even the most mild-mannered could be affected by conflict and catastrophe. Fitt may have known who would 'have control of the weapons', but he could not have foreseen what would happen in the ensuing months. So while Fitt cannot be held intentionally culpable, he can be said to have failed (like many others) to foresee the consequences of what he was engaged in. The provision of arms to committed republicans was not going to be a process that could easily have been reversed nor a situation that he could control for ever.[161]

However, Fitt's negligence pales by comparison with the actions of the Lynch-led southern government during this period. It was the withdrawal of Irish attempts to take the northern nationalists in hand, under pressure from the British, that ultimately led to the growth of the Provisional IRA from a republican nucleus to a mass movement. For it was in the political vacuum created by British absence from the no-go areas after August 1969, and southern withdrawal from assisting and directing the political organisation of northern Catholic politics, that fertile ground was created for a rebirth of armed republicanism and its fruit, the Provisionals. Within this political vacuum the republican nucleus trained hundreds of discontented, angry young men and women, who were determined that there would be no repeat of August 1969 and who trusted a local republican leadership instead of looking south to Dublin for guidance, and help as they had from the 1920s.

What is intriguing, however, in hindsight, is Fitt's later faith in the RUC when he clearly did not trust it with his life in the summer of 1969. John Kelly confirmed Fitt's fear: 'The RUC was part of daily life and Fitt like all of us would have tolerated it. But by 1969 he certainly would not have trusted them with his life. He did not feel that they would have protected him from loyalist paramilitaries and at that time he was a target.'[162]

Despite his association with the Kelly brothers, Fitt was totally unprepared for the formation of a 'Northern IRA' in 1969. Twenty years later he recalled its appearance in his home constituency. 'In the Dock area the IRA formed the Third Battalion. They were the scum of the earth. They were people who had all sorts of convictions for petty theft – social rejects, and then all of a sudden they were the IRA.'[163] Yet these are the people, the 'scum of the earth' who, according to John Kelly, he sought to arm at the time! Arguably Fitt had acted with criminal responsibility in 1969 and his road to Damascus-style conversion in the intervening years was based on a fundamental reappraisal of the situation, complete with a degree of airbrushing.

The arrival of British soldiers on the streets of Northern Ireland in August 1969 had reduced the vulnerability of the Catholic community to attack from loyalist mobs and, in the short term at least, provided an alternative to the RUC, which was viewed as representing the unionist tradition in a way that was unsatisfactory to nationalists.

In October 1969 the *Belfast Telegraph* quoted Fitt saying 'Thank God for the British troops.'[164] At this point Fitt was only expressing a widely held nationalist view – the British army was not yet the enemy. However, it would not be long before Fitt's 'republican' label and history appeared at best inappropriate and at worst somewhat ludicrous.

He had already moved away from some of his old allies. While in London on October 20 Greaves recorded in his journal what he interpreted as a snub from Fitt. 'CC [Charlie Cunningham] told me that when they all went to lobby at the House of Commons GF [Gerry Fitt] was there and, seeing SR [Seán Redmond], said 'Hello, Tom,' – This, says Charlie Cunningham, was a calculated snub, but Seán Redmond replied coolly, 'Tom's in Dublin".'[165]

Charlie Cunningham was (and remains) a Connolly Association activist and he seemed to think that Fitt had intentionally mis-identified Seán Redmond as his brother Tom.[166] Seán Redmond was general secretary of the Connolly Association. When I asked him about the incident he revealed:

> When Fitt went to Westminster first he did not know many people. I did and I introduced him to many of the MPs. But by 1969 he did not need me and the snub may have been calculated – I don't know – but he was that type of man anyway. The Westminster scene seduced him and there was an element of that too. I think it is fair to say that he had started to move away from us at that point.[167]

Redmond cannot be accused of using hindsight to form his opinion. Greaves' journal for the following day reads:

> I asked SR [Seán Redmond] about Gerry Fitt. He did not think there was anything wrong with him but absorption in himself and a some-what naive faith in the Labour Party for doing what they have. He had travelled back from Brighton with Fitt, Paul Rose and Frank Pakenham. One could detect the inner awe when he said 'Lord Longford'. All the world loves a Lord![168]

It is perhaps significant that Greaves does not refer to Fitt again in his journal. This 'snub' may have had to do with the divergent policies that Fitt and Greave's supporters were now pursuing in the post-August situation. Greaves and his supporters in the Connolly Association and those influencing the republican movement had theorised during the 1960s that Ireland was about to be re-incorporated into the UK in a federalist plan supported by compromising 'gombeen' elements that had taken over Fianna Fáil. They had inspired the republicans to oppose this process in the south through agitation and political education. They saw direct rule as a step in this process and a potentially very dangerous development as a result. So the policy of the Greaves-inspired Official Republicans after August 1969 was for a reformed Stormont with a bill of rights to protect the minority and establish the democratic gains made in constitutional form.

Fitt, on the other hand, took the mainstream nationalist view (and the position of Joe Devlin in 1920 when he opposed its establishment) that Stormont was the source of most political ills visited on northern Catholics. He called in August 1969 for direct rule as the only way of getting social justice for Catholics. It was clear that he had the bulk of Catholic support for this in the post-August situation. Seán Redmond argued:

> Fitt became confused. His basic instinct was working-class and socialist but he never worked out any coherent political philosophy in his head. He was not a deep thinking man in that sense. In the sixties his only consistent view was his hatred of unionism. The Connolly Association was opposed to the concept of direct rule because our view was that democratic politics in the North might develop on class lines if the civil rights safeguards had been introduced. We did not think destroying Stormont would destroy unionism. In fact we thought it would be a backward step. Fitt's hatred of unionism ensured that he wanted to tear down Stormont.[169]

So a situation would emerge in which Fitt, and the newly emerging Provisionals, were in one camp calling for the end of Stormont; and Greaves, the Connolly Association, the Official Republicans and John Hume were in the other, favouring a reformed northern Irish assembly. Hume had, as we shall see, from December 1969 become part of a 'shadow cabinet' of nationalists at Stormont, demanding posts from the unionist administration, and had been reported in the *Irish News* of 2 March 1970 as opposing direct rule on the basis that it made Northern Ireland an 'outpost of London'.[170]

Ultimately Fitt was to concede to Hume's policy on the formation of the SDLP. But he may have been influenced by the leadership of the British Labour Party in this. In the weeks following the August pogrom it was made clear, and Fitt could not have failed to understand, that the Labour government was intent on pursuing the traditional British policy with regard to Ulster – keeping it at arm's length as a semi-detached region of the UK and letting local representatives exercise political power. To do this local government was to be upheld at all costs.

Fitt was deeply respectful of the Labour leadership in Whitehall and – against his own political judgement – put his faith in them. He did not oppose them and campaign for greater British involvement to fundamentally address the problems of Northern Ireland – probably because he did not see Britain as being at fault, preferring to blame the unionists. Coughlan certainly felt that elements within the Labour Party had a detrimental impact on Fitt's political thinking.He told me:

> Unfortunately Fitt fell too much under mainstream (i.e. centre and right-
> wing) Labour Party influence the longer he stayed at Westminster and
> he ended up joining the majority of them in calling for 'direct rule' rather
> than the Bill of Rights, whereas a few Labour MPs, under Connolly
> Association and Greaves influence, resisted that fatal song. From then on
> Fitt was a prisoner of mainstream Labour opinion – and the bipartisan
> policy it was committed to – until he eventually rebelled to vote against
> Callaghan and Co in 1979.[171]

Fitt was totally unprepared for the impending collapse of the Stormont
regime.[172] His loose commitment to the idea of a united Ireland was no
substitute for a coherent political philosophy that might have emerged
if he had followed through on his opposition to Stormont in late 1969/
early 1970.

It was easy to aspire for a United Ireland – it is not so easy to implement it. In 1969 Fitt did not have the strategy to promote the ideal he
had espoused throughout the decade. As the nationalist mood became
more militant and civil rights aspirations were increasingly replaced with
a demand for a united Ireland, Fitt and his fellow constitutionalists fell
into a temporary political limbo, trapped by their support of a regime that
had to react in increasingly repressive fashion to the bombing campaign
of the Provos. With the withdrawal of influence from Dublin and in
the absence of mainstream nationalist leadership nobody represented
the Catholic community in any political discourse, and this was only
partly addressed a year later by the establishment of the SDLP. By then,
however, the IRA had filled the void created by the absence of British
and Irish political presence. Much of the fault for this development can
be laid at the door of Westminster and, to a lesser extent, unionism. Westminster had decided to minimise British involvement to the smallest
degree possible and to 'let unionists carry the can'. This was the worst
possible abrogation of responsibility in the circumstances. By not taking
the situation in hand the government was led to supporting all measures
that upheld Stormont authority from Chichester-Clark to Faulkner, and
this meant association with increased levels of repression, from curfew
to internment.

On 10 October, the Hunt Report was published. It recommended that the RUC should be disarmed and the B Specials replaced by a part-time military force under the control of the general officer commanding in Northern Ireland. The keynote of the document was that policing in Northern Ireland should become similar to policing in Great Britain. Fitt considered that the recommendations were acceptable to the whole community and a further vindication of the demands of the civil rights movement.[173]

However, his welcome of the new reforms altered when it was announced in November that the new force would be called the 'Ulster Defence Regiment' (UDR). He found the word 'Ulster' in the title offensive. It presumably offended his nationalist sentiment and no doubt he would have considered the title insensitive and unimaginative: 'I, in company with a large number of Labour supporters, take offence at the description of the new forces arrogating to itself (Ulster Defence). This is seen at Westminster as an attempt to give official recognition to the term 'Ulster' as it is understood by the Unionist Party.'[174]

Fitt was not the only politician who felt this name was unsuitable. Bernadette Devlin proposed that the name be changed to the 'Local Territorial Forces (Northern Ireland)', but this was defeated by 163 votes to 36.

On 3 December, opposition members at Stormont decided to form a parliamentary alliance in the hope that a united body would exercise a greater impact on the discussions and decisions taken at Stormont. A number of shadow appointments were made. Fitt was allocated the role of shadow 'Home Affairs', his contacts at the home office making him the obvious choice. This measure was the beginning of a process that eventually saw the creation of a new opposition party.

4

THE SOCIAL DEMOCRATIC AND
LABOUR PARTY

Although still essentially an old-style street politician reminiscent of the political operators of the 1940s and 1950s, the Gerry Fitt who emerged in the 1970s was somewhat different from the Fitt of the 1960s. In the 1960s – particularly outside Westminster – Fitt posed, and was perceived, as a militant and radical politician. His involvement in the Derry civil rights march and the conclusions drawn by the Cameron Commission, are the most explicit examples – actions prompted by the lack of success through parliamentary manoeuvres. In the 1970s, however, his was a voice of moderation: the violence of the summer of 1969 had had an impact on his thinking. As the decade progressed, this change of position brought him into greater conflict with more radical nationalists. He clashed with his own Republican Labour Party, then with the PD and, most bitterly, with the 'new' IRA. Nevertheless, in the early 1970s, Fitt did not relinquish his aspiration for Irish unity. He was still nationalistic (though he did not always pursue a logical nationalist strategy, as indicated by his unwillingness to pursue a link-up with the Irish Labour Party in April 1969).

However, any flirtation with non-constitutional rhetoric exhibited in the 1960s was not evident in the 1970s. Fitt consistently condemned all forms of violence, from whatever source. In the process, he became an implacable opponent of the PIRA, and he and his family showed tremendous physical courage in this period. Because of the danger of paramilitary attack from both sides of the religious divide his home on the Antrim Road in Belfast began to look increasingly like a fortress.[1]

Although the references to James Connolly are conspicuous by their near absence in this period, Fitt never stopped trying to prove that he was a non-sectarian socialist politician. He became leader of the Social Democratic and Labour Party (SDLP) which was an amalgamation of different groups within the Catholic community, its unifying thread being its opposition to the use of violence. Ideology and policy followed the recruitment of individual members. In fact, it was a party constructed from the top down. Despite Fitt's claims about the socialist credentials of the party, he was unable to convince Protestants to join it. He made attempts to bring about discussions with the representatives of the Protestant working-class, but they proved futile.[2] In short, although he established and presented himself as a socialist politician who represented Protestants as well as Catholics, he was unable as leader of the SDLP to attract the Protestant community. As with all political parties in Northern Ireland, the SDLP's policies and membership were a direct result of its position on the border.

Fitt viewed the prospects for 1970 pessimistically. He expected confrontation unless reforms were implemented quickly.[3] On 5 February, Chichester-Clark re-introduced the draconian public order bill. Fitt was conciliatory in his reaction, arguing that this was not the time to protest.[4] The clashes on the streets that had taken place since the summer of 1969 had clearly made an impression on Fitt. Captain James Kelly described one such incident, which he had witnessed in September just after Fitt had pleaded for weapons from the Dublin government for the defence of nationalists:

He [Fitt] rang Lisburn [British army HQ in Northern Ireland] and demanded the immediate dispatch of soldiers to the scene. Outside, a couple of hundred yards away, two mobs faced each other down a narrow street. The RUC lined up in front of the Protestant mob while vigilantes, with linked arms, held back the Catholics. Stolidly accepting the occasional punch from the more fanatical of their co-regionalists, the vigilantes successfully contained the heaving screaming mob until the arrival of the British army. The soldiers took up position in front of the Catholics while an officer negotiated with their representatives. He handed a loudspeaker to Gerry Fitt, who did an excellent job in calming down the crowd.[5]

If Fitt did share responsibility for 'stirring the pot of dissension' he did at least try to put the lid on. He maintained his conciliatory posture in

March 1970, when at Westminster he paid tribute to the role played by the army in Northern Ireland: 'The whole community on both sides of the political fence owes a debt of gratitude to the British army for its action over a number of months.'[6]

Fitt's attitude was bound to lead him into conflict with the uncompromising PD. At the end of March, PD held a meeting in Portadown, a mainly Protestant town, which led to a clash with loyalists. At Stormont Fitt condemned the PD for inciting trouble, and the PD in turn issued a statement in response to his allegations:

> Have you, Mr Fitt, abandoned the position you held in October 1968 when you defied law and order in the name of social justice? Do your reported comments on the Portadown meeting mean that you must now believe that law and order must precede social justice? ... Do you uphold the moral right of Orange Fascists to stone any meeting they disagree with?

The 'radicals' had a point: furthermore, the use of the term 'Orange Fascists' to describe the unionists was not dissimilar to some of the language used by Fitt in the past.

The *Irish News* asked Fitt to comment on the statement. He said:

> After listening to the questions posed by the PD, I am more than ever of the opinion that they are a group of infallible nincompoops intent on giving themselves an aura of importance which they do not deserve. The circumstances of the Portadown fracas as reported in the press would intimate to all and sundry that certain members of the PD are intent on creating the greatest possible frictions and then scurrying to their own habitats, which is normally at a safe distance from the trouble they have created.

Fitt's comments are ironic when we recall that he had in the past been involved in demonstrations in which he hoped that police would attack protestors. There was a hint of hypocrisy in his new position.

Fitt's response to the Portadown incident provides another example of his suspicion of anything that smacked of education. One reason why he held PD in such low regard was because he resented people with formal schooling encroaching on his area of competence. 'I don't have to take lessons from the PD on matters of social justice, a battle which I have been fighting before many of them had passed their 11 plus. The series of questions which they have posed on this occasion will be treated by me with the contempt they deserve.'[7]

The beginning of April saw the first major clash between Catholics and the British army. In the Belfast district of Ballymurphy there were several days of rioting sparked by an Orange parade that passed nearby. As in August 1969, there were enforced population movements – this time Protestant families were uprooted, particularly from the New Barnsley Estate in West Belfast. Fitt declared that he could not condone or forgive those responsible for intimidating people into leaving their homes 'Protestants had his sympathy and support as much as Catholics.'[8] Three days later he travelled to London to seek emergency talks on the situation with James Callaghan and the British Secretary of Defence, Denis Healey. He maintained: 'Unless the situation is resolved many thousands of innocent people, both Protestant and Catholic, are faced with misery and despair.'[9]

At Westminster, Fitt still clung to his belief that the Labour government would make the unionists toe the line. The extent to which this was possible is another question. Nevertheless, he feared the consequences of an electoral Labour defeat and pleaded for the immediate introduction of the post-August reforms. 'There is a fear in Northern Ireland that if, unfortunately this government were to be defeated at the next general election, and a Tory government were elected, the new government would not pressurise the Unionist Party.'[10]

At this point of his career Fitt was totally committed to the British Labour Party. His anti-Tory rhetoric became more frequent and more virulent because he believed the Conservatives were intent on a policy of coercion in Northern Ireland.

Wilson called the general election that Fitt feared for June. The Republican Labour Party unanimously chose Fitt to stand again in West Belfast – his selection hardly came as a surprise. Accepting his nomination, Fitt described his opponent, Brian McRoberts, as one of the most reactionary candidates to contest West Belfast and claimed, 'A tense atmosphere exists in which right wing unionism is attempting to stultify the reforms which have been won at great cost.'[11]

Further evidence of Fitt's commitment and faith in the Labour government can be seen in his support for his socialist colleagues in Britain during the election. In Manchester, he spoke in support of Gerald Kaufmann.

Referring again to the reform programme, Fitt expressed his belief that it needed the protection of a further electoral mandate for Labour and his fear that, if this was not forthcoming, there would be a serious escalation of the 'present tensions'.[12]

Encouraged by the opinion polls, Fitt was confident of a Labour victory that would enable those in the Connolly tradition of Labour supporters to undo the half-century of unionist mis-rule and Tory neglect.[13] As the election drew closer, the nationalist/republican content of his rhetoric became increasingly strident. 'Never was it more urgent for every nationalist of every shade and every republican whatever his allegiance of the moment, and every true Labour man to ensure that their voices and the people's interests are heard at Westminster.'[14] Fitt attacked his opponent for posing as a moderate, but in reality accepting the unqualified support of Mr Paisley and his 'cohorts'.[15]

As in previous campaigns, Fitt had to balance his republican and Labour links; McRoberts, on the other hand, predictably based his campaign on the benefits of Northern Ireland being an integral part of the United Kingdom. There was some debate as to how the population shifts caused by the August 1969 violence would affect the result. There was also speculation that voters would not cross the peace line (which had been erected in September 1969 between Catholic and Protestant areas of Belfast to try to prevent rioting) that divided the constituency for fear of intimidation in a 'hostile' area. The uncertainty of the election meant that Fitt would still have to woo the Protestant community to retain the support he had secured in 1966. His civil rights record would possibly work against him, with Protestants equating his headline-grabbing activities with nationalism. On the other hand, his pro-Labour Party attitude at Westminster was to his advantage.

From one of his campaign platforms on election day, Fitt displayed the latest edition of the *Protestant Telegraph* which he described as the 'most scurrilous anti-Catholic rag ever to be published in Ireland. But I am honoured to be named in this sheet as one of the rebels who Paisley says must not be returned to Westminster. This obscene publication comes out on the side of my unionist opponent, Mr McRoberts.'[16]

Despite the *Protestant Telegraph*'s influence Fitt successfully defended his Westminster seat, polling 30,649 votes to McRoberts' 27,451. He had apparently managed to transform a marginal seat into a safe anti-unionist constituency.

Fitt was not the only 'rebel' candidate to be returned to Westminster. Bernadette Devlin retained Mid Ulster and Frank McManus, a Unity candidate, won the Fermanagh–South Tyrone seat. But the general election also saw the return of the Conservative Party to power in Britain, a development Fitt viewed with a great deal of apprehension.

After his victory, Fitt claimed the result proved that Protestants had voted for him, but he reasserted his position on the national question:

> To these people I say I accept your support as a working-class represen-tative and I will in the future, as in the past, endeavour to service all my constituents. But there can be no doubt where I stand on the national question and those who supported me at the polls must be under no doubt that I believe in the eventual reunification of my country with the establishment of a socialist government for all the people of Ireland.[17]

The Falls curfew, which occurred on the weekend of Friday–Sunday 3–5 July, ensured that the Northern Ireland crisis had the appearance of a colonial conflict. Having carried out an armed search in Balkan Street, the army clashed with the IRA. The army then (illegally as it transpired) placed the inhabitants of the lower Falls Road under curfew. During the curfew five people were killed and sixty-five, including fifteen members of the British army, were injured. The result was a deterioration in army/Catholic community relations that undoubtedly benefited the Official and Provisional IRA. Fitt told the *Belfast Telegraph* that he found the situation 'heart-breaking'.[18]

On 6 July, Fitt and Paddy Devlin left for London to protest to the new British Home Secretary, Reginald Maudling, about the brutality of the British army, particularly Scottish soldiers, over the weekend. Accounts of the episode differ, but Catholic politicians were very critical. Devlin exaggeratedly suggested it was 'the most savage and brutal attack ever made on citizens in any country in the world'. Fitt called for a public enquiry and warned, 'Unless steps are taken to have such an enquiry the whole place would go up in flames.'[19]

During that meeting Fitt argued that the weekend's events showed that the Conservative government was prepared to support the Unionist Party at all costs. Maudling refused to discuss the role of the army, but assured Fitt that the Conservatives were committed to following the reform policy of the Labour Party.[20]

On 8 July, Fitt made it clear that he did not accept Maudling's assurances of Tory commitment to the reform programme. He argued that there had been a decided change in policies and attitudes in Northern Ireland, with the Conservatives supporting the Unionist Party in a very biased way.[21] Evidently Fitt felt that the return of the Conservatives to power had changed the whole complexion of politics in Northern Ireland.

Paddy Devlin gave a more considered view of the Falls curfew in his autobiography:

> Looking back on events now, the Falls curfew of July 1970 turned out to be the most significant turning point in the early stages of the Troubles. It represented a major policy change by the British, brought even more recruits to the Provisionals and bolstered their credibility, while it also triggered the formation of what was to be an important and lasting political realignment.

The political realignment had a detrimental effect on both the Belfast socialists. Devlin explained:

> Overnight the population turned from neutral to or even sympathetic support for the military to outright hatred of everything related to the security forces. As the self-styled generals and godfathers took over in the face of this regime, Gerry Fitt and I witnessed voters and workers in the Dock and Falls constituencies turn against us to join the Provisionals. Even some of our most dedicated workers and supporters, who had helped us through thick and thin at election times, turned against us. Many of them would indeed later viciously attack members of our families and our homes, eventually driving us out.[22]

John Kelly agreed that the curfew was a watershed that benefited republicans:

> I think [it was a turning point] because of the severity, ferocity in which the British army attacked the Nationalist population within that area. They just cut them off ... for 48 hours, they went in with weapons, they shot people, they ransacked houses, and I think that the whole episode really soured the Nationalist population and discouraged them and sort of made them feel again that they were defenceless, that here the British

army was, they were perceived to be the saviors of the situation, were now turning against them in a most savage kind of way. And again they turned to the IRA as their protectors.[23]

The Conservative Party and the Unionist Party had, of course, strong and close historical links. Unionist demands for a military solution would have found sympathetic ears in certain 'law and order Tory' circles. Fitt's and Devlin's allegations that the change in government at Westminster had produced a harder, more unionist line from the new Conservative administration therefore found a receptive audience in nationalist circles. But this view was a rather superficial one. In fact the Tories were only following the logic of the previous Labour administration's decision to allow unionists to shoulder the responsibility. Once Westminster ruled out taking responsibility for Northern Ireland itself it was forced into more desperate and alienating security measures, to shore up the unionist regime at Stormont. As Austin Currie concluded later:

> The Civil Rights movement wanted British troops in, but it should have been accompanied by a British political presence. The crunch mistake in 1969 was to keep Stormont, with Oliver Wright as the British government's watchdog in the North. That was the crucial period in which the Provisional IRA was founded and gained momentum.[24]

Violence continued in August. On 11 August, RUC constables Donaldson and Millar were killed by a booby-trap bomb in Crossmaglen, South Armagh. Nobody claimed responsibility, but the culprits were presumably one of the two IRA organisations. Fitt was unequivocal in his condemnation:

> I condemn with all my heart those responsible for the dastardly crime. I am filled with horror and contempt that there are still within this community such persons who have so little regard for human life. I appeal to all sections of the community to do everything possible to ensure that those guilty of this crime are brought to justice as speedily as possible.[25]

Ironically, on the same day as the killings, both Fitt and Paddy Devlin were at the funeral of the old IRA leader Jimmy Steele, who had been jailed in the 1930s and 1940s for republican military activity, and who was responsible for Provisional IRA publicity up to his death.[26] His funeral incorporated the tradition of firing shots over the coffin. In a statement Brian Faulkner noted that both Devlin and Fitt had witnessed this event, and charged: 'No one outside the Security Forces is entitled to hold arms at this time. They have a responsibility to name the men.'

Fitt, in language befitting a football manager who fails to see a particularly brutal foul perpetrated by his own player, claimed: 'I was at the end of a cortège of nearly 4,000 people and I neither heard nor saw shots being fired.' Fitt considered Faulkner's statement a 'shabby attempt to focus attention away from the problems within his own party'.[27] At this point Fitt still felt able to show some deference to the republican dead, particularly to Steele who had been adamantly and vocally a traditional physical force republican uninterested in the socialist inclinations of fellow-republicans such as Cathal Goulding, Seamus Costello and Seán Garland.

The combined aims of wresting the initiative away from the Provisionals and facilitating the Conservative government's requests for a single identifiable nationalist political party with which it could bargain finally produced the SDLP on 21 August. It appears that Fitt was also under pressure from his socialist friends at Westminster. He suggested the rumour mill was spinning:

> The British Labour Party was anxious for us to form a united opposition. There was some talk that things were going on behind the scenes and all sorts of rumours that the Knights of St Columbanus were trying to force it.[28] I never fucking met them. Priests and all were supposedly involved. I never met them. They never came to see me.[29]

This new group consisted of six opposition MPs: John Hume, Paddy O'Hanlon and Ivan Cooper (previously Independents); Paddy Devlin (elected as a member of the NILP); Austin Currie (a Nationalist); and Fitt. Paddy Wilson, a senator in the Northern Ireland parliament, also subscribed to the new formation. Rumpf and Hepburn explain the birth of the new group:

> People's Democracy never looked like taking the lead in Ulster Catholic politics, and of course never set out to do precisely that. The Nationalist Party, with its President no longer in Parliament after 1969, proved unable

to reassert its leadership. Thus there developed in 1969–1970 a growing demand for a 'United Opposition' at Stormont under the leadership of those MPs who had been active in Civil Rights. It sought to be genuine left of centre Civil Rights and Trade Union opposition, but when the NILP pulled in its horns at the end of 1969 it was left simply as a demand for unity among MPs representing Catholic seats.[30]

Fitt's high profile at Westminster and during the civil rights era made him an obvious candidate for the new party. Both he and Devlin insisted on the inclusion of the term 'Labour' in the party's title, as a condition for their participation and, as they saw it, that of the Belfast working-class.[31] How the party was named is a well-worn tale, but this is Fitt's version:

> Whatever the name of the party it would have to have the term Labour in it. Hume said 'you could call it Social Democratic Party – it's the same thing'. I said 'No, it's fucking not – the term Labour must be in.' He said, 'that wouldn't do us any good down the country', and I said, 'it won't do us any harm in Belfast'… I fought like the Hammers of Hell for the name Labour to be in the title. I wanted Labour to come first so it would be the Labour and Social Democratic Party. Then Paddy Devlin said, 'Fuck that – the LSD Party – nothing doing.' I had to agree on that point.[32]

SDLP leadership was also a crucial issue. Fitt was mentioned as a possible leader. He said:

> I have not sought any personal political advancement but I am fully convinced that real leadership must be given to the minority, and it is with this ideal in mind that I am prepared to engage in further discussions with my party colleagues in an effort to do all in our power to give expression to the real hopes, fears and aspirations of those opposed to unionism.[33]

On the same day, the *Irish News* reported that Devlin, Hume and Currie endorsed Fitt as leader. Hume said, 'I have worked for the creation of a left of centre democratically organised movement. If that can be created then Gerry Fitt is acceptable to me as leader.' Currie commented, 'I have no doubt that Gerry Fitt is the one person with the necessary experience, ability and general acceptability to lead such a grouping.'[34] The *Belfast Telegraph* commented on the question of leadership:

The choice of a leader has always been a source of potential disagreement. This time the name of Mr Gerry Fitt has been mentioned. There is no doubt that he is an able politician. But the opposition benches have accommodated individuals with strong characters and it is at least questionable if such individuality can be successfully moulded into a team with sufficient discipline to withstand all the pressures of old loyalties and ideological strands.[35]

Having accepted the leadership, Fitt presided over the party's first press conference on 21 August and announced the intention to provide a socialist alternative to unionism.[36] He claimed that his party had support throughout Northern Ireland. Fitt clarified its position that the unity of Ireland could only be achieved through consent:

Violence will not unite the people of Ireland – will not do away with the border in Ireland. There is only one way in which this country can be united, and that is by a massive process of education, by a massive attempt by this new party to go out and instill confidence into those who were formerly our political opponents or did not take any part in politics whatsoever.[37]

Fitt had abandoned any tendency to use the threat of violent scenarios as a political weapon. In the 1970s, he rejected all forms of violence as being inimical to progress in Northern Ireland. There was no call for direct rule. Importantly the SDLP agreed that reform was attainable in Northern Ireland and that there was a place for the minority. Irish unity was only one aim but an undiluted aim nonetheless. Nationalism was to be put on a shelf but always kept within reach. As Devlin later acknowledged, 'The vexed question of a united Ireland could go on the back-burner; time enough to consider it when we had healed our internal problems in the North.'[38] Despite this, and significantly in relation to Fitt's later attitude, the Irish dimension was always a key factor in the party's overall political policy on the constitutional issue. Fitt gave his commitment to the principle (he could hardly have done otherwise, having joined from the Republican Labour Party) as did all the founding members. Ivan Cooper confirms this: 'All of us signed up. We were constitutional nationalists. All of us signed up to wanting the unity of the country and all of us pushed it wherever we could.'[39]

Did the optimism and professionalism the SDLP exhibited at its inaugural press conference hide personal and ideological differences that did not augur well for the future? According to Fitt the answer is yes. In retrospect, he claimed that he was disinclined to join the party at all:

> We were all together in our opposition to the unionists and lots of people began to talk about having one party. I was all too well aware of the differences between Belfast and rural politics. I was very reluctant to do it. I did not need a party but the others did because they could not go on being just Civil Righters.
>
> Paddy Devlin was a key figure. If he had not won the election of 1969 and Harry Diamond had been re-elected we would have had our Republican Labour Party and there would not be an SDLP.

Fitt went on to again emphasise the rural/city divide; 'The differences were always there, the rural areas – farmers' interests – which I didn't have a clue about and didn't want to have a clue about.' In essence Fitt felt 'the SDLP was a resurrected and more educated version of the Nationalist Party'.[40]

Fitt also maintained that Austin Currie was instrumental in persuading him to join the party – a decision that in hindsight he considered 'disastrous'.[41] Currie commented:

> He is right. I take some responsibility for him joining and being leader. I was determined the new party should come into existence. I recognised the differences between Belfast politics and the country politics and I felt that Gerry's participation in it was essential and there was only one way Gerry would participate and he certainly was not going to accept the leadership of John Hume. He effectively became leader on RTÉ radio as a result of an interview.[42]

Fitt had accepted the leadership on the air in response to an interviewer's questions when he heard that both Currie and Hume had supported his candidacy. The SDLP was conceived by Cooper, Hume and O'Hanlon at the O'Neill Arms Hotel in Toomebridge, County Derry and born on a radio programme.

In reality, Fitt and Hume were the only realistic candidates for the leadership. When asked if he would have accepted Hume as leader, Fitt replied: 'There was no way they could have had any other leader because I was the key figure. I was the MP for West Belfast. There was no way I would have been in the party unless I was the leader.'[43] Gerard Murray, in his history of the SDLP, agreed:

> In reality, the SDLP could not have been formed without Fitt. He was essential to the SDLP to give it the necessary limelight to advance its policies and to justify its existence. It was through his contacts with trade unionists and the British Labour Party that the SDLP obtained credibility during its formative years. Fitt, with the backing of Devlin, established contacts with the Irish Labour Party through its general secretary, Brendan Halligan. A combination of Fitt's efforts and the good-will of his associates admitted the SDLP to membership of the Socialist International. Fitt's overall value to the SDLP was his ability to promote their cause beyond the borders of Northern Ireland.[44]

Paddy Devlin argued that Fitt's leadership was the product of an 'anti-Hume move'.[45] Hume claimed he was uncertain: 'I don't know because I didn't care who was leader. I genuinely wanted a political party formed and I didn't care who led it as long as it was a democratic political party. I was approached and told that if I agreed to Fitt becoming leader he would join the party. I agreed. No problem.'[46]

In the event, Hume became deputy leader. Considering the make-up of the party, and the fact that it emerged as primarily a nationalist rather than a socialist party, it was perhaps Hume rather than Fitt who was the natural leader. Hume thought so:

> Gerry never made any contribution to debate within the party, to philosophy, to policy documents, to strategy. They were all written by me. Gerry was a figurehead. His strengths were his personality. He is very personable, a man of great humour. He gets on with everybody in that sense but he had no direction. No plan for solving the problem. He was a reactor. He was anti-unionist basically. He emerged from a situation where he was a street fighter, fighting against somebody. It was Rangers and Celtic. He was a Celtic man that won.[47]

Hume's contention has validity, though Cooper, Devlin, Currie and (as the decade progressed) Seamus Mallon among others, all made substantial written policy contributions.[48] We have seen that Fitt was very much an individualist who would not have been easy with the yoke of a political party. He wanted to do his own thing and he trusted his own instinct. Cooper provides a valuable insight into Fitt's attitude:

> We were very determined to create a grass-roots membership with proper democratic structures. Gerry did not like that. He never really had a proper branch in Dock. I don't think the Republican Labour Party was a formally structured party. So when he joined the SDLP and branches started to be set up, proper democratic structures that led to proper debate, Gerry did not like it. He did not like it because of potential branch censorship. Gerry liked to make policy on the hoof. He never really swallowed the idea of a democratically structured party of which he was leader. Gerry's attitude was 'I have been elected for West Belfast, I have been elected by the people. I don't need any wee men who are school teachers[49] dictating policy to me.'[50]

Fitt was neither an organisational man nor indeed a political theorist. He was a political personality. In many ways the leadership debate was academic. Eddie McGrady, the party's first chairperson, confirmed that 'Fitt was *de jure* leader rather than *de facto* leader.'[51]

Fitt's leadership style can only have frustrated the ambitious and impatient senior figures within the party, personalities whose political apprenticeship within the Civil Rights Association had been based on a combination of idealism and intellectual discourse. Austin Currie summarised the strengths and weaknesses of Fitt as a party leader:

> Gerry Fitt was an unusual party leader. He rarely used a script. Even on important occasions, such as his annual speech to the party conference, he relied only on notes, sometimes scribbled on the back of an envelope – literally. On one occasion he quoted from John Donne, nearly causing me to fall off my chair in shock. I found out afterwards that the quote had been given to him by Conor Cruise O'Brien.[52] He did not perform a traditional leader's function at party meetings either. He did not try to impose any discipline or order, nor did he try to sum up or bring matters to a conclusion. Indeed he was invariably the worst offender in terms of digression, interrupting to tell jokes that rarely had anything to do with the subject under discussion. His strength was in his judgement of individuals, his predictions of how someone was likely to respond to

particular circumstances, and the amount of information he was able to collect from all quarters on which such judgements could be based.[53]

Fitt's individuality, while attractive to urban voters, was clearly problematic in party political and bureaucratic senses. He was both prize asset and fundamental weakness, an indispensable liability whose presence would be tolerated as much as venerated.

McGrady told me that 'Gerry saw Devlin and Hume as contenders. This whole thing about academia and practical politics was an issue. It was an issue for Devlin too. There was resentment there all the time.' Cooper put it simply; 'There was no love lost between John and Gerry.'[54] Fitt's emotional, instinctive and reactive opposition to unionism contrasts sharply with Hume's intellectual approach and his concern for policies and strategy. McGrady explained, 'Hume was never one to have a vocal confrontation. He would do the rational thing in a quiet way. There was never anything close to fisticuffs.'[55] The same could not be said of Devlin (a man of deep humanity who did, however, employ a certain pugilistic style of politics) and Fitt, who both confirmed to me that they threw misdirected punches at each other in a corridor at Stormont after a disagreement over 'political tactics'.[56]

Fitt subsequently maintained that he suspected the new party would not last long:

> I never thought it would last. It has lasted nominally but it is still not a Belfast party.
>
> Belfast has been swamped by the nationalists. It has not changed the issues. The SDLP in Belfast is irrelevant. They don't win elections and they will never win West Belfast.[57] The differences that were there then are there now.[58]

There was clear disagreement between Fitt and Hume over how the political situation developed in West Belfast. Hume had assumed that Fitt was bringing all his Republican Labour councillors from West Belfast into the new party. He did not; he brought only one, Paddy Wilson, and according to Hume, 'that division between the ones he left behind and the SDLP was a division that caused alienation between West Belfast and the rest of us, which led to the West Belfast of today.'[59]

Hume's belief regarding Republican Labour councillors was totally unfounded. Fitt's parting from his former colleagues was far from amicable.

On 24 August, it was reported that both Fitt and Paddy Wilson were expelled from the Republican Labour Party. The decision was taken by a vote of fifty-two to one. A statement issued by the party was read by Paddy Kennedy, who had refused to join the SDLP. The statement stressed that the two had effectively expelled themselves by joining another political organisation, and also emphasised that Fitt had been given no mandate, from either the party or his constituents, to form a new organisation. Referring to the SDLP, the statement noted, 'not once in the party's statement of aims had the words socialist or republican been used'. The statement also rejected the SDLP's stance on the constitutional position. 'No one section of the Irish people has the right to take a decision for that one section only without the nation as a whole being consulted.'[60] At the inaugural press conference of the SDLP, Fitt had given the impression that the Republican Labour Party supported him: 'As I see it, the representatives here have a mandate from their constituencies, whether the Unionist Party or anyone else recognises the fact, we are the opposition ...'[61] The statement read by Kennedy undeniably suggested that he did not have the support of his party. It seems that on this occasion Fitt had failed to cajole his colleagues to come around to his way of thinking. Fitt recalled his break from Kennedy:

> Paddy Kennedy was a nice wee fellow but terribly naive in politics. Between 1969 and 1970 when the Provos started to move in and they moved in on Paddy in Central and Paddy started to make Provo speeches and I said 'keep away to fuck from those murdering bastards' but Paddy was influenced by them. He started talking about 'the OC this and the OC that'. I said, 'who the fuck is the OC only some corner-boy, some lay-about and now he is the OC of the IRA'. So Paddy and I moved apart and I told him I did not want him near me in the 1970 election.[62]

Austin Currie confirmed that there was a personality clash between the two. Kennedy 'seemed determined to assert his independence from his mentor and was paying more and more attention to the newly formed Provisional Sinn Féin'.[63] Paddy Devlin also established that Kennedy had moved closer to the 'Republican' in his party title and away from 'Labour'. He had 'different priorities and allegiances we did not share' and 'Even Gerry his party leader avoided having meetings with him, thus widening the gulf.'[64]

Only days after its formation the SDLP had a problem. A new party whose leader was rejected by his former political supporters suddenly looked much less credible. At this early stage, however, there was enough good will from the wider nationalist community and elsewhere to see the party through. The new grouping had met a need for a new departure in Catholic politics, but it was seen by many as a 'green' Social Democratic and Labour party and therefore inherently sectarian.

The Republican Labour Party ceased to exist as a political force by 1973, its disintegration being, at least in part, a product of Fitt's absence. He later argued that his former constituency workers felt that the SDLP was too similar to the Nationalist Party. Some joined the Provisionals, but the more socialist inclined republicans joined Official Sinn Féin.[65] (This view contrasts with Paddy Devlin's: he recalled that their supporters joined the Provisionals.) This is perhaps an example of wishful thinking on Fitt's part, perhaps considering the 'Officials' the lesser of two evils. While the Provisional IRA would stake its claim to be the inheritor of the mantle of physical force republicanism in the tradition of Tone and the Fenians, Fitt may have viewed the rhetoric of the Official IRA as part of a more socialist lineage inspired by the radicalism of Connolly. I asked John Kelly when and why Fitt moved away from the republicans. He told me:

The split between Fitt and republicans is difficult to explain. I was away trying to get hold of weapons, but I suggest that it was not ideologically driven but more a consequence of a clash of personalities. Fitt clashed with local republicans. I think he felt let down by the movement after the service he had provided. His house had been used in August, September and October as a headquarters. He was involved in the barricades. He had sanctioned the use of republicans as bodyguards. I think he felt betrayed when republicans developed their own agenda.[66]

If Kelly is correct, Fitt was naive to believe that if he facilitated the early organisational needs of the republicans he could thereafter dictate his political agenda to them. He may have miscalculated by failing to predict how they would grow and assemble a big enough political base to make them an independent political force, one that no longer required the helping hand of a sympathetic MP. It is also possible that Fitt viewed these developments, in personal terms, as a betrayal of his benevolence. What is certain is that republicans would not dance to Fitt's tune, preferring instead to work towards their own agenda: waging a military campaign to force the British out of Ireland.

By October 1970 there were some progressive developments for the SDLP. Its new party headquarters was opened in Belfast. At the press conference Fitt declared that since the party had been launched, 1,300 applications for membership had been received, and branches set up in fourteen of the Northern Ireland constituencies.[67] The 'head without a tail' bearing of the SDLP was also remedied in October, when the NDP disbanded and defected en masse to the new party.[68] Ian McAllister interprets the SDLP's inheritance:

> The most easily traceable legacy of the NDP was in terms of political organisation. It is clear that the SDLP constitution was modelled closely on that of the NDP. As the SDLP was formed at the parliamentary level down, rather than vice versa, the experience of the old NDP members in constituency organisation and co-ordination proved invaluable in giving the new party a residue of support and ability in the country while setting up their constituency organisation. The considerable contribution of the NDP towards contemporary minority political opposition in Northern Ireland is an acknowledged if neglected fact.[69]

The NDP clearly exercised a strong influence within the newly established SDLP, and its members became the nucleus of SDLP membership. Equally important, the philosophy behind the formation of the NDP in 1965 became the foundation of SDLP thinking in the 1970s. The fact that Fitt and the NDP had an acrimonious history made his position as leader somewhat incongruous. The situation would never be fully resolved. Nevertheless, in November Fitt led the SDLP in their first talks with a British minister, Richard Sharples, Minister of State at the home office, in which he conveyed the party's view on the Northern Ireland situation.[70]

The year 1971 began with renewed rioting in the Catholic Ballymurphy area of Belfast. It seems that neither the army nor the IRA controlled the district, and youths were intent on stoning what they considered a foreign army of occupation. Fitt asked the Minister of State for Defence, Lord Balniel, to withdraw the troops for a period, claiming that their presence in Ballymurphy was heightening tension in the area and could lead to further violence.[71]

The riots led to renewed unionist calls for the re-introduction of internment, which had been effective during the IRA campaign of the 1950s and 1960s. Fitt held a meeting with Maudling to argue against its re-implementation, telling the *Belfast Telegraph* that 'the due processes of the law could be invoked to weed out any trouble makers in the community without recourse to this draconian law'. It seems that at this point he considered the unrest to be the work of a hooligan element. Maudling undertook to give serious thought to Fitt's assessment of the possible reaction to internment.[72]

The unionist demand for internment gained greater momentum in February, when the IRA moved from a defensive to a decidedly offensive strategy. Fitt told Stormont; 'This city is sitting on the edge of a volcano.'[73] Two days later the British army suffered its first fatality when Gunner Robert Curtis was shot by the IRA. (Fitt later claimed that he heard the shot that killed him.)[74] A Catholic civilian, Bernard Watt, was also killed by the British army, as was IRA member James Saunders. Fitt appealed for calm: 'The deaths of two Irishmen and a young British soldier in Belfast must surely testify to the futility of violence in the attainment of political or national objectives. To the death toll must be added the total sum of misery, fear and distress in every home of the city.'[75]

On the British television programme *This Week* Fitt was asked if he condemned the actions of the Provisionals. He answered: 'I condemn the actions of anyone in Northern Ireland who at any time, in any way, tries to escalate violence.'[76] The violence did escalate, and at the end of the month two more members of the RUC were killed in Belfast. Fitt told Callaghan, 'The heart [has] been knocked out of me.'[77] He was clearly becoming disillusioned and must have been aware that the situation was getting out of the control of elected representatives. The SDLP had been formed too late to stop the Provisionals taking a grip.

Nevertheless, prominent members of the party voiced their disapproval of the IRA. Hume appealed to members of the Catholic community not to join violent organisations. At Stormont he claimed:

> They do not defend your homes. They are leading you to self destruction. They cannot right your wrongs by creating greater wrongs ... If I feel that their methods will unite this island under their leadership then I want nothing to do with such an Ireland or with such people ...[78]

Despite these appeals, the violence intensified. On 10 March three young

Scottish soldiers, two of them brothers, were lured to their death against the background of a bombing campaign that was gaining momentum. Disorder resulted in increased pressure from right-wingers in the Unionist Party for the resignation of Chichester-Clark, who they felt was not doing enough to improve security. On 19 March, Fitt predicted civil war if Chichester-Clark was ousted by the hardliners.[79] The following day the Prime Minister was forced to resign.

The new Prime Minister for Northern Ireland, Brian Faulkner, was considered a hardliner. At Stormont, Fitt demanded that he implement the reform programme: 'To many thousands of people through the length and breadth of Northern Ireland these reforms at the time mean absolutely nothing. We have to see the legislation transformed into fact.'[80] Fitt emphasised his point and predicted with some accuracy that Faulkner might be the last Prime Minister of Northern Ireland when he told the *Belfast Telegraph*:

> This victory of Mr Faulkner's could turn out to be a pyrrhic victory. Unless he makes it quite clear to this community in the early days of his administration that he is prepared to forge on with the reform programme announced in 1969 and furthermore to enlarge it with progress so that social justice will be freely available to everyone in Northern Ireland then Mr Faulkner will find that he will go down in history as the last prime minister of Northern Ireland.[81]

Faulkner was keen to incorporate the SDLP, at least nominally, into the political system, and proposed a committee system to work alongside the Stormont cabinet to oversee control of key government departments. He offered the SDLP the chairmanships of a number of these new committees. The committees would have no Executive or legislative power but they presented the SDLP with a dilemma: here was the first opportunity for nationalists to administer the system. Some may have felt the offer was designed as much to get the British off Faulkner's back by engaging the opposition at a rather insignificant level, but it was certainly a new departure for unionism to make such an offer and to challenge the new Catholic reformist party to live up to the courage of its convictions.

The proposal was greeted with a cautious but favourable response from Fitt and his party. Devlin called it Faulkner's 'best hour' and John Hume told the *Irish News*, 'It should be made clear to all people today who say that no change has taken place, that this is simply not true. There have been changes in this community.'[82]

It was at least a start, and on 7 July the SDLP took part in what was to have been a series of all-party discussions. Optimism soon perished. On 8 July, two Catholics were killed by the British army in separate incidents in Derry. The result was a marked increase in SDLP militancy, and the first real rift in the party.

The Catholics killed in Derry were Desmond Beattie and Seamus Cusack. The army claimed that they were gunmen and bombers, but local witnesses refuted this. The SDLP issued an ultimatum to the British government demanding an independent enquiry within a week, or they would pull out of Stormont indefinitely. John Hume was convinced that such an enquiry would prove the army was guilty of deception. The statement also proposed an 'alternative assembly' and the move was clearly inspired by Hume, but he was fully supported by his colleague in Derry, Ivan Cooper:

> The Party heard a full and detailed report from Mr Hume on his investigations into the deaths. We are completely satisfied that Mr Hume's call for an enquiry into the circumstances of the deaths is fully justified and will reveal that the statements of the British army and the Stormont PM are untrue. We now reiterate our demand for an impartial enquiry ...
>
> If our demand is not met by Thursday next – exactly a week after the deaths of the two young men – we will withdraw immediately from parliament and will take the necessary steps to set up an Alternative Assembly ...[83]

This was an ultimatum of enormous magnitude. In essence it was threatening a withdrawal from the course of reform politics within the system and the adoption of a Sinn Féin approach, akin to 1919. In fact, *An Phoblacht* called it 'a move toward the policy of Sinn Féin'.[84]

On the afternoon of the killings Hume had called a party meeting. Fitt and Devlin did not attend. Fitt told me that his wife had told him about it but he had said 'Bollocks; I'm not going to any fucking meeting. I have lost constituents too. It's a Derry thing.'[85] Neither Fitt nor Devlin were notified about Hume's action. Currie was apprehensive over the reaction of the two, in Fitt's case because he 'had always been particularly strong on attendance at Stormont' and he would have been 'concerned about his

Westminster seat, since a proposal to boycott Stormont over actions of the British army under control of the British government was bound to lead to the question of boycotting the Westminster parliament as well'.[86] This was because the ultimatum was in itself flawed. The SDLP was threatening to withdraw from Stormont on an issue over which Stormont had no jurisdiction, while remaining at Westminster where the responsibility for these matters actually lay.

Currie was right to be alarmed. Fitt was angry about the ultimatum,[87] as was Devlin; 'Gerry and I were livid with anger. Just at a time when there were signs that we might be getting somewhere, the old nationalist knee-jerk of abstention was brought into play … Gerry and I made it clear from the outset that becoming abstentionist was going to leave the way clear for the Provos; indeed, we believed the party had fallen for a Provo trap.'[88]

Retrospectively Fitt went further, claiming, 'Hume was playing ball with the Provos.'[89] The truth is that Hume was keen to prevent the Provisionals gaining a foothold in Derry, as evidenced by Hume having called the party meeting after a high-profile visit to Derry by Ruari Ó'Bradaigh, the Sinn Féin president.

Currie said Fitt 'felt he could bring sufficient pressure to bear on Maudling, the Home Secretary, to achieve a face-saving formula'.[90] Both were confident and both were wrong. Before Fitt met the Home Secretary he said:

> I am not prepared to accept the army investigation. They should welcome a public, impartial enquiry because we are absolutely convinced that the evidence would prove conclusively that the two men who lost their lives in Derry were in no way connected with the throwing of nail bombs or the use of firearms.[91]

Maudling sided with the military and rejected Fitt's appeal, saying 'it is an army matter'.[92] Devlin explained the consequences: 'Faced with British unwillingness to give us some face-saving formula, although the holding of the inquests was accelerated, Gerry and I were unwillingly sucked along with the majority feeling, which was emotional rather than practical.'[93] According to Cooper the episode had a silver lining for Fitt. Although Cooper was in favour of an alternative assembly 'as a way of maintaining grass-roots support' he acknowledged that the SDLP were 'in a sense in the wilderness', a factor 'Gerry was quite happy with as he had the only political platform available and it left him in a place of leadership.'[94]

But the course of events in late July and early August 1971 puts a serious question mark over the substance of Fitt's leadership at the formative stage, particularly in the way that he was prepared to be railroaded by a subordinate colleague into a decision with immense political consequences. There is no doubt that Fitt knew the consequences of the SDLP ultimatum. He knew that political ground would be surrendered to the Provisionals, that the political initiative would be handed over to them at a crucial juncture, and that conflict would certainly intensify if unionists saw the SDLP – despite all their intentions of supporting the system – withdrawing to a nationalist assembly.

It is impossible to anticipate how events would have unfolded if the SDLP had accepted Faulkner's offer and not walked out of Stormont. Undoubtedly this would have placed the new party in direct conflict with the Provos, and there is little doubt that there would have been intense pressure on them and perhaps great short-term political damage. But it is also the case that Faulkner would have found it difficult to proceed with the policy of internment after August 1971 if he wanted to keep the SDLP on side. Internment was made probable by the nationalist withdrawal from politics because there was no reason for restraint left in unionism, and there was no reason for Britain to veto the unionists, since the only alternative was to take responsibility themselves. Internment greatly intensified the conflict and determined that political events would be shaped by the Provos rather than the SDLP.

On 16 July, Fitt led his colleagues out of Stormont and the rest of the opposition, with the exception of the lone NILP member, followed suit. The SDLP claimed the break was total. Fitt told a Belfast news conference that by withdrawing from Stormont 'we will bring home to the world the reality of the Northern Ireland situation which is that Stormont is and always has been the voice of unionism'.

He assured the conference that, contrary to rumour, there was complete unanimity in the party on its decision. This seemed not to be the case.

In reply to a suggestion that the SDLP was taking a revolutionary position, Fitt said, 'We do not support the gunmen or violence and our move is certainly not intended to lead to the position of the gunmen being strengthened.'[95] The relationship between constitutional and revolutionary nationalists was often questioned by the media.

In August, Fitt was asked by a correspondent of the London *Times* if
he and SDLP were being coerced by the IRA. He replied:

Since the day I entered politics I have never been prepared to let myself
be subjected to pressure from any extremist organisation, be it the IRA,
the Ulster Volunteer Force or anything else. I would rather resign both
my seats than be the voice of, or accept the dictates of, any extremist organisation in Northern Ireland.

He was also asked if he was in any way personally afraid of the IRA:

I am a married man and we have five daughters. I truly love each and
every one of my family. I have talked the whole matter over with my wife
and my daughters and we have frankly discussed the possibility of me losing my life under certain circumstances. I would have no regrets if I lost
my life as a result of standing by the principles I believe in.[96]

As leader of the SDLP, Fitt constantly made it clear that he was opposed
to all types of violence, from whatever source. Undeterred, the IRA continued its bombing campaign. The pressure to apply internment became
greater and on 9 August the raids began. By that evening, 342 men
had been picked up, all but two from the Catholic community. One
of the two non-Catholics belonged to the PD and the other was pro-
republican. Rumours quickly circulated that the internees were being ill-
treated. Coogan has noted that 'Internment did not crush the Provos but
unleashed them.'[97] John Kelly confirmed that the British got it badly
wrong:

It was devastating (internment), absolutely and totally devastating. Again,
throughout the whole community, the Nationalist community, because
of the one-sided nature of it, because of the haphazard way in which
it was carried out, where people were just taken who had absolutely no
connections to the Republican movement. It was a devastating blow
psychologically, morally to the whole Nationalist community, the entire
Nationalist community. I think it was the most devastating mistake that
the Brits made in the last 25 years.[98]

There can be no doubt that it was an ill-advised policy decision and failed as an attempt to reassert the authority of the Stormont parliament. Nevertheless, internment continued. Fitt retrospectively explained his attitude to it:

> I always had a rather confused attitude about internment. Some of the people in the New Lodge Road [a Catholic area of Belfast], I would have interned them myself. They were a bunch of bad bastards. There were others that should not have been interned at all, but there was no way you could differentiate or identify them. I was always qualifying my condemnation of internment. That was no good to the IRA. They wanted outright condemnation. The others in the SDLP were anti-internment. Particularly the rural areas. Paddy Devlin was on the Falls – he had no choice. I stood up to the Provos, that is why I have a bodyguard now.[99]

Ivan Cooper is adamant that Fitt's recollection was total fabrication. 'Fitt was as much opposed to internment as any of the rest of us. No question. He had no reason not to be leading the campaign against internment. I have no doubt that he was in sympathy with the protest. The rift with his constituents came later.'[100] There is certainly ample evidence to support Cooper's contention, but one thing is certain: after internment the mood of the Catholic community was more confrontational. The SDLP had no choice but to intensify its militant position and again pledge that it would not return to Stormont or co-operate with the Westminster or Belfast governments until internment was terminated. Any other position would have been incomprehensible and politically damaging. Fitt reported his protest to Maudling: 'I said it had been introduced as a short term solution with the intention of propping up the Faulkner government but it had been an appalling failure up to the moment.' He also demanded the recall of the Westminster parliament from its summer recess because of the gravity of the situation in Northern Ireland.[101]

An example of how far removed Fitt had become from his former colleagues in the Republican Labour Party was indicated by the fact that at a widely publicised press conference, Paddy Kennedy shared a platform with the northern divisional commander of the PIRA.[102]

In an attempt to end interment, the SDLP and the Nationalist Party orchestrated a campaign of civil disobedience. They called for a complete refusal of all payments of rent and rates to public authorities until the last internee had been released. Fitt claimed this was 'an attempt to bring down the system in a non-violent way'.[103] The SDLP also withdrew its representatives from a number of public bodies.

On 24 August, Fitt left Dublin for the United States on a trip to include the cities with large Irish-American communities – New York, Boston and Chicago. He told journalists the reason for the tour:

> I want to tell the people what has really been going on in Northern Ireland since internment and about shocking brutality by the British army. We want to try and get America to exert some diplomatic influence on Britain and the wrong headed policies pursued by the obstinate pig-headed Mr Heath and the Tory government in Westminster.[104]

While in the States, Fitt had talks with U Thant, the secretary general of the United Nations. He gave him copies of statements alleging acts of brutality by British troops committed under internment regulations in Belfast and other centres. After the meeting, Fitt told reporters that he did not think the UN could take any drastic action because Northern Ireland was a part of the United Kingdom and high politics were involved.[105]

Fitt reverted to a more nationalistic position in Boston and urged Irish Americans there to make their views on the situation in Northern Ireland known to their representatives in Congress. 'Congress could then make the feelings of the people known to Prime Minister Edward Heath.' He went on: 'I also have no doubt the American delegation to the United Nations could make their feelings known to the British delegation. The war in Northern Ireland must end now without the shedding of another drop of blood, but there can be no peace until there is only one government.'

Fitt also proposed that parliament should be suspended and a commission set up in its place to represent all the people of Ireland equally. He said the transition to the commission might even take years, but it would result in a 'United Ireland'.[106] Fitt found it easy to be a nationalist in the United States where political pronouncements on Ireland were less likely to be forensically analysed by either his supporters or his detractors.

Back in Northern Ireland internment had produced a tremendous escalation in violence. At the end of August, a British armoured car was ambushed near the border and one soldier was killed. When he returned from the United States, Fitt said, 'That is just another unfortunate and tragic sequence of events since the British army became so involved in acting on behalf of and at the instruction of the Unionist Party.'[107] August had seen 100 explosions and thirty-five deaths – one more than in the previous seven months. As Farrell concluded, 'by any standards internment had been a disaster'.[108]

In September, Fitt was admitted to a Dublin hospital for treatment for a slipped disc. While bedridden, he granted an exclusive interview to the *Irish Independent*, which revealed his political thoughts at this time. He predicted an end to the border by the mid-1980s and the reunification of Ireland within fifteen years. His words imply that Catholic political agitation was designed to end partition. He said: 'In view of present events in Northern Ireland this might seem like a long time to wait, but when you consider that it has taken 400 years to create the present situation, I do not think it is too long.'[109] This disclosure adds further fuel to the charge that despite some of his rhetoric Fitt's politics were essentially anti-partitionist. His prediction for a united Ireland within fifteen years was wildly optimistic.

London and Dublin, on the other hand, feared an all-out sectarian war, and were anxious to prompt the SDLP into political discussion. The *Belfast Telegraph* reported that members of Fine Gael and the Irish Labour Party visited Fitt in hospital to persuade him to adopt a less rigid attitude to possible talks, since it was felt that he may have been more flexible than his SDLP colleagues.[110] Evidently some politicians in the Republic considered Fitt to be more pragmatic than his partners.

Fitt was well enough to return to Westminster for a two-day recall to discuss the continuing crisis in Northern Ireland. Maudling had proposed round-table talks before the termination of internment but the SDLP demanded the release of internees before any discussion.

During the debate, the shadow Home Secretary James Callaghan took the unusual step of putting a question directly to Fitt. Callaghan asked that if there was a solution to internment would the SDLP, without giving up its long-term aspiration for a united Ireland, agree to participate in government with unionists. Fitt replied:

> Without hesitation, I can tell the House that if there is a satisfactory solution of the problem of internment which at present besets Northern Ireland the SDLP, being the largest opposition party, would in company with other members who have withdrawn from the Stormont government be willing and anxious indeed to enter into negotiations to bring about a satisfactory solution in Northern Ireland.[111]

Callaghan's question proved academic – the Conservatives were content to persist with internment – yet the dialogue shows the SDLP's dilemma. If they had agreed to negotiate while internment existed, they would have represented no one, yet they were committed to constitutional government.

The PIRA maintained the bombing strategy and the death toll continued to rise. Fitt continued to condemn the bombers:

> They had managed to eliminate from their thinking one million of their Protestant fellow-countrymen when they claimed that their struggle was solely against the British army. That they can ignore the political opposition to a united Ireland on the part of one million fellow Irishmen must be beyond the comprehension of all sane people. If I am to be true to my political principles, then when I condemn the political use of British bayonets in Northern Ireland, I must also condemn the political use of an IRA bomb.[112]

The SDLP held its first annual conference in Dungiven on the weekend of 23 and 24 October.

The party re-affirmed its commitment to the campaign of civil disobedience, passive resistance and abstention from Stormont in an effort to end internment and change the system of government. Fitt outlined its policy of 'reform, reconciliation and re-unification'. He also urged Protestants to join the party and called for accommodating gestures from the government of the Republic. 'I would say those sections of the Constitution which offend the Protestant conscience should immediately be taken out of the Constitution.' He argued that if Protestants accepted his invitation to join the SDLP, the gunmen and explosions would stop.

He also maintained that there was no ambiguity about the SDLP: it was a 'socialist party'.[113] Fitt may well have been sincere in his claims but there was no doubt that his party was basically a Catholic party in the process of setting up a nationalist assembly. As a socialist, Fitt wanted Protestant as well as Catholic support, but he was the leader of a party that had a fundamental objective of Irish unification. Fitt wanted that objective achieved by consent, but he must have realised that such consent would not be given by working-class Protestants, the very people to whom he tried to appeal.

The John Hume/Ivan Cooper-inspired 'alternative assembly' met on

26 October in Dungiven Castle, its creation being evidence of the total breakdown of political consensus. Hume set the tone of the gathering by quoting Edward Carson's words, 'we do not care twopence whether its treason or not'.[114] It is significant that Fitt missed the opening of the opposition 'parliament', since he was arguably the least militant of the leading figures in the SDLP, and possibly wanted to distance himself from the proceedings. Hume apologised for Fitt's absence, saying that he was attending a funeral.[115] The assembly held only one other meeting. It was a pale imitation of what had happened in 1919/1921 – if that was ever the intention – and nothing of substance came out of it.

In November James Callaghan followed up his direct question to Fitt at Westminster regarding the sharing of power. Paddy Devlin reported:

> Gerry Fitt, John Duffy[116] and myself met Callaghan and Benn at the Dunadry Inn, a hotel near Belfast airport, on 11 November 1971. Callaghan immediately wanted to know if we would join an administration that would include unionists, in order, he said, to bring Northern Ireland and its people back from the brink of anarchy. Gerry replied that we would be willing to negotiate such a settlement – the first time anyone had formally proposed power-sharing to us – but we also outlined the formidable obstacles in the way of any settlement, not least the continuation of internment, the heavy-handedness of the army and our doubts whether control of security policy should remain with what we now regarded as a completely discredited Faulkner administration.[117]

Devlin appears to have been unaware of the exchange at Westminster, and anyway Callaghan was in opposition and not in a position to offer anything. Nevertheless it was certainly food for thought for Fitt and the SDLP. The party at its formation said it did not favour the abolition of Stormont, so there was nothing contradictory in Fitt's apparent enthusiasm. But the party had little room for manoeuvre. Paul Bew and Henry Patterson explain the condition of the SDLP at the turn of the year:

> The continuation of internment and detention, the dense army presence and the incapacity of the state to control sectarian assassinations combined to produce rather conditional support for the SDLP among Catholics. The effect of the post-68 mobilisations had been to create a whole range of local defence groups, community associations and smaller leftish and

republican groups which, together with the Provisionals, increasingly criticised the SDLP and argued that it would shortly be absorbed and co-opted.[118]

The year ended on a particularly bad note for Fitt. On 4 December, fifteen people died in an explosion at McGurk's bar, a Catholic public house on the New Lodge Road. This was the single largest loss of civilian life in one incident in Northern Ireland until the Omagh bombing in 1998. Fitt said 'I am personally so shocked that I cannot think clearly what next week will hold. All I know is there will be 15 funerals from my constituency and that is all I can think of.'[119]

There were 174 fatalities in 1971: 115 civilians; forty-three members of the British army; nineteen IRA activists; eleven members of the RUC; and five members of the UDR.

The SDLP position hardened through its abstentionist period and Austin Currie issued a very intransigent new year's message at the Falls Park at a civil disobedience rally:

> Within the next six or seven months, Faulkner and his rotten Unionist system will have been smashed … The so-called British Home Secretary has once again come on to TV and said that the SDLP ought to be prepared to talk. But I say to Maudling: 'Why the hell should we talk to you? We are winning and you are not … Even if Maudling got down on his bended knees and kissed all our backsides we would not be prepared to talk … The aim of this campaign is not only to end internment but to destroy this government because all the evils of this community are symptoms of that basic disease – unionism.[120]

Currie's speech illustrated how far the SDLP had travelled in the five months since Faulkner's offer had encouraged Hume to say that unionism had changed. Now Currie was calling for its destruction. It is not clear what his party leader would have thought of such rhetoric.

On 30 January 1972 thirteen men were shot dead by British paratroopers in Derry's Bloody Sunday. The shootings occurred during an illegal march organised by the Civil Rights Association to protest against internment. The army claimed that they had been fired upon first, but nationalist and Catholic Ireland rejected this, and a wave of intense anger swept the country. Fitt fulminated: 'It must now be evident to all that the

British army in Northern Ireland has now taken on all the trappings of an army of occupation determined to use their superior military might to keep in power a corrupt and discredited government that has gained the odium of the world.'[121]

At Westminster, Bernadette Devlin claimed, 'The government may well have lit a fire in Ireland, the flames of which may not die out until the last vestige of British rule has gone from that country.' Fitt's contribution to the debate saw him endorsing Devlin's sentiments, demanding the suspension of Stormont and urging the withdrawal of the British army. His speech was charged with emotion:

Until last Sunday I regarded myself as a man of moderation. I have consistently condemned violence. I have condemned every life that was unnecessarily taken, every shot that was fired and every explosion that has taken place. But I am consistent with my own conscience, with the fact that I was born and reared, and will be until the day I die, an Irishman. If I condemn the violence of anyone in Northern Ireland I must condemn the violence of the British army that was meted out to the Irish people in the city of Derry last Sunday.[122]

Fitt's emotion was similar to that expressed in the Republic, where the British embassy in Dublin was burned to the ground during a national day of mourning on 2 February.

Interestingly, Fitt later claimed that at a meeting of the SDLP on the Friday before the tragedy, John Hume had expressed real apprehension about the march, an event the party had hoped to use to its advantage by having one of its high-profile members arrested and imprisoned. Fitt told me that Hume was wary of involvement and had said; 'I don't know – there are all sorts of strange people running around Derry who are not Derry people at all and I think there is going to be shooting down there. I don't want to be there at all. I think the IRA are going to start a shooting war.'[123] It is difficult to determine the truth of Fitt's assertion, which needs to be seen in the context of his ever-increasing resentment of Hume and his hatred of the IRA.

In the following week Fitt attended a civil rights march in Newry, along with thousands of other protesters. There were great concerns over this event since there had been calls for all of nationalist Ireland to be there. In the event 20,000 appeared. Fitt addressed the crowd and claimed that the march represented a total rejection of Stormont. He also claimed the demonstration was an indication that the vast majority of those opposed to unionist government supported a non-violent movement:

> Newry has indeed reason to be proud tonight. It will be remembered that the first violence of the Civil Rights movement unfortunately and tragically took place in Newry in January 1969 and it was only right that this historic town should have availed itself of this opportunity before the eyes of the world to prove its solidarity and support for non-violent action in its endeavour to rid itself forever of the injustices perpetrated under unionism and so ably by the Tory administration at Westminster.[124]

After Bloody Sunday and the Newry march, the whole minority community seemed united in its opposition to Stormont.

Edward Heath appealed to the northern minority representatives to re-think and agree to peace talks without pre-conditions, but Fitt rejected this request: 'I find the whole matter rather confusing. On the one hand Mr Heath is asking for talks while at the same time we are being told in Newry from a helicopter that we are all going to jail for six months.'[125] Fitt was referring to the mandatory prison sentence of six months for anyone convicted of participating in an illegal march.

Meanwhile, the violence continued. On 22 February, the Official IRA bombed the paratroopers' headquarters at Aldershot in England, killing six civilians and an army chaplain. Three days later, Northern Ireland Minister of State and Home Affairs, John Taylor, was seriously wounded in an Official IRA assassination attempt.

On 4 March, two women were killed and 136 people injured by a bomb in the crowded Abercorn restaurant in Belfast. Fitt considered this the most serious tragedy since the outbreak of the Troubles: 'This barbaric act will have repercussions on the Irish people throughout the world for generations to come, and will have sullied the name of the Irish race.'[126]

As a consequence of the civil disobedience campaign, Fitt had not attended Belfast Corporation and was therefore due to be expelled. However, the anti-unionist streak in him was too strong to relinquish his hold on the Dock Ward without a fight. He therefore made a token appearance at the City Hall which enabled him to keep his seat. This displeased his SDLP colleagues and the Andersonstown PD severely criticised Fitt for his decision:

This action should come as no surprise to anyone who has watched Mr Fitt's cheap political manoeuvring throughout the present struggle. While the people have been demanding the unconditional release of all internees and political prisoners and a no to the Special Powers Act, Fitt has attempted to wriggle out of his 'no talks' dilemma by demanding that the internees be released or charged. The peoples' demand still stands; we have no intention of watering them down to allow Fitt and co. to crawl to Maudling's sell-out table.

The people have withdrawn consent from Stormont and rejected the corrupt sectarian structures which are necessary to keep it standing. Fitt by continuing to hold on to his Council seat, and attending – however briefly – a council meeting has shown that he has not withdrawn from the system, he is merely hibernating until Maudling can fix him up a seat in the Cabinet.[127]

Fitt's old colleagues in the Republican Labour Party also chastised him for his decision to appear at City Hall.[128]

When the other Dock seat fell vacant due to SDLP abstention, the prospect of a unionist taking over was again too much for Fitt. He announced that his wife Ann would contest the seat, but if victorious she would, like her husband, boycott council meetings. Redevelopment and slum clearance had changed the religious demography of the Dock Ward to such an extent that by 1972 Catholics were in a majority of two to one. The only hope of the other candidate, David Robb of the Constitution Party, was that enough SDLP voters would decide to boycott the election.

In her election address, Ann Fitt argued that her husband would fail in his duty to the Dock residents if he did not provide an opportunity for them to decide whether they were prepared to allow 'sectarian bigots' to return to the area where they had been previously 'totally and firmly rejected'.[129] She had a comfortable victory. Robb lost his deposit.

The City Hall episodes are further evidence that Fitt's politics was based on personality. His SDLP colleagues Paddy Devlin, John Hume, Austin Currie, Ivan Cooper and Eddie McGrady all told me that Fitt had little organisational ability and indeed no interest in it. They also indicated that he provided little input into policy and strategy. Fitt himself readily admitted he was not the ideal party leader. He relied on his own political instincts even at the expense of his own party responsibilities, and he was loath to give up any political forum.

After Bloody Sunday, as the state drifted towards total anarchy, Edward Heath came under increasing pressure to adopt some sort of initiative in Northern Ireland. Fitt was one of the more vocal complainers: 'It is disgraceful; all their plans seem to be in the Sea of Tranquility.'[130] In retrospect, it seems likely that Heath had already decided to close Stormont.

On 20 March, a no-warning bomb killed six people in Belfast, bringing the total number of deaths in 1972 to seventy-six. Since the Troubles began, 282 people had died, 219 of them since the introduction of internment. On 22 March, Faulkner met Heath in London and was told that Westminster was going to take all security powers away from Stormont. Right-wing pressure from within the Unionist Party would not allow Faulkner to relinquish control of security. It seemed that his position was untenable. Fitt commented that any announcement of the resignation of the Stormont government would cause no regret in the minority community: 'This was the only possible step for the Conservative government to take and one hopes now that they will be prepared to use all their resources should any attempt be made to give a re-birth to unionism by a show of force by unionist extremists.'[131]

On 24 March, Heath announced that the Faulkner government was resigning, that Westminster was suspending the Stormont parliament, and that William Whitelaw was to be the new Secretary of State for Northern Ireland. Two and a half years after the arrival of British troops, direct rule had arrived. Of the task ahead, Fitt said, 'Our sole motivation in this endeavour will be what is good for the people of Northern Ireland.'[132] Fitt recalled the fall of Stormont:

> Some people said that we should have stayed in Stormont and reformed it. Others said, and I think I was one, that you could not reform Stormont because the unionists were so deeply entrenched in there. Looking back, in retrospect, it may have been better not to call for the abolition of Stormont but reform it from within.[133]

Fitt's view certainly changed. On the day the resignation was announced he told the *Belfast Telegraph*: 'I have always regarded Stormont since its inception in 1930[134] throughout the long years of its history as being an absolute disaster for the communities in Northern Ireland and for the people of Ireland as a whole.'[135]

Fitt's position after direct rule was still essentially nationalist, although for the first time there is an indication that the sentiment was somewhat diluted. We can only speculate on the reasons for this. It was perhaps due to the removal of Fitt's and the Catholic community's fundamental source of grievance – the Stormont system. Catholics certainly tended to experience less alienation from the system as the specifically local unionist manifestations of it were removed and the British state began to play a greater part in governing them. This factor may have been the greatest influence on Fitt's subsequent political path, which ultimately led him to the House of Lords, and which is perhaps analogous to Ulster Presbyterians' acceptance of the British connection after the dissolution of the Ascendancy Parliament (with all its Anglican exclusivity) under the terms of the 1801 Act of Union.

Whatever the reason, Fitt's nationalism became more measured and he admitted that a united Ireland might take a long time to materialise. He spoke at Westminster on 28 March:

> We should be realistic and recognise that we are always going to have the Irish problem with us until the day when Ireland is reunited. No one can say when that will be, whether it will be 5, 10, 15, 20 or 30 years hence. Some day it will happen. Some day it must come. No one can say when or how it will be brought about ... Therefore if we are to take steps now effectively to preclude the achievement of that deal at any time in the future, we are only stirring up trouble for ourselves in the years to come.[136]

As Farrell points out, the advent of direct rule also had a profound impact on minority politics: 'the suspension of Stormont had fragmented the almost total solidarity of the Catholic population produced by internment and reinforced by Bloody Sunday'.[137] Fitt and the SDLP led the body committed to compromise – a point noted by an editorial in the *Belfast Telegraph*:

> It may stick in many a Protestant throat to admit it, but the most effective instrument for peace in the Catholic community now is the SDLP, and MPs like Mr Hume and Mr Fitt are fully accepting their responsibilities. They are confident they have popular support for their plea to give peace a chance and the people must show it in every way they can.[138]

Fitt did indeed call for the cessation of violence, but without success. Shootings and bombings occurred sporadically throughout Northern Ireland, and on 15 April, British paratroopers shot dead Joe McCann, leader of the Official IRA. The complex position of the SDLP was exposed by the fact that both Paddy Devlin and Paddy O'Hanlon attended his funeral.[139] However, by the end of May, Fitt and the SDLP acknowledged that they were in direct competition with the IRA. Fitt said: 'In this situation, the position is now clear. We are opposed to the men of violence and we will fight them at each and every opportunity that is given to us.'[140]

On 28 May, an IRA bomb exploded prematurely in the Short Strand area of Belfast, killing eight people. On the following day, the Official IRA ordered an indefinite ceasefire after unfavourable reaction to its killing of Ranger William Best (a Catholic) while he was visiting his family in Derry. Fitt was pleased by the Officials' cessation of hostilities and hoped the Provisionals would follow suit.[141]

The Provisional IRA did indeed come under considerable pressure to follow the example of the Officials. They offered to meet Whitelaw – an offer their commander-in-chief, Seán MacStíofáin, said was a 'further expression of the republican movement's desire to secure a lasting peace'.[142] Whitelaw quickly dismissed this overture, saying he 'could not respond to ultimatums from terrorists who are causing suffering to innocent civilians in Northern Ireland and shooting British troops'.[143] The SDLP had considered the Provisionals' offer to be a 'sincere attempt to produce an atmosphere for a peaceful settlement of the North's problems and representative of their willingness to engage in peaceful and political activities'.[144] More important, the IRA offer gave the SDLP the opportunity to act as intermediaries in trying to arrange talks between the IRA and the British government.

Meanwhile, Fitt had been the main sponsor of a motion at Westminster urging Whitelaw to review the case of prisoners claiming political status. Thirty Labour MPs, along with Bernadette Devlin and Frank McManus, had signed the motion.

At this juncture the republican movement's political leadership in Provisional Sinn Féin was very much subordinate to the IRA, so John Hume and Paddy Devlin effectively filled the vacuum. Both held a meeting with representatives of the Provisionals in Derry on 14 June, which led to secret meetings between Whitelaw and the leaders of the IRA.[145] The IRA said they would not meet Whitelaw unless paramilitary prisoners were granted 'special category status', and this demand was met. This meant that IRA prisoners would be housed separately from non-political prisoners, and ensured that they could wear their own clothes, have more frequent visits and no longer undertake penal work. In short, the IRA was granted a measure of political legitimacy that implied that the organisation was not merely a group of gangsters and thugs. Fitt's manoeuvring at Westminster shows that he was in favour of the move. The talks ended a republican hunger strike that was reaching a critical stage, and prompted the Provisionals to announce a ceasefire for 26 June, calling for a reciprocal response from the British.

This truce proved to be very fragile and ended on 9 July, after a clash in the Lenadoon area of Belfast. Fitt, speaking from London, said that he had been saddened 'almost to the brink of despair.'[146] His gloom would have been accentuated by developments in the Protestant community.

In September 1971 the Ulster Defence Association (UDA) began as a co-ordinating body for loyalist vigilante groups and it quickly became the largest Protestant paramilitary organisation. Fitt argued that Whitelaw's efforts were being undermined not only by republican forces, but also by fear and frustration in the minority community caused by intimidation by the UDA. He also recognised that this pressure could lead Catholics to give at least passive support to the IRA. Fitt continued to attack internment: 'while internees are still interned, it still will create a running sore throughout the minority community in Northern Ireland'.[147] Nevertheless, internment remained and the Provisional's campaign continued. On 21 July nine people were killed when twenty-two bombs were set off in Belfast's 'Bloody Friday'.

Catholics began to feel the Protestant backlash as the UDA embarked on a campaign of sectarian assassination. Until then there had been only sporadic incidents, but from February 1972 a sustained campaign gathered momentum. The day after Bloody Friday saw the discovery of the bodies of a Catholic couple in North Belfast. They had been tortured and shot by the UDA. On 27 July, the hooded body of Francis McStravik, a Catholic, was found in Sandy Row, a loyalist area of the city. He had been shot through the head. Fitt launched a strong protest to Whitelaw against what he called the apparent inability and unwillingness of the security forces to track down the perpetrators of the series of foul murders in Belfast.[148]

Whitelaw responded to Bloody Friday on 31 July, launching Operation Motorman, when the army moved into both Catholic and Protestant 'no-go' areas at 4.30 a.m. He was determined to act against the Provisionals, who for their part did not resist, being unwilling to engage the army in open combat. It turned out to be the biggest British military operation since the Suez crisis. The Protestant community helped the army take down their barricades, claiming that they had been a response to republican 'no-go' areas. West Belfast saw the beginning of a period of military occupation.

After dialogue with and encouragement from the Irish government, Fitt and the SDLP decided that its refusal to enter into talks with the British was preventing political progress. The Provisionals had engaged with the government while internment remained, so why shouldn't the SDLP? In retrospect Ivan Cooper considered that the no-talks-until-internment-ended position was 'a silly policy – we were hung up on a hook'. He added, 'Fitt was particularly uncomfortable because he was always receiving criticism from Westminster MPs when he was in London.'[149] On 7 August the party held its first meeting with Whitelaw, demanding an end to internment, arms searches in Protestant areas and an easing of army pressure on the inhabitants of minority districts. Whitelaw responded by releasing forty-seven internees and promising to inform Heath of their views.[150] Heath argued that he could not end internment but encouraged the SDLP to attend a conference being organised by Whitelaw at Darlington.

The fact that the SDLP met the British while internment still operated (and unionism had not been destroyed!) drew criticism from PD. The PD weekly paper *Free Citizen Unfree Citizen* claimed, 'They are out to channel the discontent of the Northern minority away from the dangerous revolutionaries and back into the Parliamentary system.'[151] On 22 August, nine people were killed in a Newry Customs Office bombing.

The SDLP was unconcerned about criticism from the marginalised PD because by this time there were stirrings in the Catholic community that made political re-engagement necessary.[152] By June 1972, 60,000 people in West Belfast had signed a peace petition. Revulsion at the effects of the republican bombing campaign (which had become far less restricted after direct rule), the loyalist assassination response and the appearance of large numbers of UDA on the streets signalled that, far from demoralising or destroying unionism, the Provos' campaign was provoking a substantial response from the Protestant community. It was impossible to assert in mid-1972, as Currie had at the start of the year, that 'we are winning', and that talking was unnecessary. Signals were also coming from the south (in the form of an Offences Against the State Act) that Dublin no longer saw the PIRA campaign as a reflex against oppression. In deciding to talk the SDLP was responding to the realities of the situation.

In September, the party published a policy document entitled 'Towards a New Ireland', which called for joint sovereignty over Northern Ireland, a power-sharing government and a British declaration in favour of eventual unity. John Hume had drafted the final version, published on 20 September. Whitelaw set out proposals for the creation of special tribunals to deal with internees. Fitt felt that these proposals did not go far enough and refused both to end the boycott on talks and to attend the conference in Darlington to discuss political initiatives. He was adamant: 'I am not prepared to sit at a Conference table when my constituents are held in internment without trial, when they are being held as political hostages. While people are interned without trial the SDLP feel unable to engage in any meaningful discussion with the government.'[153]

The attitude of the SDLP changed after the publication on 30 October of a Green Paper on the future of Northern Ireland. Although the document re-affirmed that there could be no change in constitutional terms without majority consent within Northern Ireland, it did recognise an all-Ireland dimension:

> A settlement must also recognise Northern Ireland's position within Ireland as a whole … It is therefore clearly desirable that any new arrangements for Northern Ireland should, whilst meeting the wishes of Northern Ireland and Great Britain, be so far as possible, acceptable to and accepted by the Republic of Ireland.[154]

The paper also proposed a measure of meaningful power-sharing, with the minority exercising Executive power.

The acceptance of an Irish dimension and the prospect of political power proved sufficient bait to lure the SDLP back to participation in northern politics. At their annual party conference in November, a substantial policy change was adopted, and the decision taken to enter into discussions with Whitelaw. The party had brought to an end its policy of not negotiating while internment lasted. Dialogue was the only way forward, the party argued. Apparently the internees were no longer 'political hostages'. In his address Fitt said: 'Now is the time for the SDLP to make its voice heard in any talks that are taking place. If the British government think they can issue a White Paper based on the charade that took place in Darlington then they can have another think.'[155]

In an attempt to reassure unionists of the intent of the Green Paper, the British government held a referendum on the border on 8 March 1973. All anti-unionist groups, including the SDLP, called for a boycott. Fitt was blunt: 'Take no part in it.' He claimed:

> This is the only election in which the result was pre-determined over 50 years ago at the setting up of this state, when borders were deliberately drawn to give a permanent majority to Protestant ascendancy in the North … In these circumstances we will not allow ourselves to be used by the forces of reaction, and we urge all those who have opposed and have been oppressed by unionism not to participate in this election.[156]

The boycott had been effective: only fifty-seven per cent of the electorate took part in the poll. As Fitt said, 'It had merely shown that there were more Protestants than Catholics and more unionists than nationalists in Northern Ireland.'[157] The survey had proved nothing that was not already known, merely highlighting a rather uncomfortable fact of life for nationalists.

Having reassured the unionist population with this referendum, on 20 March the British government published a White Paper outlining its new proposals for the governance of Northern Ireland. A new Executive was to be responsible to a new single seventy-eight-seat chamber assembly, which would be elected by proportional representation. The innovation in this new political initiative was compulsory coalition. The Irish dimension was also recognised. Periodic referenda were to be introduced to test opinion on Northern Ireland's constitutional status in relation to the UK and the Republic. There were also institutional arrangements for consultation and co-operation between Belfast and Dublin. The scheme was embodied in the Northern Ireland Constitution Act of August 1973.

Fitt and the SDLP were cautious in their response to the new proposals. Fitt told a press conference that they recognised that the proposals could represent an advance of position in some areas, while in others, 'we must express both our reservation and our disappointments'. The SDLP felt that the Irish dimension was not sufficiently meaningful. Fitt endorsed this:

> We asked for a strong all-Ireland institution with clearly defined powers. We did not get it. Instead what we got is something that we asked for one year ago – a formula for quadripartite talks involving representatives from both sides in the North and South and Britain.

At such talks we will continue to press our views as to the nature of any all-Ireland institution, and we believe that these views will become increasingly more meaningful to those who have opposed us.

The White Paper also failed to address the future of policing and this was also a concern for the party – radical reform, including a change of name, was a minimum requirement. In September 1973 the chairman of the Police Federation declared that the RUC was unwilling to reform itself and the government made no attempt to overrule him.

The SDLP did, however, decide to contest elections to the new assembly.[158] The White Paper was approved at Westminster by 329 to five. Fitt abstained, a reflection of his party's reservations.[159] He and the SDLP were evidently not satisfied by the British government's failure to clarify its position on the evolution of the proposed Council of Ireland and its unwillingness to constitute a new police service. Yet the SDLP was sufficiently happy with some of the proposals – hence their agreement to contest elections. Fitt and his colleagues rationalised that a strong showing in the elections would force the British to take note and end internment. The party miscalculated. Internment remained, as Fitt had put it, 'a running sore throughout the minority community'.

The Provisionals, on the other hand, rejected the White Paper's proposals. There was no let-up in their military campaign and on 11 April the death of a British soldier shot in the Bogside area of Derry brought the total number killed since August 1969 to 769.

The unionists were also unimpressed with the proposals. William Craig formed the Vanguard Unionist Progressive Party (VUPP) and resolved to fight the assembly elections in alliance with the Democratic Unionist Party (DUP) in opposition to the document.[160] The Alliance Party, a non-sectarian unionist party formed in 1970, was the only group fully to endorse Westminster's plans.

Although Fitt was an implacable opponent of the Provisionals, he did think its political wing, Provisional Sinn Féin, should be allowed to contest the election. He argued that every political party should be permitted to contest elections in order to ascertain the feelings of the electorate.[161]

A dress rehearsal for the assembly elections was provided on 30 May by the first local government elections for six years. Fitt was characteristically positive. 'I am superbly confident. I was never more confident entering into an electoral battle in all my years of experience.'[162] He announced that he too would be seeking election as a local councillor for the newly designated Area G. Area G included Dock, strongly republican areas and equally strong loyalist areas. The PD and Provisionals decided to boycott the elections. Fitt and the SDLP remained unrepentant. On the day of the poll Fitt argued:

> This is the first opportunity that the people of Northern Ireland have had of using one man one vote to undo the damage of the unionists in six-county local government, and they are being asked to abstain and boycott the use of a reform which was won after so much suffering by the ordinary people. I believe it is completely irresponsible and if acted upon will only ensure that the Unionist Party will once again be in a position to establish their sectarian policies. We, the people of this area, would be brought back again to the position we were in before 1969.[163]

The turnout for the poll was high, except in hard-core republican enclaves. The SDLP, in its first major electoral test, wiped out all other anti-unionist groups, winning eighty-three of the 103 anti-partition seats and obtaining 13.4 per cent of the vote. Fitt was elected on the first count. The NILP, the Alliance Party and the Republican Labour Party all polled badly. Fitt's success, however, was soon tarnished.

On 26 June, SDLP Senator Paddy Wilson and a companion, Irene Andrews, were stabbed to death in Belfast by the Ulster Freedom Fighters (UFF), a name used by the UDA as a flag of convenience. John White (later a loyalist political spokesperson) confessed to the murder in 1978 and was sentenced to life imprisonment.

Fitt and Wilson were close friends, the latter having been Fitt's only colleague in the Republican Labour Party to join him in the SDLP. Fitt showed admirable restraint and appealed for peace: 'It is imperative that we should all try to be calm. I know that young, misguided people might be tempted into taking some form of retaliatory action. In God's name, don't. There has been enough, and more than enough of killing.'[164]

Two days later the elections for the new Northern Ireland assembly took place, with Fitt contesting North Belfast. The Provisionals and PD again urged a boycott; but Fitt called on electors of all religious persuasions to vote wisely in the interests of peace.[165]

His appeal was answered by another high poll and he topped the North Belfast ballot, being elected in the first count with 8,264 first preference votes. His nearest challenger was Johnny McQuade of the Democratic Unionist Loyalist Coalition, who polled 5,148 first preference votes and was elected on the eleventh count.

The SDLP, equipped with a manifesto entitled 'A New North – A New Ireland' gained nineteen seats. Paddy Devlin, Hume, Cooper, Currie and O'Hanlon were also elected on the first count. The party gained 22.1 per cent of the total poll, and had established itself as the official representatives of the northern minority. Republican Club candidates received only 1.8 per cent and the Nationalist Party 1.4 per cent.

On the unionist side, the reverse occurred – unionism had fragmented. The moderates, led by Brian Faulkner, who had hesitantly accepted the White Paper, received 29 per cent of the poll, whereas the anti-White Paper unionists, the Vanguard Unionist Loyalist Coalition led by William Craig, and the Democratic Unionists, led by Paisley, secured 31 per cent. The middle ground gained only 12 per cent, the Alliance Party doing worse than expected.[166]

Fitt had considered the assembly nothing more than a conference table, though he did believe it represented an opportunity for spokesmen from both Protestant and Catholic working-class to establish links:

> It is the working-class of both religions who have suffered so disastrously in the past four years of turmoil and tragedy and it will be the immediate task of the Social Democratic and Labour Party to have discussions with the Protestant representatives who can speak with an authentic voice on behalf of the community.[167]

These thoughts proved naive. The first meeting of the assembly broke up in pandemonium, and the speaker Nat Minford was forced to suspend the sitting due to loyalist disruption.

Why did the SDLP change its position? It initially took a very cautious attitude to the assembly, perhaps due to fear of going too far too soon in recognising the legitimacy of the state. But an *Irish Times* editorial on 3 July 1973 revealed that the Taoiseach 'is not among those who think that the Northern Assembly is a conference table ... He clearly told the assembly men and women that their job is to get down to it and produce an Executive quickly.'[168] Southern pressure was applied to the SDLP to change its view of the assembly as a mere conference table and to end its stalling operation. The northern nationalist press followed suit. On 14

July the *Irish News* editorial urged the SDLP to see it as 'a basis for power sharing' that 'could develop into an enterprise of real success' even though the assembly 'was not an instrument for realising the political ideals … What alternative is there at the present time?' it asked.[169]

The thing that seemed to really concentrate the minds of the SDLP, however, was a statement by British Prime Minister Ted Heath, who warned in mid-September that the stalling could not go on forever: 'I would favour the total integration of N.Ireland with Great Britain if the proposed Executive is not set up by March, as required by the Northern Ireland Constitution Act.'[170] This placed the ball firmly in the SDLP's court. Integration would have been favoured by many unionists but would have been totally anathema to nationalists, so if the SDLP did not alter its position it would be faced with a much worse political scenario.

Despite the stalling and the setbacks in the assembly, Whitelaw held separate talks with the parties that had voiced nominal approval of the White Paper – the Faulkner unionists, the SDLP and the Alliance Party. At the end of the month, the SDLP finally took the initiative and issued an invitation to the other two to engage in power-sharing talks.

On 5 October talks began on the government of Northern Ireland. On the first day there was movement on social and economic areas. Whitelaw claimed: 'Steady progress has been made. There has been certainly a determination on all sides to seek to resolve contentious matters in a spirit of good will.'[171] That morning, Fitt as party leader had laid out the SDLP position. He proposed that 'nothing was agreed until everything had been agreed'. He then stated that the Constitution Act was not an issue since the SDLP was committed to the consent principle, and maintained that the rent and rates strike would end once internment had gone. He concluded his address by stressing that the ending of internment, reform of the police and the Council of Ireland were all important.[172] The SDLP had made an important concession – there could be no change in the status of Northern Ireland until the next border poll in ten years' time.

Agreement was reached on 21 November, and on the following day Heath announced the formation of an Executive designate with eleven members – six unionists, four SDLP and one Alliance. Brian Faulkner was to be chief Executive, and Fitt his deputy. There would be a tripartite conference involving London, Belfast and Dublin to negotiate details of a Council of Ireland.

Fitt had played a part in this success. He had managed to both amuse and bemuse Faulkner with his humour and on one occasion 'lacerated' him 'for demanding a majority on the Executive'.[173] After the agreement Fitt declared: 'We are highly satisfied.'[174]

Fitt and the SDLP may well have been pleased with the outcome, but militant nationalists and republicans were not. Ruari Ó'Brádaigh commented: 'The Provos are about to win the battle and lose the war ... The SDLP are about to cream off all the Provisional successes. They are poachers turned gamekeepers.'[175] The Provisionals viewed Fitt and the SDLP as arch-collaborators and made it clear that they intended to pursue and intensify the armed struggle. A statement from Provisional Sinn Féin contained a threat to both Fitt and Hume, whom they regarded as partitionist nationalists: 'We hope they understand the consequences of their treachery.'[176]

At Westminster, Fitt and Bernadette Devlin were involved in a bitter exchange, Fitt maintaining that Devlin was 'a total and absolute irrelevancy in Northern Ireland'.[177] Devlin countered in a statement to the *Irish News*:

Too many people have died in the past four years to allow the fight to be left in the hands of their orphans. Ireland's history is full of Gerry Fitts who, however well-intentioned, called a halt at the eleventh hour and were hailed as heroes by a people who realised their mistake too late. It cannot be allowed to happen again. There are those of us who are not prepared to see it again and that in the eyes of the SDLP is a crime.[178]

Although antagonism and pessimism were not universal, the opposition to power-sharing from militants in both communities did not augur well for the future. An editorial in the *Belfast Telegraph* expressed some hope, however:

Thanks to Gerry Fitt the tough-talking in-fighter has graduated to the big league. He and his party have not made the mistake of getting themselves cornered. They have left their options open and their sights on community peace. They have opted for politics rather than confrontation which is a new direction for Irish nationalism.[179]

The *Telegraph* was incisive: the SDLP was committed to a compromise settlement. This policy of working within the Northern Ireland context

left Fitt and the party hierarchy open to criticism of collaboration, with
the issue of negotiations while internment still operated provoking the
most disparagement, particularly after the party's earlier position and
statements. The SDLP had insisted that it would not co-operate with any
Westminster initiative until internment was ended, but was persuaded
from that position by the prospect of power-sharing and the adoption
of an Irish dimension. The party argued that with the establishment of
normal politics the necessity for internment would disappear.

This clearly did not satisfy some elements in the Catholic community
who considered it an insult to see Gerry Fitt prepared to work alongside
Brian Faulkner, the architect of internment. Even within his party there
was a desire for a different type of leadership. As early as October 1972
an unidentified SDLP spokesman felt it necessary to say 'Gerry is a good
attacker. He has to prove yet, and so does the party, that the record can
be as good when a more constructive approach is required. You have to
take a party like ours by the neck. You don't lead it merely by talking ten
times faster than anyone else.'[180] Fitt told me that he came to resent these
nameless spokesmen who expressed 'concern' to the press. To him they
were nothing more than 'cowardly bastards'.[181]

The Catholics in Fitt's West Belfast constituency had suffered a great
deal under the Conservative government's 'get tough' policy. House raids,
internment and the Diplock courts[182] had succeeded in alienating the
population from the British. Fitt voiced opposition, but among constituents
raised on an education of England's treachery to Ireland the damage had
already been done.[183]

Although the Provisional IRA, with some justification, claimed that
it was they (and not the SDLP's 'middle-class collaboration') who had
finally forced the demise of Stormont, events such as Bloody Friday and
a general war-weariness lost the movement a lot of support, except in
the republican urban ghettos. The failure of the PIRAs and PDs boycott
of the assembly elections showed that the minority community had
given Fitt a mandate to lead the SDLP in talks aimed at power-sharing
within Northern Ireland. Despite the breakthrough on the Executive and
six weeks of negotiations there were still major outstanding issues to be
addressed, mainly internment, reform of the RUC and – crucially – the
rather ambiguous Council of Ireland. With the best will in the world these
issues could hardly be described as loose ends.

But Fitt and the SDLP were taking a new road for Catholic politicians in the Six Counties. This was a road that would test their ability to balance all-Ireland nationalist ideals with the need to develop an effective power-sharing government in Northern Ireland that would help stabilise the state and bring to an end the communal antagonisms that had torn it apart.

5

THE EXECUTIVE AND AFTER

In the mid-1970s Gerry Fitt's nationalist position underwent a discernible transition. This conversion was influenced by political processes initiated by the British government. Fitt became less focused on the Irish dimension. He began to think it was desirable to concentrate less on southern political involvement in the administration of the north and more on an accommodation with Ulster Unionists. In practice, however, Fitt gave in to party pressure that insisted on a strong Irish dimension. The implication is that Fitt himself was not a very forceful character in the political dialogue, and that he simply went along with policies decided by other people, acting merely as a party spokesman and figurehead.

In the crucial period of the Executive's existence (when the future of Northern Ireland lay in the balance) both the SDLP and its leader were in two minds.

Expressing hope for the future at the third annual SDLP conference in December 1973, Fitt still acknowledged the difficulties that lay ahead:

I never believed that I would see a day as this when there is such hope, when unionists and republicans, Protestants and Catholics, representatives of Orange and Green are prepared to sit down and discuss their differences to find areas in which it may be even more difficult to find agreement.[1]

No one section of the community could claim victory over the other, he said, adding pointedly, 'We are not claiming total victory. No, we have been kicked for far too long, for too many years, to want to inflict the same treatment on our fellow countrymen.' He again said that the SDLP was a socialist party with an equal claim to Protestant and Catholic support. He explained the party rationale in pursuing a policy of power-sharing and asked:

What should we have done? Should we have waited and not talked until we had achieved total victory? And should Brian Faulkner not have talked until he had achieved total victory? If this had been done, the result would have been that the gunmen would have won and there would have been more death and destruction. There would have been no prospect of peace and reconciliation in this community.

The motion confirming the SDLP's deal with the Faulkner unionists and the Alliance Party was carried by 235 votes to twenty-two. On the rent strike, the party leadership secured endorsement by 182 votes to twenty-two for a motion giving local leaders the freedom to call off the strike.[2]

The conference was a great success. It showed, according to *Fortnight*:

> ... why Gerry Fitt has remained firmly in control of the top job. His speech
> – and the much reported promise of an inexhaustible supply of new men
> to take over if the men of violence should strike him down – lifted the
> Conference on to a new level with a vision of a job to be done and no
> other way of doing it. This was the stuff of leadership.[3]

Events would show that this view of Fitt's leadership was a very superficial one. His influence was limited from the beginning and waned as the decade progressed. Ivan Cooper said, 'Gerry became very isolated. He was not a party man. He was a man who had the feeling of being constantly under threat. He was very insecure. Unless people around him were telling him he had performed well he was unhappy.' Cooper's affection for both men was absolute, but he did feel that Hume could have done more to develop a healthier relationship between the leader and his party colleagues. He told me:

> John was not as supportive of Fitt as he could have been. He had ambitions
> on the leadership himself. Politics is that type of game. He was to some
> extent dismissive of Gerry.[4]

In short, Hume was the leader in waiting – waiting for the figurehead to fail or fall on his sword.

At the Sunningdale conference, which began on 6 December, the SDLP, the Alliance Party, the Faulkner unionists and both the Dublin and London governments met to finalise an agreement on the Council of Ireland, without which the SDLP would not participate in the Executive. (It was the first time since 1925, when the boundary commission was abandoned, that the Prime Minister, Taoiseach and Northern Ireland government – in the form of the Executive designate – had attended the same talks on the future of Northern Ireland.) Ominously, on that same day in the Ulster Hall in Belfast, 600 delegates from Unionist Party constituency associations, Vanguard, the DUP and the Orange Order voted to form a new United Ulster Unionist Council (UUUC) to provide a common leadership to oppose and bring down the power-sharing Executive.

On 3 December, Whitelaw was transferred from his post as Secretary of State for Northern Ireland to the Department of Employment, where Heath thought his talents would be better used in dealing with the miners' strike in Britain. Fitt was disappointed by Whitelaw's removal from the Northern Ireland scene only three days before such crucial talks: 'One would have thought that he should have been allowed to remain throughout the course of the tripartite talks in an effort to bring that to a successful conclusion.'[5] Francis Pym, Whitelaw's successor, had comparatively little knowledge of Northern Ireland and according to Paddy Devlin was 'a cold fish and certainly not as adroit a politician' as Whitelaw.[6]

But this was another instance of the British attitude to Northern Ireland. When force was applied and violence threatened to get out of control in the state, the resources of the British state were applied to problem solving. When things began to settle down again Northern Ireland was relegated to the bottom of Westminster's priorities – there being no votes to be won or lost there. And this lesson was one that was never lost on republicans.

Fitt later underplayed the importance of the conference: 'I myself don't think Sunningdale itself was necessary because Whitelaw got us together in Stormont with Brian Faulkner. We in fact, agreed on the Executive at Stormont. That was all agreed without ever going to Sunningdale.'[7]

Fitt also minimised the importance of the idea of the Council of Ireland. In contrast, Paddy Devlin, in his book *The Fall of the Northern Ireland Executive* described the SDLP approach at Sunningdale as follows. 'The general approach of the SDLP to the talks was to get all-Ireland institutions established which, with adequate safeguards, would produce the dynamic that could lead ultimately to an agreed single state for Ireland.'[8] Fitt's assertion that the conference was unnecessary does not stand close examination, even if the Council of Ireland is taken out of the equation. Major issues needed to be addressed, not least what degree of recognition the Irish government would give to the constitutional status of Northern Ireland. In addition, law and order, internment, policing (the British were adamant that the RUC must continue to provide the police service for Northern Ireland), security, finance for the operation of the Executive, extradition and an all-Ireland common law enforcement area all had to be debated.

Devlin, Cooper, Currie and Hume all maintained that Fitt did not play an important role at Sunningdale. Negotiation was not one of his political strengths. He himself admitted to being largely a spectator: 'I did not take part in any of the discussions because as far as I was concerned the discussion had been concluded at Stormont.'[9] When negotiations moved to sub-committees Currie said, 'Gerry decided he was best suited for a roving commission.'[10] According to Cooper, 'Gerry would have been going round doing PR work more than anything else.'[11]

This was not a situation where the delegation's best player and leader was left at home, as was the case in the Anglo-Irish Treaty negotiations of 1921. Although Fitt, like de Valera, sidelined himself, in this instance it was as the weakest player and leader that he was left on the bench. The hard bargaining was best left to Hume, Currie, Cooper, Devlin and McGrady, all skilled negotiators. While Devlin may not have had the subtlety and guile of Hume, his trade union background had made him an experienced and capable deal-maker; according to Cooper he was 'the key man at Sunningdale'. Fitt did not take a ministerial portfolio in the Executive. His talents lay elsewhere, and many people in the party realised that he would have been incapable of running a department effectively. Cooper confirms this:

The reality was that Fitt could not discipline himself to run a department. He wasn't prepared to sit down and spend time reading documents and seriously study documents. He could therefore not develop a coherent policy. I met Wilson with him when Wilson was prime minister and Gerry had nothing prepared and the meeting was nothing more than a public relations exercise. As deputy chief minister Fitt had nothing to do. He had a magnificent office but he didn't do any ministerial work or anything. He was a very undisciplined man.[12]

Fitt and the SDLP clearly made a good call; the party performed well at Sunningdale – perhaps too well as events turned out. Despite his minor role, Fitt's later claim that there was no need for Sunningdale is incorrect when the importance of the institutionalised Irish dimension to his party and his constituency is considered.

The real problem was that there was no one in the party who would advise it to lower its sights when the future of the Executive lay in the balance – primarily over the ambiguity of the Council of Ireland. That role should surely have been played by its leader, particularly because Fitt (who had at least some knowledge of the Belfast Protestant working-class) seemed to understand the predicament better than his more idealistic colleagues. But Fitt did not have the status or authority to change the direction of the party.

The Sunningdale conference lasted three days. On 9 December a communiqué was issued that declared an agreement in principle to establish a Council of Ireland. What had been agreed between the two governments was to be ratified later and solemn declarations registered at the United Nations. The council would have Executive powers: in return the Republic would recognise the constitutional position of Northern Ireland and acknowledge 'that there could be no change in the status of Northern Ireland until a majority of the people of Northern Ireland desired a change in that status'. The council would have two tiers: Executive and consultative. The Executive tier would comprise fourteen ministers, seven each from the assembly and the Republic's government. This body would deal with tourism, agriculture, transport and electricity on an all-Ireland basis. The second tier, the consultative assembly, which would comprise thirty members each from Dáil Éireann and the Northern Ireland assembly, would have a purely advisory role. The British government agreed that 'If in the future the majority of the people of Northern Ireland should indicate a wish to become part of a united Ireland, the British Government would support that wish.' On security matters, a joint law commission was to be created to look at the issue of extradition, and the possibility of an all-Ireland court would be investigated. The SDLP would have been satisfied with the agreement that 'the Council would be invited to consider in what way the principles of the European Convention on Human Rights and Fundamental Freedoms would be expressed in domestic legislation in each part of Ireland', but less pleased with the levels of progress in policing and detention without trial. These issues were not resolved to the SDLP's satisfaction, which undermined the party's participation in the Executive.

The leaders of the parties involved presented a united and optimistic front. Faulkner said, 'The agreement heralds a new dawn not just for Northern Ireland but for the whole of Ireland.'[13] Oliver Napier of the Alliance Party declared, 'This is a very proud day', and Fitt maintained, 'All our objectives have been achieved.'[14] This was not true, but Fitt can be forgiven for not dwelling on the fact. Policing had been the most difficult problem. The SDLP had wanted a symbolic break from the past – a change of name and uniform would have had an impact on the nationalist community, among whom there was little support for the RUC. Even stronger policing links with the Council of Ireland would not encourage nationalists to identify with the RUC. The SDLP remained unconvinced by the treatment of the policing issue at Sunningdale although it was promised that an all-party assembly committee would look at 'how best to introduce effective policing throughout Northern Ireland with particular reference to the need to achieve public identification with the police'. The issue of internment was equally muddled. Heath had promised to phase it out 'as soon as the security situation permits'. It continued for another two years. When the talks came to an end Fitt quoted William Gladstone, the nineteenth-century Liberal Prime Minister, who had declared it his mission to pacify Ireland. Fitt had said to Heath, 'He didn't succeed, but I hope you have.'[15] Decisive action on internment might have been a good start.

On the same day as the Executive had confidently greeted the press, a new Ulster Army Council (UAC), made up of UVF and UDA paramilitaries, declared their intention to oppose any progress towards a Council of Ireland.

The Sunningdale Agreement itself was dextrous – unionists and nationalists could both claim victory, and the Council of Ireland proposal had deliberately been left open to interpretation.[16] Farrell concluded that it was a 'masterpiece of balance and ambiguity'.[17] But Fitt was confident that a new era had dawned and that the power-sharing concept had enough support to be successful. He declared, 'I can see very clearly a hope that has never been seen before in Northern Ireland.'[18] It was a political high point for Fitt and the SDLP.

On 1 January 1974, the Northern Ireland Executive officially took up duty. Fitt was deputy chief minister; Hume, minister for commerce; Currie, minister for housing; and Paddy Devlin, minister for health and social security. Cooper, who was not on the Executive, was minister of community relations. Fitt revealed some of the tensions that arose over the appointments:

> When it came to the handing out of ministries they were fucking killing each other for jobs. I told John to take education as he had been a school teacher. No way would he because it was a hot potato, what with the Catholic Church.
>
> There were six of us. And I didn't want a ministry. I had enough to do in Westminster and not only did I not want one but it was a way of leaving a vacancy for someone else, because they all wanted ministries.[19]

The cracks were papered over, and Fitt swore, 'I will uphold the laws of Northern Ireland and conscientiously fulfil my duties under the Constitution Act in the interest of Northern Ireland and its people.'[20] He had no qualms about taking the oath:

> I am happy with the oath which I have sworn before the Lord Chief Justice. It is one I can take in all conscience and all honesty because I have taken the oath to serve all the people of Northern Ireland. I know that I can speak for all my colleagues that they are activated by the same emotion. I believe we are entering into a new era, and it will not be easy. There will be many people who will spare no efforts to bring the administration to an end. But being born in Northern Ireland and living all my life in the city of Belfast, I am confident that the Executive speaks for the overwhelming majority of the people. They want this administration to succeed.[21]

Despite Fitt's good spirits, within four days there were ominous signs for the future of the Executive. On 4 January, the Ulster Unionist Council (the policy making body of the UUP) rejected the Council of Ireland by 427 votes to 374. Before Sunningdale, Faulkner had survived with a ten-vote victory for power-sharing, a clear indication of vulnerability. On this occasion, he was defeated by fifty-three votes. While Fitt was not surprised by the result, he remained positive, claiming that if the Executive were to function for six months and be seen to be governing in the interests of all, there would be massive support for it, even in the Unionist Council.[22]

On 7 January, Faulkner resigned as Unionist Party leader. He considered it the only honourable course in the face of what was essentially a vote of no confidence.[23] Fitt commented, 'I believe Mr Faulkner realised that he would find it extremely difficult to drive the more backward sections of the Unionist Party into the twentieth century.'[24] The minutes of the Executive reveal Faulkner's unease. 'The Chief Minister said that views were divided as to whether the vote at Friday's meeting of the Unionist Council accurately expressed Unionist opinion in the country. There was no doubt that there was great concern among Unionists about the Council of Ireland.'[25] Despite this Faulkner's memoirs indicate that he was as confident as Fitt that the Executive could convince both communities of the benefits of power-sharing. His confidence was based on the low attendance that anti-agreement rallies were getting from the Protestant community. His resignation, however, divorced him from the Unionist Party machine and this had important repercussions in the following month.

As for the SDLP, its position was totally transformed from that of the previous year. The SDLP had once relished unionist leaders' problems and splits in the unionist camp, but now the SDLP realised that Faulkner's problems were its own. The architect of internment was by now indispensable to the survival of the Executive, so efforts were made to help him. The SDLP stopped raising grievances and criticising unionism, and John Hume went off to the US to encourage investment in Northern Ireland.

The Executive suffered a major setback when Kevin Boland, a former Fianna Fáil cabinet minister and staunch republican, challenged the legality of the Republic's recognition of Northern Ireland's status in the Sunningdale Agreement. Boland argued that the constitution of the Republic laid claim to all the territory of Ireland and therefore it was illegal to recognise Northern Ireland's status as part of the United Kingdom. However, the Irish government argued successfully that it had not agreed that any part of Ireland belonged to the United Kingdom. Its recognition of Sunningdale would not affect the right of any future government of the Republic to make a claim of sovereignty. It had been a *de facto* rather than a *de jure* arrangement – something akin to a policy statement.

To many people the agreement meant that the Irish government had decided temporarily not to enforce its claim on Northern Ireland against the wishes of the majority. In essence the ruling implied that the reunification of Ireland did not require the consent of the Protestants. The legal proceedings were highly publicised and the judgement was a major blow to the Faulkner unionists, who would not be able to sell the Council of Ireland concept to the majority community without the Republic's recognition of the status of Northern Ireland. Faulkner travelled to Dublin to meet Cosgrave in the wake of the ruling and was 'satisfied that there was no going back on the Sunningdale declaration about the status of Northern Ireland'. He had let the southern government know what he really wanted: 'The Chief Minister had made it clear to Mr Cosgrave that the apprehension of prominent IRA men like Martin McGuinness would do more to satisfy Northern Ireland people than anything else.'[26]

It was curious that the Republic's government, which included both Garret Fitzgerald (considered a moderate nationalist) and Conor Cruise O'Brien (in latter years a professed unionist), felt it unnecessary to argue for a referendum on articles 2 and 3 at this time.[27] Alternatively, it did not seem to occur to them that postponing the establishment of the Council of Ireland until after the Executive had bedded in might have taken the pressure off Faulkner and helped his survival. To be fair, though, both were likely to have been under considerable pressure to abide by government policy agreed in cabinet.

The fact that nothing concrete had been agreed at Sunningdale in relation to the Council of Ireland was bound to create problems. This is reflected in a memo sent by Faulkner to his colleagues in the Executive on 22 January.

> In my view, it would be a great mistake to consider any single aspect of the 'Sunningdale' package in isolation, that 'package' contained elements which were in varying degrees acceptable to each participating party, and if the various objectives should now be pursued within different time scales, the whole delicate balance of the agreements could be upset, with adverse results for all of us.[28]

On the same day eighteen loyalist protestors were forcibly removed from the assembly.

The ambiguity surrounding the Council of Ireland had to be clarified after the Boland case. In early February, Fitt clarified the SDLP's position on the Irish dimension, doing Faulkner no favours in the process. He was asked in the assembly whether he and the SDLP would still participate in the Executive if the southern government did not carry out its obligations and there was no Council of Ireland. He replied: 'No, as I see it that would be a betrayal of the whole Sunningdale Agreement. The Agreement was reached on the basis that there would be a Power-Sharing Executive, that there would be a Council of Ireland and that the Southern government would take up a certain stand in relation to them.'[29]

Fitt was emphatic and unequivocal in his answer. At this point we must assume that he was, like his colleagues, in favour of a Council of Ireland. But the problem now was not the idea of the Council of Ireland but what it actually constituted.

Despite the problems, the Executive strove to counter the initial resistance. Faulkner noted:

> Early in February a reception for industrialists was held in the Ulster Office in London. It struck me very forcibly how much more effective our sales story was made for the 250 or so powerful men who came along by the simple fact that Gerry Fitt and I were standing side by side at the door to welcome them, and showing the same concern for jobs and living standards in the province we now governed.[30]

Adverse developments for the Executive partners continued. In Britain, the miners' strike was crippling. Heath, remaining steadfast against it, decided to seek the electorate's approval for his position. Pym, Whitelaw, Faulkner and Fitt all warned him on the detrimental effect of a general election on the Executive. Paddy Devlin explained:

> We knew that we would not be able to compound our position as a Power-Sharing entity unless we had an extended run; Two months in office could demonstrate potential but not practical results in our favour. Potential results would never be realised in the white heat engendered by a tribal election.[31]

The election was called for 28 February. The UUUC were to fight the election as a single party, in sharp contrast to the Executive parties, who did not make any electoral pact. The election was in effect a referendum on power-sharing and the Council of Ireland.

Fitt again defended his West Belfast seat. He was challenged by McQuade of the UUUC, Brady (Republican Clubs), Boyd (NILP) and Price (Independent). Albert Price was the father of Dolores and Marian Price, two sisters who were members of the Provisionals and had been convicted of bombings in Britain. At the time, the two were on hunger strike in Brixton Prison in an attempt to be sent back to Ireland to serve their sentences. Paddy Kennedy, who was to have stood for the Republican Labour Party, announced his withdrawal: 'I am now standing down and I now call on all anti-unionist candidates to do the same. The issue in West Belfast must be the plight of the Irish political prisoners.'[32] The SDLP ignored such sentiment and confirmed that they would contest all twelve Westminster seats. Fitt declared, 'Now we have created a system to end this conflict and through which people will learn to live together rather than die together.'[33]

Fitt remembered this election battle as being particularly 'vicious'.[34] Republicans printed election leaflets showing a picture of him superimposed on a union jack, with the words 'Vote Fitt for the West and support your Republican-Unionist candidate', suggesting that Fitt had betrayed his original political ideals.[35]

Paddy Devlin recalled that republicans tried to hijack Fitt's campaign with a 'sophisticated dirty trick'. They spread a rumour that, as a member of the Executive, Fitt was not eligible to defend his West Belfast seat because of the provisions of the 1957 House of Commons Disqualification Act. 'By breakfast time the groundless allegation was being broadcast on the local airways and promoted by loudspeaker throughout the West Belfast constituency.'[36] The smear was corrected quickly, but it was feared that the republican tactic might have affected Fitt's vote.

Since the 1970 Westminster election (which Fitt had won with a majority of 3,198), the West Belfast electorate had increased by 6,000 to 70,000 due to an extension of the boundary into South Antrim, taking in Catholic Andersonstown. McQuade's only chance, therefore, lay in a decisive split in the nationalist vote. Fitt's weakness was the internment issue, and both Brady and Price (the latter with PIRA support) hoped to capitalise on this. The *Irish News* reported that political observers in the constituency were giving Fitt a fifty-fifty chance of retaining the seat.[37] On the eve of the poll he declared that he would be the 'true voice of moderation' in the next Westminster Parliament.[38] Fitt was no longer inclined to be seen as a radical.

Fitt retained his seat, but with a reduced majority of 2,180. He polled 19,554 votes. McQuade polled 17,374, Price 5,612, Brady 3,088 and Boyd 1,989. Price's vote had shown that there was a nucleus of support for the Provisionals.

Although Fitt was victorious in the election, the other results were disastrous for the Executive parties. The UUUC took eleven of the twelve seats, with Fitt the only anti-unionist candidate to survive. The UUUC, with the unionist election machine that Faulkner had relinquished on his resignation, had secured fifty-one per cent of the vote. Having received over half the total votes cast, it claimed that the result was a vote of no confidence in the new administration. The Faulkner unionists obtained only 13 per cent of the vote, and no seats. The SDLP actually increased its vote by 24,000 from June 1973, but as a result of the UUUC decision to put up a single candidate against the divided Executive parties, three UUUC candidates were elected despite a pro-Executive majority in their constituencies. Bernadette Devlin and Frank McManus were defeated in mid-Ulster and Fermanagh–South Tyrone respectively.

The February 1974 election had put the Sunningdale package and the concept of power-sharing to the test of public opinion before the Executive had time to prove itself. The election results reflected traditional communal polarisation. As Basil McIvor, minister of education, remarked, 'it was the phrase "Dublin is just a Sunningdale away" that had beaten us in the election'.[39] The Executive had been seriously undermined.

Faulkner interpreted the results of the election in a meeting of the Executive that Fitt did not attend:

> The Chief Minister regarded last week's vote as a clear warning. The Union-ist Assembly party were willing to continue support of the Executive but were not prepared to support a Council of Ireland without solid action by the Republic on status, extradition and in dealing with violence. He was convinced that the priority was to preserve the concept of power-sharing on the foundation of the Constitution Act but he was equally convinced that there was no possibility of making progress towards ratification of Sunningdale without action by the Republic

Hume had his own warning: 'A short time ago there was no support for power-sharing until it was seen to work. The same would be true for the Council of Ireland. If the Council of Ireland were to be removed, his party would go, and we would be back into the hands of the extremists.' Roy Bradford, minister for the environment, was particularly shrill. He claimed that unionists were asking, 'Where has co-operation got us?' 'Has violence diminished?' 'Have the South co-operated?' According to him the election results were a 'protest vote – he would not agree to ratification unless and until others delivered and were seen to deliver. The onus was now on the Republic to act.'

While alarm was widespread in Faulkner's immediate circle, Hume was keen that a statement be released to hide any signs of division in the Executive. A split was already evident and was only likely to get wider. Ministers agreed on the following wording:

> The Executive are united on policy but agree that its successful implementation will demand not only resolution and determination by them, but a delivery, in the letter and the spirit of those commitments entered into by the British and Irish Governments.[40]

The Executive was not the only casualty of public opinion in February 1974. The British electorate failed to endorse Heath's leadership and the Labour Party was delivered into power, with Harold Wilson once again occupying Number Ten, albeit without an absolute Commons majority. On 5 March (the same day the Executive's statement was released) Merlyn Rees was, as expected, appointed the new secretary of state. The 'resolution and determination' the Executive craved would not come from Rees. His position was weakened by the fact that the Labour Party had formed a government with a minority vote. Fitt had already been reported to be happy about the prospect of Rees succeeding Pym.[41]

The new secretary of state, according to Devlin, 'assured everyone in sight that the Sunningdale Agreement would have his support and we would be given time to show the fruits of our work'.[42] Consequently the Executive ploughed on, hoping that its performance would improve its chances of survival. The SDLP had clearly not lost sight of the agreement. In the wake of the election results a 'senior member' of the party felt it necessary to put the party's position on record:

> The SDLP would be most unhappy if it was attempted to put new conditions into the Sunningdale package before final notification because of an unfortunate set of electoral statistics which were totally freak ... there is no question of allowing hysteria to blow us off course. To allow this could lead to the loss of a landbase. It would be fatal for any political party to allow themselves to be placed in that position.[43]

The resolve expressed by this spokesperson was probably not shared by Fitt, though his faith in Westminster remained: 'Many people in Northern Ireland may believe that the eleven voices of the UUUC coalition will cause great consternation at Westminster but I can assure them that all the major British political parties are well aware of what the true position is.'[44]

But were they? Fitt's faith in the steadfastness of the British government and Northern Ireland Secretary of State (especially Labour) is difficult to excuse, especially given the complex arithmetic that dominated proceedings at Westminster. During his career he showed increasing willingness to be dictated to – even fobbed off – long after such an attitude could be justified. The reasons could be weariness or lack of imagination on Fitt's part. It is also probable that Fitt underwent a process of 'embourgeoisement' in the comfort of Westminster with all its attendant flattery: Seán Redmond had noticed such a process as early as 1969 and Eamon McCann felt that Fitt was 'seducible'.[45] It may be that Fitt became enamoured with Westminster – something he had said would never happen. Ivan Cooper added some credibility to this view:

> The problem with Gerry was that he was at Westminster regularly. He formed relationships there. When the Provos started attacking his house he escaped there. Whenever he got into any political difficulty he escaped there. He liked the institution because he was able to get copy. The reporters were there from all the Irish newspapers. It was a great club, a great club to be a member of.[46]

Fitt told me that he felt vulnerable when in London. It was a case of 'while the cat's away the mice will play' as his colleagues at home 'tried to assert themselves' so they would not look like Gerry Fitt's minions.[47] Both recollections confirm that at times relationships between the leader and his colleagues were far from healthy.

The unionists in the Executive felt they had to respond to Protestant fears reflected in the election results. They wanted to reappraise the Council of Ireland, in view of the fact that the Republic's government had not met its pledge on constitutional recognition and extradition.

On 4 March the Faulkner Unionists in the assembly decided that there should be no ratification of Sunningdale unless articles 2 and 3 of the Irish constitution were repealed. On 11 March twenty-one assembly members, headed by Ulster Unionist John Laird, upped the ante by putting their names to a motion calling for a renegotiation of what was agreed at Sunningdale. A statement made by Cosgrave in the Dáil on 13 March, which said the position of Northern Ireland within the United Kingdom could not be changed except with the consent of a majority of the people of Northern Ireland, was not enough to calm their fears. The Boland case was out of the way but the damage had already been done. The status issue was confused. Things got worse when the report of the Anglo-Irish law enforcement officers rejected extradition because of constitutional implications. This in effect meant that the Republic could not or would not take action against 'fugitive offenders'. Despite these developments Fitt remained confident about the new institution's prospects. On 18 March he claimed:

> The new Executive was given a job to do. Its members have got their heads down and got on with it. It has plenty on its plate. Legislation under way or in the pipeline ranges over the whole spectrum of life in the Province. More and more, the Executive is being seen to speak and act for the real Northern Ireland. Its success is clearly causing dismay to the men of violence.[48]

Five days later the Ulster Workers' Council (UWC), an organisation with connections to loyalist paramilitary groups, particularly the UDA, and loyalist politicians (most notably Vanguard leader, William Craig) demanded the dissolution of the assembly and new elections. The UWC became the main mobilising force for loyalist opposition to power-sharing arrangements and the Council of Ireland. It is debatable which component it detested most.

There were rifts in the SDLP in April, when Austin Currie, one of the instigators of the rent and rates strike against internment in 1971, now in charge of housing, said that all arrears must be paid in full and that there would be an increase in the amount that could be deducted from social security benefits. In addition – and most controversially – there would be a new collection charge of 25 pence per week to cover administrative costs.[49] It was a difficult position for Currie, and his reputation was unfairly tarnished by it. How could a member of government sanction civil disobedience? Granted, internment still operated, but if the SDLP honoured its undertakings made at Sunningdale the British would too. Or so it was hoped. Despite this argument, Paddy Devlin was most zealous in his opposition to the measure, urging that it would be 'fairer and more effective to solve the problem by appealing to the tenants to clear up their arrears'.[50]

After fruitless discussions with Rees on internment, Devlin resigned from the Executive, which put Currie, who was uncertain about his colleague's motivation, in an awkward position.[51] Devlin later asked for his resignation to be 'frozen'.[52] These issues were trivial and subsequently academic, because by the beginning of May the Executive was in serious trouble.

By this stage Faulkner, to ensure its survival, was intent on making the Sunningdale package more acceptable to loyalists. On the other hand, watering down the Council of Ireland was anathema to the SDLP. To what extent this view was shared by the party leader is open to question. In retrospect, Fitt claimed that he tried to play down the importance of the Council of Ireland in order to prevent the collapse of the Executive.[53] Faulkner's memoirs confirm this: 'It always seemed to me that Gerry Fitt did not really care if there was a Council of Ireland or not, but had to go along with it because his party was insisting'.[54]

Faulkner's notion confirms two points regarding Fitt. First, Fitt felt that the Irish dimension represented an impossible obstacle to power-sharing in the north. Second, Faulkner indicated that Fitt was merely a figurehead rather than a leader who was orchestrating party policy. He was a commentator on the political scene rather than a key actor in it.

The problems affecting the continued operation of the Executive were not, therefore, confined to the streets: divisions within the group as well as political pressures from without threatened to undermine the entire power-sharing project. During a meeting of the Executive on 7 May Fitt 'mentioned the depressing news of the latest violence, the air of disenchantment among backbenchers at Westminster and the growing pressure from the left wing to review the Government's attitude to Sunningdale'. It is possible that Fitt shared this 'left-wing' view and just wanted to get on with sharing power. 'He was convinced that the Executive must do what it had to do and he was hopeful that it would act unanimously.' The cohesion that Fitt hoped for was not apparent in the contributions from the unionist ministers.

Faulkner made the point that 'it was most damaging to the Executive that we could not as an Executive wholeheartedly support the police'. Herbie Kirk, minister of finance, 'doubted whether a hundred per cent ratification of Sunningdale would have any different effect on terrorists, who were, in his opinion, to a large extent internationally inspired and supported'. He argued for a 'lower key' implementation of Sunningdale. Roy Bradford agreed. He was convinced that there was 'deep-seated opposition, especially to the giving of Executive functions to a Council of Ireland, and therefore it was not possible to implement as fully as envisaged'. Leslie Morrell, head of the department of agriculture, argued that 'one of the matters causing most trouble among Protestants was the lack of support of law and order by some members of the Executive. If they would be able to offer support after the ratification of Sunningdale but not do so now, there must be something very terrible in Sunningdale – that was how the argument ran.' John Baxter, minister for information services, followed the same line and pressed 'for a much less frightening version of a Council of Ireland'.

It is perhaps significant that Fitt did not contribute further to the debate. Did he agree with his unionist colleagues? John Hume certainly didn't. He was robust in his response, making the point that 'all parties had committed themselves to a concept which he felt should not be diluted for the sake of political expediency. Any weakening would be a victory for our opponents both IRA and Protestant extremists'. As regards policing and the outcome of indecisive action by the Executive he claimed:

> Sunningdale could not have achieved a reduction in violence but its implementation would allow his party to support the police. The Executive should show strength and ratify. If Sunningdale were ratified opposition and violence would collapse. If it were not the British would pull out and the Protestants would be the long term losers.

Faulkner efficiently and impartially summed up the state of play after the discussion by affirming that the SDLP 'must be enabled to demonstrate that they are not selling out' and the assembly unionists 'must be able to show they are not bringing it (the Council of Ireland) in by stealth'.[55] Despite the opinion of Hume and others in the SDLP, persistent pressure from Faulkner to phase in the Council of Ireland resulted in the Executive setting up a sub-committee with the intention of creating a two-stage implementation process.

In early May the UWC announced that it would lead a 'full-scale constitutional stoppage' throughout Northern Ireland in protest at the

continuing operation of the Executive, if a motion requesting the re-nego-
tiation of the constitutional arrangements was not accepted. On 14 May,
the Northern Ireland assembly endorsed the Sunningdale Agreement
by forty-four votes to twenty-three. The UWC then announced that the
strike was to proceed.

Few workers joined the strike on its first day. However, when barricades went up and intimidation grew, the numbers of strikers escalated.
Rees refused to negotiate with the UWC and on 17 May tension was
heightened by three car bombs that killed thirty-three people in Dublin
and Monaghan. The SDLP correctly believed that support for the
'stoppage' stemmed from loyalist paramilitary threats and urged Rees to
order the dismantling of the barricades.

By 19 May the state's electricity supplies were dwindling. Rees responded by declaring a state of emergency to protect all essential services
and he met Wilson for talks. On the following day 500 additional troops
arrived in Northern Ireland and it was reaffirmed that the government
would not bargain with the UWC. The Executive approved this position:
'Ministers were generally agreed that alarming as the situation was it
would be wise not to attempt to enter into any deal with the strikers but to
support the Trade Unions and, as an Executive, to try and reach agreement
on Sunningdale as a matter of urgency.'

Rees was also keen for the Executive to move on Sunningdale. He
'reaffirmed that the British Government were prepared to stand firm in
support of the Executive' but asked that the Executive should, 'as a matter
of urgency, deal with their part'. The SDLP was reluctant to budge, arguing that 'support for the strike was based on a false understanding of Sunningdale. Once this had been removed by a clear agreed statement from
the Executive support for the strikers would diminish.'[56] This was a forlorn
hope, which largely contradicted what was happening on the ground. The
strike continued.

On 21 May, Len Murray, the general secretary of the British Trades
Union Congress, led a group of 200 people on a 'back to work' march. It was
an unmitigated failure. The Executive, meanwhile, had begun to unravel.
Bradford argued strongly 'for opening a dialogue with the strikers on the
grounds of their very wide support and the realities of the situation'. He
had gone public on this issue two days before without informing Faulkner
or the Executive. Despite his stance, 'Ministers were generally in favour of
taking firm steps to oppose the strikers.' The minutes also show that the

Executive approved a Sunningdale draft statement agreeing to postpone certain sections of the agreement until 1977. This diluted the immediate impact of the Council of Ireland. Pressure within the Executive was severe. The IRA and loyalist paramilitaries were destroying life and property with apparent impunity. Faulkner claimed, 'time was running out. If any benefit was to result from the agreed statement it should be announced as soon as possible.'[57]

SDLP backbenchers viewed developments with understandable apprehension and anxiety. The party had agreed to participation in Stormont in return for unionist agreement to participate in an all-Ireland institution. To them the Council of Ireland was part and parcel of the whole deal. The watering-down rumours were bound to cause dissension and it was not going to be easy for the leadership to pass anything through the assembly party that smacked of surrender. The SDLP assembly party met on the morning of 22 May. The leadership had accepted that the party would have to agree to Faulkner's proposals for the council to be introduced in two phases.

The Executive members, apart from Paddy Devlin (he was opposed, not to the 'phasing in' but to the timing of the announcement, fearing it would strengthen the UWC position), voted with the leadership, but were defeated by eight votes to eleven. There was implied but no direct criticism of the leadership, which had failed to convince all their colleagues that Faulkner was not bluffing.[58] Faulkner recalled the aftermath of the meeting:

> The SDLP Executive members had a meeting of their backbenchers to secure final approval, but when they came back they were more disappointed than I had ever seen them. 'I'm sorry,' said Gerry Fitt, 'we can't get them to agree.' It seemed as if the Executive was about to break up on this issue, as neither Alliance or ourselves were prepared to go back on what had been agreed. I got up from the Executive table and said 'well, if that's the case I am afraid it means the end of the Executive. I am going into the Assembly to announce the resignation of the Executive because of the failure to agree on the re-negotiation of the Council of Ireland'. I was at the door when Gerry Fitt stopped me. 'Give us another half an hour and we will try again, Brian,' he said.[59]

According to Paddy Devlin, Stan Orme, Fitt's old friend and now Rees's deputy, had contacted Fitt and asked him to convene another meeting of the assembly party.[60] Orme addressed the SDLP assembly group and told them that there would be strong action against the strike and an end to internment. In the second vote, the earlier decision was reversed and the compromise was carried by twelve votes to five. Faulkner also recalled:

> It was about an hour later that Fitt and his colleagues returned looking more cheerful. 'We had another vote and a majority have agreed,' he said. I went straight to the Assembly and announced the new proposals. It later transpired that Orme had been rushed up from Stormont Castle to address the SDLP back benchers, and had played a major part in changing their attitude.[61]

Interestingly Currie suggests that, despite Faulkner's testimony, it was the chief Executive himself who had initiated Orme's intervention.[62] Orme's performance at the meeting was something of a *tour de force*, but Fitt missed it: finding the whole situation too tense he went for a drink.[63] Despite the stress and strain on all those involved, the announcement of the phasing in of the Council of Ireland had no impact on the strike. And Orme's promise of effective action against them and movement on internment never materialised.

On the day after Orme's address to the SDLP the security forces did begin to remove barricades, but they were put back up as quickly as they had come down. Seamus Mallon was one of the five SDLP members not fooled by Orme:

> Orme was brought in to say 'if only we would dilute the Irish dimension'. 'If only we would put it to one side – postpone it – that would save unionism and the Executive.' How many times have I heard that? I have lived with that sentiment all my political life. I could not understand how you could have viable political beliefs to negotiate in a proper democratic fashion and then be required to suspend or postpone to satisfy those that don't like it.
>
> Orme also promised an end to internment. I said, 'there is a bit of paper there, Stan. Would you write that down?' Needless to say he didn't.[64]

In any case what had happened had been a case of too little too late. If such a concession had been made earlier – after the February elections, for instance, or when the rallies against the Executive consisted of only a motley crew of extremists – the crisis could have been headed off, if only temporarily. But politicians who ignore election results that reveal a change in public mood do so at their peril. And yet how else could the SDLP have reacted? It did not see the loyalist action simply as a strike that challenged the new political dispensation, but as an attack on the capacity to lead a normal life.

Normality was further away than ever and the Executive struggled to meet its responsibility of the governance of Northern Ireland. Nevertheless, ministers adopted a 'fuel oil plan' designed by Hume to take complete control of supplies. They agreed 'that there was no acceptable alternative to this demonstration of the Executive will and determination to govern'.[65] On 24 May Fitt, Faulkner and Napier travelled to England to meet Wilson at Chequers. They received the 'clear impression that Mr Wilson was firm in his desire to do whatever was necessary, and within his capability, to stand by the Executive'. The delegation was also buoyed by the fact that 'the Prime Minister intended to make a statement on television the following evening'.[66]

Wilson's commitment to the Executive, despite what he had said, was questionable. What was not in doubt was the British army's reluctance to fight a war on two fronts: against the IRA and loyalism. Faulkner and Fitt, and others in the Executive, were, however, keen on using the army to break the strike. Faulkner's position would have been more difficult than the SDLP's on this issue, but his memoirs show that he was in favour of military action.[67] Rees also confirmed that Fitt took the opportunity to criticise the BBC for its 'pro-loyalist policy' and the RUC 'for lack of arrests of those organising the road blocks'.[68]

As disruption became more widespread, Fitt became increasingly desperate. In an impassioned speech in the House of Commons he spoke of how 'a band of unelected people, people who have never had a single vote cast for them in the ballot box, people who misname themselves the Loyalist Ulster Workers, are holding the entire community to ransom.' Fitt, used to defending the rights of workers, rightly claimed that it was not an industrial strike: wages and conditions of employment were not the issue. He demanded the use of British troops to ensure that the essentials of life would be made available to everyone in Northern Ireland. His concluding words have a familiar ring: 'I believe that the British government must accept their responsibilities. I regret that it has to be a socialist party that must face the position, but knowing the men who compose the government, and having known Labour backbenchers for some years, I feel that the government will show the courage that they undoubtedly have.'[69]

Fitt's confidence was again misplaced. Far from improving the situation, Wilson's television broadcast made it worse. He attacked the UWC for 'sponging' on British democracy, which merely inflamed the situation. But he did not promise any action against the strikers, and all he succeeded in doing was to needle the Protestant community and ensure greater support for the strike.

On 27 May, the army was finally used to take over selected petrol stations, but it was too late to halt the momentum of the strike. Faulkner was beginning to lose his nerve. He told the Executive, 'Messages were coming in from an increasing number of sources – employers, the Farmer's Union and influential people in all walks of life asking that there should be some communication with the strikers.'[70]

The chief minister wanted to negotiate with the UWC, and the following day Faulkner said, 'He and his party colleagues were convinced that the proper option was to seek agreement from the secretary of state to the initiation of discussions through intermediaries'. Hume disagreed totally:

> In his view the Executive, having asked the Secretary of State for certain action and having been assured of the Army's capacity to follow through with any consequentials, should stand firm. There were fundamental political principles not only for the authority of the Executive, but for British authority in Northern Ireland. He was convinced that if power could be restored the public would get back to work. He would not resign.

Fitt was also not in favour of negotiation. He was still loyal to the Labour Party, believing they would use troops as had been promised.

> The Deputy Chief Minister recalled that the Executive had made a united request to the Secretary of State to which he had responded. He was therefore entitled to loyalty from the Executive. If not the result would be a very hostile United Kingdom ... He did not want to see Northern Ireland dragged down into the mire. He saw no possibility of a change of heart by the strikers who wanted to bring down the Constitution. He did not see how a mediator could talk to the strikers with any hope of

change. The Secretary of State was prepared to talk to politicians but they obstinately wanted him to make the first move.

Fitt also retained his faith in the power-sharing concept, still believing 'that there was a vast residue of people who wanted to work and wanted to support the Executive' and asserting that a vast number of Protestants did not want to live under Craig and Paisley. Currie was also against capitulation. He compared the situation with the Germany of the Weimar Republic. He claimed that the UWC strike represented 'a fascist takeover and reassertion of Protestant ascendancy which would never be accepted by the Catholic population, who would in consequence be driven into the arms of the IRA'. He also claimed that 'civil war would be inevitable' and advocated 'immediate progress towards Sunningdale II'. Only then 'when control had been asserted and some direction shown, the Executive could bring in mediators'. He concluded by saying 'The Executive had chartered a way and should brazen it out'.

Clearly there was no consensus within the Executive. Bradford had maintained, 'There were only two courses, the first to press on with attempts to break the strike and the second, to talk. The army had obviously made it clear that the first course was not a feasible one.' He had no doubt that the Executive should talk, or the country would slide into anarchy.

Faulkner reported to Rees that a majority view within the Executive wanted to open a channel of communication with the strikers, 'preferably by way of mediation'. Rees was not prepared to agree to arbitration and Faulkner, fully aware that the consent needed for the perpetuation of the Executive had been lost, resigned.[71] With the withdrawal of the unionist members the Executive collapsed, ensuring that after thirteen days of strike action, and intimidation, the UWC had achieved its immediate aim.[72] The SDLP and the Alliance Party did not resign, but were dismissed the next day. For twenty-four hours, therefore, Gerry Fitt was acting chief minister for Northern Ireland. Ultimately, Fitt's optimism that power-sharing would work proved misguided. He was visibly upset at the fall of the Executive.[73]

Many reasons can be put forward for the failure of this political experiment, although in retrospect Fitt was adamant that the Council of Ireland was the most significant issue. He felt bitter about the militant nationalism of certain members of the SDLP and argued:

As far as I was concerned we had got an Executive composed of Protestants and Catholics representing the unionists and nationalist communities. For me that was the biggest development in Irish politics, certainly in northern Irish politics, that had happened within my lifetime. I never believed that you would ever have a power-sharing Executive. As far as I was concerned that was it – I didn't want anything else. But the nationalists outside of Belfast, they said 'oh no … no … the Council of Ireland'. We have to have this Council of Ireland – article 12. I said, leave that alone. That's going to drive the Prods mad. It'll drive them up the wall … The Prods will accept very reluctantly, but they will accept that the time has come to have a power-sharing government but that business of the Council of Ireland; it scared the living daylights out of them

Fitt went on to express bitterness at the role of the Republic:

When we went to Sunningdale, that's why we went there to involve the government of the Republic in Sunningdale and this was the government of the Republic – macho getting in on the act. You know. Sunningdale came about because of the blood that was spilt on the streets of Northern Ireland, Catholic and Protestant and army. It had nothing to do with the Free State, nothing to do with it.

Clearly Fitt's position had changed considerably from the late 1960s, when he had occasionally criticised the southern administration for their lack of resolve in pursuing an end to partition. By the late 1980s, however, he was totally convinced of the detrimental effect of the Irish dimension: 'There was nothing in the Council of Ireland proposals which was a danger to the unionists but it was symbolic. They said it is the thin edge of the wedge. It was the Council of Ireland proposal that killed power-sharing.'[74]

Fitt's claim about the 'nationalist's' attitude does have some validity. It does seem from the minutes of the Executive that John Hume was particularly strident in his defence of the agreement and was, for example, adamant that Faulkner should not have gone to Rees with his mediation proposal.[75]

Fitt found another villain. He told me and anyone else who was prepared to listen that a speech by SDLP member Hugh Logue was primarily responsible for the fall of the Executive. It was a position he never relinquished and often spoke about. In 1998 he told the House of Lords, in the wake of the Good Friday Agreement:[76]

> When the Sunningdale Executive was set up, the cross-border bodies were then referred to as the Council of Ireland. One section of political thought in Northern Ireland said that the cross-border bodies were absolutely no danger to the unionist majority in Northern Ireland; the other section of politicians were saying the opposite. In fact one member of my own party, Mr Hugh Logue, in discussing at a press conference the Council of Ireland proposals – namely, what we have now in the north-south body – asked whether people did not realise that setting up the Council of Ireland proposals was the vehicle that would trundle the unionists into a united Ireland. Once that appeared in the press it spelt the end of the Sunningdale Executive, because that was exactly what the opponents of Sunningdale were saying.[77]

On 17 January 1974 Hugh Logue, then an SDLP assembly representative for Derry, made a speech at Trinity College Dublin, in which, it was reported, he claimed that the Council of Ireland was the 'vehicle that would trundle the unionists into a united Ireland'. Logue has clarified his position many times since, claiming in 1997, 'The line is misquoted from a speech which 24 years ago was outlining that even if the direction is set for Irish unity, the speed of movement towards its achievement depended upon consent.' He added, with some justification, 'It was outright non-sense to suggest a misquoted remark brought down a government or brought thousands of loyalists onto the streets four months after the speech was made.'[78]

The truth of the matter was that Fitt didn't like Logue and considered him one of the 'cowardly bastards'.[79] Fitt did not forgive and forget easily.

Fitt's interpretation of the detrimental impact of the Council of Ireland was a minority view within the SDLP. John Hume argued: 'It was that people did not like to see the likes of us sitting in charge of government departments and they did not like to see Fitt as the virtual deputy Prime Minister of Northern Ireland. That's what it was and that's what they said at the time.'[80] Eddie McGrady, who had been responsible for Executive planning and co-ordination, was equally candid: 'For God's sake, Hume was Minister of Commerce – unionists could not countenance that.'[81]

Denis Haughey, who was then SDLP party chairman, later said, 'A number of senior unionist politicians at the time expressed the opinion to me that the real irritant to extreme unionism was not the Council of Ireland but the thought of John Hume, Austin Currie, Paddy Devlin and Gerry Fitt exercising ministerial authority in Northern Ireland.'[82]

These opinions are given weight by the view of two of the principle unionist leaders of the time. In a letter written on 8 February 1976, a few weeks before his death in a riding accident, Faulkner wrote, 'certainly I was convinced all along that the outcry against a Council of Ireland was only a useful red-herring – the real opposition was to sharing of power'.[83] Perhaps more surprising is the admission of William Craig. His objection was not, as was widely thought, to the council but to power-sharing, which he considered a 'denial of democracy'. He added, 'I was always prepared to have a relationship with the Irish Republic provided that their relationship with us was correct. And those who say that the Council of Ireland was what tipped the strike off are talking nonsense.'[84]

This may be true, but the detrimental impact of the Irish dimension as Fitt saw it had a significant effect on his political thinking and direction. Ivan Cooper's assessment, however, claims that Fitt shifted ground much later: 'All of us in the SDLP signed up to the Council of Ireland, including Gerry. It was only later that he said we had made it too difficult for the unionists with the cross-border bodies. This was nonsense. The real problem was that the unionists didn't try and sell it.'[85]

Faulkner's memoirs do imply that Fitt's nationalism was less 'green' than some of his colleagues. Power-sharing can therefore be seen as a watershed in Fitt's career. In the 1960s, his socialistic rhetoric had always had traditional nationalist aspirations. However, in the early 1970s he and his party rejected the simplistic notion that the ending of partition was the solution to the conflict. By 1974 he appears to have gone further and begun to favour an internal resolution.

Fitt's reflections were probably pragmatic and perhaps worthy of consideration; but they remained private thoughts. If he really had any convictions he should surely have spoken out and fought for them. If Faulkner's reminiscence is correct, Fitt's nationalism in 1974 was essentially toeing the party line. Privately his politics had changed. Publicly they had not. The problem for Fitt was that he led a party that was not prepared to put the Irish dimension to one side and work in a purely Northern Ireland context.

If Fitt was convinced about the role of the Council of Ireland in the downfall of the Executive he did not seem to have had the political *nous* to realise this when it counted – when he was deputy chief of the Executive and leader of the SDLP. If he did realise it he kept his views to himself. Perhaps he felt he did not have the ability to argue his case with his political colleagues in the SDLP and convince them that (in his view) they were on the road to self-destruction. He must have believed that the survival of the Executive depended on the survival of Faulkner. This meant that concessions had to be made to guarantee Faulkner's position by ensuring that the bulk of the Protestant community was kept on side. Fitt, however, remained strangely quiet, emasculated by his party colleagues and perhaps by the sense that he was a prisoner of his earlier nationalistic rhetoric.

Despite his silence at the time, there was probably a fundamental division between Fitt and his colleagues. Fitt believed that the Executive experiment was worthy as a transforming mechanism of Northern Ireland without the Council of Ireland and that the all-Ireland dimension could be put in abeyance until progress could be made – if that would ensure the survival of power-sharing. His colleagues believed, with some justification, that power-sharing without the Irish dimension was merely an internal solution that could not be defended against the Provisionals.

Whatever the case, the SDLP wanted to have its cake and eat it. The desire for both power-sharing and an all-Ireland dimension was, after all, the agreement. The party believed it could have unionist agreement to power-sharing and a Council of Ireland at the same time. It gambled that Labour resolution and British army power would enable the SDLP and Faulkner to govern a society in which popular support was absent, or largely inert, against the powerful forces that had been unleashed by the previous years of conflict. It was wrong. The result was twenty more years of conflict. And nationalism would never again enjoy a unionist leader of the calibre and ability of Faulkner. Ironically for unionism, future attempts at negotiating a new political dispensation for Northern Ireland would force distinctly less palatable options on them.

In the period of the Executive, Fitt again showed his faith in Westminster and his socialist colleagues, but again they let him down. Rees' promise that Sunningdale would be ratified did not materialise. Orme's pledge to the SDLP that the Northern Ireland Office would act strongly against the strikers and move on internment was a total fabrication born from expediency. Wilson's speech to the loyalists was counter-productive. Paddy Devlin considered it 'a massive anti-climax offering a pathetic intervention that delivered nothing of what was promised'.[86] The Executive depended on Westminster for its survival, but the Labour government showed no signs of the courage that it 'undoubtedly had'. Fitt's confidence was misplaced: he (and others) failed to appreciate that the government would sacrifice its ideological commitment to power-sharing in order to avoid civil conflict.

The amazing things about Labour's handling of the crisis were their failure to countenance concessions to the opposition when they might have had an effect; and the extravagant surrender the government made to the strikers at the end. Acting in a part of the UK where the normal structures of civil society and representative government did not exist, they had to behave almost like pro-consuls in a colony.

Republicans were as delighted as the UWC with the fall of the Executive. They had constantly condemned both it and the Sunningdale Agreement, maintaining that Fitt and the SDLP had 'sold out' in the unification struggle. The fact that the experiment failed in the face of loyalist intransigence and British inactivity gave credibility to the republican sentiment that it was yet another example of the collaborators' blind faith in perfidious Albion, a faith that resulted inevitably in the crushing of the rights and aspirations of the minority community.

The post-Executive period would be a difficult one for the SDLP. Not only would it have to endure the gloating of loyalists and republicans, it also needed to perform effectively despite its internal differences on the Council of Ireland concept. Picking up the pieces would not be easy. Although disappointed by the disintegration of the Executive, Fitt did not despair. On 29 May, he claimed with all the accuracy of a builder's estimate that the power-sharing process had begun in Northern Ireland and it could not be stopped – it had merely received a severe temporary setback.[87] But no immediate alternative policy existed – other than a return to direct rule, which all the parties agreed was no solution. Despite any private reservations he may have had, Fitt made it clear that the SDLP would not relinquish its political *raison d'être* to maintain a minority presence in government and a formalised link with the Republic: 'The Catholic community must be allowed to aspire to the peaceful re-unification of Ireland by consent. If the Catholic community was to be asked to become unionists as such then power-sharing wouldn't be possible.'[88]

A political impasse had been reached: the Protestant community had already rejected such proposals. The Official Unionists, now under the leadership of Harry West, presented a plan for majority rule in a Stormont government with the offer of opposition participation in parliamentary committees. The proposals were strongly attacked by Faulkner and his new Unionist Party of Northern Ireland, and by Fitt, who said:

> It is in fact an attempt to resurrect the old Stormont and ascendency government which existed before direct rule, and as such, would not be acceptable and would be completely rejected by the minority in Northern Ireland. In doing so they would have support from the democratic world.
>
> If this is the final position of the Official Unionist Party, then one can only predict serious political difficulties in the future.[89]

Fitt was aware of a possible drift away from constitutional nationalism in the political vacuum that now existed. In an attempt to fill this vacuum, Rees declared that a new Northern Ireland Bill would make the Secretary of State responsible for government in the state. The Bill would provide for an elected constitutional convention, which would 'consider what provisions for the government of Northern Ireland would be likely to command most widespread acceptance throughout the community'.[90] The White Paper was somewhat vague and imprecise. It did not contain compulsory provision for power-sharing and even if it did the SDLP was, understandably, no longer convinced of British resolve. Although the White Paper mentioned the Irish dimension, it did not suggest that it would have to be acceptable to the Republic's government. The document also failed to recognise the long-term aspiration of the minority for unity. As Barry White pointed out; 'Without a strong commitment to power-sharing or an Irish dimension, the Convention would be seen as a calculated insult to the SDLP and a surrender to Protestant intransigence.'[91]

Fitt's reaction at Westminster to the new Bill reflected the SDLP's pessimism:

> I believe that the introduction of the White Paper and the Bill today represent an abject and total surrender to those forces in Northern Ireland which set about using every endeavour to bring to an end the system of government that we had under the Sunningdale Agreement. That is the way in which this measure is being interpreted in Northern Ireland.[92]

Unimpressed by developments in Northern Ireland, many SDLP members adopted a tougher line. Eddie McGrady, assembly member for South

Down, had already urged the British government to announce their intent to withdraw from Northern Ireland,[93] and after the implications of the White Paper became known Paddy Devlin, Hugh Logue, Paddy Duffy (party treasurer) and John Duffy (general secretary), all made scathing attacks on Rees and the British government.[94]

On 20 July, the UDA, which had provided the muscle behind the UWC strike, resigned from the council. Its chairman Andy Tyrie invited representatives of the Catholic community to take part in talks. He said: 'The SDLP are elected representatives and I think we would be quite prepared to speak to them. They can put across the views of ordinary Catholics. We think we will get a good response and our attitude is that we cannot go on fighting forever.'[95] Fitt was keen on talks – his socialist orientation always made him open to Protestant overtures. Discussions were held on 1 August, but the meeting proved unsuccessful. The UDA spokesman said there would be no discussions until the SDLP gave up its aspiration to a united Ireland. For his part, Fitt claimed:

> The tone and content of the UDA statement certainly does not reflect in any way the meeting which had taken place. I can only presume that there are elements within the UDA who are determined to pre-empt any useful discussions and to make certain that no useful dialogue can take place. I realise that there are many thousands of people throughout Northern Ireland who feel disappointed that nothing constructive has emerged from this meeting, and I can only reiterate that the SDLP while clinging tenaciously to its policies, will make every endeavour to unite both communities in Northern Ireland.[96]

The extent to which Fitt clung tenaciously to SDLP policy can be disputed, but the same cannot be said for Hume. On 8 August, he and some of his SDLP colleagues attacked the British, taking a more militant line. He told a party meeting in Derry that the British faced a clear choice: 'confrontation with violence or withdrawal'.[97]

At the end of the month, Fitt was part of a six-man delegation that flew to London for talks with Labour, Conservative and Liberal Party leaders, to express moderate nationalist feelings about the lack of firm direction and the continuing internment issue.[98]

The SDLP followed the trip with a conference to review party strategy. Taking part were the nineteen assembly members and the party Executive.

The conference also intended to plan policy for the forthcoming elections to Westminster and the Northern Ireland Constitutional Convention. Fitt said: 'We have said that the British government must spell out what it will accept from the political parties in Northern Ireland and what it will not accept. Otherwise people will be asked to vote at the Convention elections without being sure what they are voting for.'[99]

Increasingly disillusioned SDLP members were not helped by the attitude of the Irish government. After the failure of power-sharing, the Dublin administration showed a distinct intention to disengage from Northern Ireland affairs. On 13 June, Cosgrave said: 'They (citizens of the Republic) are expressing more and more the idea that unity or close association with a people so deeply imbued with violence and its effects is not what they want'.[100]

In September, another SDLP delegation met Harold Wilson. Before this meeting Fitt remarked: 'The situation in the North from the minority point of view, is showing daily deterioration mainly due to military bias against the Catholic population. There will have to be an end to this.'[101] He was pleased with the outcome of the meeting:

> It was a most satisfactory meeting – one of the frankest the SDLP has had with the British prime minister. Every aspect of the political situation in the North was discussed, including internment, the role of the British army, the role of the police and in particular what appeared to be unclear attitudes expressed by the British government.[102]

The SDLP seemed convinced of Britain's commitment to power-sharing and an Irish dimension and entered the October general election with this in mind. Fitt was asked by the *Belfast Newsletter* what he felt was the most important issue in the election. He replied: 'The acceptance by the whole community in Northern Ireland that there must be partnership in government and the recognition of the legitimate aspirations of this divided community, consequent upon this a complete rejection of violence.'[103] By 'legitimate aspirations' he presumably meant an Irish dimension.

Fitt was opposed in the West Belfast constituency by Johnny McQuade (the nominee of Paisley's DUP, standing on the United Ulster Unionist Coalition ticket and who had come second to Fitt in February), Kitty O'Kane of the Republican Clubs, Sam Gibson, chairman of the UVF's political wing, the Volunteer Political Party (VPP), and a Communist, Patrick Kerins.

The previous April, Rees had removed both Provisional Sinn Féin and the UVF from the list of proscribed organisations. The UVF decided to contest the election, but Provisional Sinn Féin declined. Republican criticism of the SDLP therefore came from O'Kane:

> The SDLP talk about the power-sharing Executive as if it were a golden age and have made its restoration their main political aim. The power-sharing Executive was in essence a Tory government bribe to the middle-class SDLP leadership, which helped them accept Brian Faulkner as their leader in return for whatever patronage and prestige they might get out of it.[104]

O'Kane's criticism did not stop people voting for Fitt. Despite a five per cent drop in turnout since February, he retained his seat, increasing his majority to over 5,000 votes, aided by the split in the unionist camp. O'Kane unexpectedly lost her deposit. Fitt was also possibly helped by the fact that there was no Provisional-backed candidate.

In each of the twelve seats in Ulster the UUUC put up a single candidate and had ten MPs returned. It secured fifty-eight per cent of the vote, consolidating its post-Executive position; but it lost the Fermanagh–South Tyrone seat. Before the October poll, the SDLP and McManus (the former MP for that area) had agreed on a compromise nationalist candidate – Frank Maguire. Maguire had been active in the republican movement and was interned for two years in the late 1950s. (Fitt told me that Maguire was the 'nicest man you could meet as a drinking companion but he didn't have a clue about politics'.[105]) The fact that the SDLP secured such an agreement indicated a shift of emphasis and a more nationalist attitude. Maguire's victory showed that the anti-unionist population of the area preferred any nationalist to a unionist.

The SDLP itself managed to retain the twenty-two per cent share of the vote it had achieved in February, and its total vote fell by only 4,000, despite the fact that it contested only nine out of the twelve seats. In Britain, the Labour Party increased its majority.

The October election in Northern Ireland did little more than re-confirm what the February election had already demonstrated. Although the UUUC had one less seat, they had increased their vote by 40,000.

Faulkner's Unionist Party obtained only 20,754 votes – a mere three per cent. On the basis of the October result, the UUUC would win an outright majority in the convention elections. The middle ground that had created power-sharing and Sunningdale had gone – Northern Ireland was again polarised. After the election Fitt remarked:

> I hope the Loyalists do not see the vote as a mandate to say there will be no partnership between the communities. I hope they will use their position to try to take whatever steps they can to recognise that there are two communities and that both must work together if there is to be any future for this province.[106]

There was little confidence within the SDLP, however, that this hope would be realised.

October saw an increase in sectarian attacks on Catholics from the Ulster Protestant Action Force, with ten people killed in a month. Speaking before a meeting with Wilson in which he was to ask for emergency measures to halt the murders, Fitt said; 'People are being murdered going to and from their work ... We are now at the stage where members of the public are afraid to be on the streets of Belfast.' He maintained that he would plead on behalf of all the decent people of Northern Ireland, Catholic and Protestant:

> I am not being selective. All these killings have got to stop otherwise there is no hope for Northern Ireland. There must be fathers, mothers, brothers and sisters who know the identity of these murderers and are harbouring them. Surely, they can see that only they, the community, can reject them and stop Northern Ireland bleeding to death.[107]

Rees appealed, 'I am calling once again on all responsible leaders of every section of opinion to give practical support to the RUC in their fight against criminal violence'.[108] Although not specified, Rees' appeal would have been directed primarily at the SDLP. Fitt and his colleagues did not respond.

As the PIRA campaign continued in tandem with loyalist assassinations, the pressure increased on the SDLP to give active support to the police. Hume had shaped a policy advocating that nationalists must have a role in government before the SDLP would fully endorse the RUC.[109] At the end of October he still insisted that the RUC were not acceptable to his party, although he told the *Irish News* there was no difference of opinion between himself and Fitt.[110] The subtext of his statement suggests that there probably was some disagreement. Fitt may have been leader but Hume was pulling the strings. On the following day, the SDLP assembly party reaffirmed Hume's stance.[111]

In November the SDLP's Executive committee endorsed the stand taken on policing by the party's assemblymen. Fitt did not make his opinions known to the press, suggesting he was again toeing the party line. Despite the SDLP position on the police issue, it had not endeared itself to republicans. For example, when it was announced that both party and public representatives were to visit the Long Kesh prison, where there had been some serious rioting in mid-October, republican inmates told them 'Stay away. You are not welcome.' Fitt was singled out for criticism: 'The party leader, Gerry Fitt has never visited the camp and therefore knows nothing of the conditions even though he claims to be the all-time expert, when speaking in parliament. This is pure hypocrisy and should be recognised as such.'[112]

In parliament, however, Fitt was receiving plaudits from British politicians for a speech that was considered moderate and courageous. He actually accepted a watering down of the Irish dimension:

> I concede that the Irish dimension that we envisage may not initially or in the short term have anything approaching what we had under the Sunningdale Agreement – a Council of Ireland. I shall continue to work for such an establishment. If people in Northern Ireland learn to live together, it will be essential for some means to be found to enable the Northern Ireland majority, both Catholic and Protestant, to communicate with the rest of the people in the small island of Ireland.[113]

Rees later remarked, 'Would that such an attitude have been taken in March 1974 when I arrived in the province: the UWC strike may have been prevented'.[114] Such temperance would not have been universally welcomed in the SDLP, however. Fitt also claimed, 'I have never in this House or in Northern Ireland – nor has any member of my party – condemned the RUC in total as being unacceptable.'[115] Fitt was not straying from SDLP policy, but this might have been better left unsaid. The RUC was not acceptable to a large number of Catholics, particularly since its actions during the UWC strike, and his party colleagues found it hard to praise the force. In short it seems that Fitt and Devlin did not seem to share the antipathy for the RUC of some of their colleagues and constituents. I asked Cooper if this was fair comment. He replied:

> Yes that is largely true. I didn't have much regard for the RUC because I met some of the bully-boys at first hand. It is true that Gerry had sympathy and so did Devlin. They were talking to some of the senior officers. Gerry came to the stage that he was depending on the RUC. Hume and I never had to rely on the police for protection. Gerry developed relationships because he had these official police drivers that led to relationships with senior officers.

Cooper went on to explain that there were some benefits from the relationships that Fitt cultivated.

> I can tell you this. Gerry could get information that none of the rest of us could get. The sort of information the DUP obtain now Gerry could get. He was close to police officers and he obtained 'dirt' on all sorts of people. He had 'dirt' on unionist politicians, 'dirt' on a Dublin journalist, and 'dirt' on television men. Philanderers mostly. All that came from his relationships with the RUC. He was extremely well informed. Gerry knew everything that was going on. He knew something about everyone. That was his style.[116]

The PIRA had been far from idle since the end of the UWC strike. It had witnessed the re-election of the Labour government, which it felt had surrendered to force during the strike. In an attempt to compel the British to finally pull out of Ireland, the Provisionals embarked on a campaign of violence in England. In July 1974 a woman was killed and thirty-six people injured, many seriously, by a no-warning bomb in the Tower of London, and in October five people were killed and fifty-four injured when no-warning bombs exploded at two pubs in Guildford. In early November, a bomb in Woolwich, outside London, killed two people. Finally, on 21 November, two bombs in Birmingham killed twenty-one people and injured a further 182. In response to the carnage there was an upsurge of anti-Provisional feeling in nationalist areas in Northern Ireland.[117] As a result, the Provisional leadership was receptive to a peace initiative brokered by a group of Protestant clergymen led by the Revd William Arlow, secretary of the Irish Council of Churches.

A few leading republicans met the churchmen on 10 December 1974 at Smyth's Village Hotel in Feakle, County Clare. The republican group made it clear that they were prepared to discuss a cessation of violence and immediately after this meeting contacts were made with the Northern Ireland Office (NIO) and British officials. On 19 December, the Labour government signalled its willingness to proceed with talks On the following day the PIRA council announced it would suspend operations for eleven days between 22 December and 2 January. Fitt's response to the ceasefire was:

> I welcome this announcement. Under any circumstances it is to be welcomed if it means there will be even a temporary respite from the murders and the bombings in the terrorist campaign. I fervently hope and pray that it will be continued and that we will see an end to this campaign which we have witnessed for the past five years.[118]

The general optimism was boosted further when, on 2 January 1975, the Provisionals announced that they would extend their Christmas ceasefire by fourteen days. Fitt warned, 'If after the period of ceasefire ... anyone in the PIRA was insane enough to order the resumption of hostilities then thousands of lives would be lost in a period of violence much worse than anything experienced up to the present. In such a situation the IRA would have no support.'[119]

The extension of the ceasefire had followed indications from the Northern Ireland Office that they would consider PIRA proposals – principally an end to internment in the near future and a withdrawal of British troops to barracks – if the ceasefire was extended for a further two weeks. These hints, however, were not followed by any tangible gesture and the truce was allowed to lapse. Fitt had been correct in predicting a negative reaction in nationalist areas to the resumption of the campaign. This was shown by peace marches in Belfast and Dublin on 19 January and further gatherings in Derry and Newry at the end of the month. Partly as a result of these, contact was re-established between the Provisionals and the British.

Rees was intent on trying to draw the Provisionals into the political process. On 5 February he said in the House of Commons that if the

Provisionals ceased offensive operations, the army would be gradually reduced to peacetime levels and eventually withdrawn to barracks. He also suggested that internment could be phased out.[120] Rees considered this the most important speech he had made on Northern Ireland.[121] Paddy Devlin, on the other hand, later maintained that Rees was embarking on a 'fruitless flirtation with the Provos'.[122]

On 10 February, the Provisional army council began an indefinite cease-fire, and the following day Rees announced that 'incident centres' would be set up in various parts of the state to monitor the ceasefire. The centres were set up in existing Provisional Sinn Féin offices, where possible, and were supplied with telex machines, telephones and typewriters – compliments of the NIO. The centres were staffed by members of Sinn Féin, who liaised with government officials. The prestige of the republican movement, as the Provisionals saw it, had been greatly enhanced. The creation of the centres had significant grass-roots consequences, which became clearly identifiable by the 1980s. They helped develop 'a strong community structure for Sinn Féin which the SDLP was never able to compete with'.[123]

The SDLP leader was dismayed by the preferential treatment apparently being offered to the Provisionals. In mid-January, Fitt made it clear he was against any 'political role' for republicans and had spoken out against direct peace negotiations between the Provisionals and the British government: 'That would prove that people could bomb their way to the Conference Table.'[124] There is some irony in the fact that Fitt (who had made it clear he was against any legitimation of PIRA) had opened talks with the UDA the previous August. While the UDA was not then proscribed, its association with loyalist terrorists was well known. Fitt's discomfort with concessions to republicans may have been based on the fact that loyalist subversion did not directly affect his political fortunes and so he could afford to take a risk.

The establishment of the 'incident centres' only increased tension be-tween the SDLP and Rees. At Westminster, Fitt asked: 'Will he give, through me, to my constituents an understanding that in any talk about policing or law and order in the areas concerned, the elected representatives will be listened to before the Provisional Sinn Féin spokesman?'[125] He told a *Belfast Telegraph* reporter:

> On the one hand, the government is saying that it is designed to prevent a breakdown of the ceasefire, but the IRA on the other hand are claiming

that it gives them further recognition. This is something which will have to be clarified by the government. Elected representatives on either side – whether they be unionist or SDLP – would certainly object to any influence given to paramilitary organisations which have been rejected at the ballot box.[126]

Rees' apparent placation of the Provisionals was part of a policy to try and politicise them and create a stable environment for elections to a newly instituted convention plan.

Hume had re-affirmed the SDLP position at the party conference in January 1975:

> The central element in our philosophy is that the evils of our society derive from the divisions which can be resolved in one of two says – by one side trying to dominate the other, or as we do, by abandoning the path of conflict and trying the road that has never really been tried, the way of partnership. It is simple, clear, sensible and constructive and is the essential principle of our whole analysis. We would be abandoning our total approach if we abandoned the Irish dimension.

Fitt made his customary appeal to Protestants 'who may have had fears and differences with the SDLP', to have the courage to take the possibly dangerous course of joining 'this socialist party and helping to evolve its policy'. He added, 'If this was a Catholic party, I would not be its leader. It is a socialist party'.[127]

Fitt's grip on reality must be questioned. The only evidence to suggest the SDLP was not a Catholic party was the fact that it had one Protestant founding member, Ivan Cooper. The media referred to the 'mainly Catholic SDLP', but the party would have been hard pressed to point to any significant Protestant membership. The SDLP represented, in a practical sense, the majority in the Catholic community who disapproved of the Provisionals' campaign. Protestants would not vote or join the SDLP because they knew that doing so would be interpreted as showing, not their socialist orientation, but their support for a united Ireland. As a result, the Protestant community steered well clear of the SDLP, ensuring that the party remained a tribal Catholic one. Fitt refused to acknowledge this.

There was a sense of lost opportunity among moderates in Northern Ireland since the collapse of power-sharing and the reinforcement of unionist resistance to change in the October 1974 parliamentary election. The SDLP did not approach the convention election with much hope of success. The conference had voted for power-sharing and a strong Irish dimension as a prerequisite for the return of the SDLP to Executive government. This was reflected in the party manifesto, 'Speak with Strength', formulated for the convention elections.

> There is an Irish dimension to the problem. There is a British dimension to the problem. Any solution must take account of both. The principles on which our solution is based take account of both dimensions, as well as the most important Northern Ireland dimension itself, and do in fact command the most widespread acceptance among the people of these islands.[128]

Fitt displayed some optimism. 'If I thought the Convention was going to break down in a couple of weeks we would not be fighting this election.'[129] Such optimism was misplaced: the UUUC manifesto was virtually the antithesis of the SDLP's, calling for majority rule and no Dublin interference in Northern Ireland's affairs. Provisional Sinn Féin called on nationalist voters to boycott the election, arguing that the convention experiment was simply pointless. PSF's claim that fifty-three per cent of the people of Andersonstown would boycott the convention election was rubbished by Fitt:

> I think Sinn Féin are inclined to take themselves much too seriously; certainly more seriously than anyone else is prepared to take them in either the North or West Belfast constituencies. It is absolutely laughable that the poll which they allege they have conducted should have shown that 53 per cent of the people in Andersonstown were not prepared to vote. I would like to know who these people are as I understand from my colleagues that our own canvass returns indicate overwhelming support and that the SDLP can win four seats.[130]

At this point, Fitt was clearly confident of both his and the SDLP's position in Belfast.[131]

As the election grew nearer, Fitt told the *Belfast Telegraph*:

> There can be no running away from our obligations in this election – the

whole future of this country depends on it. There is no such thing as a no vote for that will be a vote for Loyalist ascendancy and for domination politics to continue. That can only lead to a continuation of bitterness and dissension.[132]

Provisional Sinn Féin continued to attack the SDLP:

Parties like the SDLP which crawl to this conference table will be indulging in masochistic ritual self-humiliation ... There is nothing for the Catholic people of the six counties in the proposed Convention and the SDLP knows it. They have gone one step too far, and have left the electorate behind.[133]

The election results showed that the boycott had failed to win many converts from the SDLP. The party received 156,000 votes (23.7 per cent of the first preference vote), only 4,000 less than the high in 1973. This drop, however, did result in the loss of two seats from the nineteen in the assembly. But the SDLP could say that it had maintained its political mandate, and Fitt topped the poll in his native North Belfast. The UUUC had forty-seven members elected to the Convention (54.8 per cent of the first preference vote), a substantial majority over the opposition and, in its view, a mandate to oppose change. After the election Fitt remarked, 'If we do not find the solution this time, we could find the world watching a lot of dead people here.'[134] He was correct in his analysis. The results showed that there was little desire for moderate politics and policies. Compromise would be difficult and as a result many in the SDLP toughened their stance on constitutional issues.

Nonetheless, the Northern Ireland Convention members began the job of finding an acceptable political future for Northern Ireland on 8 May 1975, and Rees hoped that 'Ulster nationalism' could formulate a system of government that would be widely accepted in the country. In his opening address, however, Fitt again emphasised the SDLP's commitment to an Irish rather than an 'Ulster' dimension:

... again I must say that however evocative, emotional or frustrating the term may be, there is an Irish dimension to Northern Ireland and its problems. We all live on this island and if we are ever to eradicate violence from these shores it must be done in co-operation with all those governments and authorities who have the power to do so. From that one viewpoint alone, I would suggest that there is a clearly defined Irish dimension. This is not the time to go into all the contentious issues that will be discussed later at the Convention but I think it is right to put on record my feeling at this time.[135]

It is difficult to ascertain to what extent these 'feelings' were his own or those of his party. What is certain is that his stance did not bode well for the convention's prospects of success. If Fitt was merely mouthing party principles, he was guilty of lack of conviction in his own political instincts. The UUUC candidates were pledged to reject power-sharing in any form, and they were emphatically against an Irish dimension. As the convention approached its summer recess, there were few signs of progress.

In August, however, an opportunity for political progress came from an unlikely source. William Craig put forward a proposal for voluntary coalition for the duration of 'Northern Ireland's emergency'. His idea was to institute a temporary partnership between the UUUC and SDLP, similar to British wartime coalition governments. Hume, Devlin and Currie represented the SDLP in talks that proved fruitless and were finally scuppered by Paisley having heard that members of his church had no desire to share power with the SDLP.

Fitt was not involved in the talks, probably for the same reasons that he stayed in the background during the crucial discussions at Sunningdale: his political skills were best used elsewhere. But Eamon Phoenix gives a fascinating insight into Fitt's political thinking in an 'extraordinary memo' recording a private meeting between Fitt and the convention chairman, Sir Robert Lowry. The memo is dated 25 August 1975, when talks between the SDLP and the UUUC had reached crisis level. Fitt's negativity was very clear. He was pessimistic about the chances of agreement coming from the convention and feared this might be the mechanism to facilitate a British withdrawal:

At the meeting Mr Fitt expressed gloom at the prospects of the convention. He considered that most of the British Labour Party and many Conservatives were keen to disengage from Northern Ireland once the convention had failed to provide a solution and a further period of direct rule had elapsed. He thought that the prime minister, Harold Wilson, would be one of the main advocates of this method of 'solving the Irish

Question'.

Fitt suspected that the UUUC wanted independence, an outcome that would, Fitt believed, lead to a bloodbath.

Fitt took the view that the recent attacks on the secretary of state by the UUUC indicated a wish by the latter for independence. He foresaw that such a step would be economically disastrous and would result in the slaughter of many Catholics. At one time his friends in England would have tried to avoid such a severance, if only because of the fear that violence would spread to Britain; they did not now fear this and they believed that the new anti-terrorist laws were a protection. The Irish government, on the other hand, 'dreaded the effect of mass deportations' of undesirables from England to the south'.

The memo included Fitt's personal verdicts on certain individuals.

Fitt said the Belfast lawyer and former DUP chairman Desmond Boal was 'a sinister influence who held court at home and entertained Paisley, Devlin and others. Boal favoured some kind of independence and was consumed by hatred of all things England'. His SDLP colleague, Paddy Devlin, was 'a good man but susceptible to flattery'. John Hume was described as 'an inflexible fanatic who saw everything in terms of Derry and could not take a wider view'. Austin Currie, on the other hand, was 'very intelligent, able and sincere'.

The memorandum also reveals the concern expressed by Fitt and the SDLP that the British were in effect suspending constitutional politics while negotiating with the PIRA:

Fitt complained at the NIO attitude to the IRA and their recent evasions concerning the possible arrest of the IRA leader Seamus Twomey. 'According to sources, Twomey had been spotted in Belfast but the authorities had failed to arrest him owing to the IRA ceasefire.'

Mr Fitt continued: 'Dublin were disgusted, considering that for years the British government had been regarding Twomey as one of the most wanted men.' Leading IRA figure Daithi O'Connell had, Mr Fitt thought, got himself arrested in order to be out of the way during forthcoming violence.

Phoenix also reported the response from Lowry, which reflected both the rigid party positions and stagnant political situation:

> The SDLP leader stressed that his party considered full power-sharing essential and their contribution to a compromise would be to support the institutions of the state. (Sir Robert noted: 'This was exactly Hume's line when I saw the SDLP negotiators.')
>
> Responding to Mr Fitt, Sir Robert observed that both the SDLP and UUUC considered agreement to be vital, but each considered that the other party was bound to 'see sense and abandon its position'. He said he did not think it likely that power-sharing would be imposed or, if imposed, that it would bring a peaceful solution.

Sir Robert concluded his note: 'We agreed that it was most important that the parties [at Stormont] should keep talking in case something could be found on which they agreed and also because it would look absurd to admit failure after the comparatively short discussions already held.'

No wonder Fitt was so gloomy. The political situation was deadlocked and the power-sharing concept he held so dear was a non-starter. No wonder also, considering some of Fitt's remarks, that the dossier that contained the memo was labelled by Lowry's own hand, 'Not for file until conclusion of Convention'.[136]

Fitt of course still had his public persona as the lone SDLP voice at Westminster and he continued to complain about British co-operation with the Provisionals, maintaining that this would give the PIRA respectability in the urban ghettos.[137] He also kept up his incessant attacks on the 'men of violence'. Speaking at the inaugural meeting of the new SDLP branch in South Antrim, he said 'Make no mistake about it but the murdering gangs who are now rampant have one ambition only – to wreck the Convention and thus keep the community in turmoil. The wild men must be rejected both by the politicians and by the people otherwise the future will be very dark indeed.'[138]

Fitt was repeating his criticisms because of ceasefire problems for the republicans. The ceasefire was formally agreed only with the army and the RUC, and the PIRA reserved the right to 'protect' the nationalist community. The organisation could not always maintain complete discipline, and many maverick Provisionals who were unhappy with the ceasefire set out on their own missions: and sectarian violence continued. On 31 July, the UVF killed three members of the Miami Showband near the border. On 15 August, five people were killed and forty injured in a PIRA attack on a pub in the Shankill Road in Belfast. On 1 September, four Protestants were killed outside their Orange Hall in South Armagh.

It was against this bloody backdrop that the unsuccessful talks between the SDLP and UUUC took place, and such atrocities were not conducive to concessions on power-sharing. The unionist majority pushed its own report through and the SDLP effectively ceased to participate. The convention wound up in early November with the unionist report calling for majority rule as its main proposal. The British government refused to accept such a hard-line recommendation. During the convention's final debate Fitt said that the institution had at least identified 'those members who were prepared to try and find a solution and those who were not'.[139] Indefinite direct rule loomed large.

The convention was in almost total disarray, the truce between the British and the Provisionals had become increasingly meaningless and it was clearly evident to all sides that the ceasefire had effectively ended. Rees made this official on 4 November, when he announced that 'special category status' was to cease.[140] The British had decided to adopt the criminalisation approach to Northern Ireland: the Provisionals, both within the prison system and without, were to be represented as hooligans, thugs and gangsters.

In the absence of cross-party agreement, Rees' methodology can be summed up as 'Ulsterisation', the intention being similar to the United States' policy of 'Vietnamisation' in South East Asia. President Nixon's plan was to encourage the South Vietnamese to take more responsibility for fighting the war, hoping that this would eventually enable the United States gradually to withdraw all its soldiers from Vietnam. In essence it was an exit strategy. Rees likewise hoped progressively to withdraw the British army and replace it with the RUC and UDR. An important component of the British plan was completed on 12 November, when Rees announced that the incident centres were to be closed.[141]

At the end of November the SDLP held its fifth annual conference. Fitt claimed that nine of the ten unionists MPs were trying to bring about total integration of the north with Britain.[142] It was a perturbed conference. At previous conferences political initiatives beckoned: the assembly election, the formation of the power-sharing Executive and the convention elections. All had failed and the party seemed to have no means of influencing the British government. There was one bright spot, however. On 5 December, internment ended. The continued use of detention without trial had always been a thorn in the SDLP's side, and consistently undermined its credibility. Its termination was welcomed by Fitt:

> I am thankful that the evil scourge of internment has been brought to an end. From the very second of its inception, we recognised the political disaster that it would be, antagonising as it did the entire Catholic community. Thousands and thousands of the minority were alienated by the imposition of this scourge of their fellow co-religionists. People who, in normal circumstances, would give no support whatsoever to any men of violence felt themselves alienated from every political institution in Northern Ireland. After four and a half years of personal tragedy to those who were interned, and particularly their wives and families, we have now come to the end of an era in our political development.[143]

At Westminster Fitt told Rees, 'Now that we have got rid of the running sore of detention, I and my colleagues will do everything in our power to involve the minority community in your attempt to reject the gunmen there'.[144]

However, 1976 began violently when loyalists killed five Catholics in South Armagh on 4 January and republicans shot dead ten Protestants at Kingsmills the following day. The victims had been ordered out of a hijacked workers' minibus and the only Catholic present ordered to step aside before the appalling act was committed. Fitt condemned both deeds:

> There are no words in any language which could adequately express the shock, revulsion and anger I feel at the barbaric crimes committed in Co. Armagh. I hope to God the people who know the identity of these murderers will take the necessary steps to rid them from our midst. I would also make an appeal to all those who would listen to my voice not to think for a second of revenge. This can only bring further tragedy.[145]

Rees, who was becoming increasingly desperate, again tried to get talks underway. In mid-January he announced at Westminster that the convention was to be reconvened from 3 February. Fitt was asked by an *Irish News* reporter if he felt Rees' move had bolstered the SDLP's position. He answered:

> I would not want to say he has bolstered the SDLP position because that might create antagonism. The Secretary of State had however, reinforced the SDLP view that there would be no return to a devolved government on the lines of the old Stormont but that there would be a government which would embrace both communities.[146]

On the day the UUUC–SDLP talks were due to start, news came of the death of Frank Stagg, an IRA hunger-striker in a British prison who had demanded special category status and a return to Ireland to serve his sentence. There was considerable violence in West Belfast and other Catholic areas, and, just as in the previous August, the atmosphere was not conducive to compromise. On the same day, the SDLP, perhaps fearing a loss of support to more extreme republicans, withdrew from the talks, claiming that the UUUC was not prepared to discuss power-sharing. The talks had lasted for an hour.

On 5 March, the failure of the convention was officially acknowledged and Westminster formally dissolved it. Fitt was under no illusions about who had held back progress: 'The man personally responsible for the downfall of the Convention was none other than a Member of this House, the Hon. Member for Antrim North, Mr Ian Paisley.'[147] The dissolution of the convention strongly indicated the non-existence of a middle ground; for most people direct rule was the best solution. On 25 March Rees officially announced the 'Ulsterisation' of the conflict, or, as he termed it 'police primacy'.

The post-Executive period was a difficult time for the SDLP. Despite individual party members voicing more militant opinions and the SDLP/McManus deal over participation in the Fermanagh–South Tyrone constituency, the SDLP did not radically change its politics. The British government's failure to accede to the party's requests and its courting of republicans could well have tempted the party to revert to republican orthodoxy in a form reminiscent of the old Nationalist Party. However, the SDLP was committed to constitutionalism and compromise and in the end agreed to participate in the convention.

In its eight-month existence the Constitutional Convention accomplished nothing. The SDLP's twin aims of power-sharing and the Irish dimension had been rejected. The future of the party looked bleak and, apart from its one MP at Westminster, it was not represented in any forum. As a consequence there was some in-house reflection. The SDLP still wanted an equitable system of government and a strong Irish dimension, but the unionist veto had obstructed any progress. Therefore the veto would have to be sidelined. This could only be achieved by a political framework that recognised the existence of two distinct identities and insisted on an Irish dimension.

Fitt's rhetoric had upheld the SDLP's aspiration for an Irish dimension. If (as is probable) he was not as committed to it as some of his colleagues, his reservations were disguised. It is possible that he tried to direct the SDLP away from nationalism. Or perhaps he was happy with the party direction and only later distanced himself from nationalism and the Irish dimension. It is difficult to be certain.

In the period after the Executive the Labour Party again disappointed Fitt. Despite all his pleadings, Rees had belittled the importance of elected representatives by bargaining with the Provisionals. When 'special category status' was eventually terminated, it was too late, since the PIRA had gained further credibility. The ending of internment also came too late for the SDLP to gain any benefit.

Fitt continued to urge Protestants to join the SDLP, but his unstinting claim that his was a socialist and not a Catholic party fell on deaf ears. He was likewise unstinting in his attacks on the Provisionals. In November 1975, he claimed the 'Provos had sullied the name of republicanism and had dragged the Irish Tricolour and the Starry Plough into the gutter'.[148] However, the Provisionals were a reality and, although in their political infancy, they were waiting in the wings ready to capitalise on SDLP failures. It was significant that the two seats lost by the SDLP in the convention elections were in the republican strongholds of South Armagh and South Derry. In May 1975, Fitt's leadership of the party was assured when he was re-elected.[149] Ciaren McKeown reported on the SDLP's fifth annual conference in November 1975:

> ... Familiarity with their leaders has brought respect rather than. contempt. And Gerry Fitt, with that unique blend of humanity, wit and native intelligence which is the secret of his political flair, has no serious rivals for the leadership. There is, of course, a residual faction of the more academic or formal, whose instincts are for a more controllable leader,

but he can usually make them laugh too. Shortly after acknowledging an outstanding ovation for an address in which he had them laughing and cheering he was jokingly asked 'so it looks as if you're going to stay in the party for another while, Gerry?' 'Aye, as long as it's going my way', he replied. There is more than a grain of truth in the observation that if the time ever comes when he is totally happy with the party, either he will be finished or the party will.[150]

McKeown's comment was prophetic. The responsibilities of leading a democratic party did not sit easily with Fitt. Individualism was fine and workable in his circumstances in the 1960s, but the 1970s had produced different and, in many ways, more complex circumstances. After six years the SDLP had no tangible gains to boast of. In the years to come it was to change course, and this shift in direction would see Fitt increasingly isolated and would eventually lead to his resignation.

The fall of the Executive and the failure of political initiatives following its collapse placed the SDLP in a position of political impotence. The party's main activities would be conducted in diplomatic, inter-governmental and trans-Atlantic contexts by those with the necessary skills. The days of the agitator had gone and the days of the statesman had come. This was the domain of John Hume, not of Gerry Fitt.

6

ISOLATION AND RESIGNATION

On 28 October 1975 Fitt told the *Belfast Telegraph*: 'I have always identified myself with the Labour Party since I was elected ... I cannot
foresee any situation in which I would lend my support to the defeat of
the present government'.[1]

By March 1979 he had radically altered his position and was prepared to allow a Conservative administration to attain power, a fateful
decision that led to eighteen years of Tory government. He told the same
newspaper, 'I certainly will not support the Labour government in a vote of
confidence. My constituents' interests and those of Northern Ireland must
be paramount.'[2] Clearly, Fitt felt that circumstances had changed to such
an extent that he had to subordinate his socialist leaning to a nationalistic
position. The irony of this was that Fitt resigned from the SDLP in the
same period because he felt it had become too nationalist. How this
paradoxical situation came about is worth investigating in detail.

Although the British Labour Party had improved its position in the
October 1974 general election by gaining eighteen seats, its overall majority in the House of Commons was only three. Fitt and Frank Maguire (MP
for Fermanagh–South Tyrone) were considered important 'independents'.
Fitt seemed intent on supporting the socialist policies of the Labour Party
as he had done since 1966. A week after the failure of the convention he
said, 'However harsh the present Labour government may have shown
itself to be over the expenditure cuts, they are infinitely preferable to a
government which might be led by Mrs Thatcher[3] and her cohorts.'[4]

When James Callaghan took over the premiership from Harold Wilson
in April 1976, Fitt continued to believe that the administration would
remain committed to finding an agreement between both communities
in Northern Ireland.[5] By the end of April, however, he had changed his
tune, telling the Labour Party Whips that his support in the lobbies could

not be taken for granted. He felt the government was being lulled into viewing direct rule as an acceptable short-term solution.[6]

Fitt was looking for some political assurances about Northern Ireland policy from the new Prime Minister before renewing his loyalty to Labour, and in the following week he received them. On 4 May, he met Callaghan to discuss his concern about government policy. During this meeting, he was apparently told that there was no change in Labour policy and afterwards said:

> Beforehand I was concerned that the government might have been tempted to swallow the view put around by some unionist politicians – particularly Mr Enoch Powell – that nothing should be done in Northern Ireland in the hope that total integration would be acceptable as a solution. I am convinced that it is not a solution and never will be.[7]

At this point an abstention by Fitt would not have been crucial, but the episode does show where his allegiance lay. On this occasion, his misgivings were mollified, but Fitt was essentially pragmatic in his relations *vis-à-vis* London, so his local focus would mean any support for Callaghan would be conditional.

While Fitt was occupied at Westminster, his SDLP colleagues had ample time to dwell on their political impotence. Some of them began to question fundamental party principles.

In June, Paddy Devlin argued for an independent Northern Ireland, maintaining that this would remove the British presence and thus the basis for republican paramilitary violence. The 'negotiated independence' idea would promote reconciliation and 'allow Northern Ireland to develop and prosper as an independent entity'.[8] Mainstream unionism was horrified at such a proposal, as was Fitt. He totally rejected the notion of 'negotiated independence', claiming that only reconciliation between the majority and minority communities in the north within a British–Irish context offered the hope of real political progress.[9] At this point he feared the political domination of Catholics by Protestants, without the safeguards underwritten by the two governments. (Devlin himself ultimately lost interest in the scheme when a loyalist group whose remit it was to explore the virtues of the plan managed only to come up with the blueprint for a new flag.)[10]

Fitt continued to clash with the Tory opposition at Westminster. The

Conservative spokesman on Northern Ireland, Airey Neave, was extremely critical of government policy in the state and advocated integration, as well as tough military measures against the IRA. He criticised Labour policy towards guerilla warfare in Northern Ireland as 'half-hearted', and demanded, 'They should go on the offensive and declare war on the terrorists now.' Fitt predicted that any military solution sought in the event of a Tory government coming into power would bring nothing but tragedy and disaster to Northern Ireland.[11]

Although it was the Conservatives who had abolished Stormont and formulated the Sunningdale experiment, Fitt was still instinctively anti-Tory. He still had a naive faith in the Labour Party and his adherence to socialism clouded his judgement on what Tory or Labour governments might offer Northern Ireland.

Despite Fitt's vociferous campaigning at Westminster against any military solution, there were elements in the nationalist community who were turning against him. This was largely a result of his criticism of the PIRA. On 9 August, the fifth anniversary of internment, Fitt was forced to hold an angry mob at bay with a revolver after they burst into his home. He, his wife Ann and daughter Geraldine were treated for shock. Fitt remained characteristically defiant: 'I have taken a stand throughout my political life. I am opposed to violence in all forms. I might die, my wife might die, but I am not going to be intimidated. I will go on saying what I believe to be right.'[12]

He described the ordeal in the *Irish News*:

I picked up my gun and went to the bedroom door and there they were standing at the top of the stairs. I pointed the gun at them and said: Move, get down the stairs or you're dead. They began backing off and I followed them down the stairs until I was standing at the bottom holding them at bay in the hall ... If I hadn't had a gun, I'm sure I would be dead now. I don't think they would have shot me, but they would probably have kicked me to death.[13]

The following day he again attacked the Provisionals: 'The only way the Provisional IRA can be defeated is by the Catholic population standing together and rejecting them. The Catholic people must make their voices heard against violence and intimidation ... The IRA will not be driving me out'.[14]

Reaction to the attack was predictably mixed. While many Protestants were sympathetic towards Fitt, they took issue with his public position on the RUC. *Ulster*, the newspaper of the UDA, declared:

> Yes, Mr Fitt, we condemn this cowardly attack on your home by republican scum. But we also condemn the way you used the TV and newspapers to go police bashing. [Fitt had called for an enquiry into why calls for help to the RUC and army went unheeded. The security forces arrived too late to thwart the attack.] You cannot expect law and order in either Catholic or Protestant areas if you do not fully support those who carry it out. The amount of Loyalists and Protestants behind the wire at present proves that the police are doing their duty impartially but as long as you advocate that the police will not be accepted in Catholic areas you only leave the Catholic supporters at the mercy of republican scum who by force and intimidation regard themselves as the rightful heroes of Irish destiny.[15]

The *Orange Standard*, in a tone of patronising irony, deplored the publicity attracted by an incident in which no fatalities occurred. This, it stated, was in sharp contrast to the recent murder of an RUC constable, an event that had brought no flowers from Prime Minister Callaghan.[16] These sentiments contrasted sharply with editorials in English newspapers, which showered him with praise. The *Daily Mirror* chose to reinforce unflattering stereotypes of the Irish by asking:

> What were the mob remembering this time? It could have been the anniversary of the day King Billy's garter snapped. Or the day Daniel O'Connell had his wisdom teeth removed.
>
> It's all the same to the gangs who rampaged through Belfast on Sunday night, and the bully boys who forced their way into Mr Fitt's home.[17]

In a similar vein, the *Sun* suggested 'August is for holidays in the rest of Britain. In Ulster it is the month of the terrorist and the hooligan. If there is to be any hope for the battered province it can only come – in the words of the courageous Belfast MP, Gerry Fitt – from standing up to intimidation.'[18]

The tabloid press was not the only medium to express admiration of Fitt; the *Guardian* did likewise:

That Gerry Fitt lived to tell his story yesterday may well have been due to his courage and to the gun which – reluctantly – he has kept by his side, knowing how totally exposed he has been over the past few years to the retribution of those who seek solutions in Ireland wholly by terror and destruction.[19]

Condemnation of the attack on the Fitt family appeared in the pro-Conservative *Daily Mail*, which devoted a full-page article to the incident entitled 'The defiant family Fitt declare: We will not be moved.'[20]

The British media had always been sympathetic to Fitt since the injury he sustained in Derry in October 1968. Throughout the 1970s he had been presented as a man of moderation faced by overwhelming odds. This latest incident served to endear him further to the journalists of Fleet Street. There was no denying Fitt's physical courage, but it is clear that the right-wing British press was quite prepared to exploit him for propaganda purposes. Interestingly the Reverend Martin Smyth, Grand Master of the Orange Order, who had been elected to the constitutional convention for South Belfast, and Gerry Adams (not a natural ally by any means) both later suggested that there was something 'theatrical' about the whole incident.[21]

Against this backdrop of republican harassment, Fitt would in retrospect be resentful that his SDLP colleagues (in his opinion) took 'Hume's advice' and 'kept their heads down', the 'rural element' qualifying its condemnation of the IRA by arguing that the Provos were 'Catholic Irish' and therefore, by implication, defensive. Fitt was clearly unconvinced:

I said 'Catholic Irish; bollocks. They are a crowd of fucking murderers.' So I was always pinpointed by the IRA and Sinn Féin. They would say 'That bastard, he means what he says.' They would say things like 'But John Hume he is different and Paddy Devlin was an ex-internee. They are all right, but Fitt's against us.' So they started attacking my house. They didn't attack anybody else's house. John Hume never had a window broken in his life. Neither did the rest of them.[22]

Fitt's sense of victimhood was entirely understandable given his experience, although he omitted to mention that colleagues such as Paddy Devlin and Austin Currie had in fact been persecuted by republicans for their outspoken political views.

The day after the attack on Fitt's home, soldiers were pursuing an injured PIRA gunman in a car, which went out of control near Finaghy, killing the three children of Mrs Anne Maguire. The next day, the 'Northern Ireland Peace People' movement was formed by Mrs Maguire's sister Mairead Corrigan and her friend Betty Williams. Some 10,000 people marched at its first rally on 14 August, and double that number on 28 August. Momentum grew as both Catholics and Protestants joined the movement. Fitt welcomed their appearance:

No politician worthy of the name can now show less courage than that seen in our streets within recent weeks by these women and men. Politicians must now listen to the clear voice of their own constituents which has united with that of their political opponents in a demand for action along the lines indicated by them.[23]

This public display of support contrasted with his private thoughts, however. Ivan Cooper maintained:

Gerry didn't like the Peace Women. He didn't like the leaders Betty Williams and Mairead Corrigan. He simply did not like them. The primary reason for that was that here were people commanding headlines and having a reasonable amount of public support. Gerry didn't like people leading a mass movement other than him. He was intolerant.[24]

Once again, Fitt was expressing private concerns about a potential threat to his power base in the West Belfast constituency, just as he had done – for entirely different reasons – when PIRA appeared several years earlier.

Despite Fitt's reservations a general and genuine war-weariness and the glare of the media ensured that the Peace Movement found a very receptive audience. Paddy Devlin had warned the Peace People not to 'go political', but the movement became more and more identified with condemning Provisional but not security force violence. In short, the organisation became perceived as anti-republican in its West Belfast cradle, and this would prove fatal. Kevin Kelley describes the reason for the crusade's demise:

If nothing else, the Peace People proved that no public group can possibly be non-political. Even when an organisation claims not to be interested in economic or social debates, it is necessarily taking a political position – one that favours the established order by default. It was this wilfully ignored factor that ultimately caused the movement to peter-out less than one year after that hot August afternoon in 1976.[25]

Fitt himself saw the political realities of the situation:

I repeat that the SDLP wants to see every success visited upon the Peace Movement in Northern Ireland, but at the end of the day political decisions will have to be taken, and I know that the people who are marching in support of peace will have to depend on their elected representatives. I only hope that I will be one.[26]

At the beginning of September, the British government changed officials but not policy in the Northern Ireland Office, and Roy Mason, the man chosen by Callaghan to replace Rees, personified the policy shift towards the criminalisation of PIRA. Fitt considered it 'disastrous'. He told me: 'Mason was an arrogant bumptious little bastard. A nasty wee c***. The way he spoke on the TV was even driving me into the arms of the IRA. I was even beginning to think they were right. He drove the SDLP to become more green – more nationalist – because of his arrogant manner.'[27] This suggests that he identified more readily with what he termed the 'green wing' of the SDLP during Mason's tenure in Northern Ireland.

Mason was a very direct Yorkshireman, a coalminer at the age of fourteen, and very much on the right wing of the Labour Party. Before his appointment he held a position in the Ministry of Defence, and his security background seemed ideal for implementing a series of measures designed to crush the Provisionals. He showed little interest in promoting political initiatives, calculating that such innovations had in the past created more conflict. A period of stable and resolute government was necessary. This annoyed the SDLP, which felt it was the responsibility of the British to create the necessary conditions for political progress.

Fitt's opinion of Mason changed little. On the night of the appointment he commented, 'He is an anti-Irish wee get',[28] and was so upset at the arrangement that he refused even to meet Mason.[29] There was a personal element in the political differences between the two men. Mason was not particularly enamoured of Fitt. In a television interview he described Fitt as being 'like a tap, he can switch on and switch off and he can turn from hot to cold'.[30] Despite their similar backgrounds, the relationship between the two men was acrimonious, and such a discordance was detrimental for Northern Ireland politics. Both would end their political careers in the House of Lords. The unionists, though, were delighted with the new man, who they thought would listen to the army and prioritise security.[31]

In response to Mason's appointment, the SDLP issued a statement asking for clarification of the British position. It declared: 'The first thing the British government must now do is state bluntly what are their intentions, both short-term and long-term, for the future of Northern Ireland.' The party wanted assurances on power-sharing and the Irish dimension. It also asked if the British were hiding behind a loyalist veto:

> When the British government repeatedly underline their guarantees to the unionist population of membership of the United Kingdom, are these guarantees unconditional? Are there any terms to be fulfilled in order to retain membership of the United Kingdom? If so, what are they? If not, is a section of the unionist population, a tiny percentage of the UK population, to have a permanent veto on how Northern Ireland is to be governed within the UK?[32]

The language and tone of the statement indicated that SDLP politicians felt their hopes and aspirations were to be subjugated to the interests of political unionism, which would make their own strategy redundant. This suspicion was not unfounded. Mason felt a devolved administration was a non-starter. He wanted a policy that would wean support away from the Provisionals by improving social and economic conditions. As a result the SDLP turned to Dublin. A four-man delegation – Fitt, Devlin, Hume and Currie – urged the Irish government to impress on Britain that new initiative was needed to end the political deadlock in the north.[33] This course of action proved fruitless. Cosgrave's administration was still reluctant to get involved, particularly after the Dublin/Monaghan bombings; and Callaghan, like Mason, did not prioritise political advance, apart from occasionally mentioning that there would have to be partnership government.

Fitt finally agreed to meet Mason in October after a brief escalation in sectarian violence.[34]

In Britain meanwhile, the Labour Party had been defeated in two by-elections, which meant that Fitt and Maguire became more important during a period when the government hoped to push some controversial bills through the Commons. Maguire came close to practising the abstentionist policy favoured by republicans and had rarely attended at Westminster. On this occasion, however, he was believed to have told Labour Whips that he would turn up to vote with the government. Fitt explained his own position:

> As far as the two by-election defeats are concerned, it will not affect my view about the necessity to support the government on this occasion. On such socialist measures as pay beds, aircraft and shipbuilding nationalisation and comprehensive education, I will certainly be supporting the government. However, on other matters – particularly those relating to Northern Ireland – I will have to review the situation as it comes along.[35]

On his election to Westminster in 1966, Fitt had simply demanded British rights for the citizens of Northern Ireland. By the mid 1970s, however, he had drawn a sharp distinction between British politics and Northern Irish politics. In the event, the two nationalist representatives duly came through for the Labour Party, which won by a single vote a motion to cut short discussion on the Shipbuilding and Aircraft Nationalisation Bill. Afterwards Fitt reaffirmed his position:

> I only hope to be able to continue my representations to a socialist government on behalf of my constituents, but if the time should ever arise when there appears to be a conflict between the interests of a British government and the welfare of my constituents, I will have no hesitation in placing that welfare in first priority.[36]

What did Fitt mean by the 'welfare of his constituents'? It seems he wanted the benefits of British socialist measures while at the same time making it clear that his socialism would be subordinated to nationalist principles. This posture was paradoxical when we consider that, privately at least, Fitt felt that SDLP nationalism was too strident. Fitt's justification for keeping an ailing administration in power needed to be justified, so bland statements like this were recounted regularly to deflect any local criticism of his position.

The tensions within the SDLP became apparent at the party's annual conference at the end of the year. It became clear that some members wanted a change of direction, or at the very least an exploration of alternatives to the policy of power-sharing with an Irish dimension. There was anger at both unionist inflexibility and what was perceived as British inactivity. An attempt to challenge the policy of partnership government within the United Kingdom was met by Fitt: 'In the end we will be proved right. We believe that our policy of partnership and reconciliation is the correct one and that it is the only policy that will bring peace to Northern Ireland.'[37] The motion was defeated but a significant one-third of the delegates present voted for a proposal to refer back to the SDLP's ruling Executive a document on party policy.

Paddy Devlin raised the question of negotiated independence and was supported by Seamus Mallon, who considered it a 'viable halfway house' on the way to unity.[38] Fitt was again totally against this idea: 'I cannot foresee the day when I would support the idea of independence for Northern Ireland. It would leave the Catholic community in a very vulnerable position'.[39] The conference agreed by 147 votes to fifty-one that the party should make its own study of the prospects of negotiated independence, although it was emphasised that this did not mean that the party accepted the principle. The *Belfast Telegraph* reported that Fitt would reconsider his position if the party adopted independence as a policy.[40] He clearly did not think the unionists would play fair in an independent Northern Ireland. He envisaged a situation in which the majority would attempt to re-impose its will on the nationalist community, negating all the gains that had been made since the dissolution of Stormont in March 1972. When it was made clear that Mason had no intention of pulling out, the idea lost any appeal that it may have had.

The most serious challenge to party policy was a resolution calling for British withdrawal. This was put forward by Paddy Duffy, an SDLP representative for mid-Ulster: 'We have to realise that any settlement for the North will have to be put to the people of the South in a referendum. The fact that a British presence continues to be a referee between the two sections of our community prevents us from getting together to solve our problems.'[41] Mallon seconded the motion: 'We oppose the British presence. This party fundamentally wants to see the end of British rule in this part of Ireland.'[42] Fitt, Hume and Currie argued against the proposal.[43] The motion was defeated by 158 votes to 111, but the result indicated a further swing to old-style nationalism.[44] Furthermore, of the seventeen SDLP convention members, ten voted for the motion, including Devlin, Cooper, McGrady and Joe Hendron, then an SDLP representative for West Belfast.

The SDLP had renewed its strategy of partnership government – but only just, and in the midst of irreconcilable attitudes. Many (not only in the rank and file) believed the British presence in Northern Ireland was the greatest hindrance to political progress. Maintaining a cohesive political party would be difficult for Fitt and the leadership. Currie read the situation accurately:

> It was a chastening experience for the Leadership. We had won the day, but the fact that so many of the leading lights in the party supported a radical change in direction could not be ignored. The fact that a majority of the Assembly party, which had elected the leadership, had opposed Gerry, John and myself on the crucial policy position could clearly have repercussions for us.[45]

This torpid political scenario extended into 1977 with Fitt continuing to urge Mason to adopt some form of initiative.[46] Mason was unmoved by such promptings: 'I should not like to say emphatically and dogmatically that there will be no political initiatives from Her Majesty's Government, but I am not satisfied that the time is right or opportune.'[47] Hume voiced his opinion of the consequences of political inertia: 'The terrible danger is that if constitutional political parties such as the SDLP are seen to be having no success, people will turn away in another direction and the only direction being offered is the gun.'[48]

Despite the grim warnings, Mason's term in office proved successful: the level of conflict in the state began to fall after the previous years of chaos. There was a sharp decline in loyalist violence and the IRA activities were curtailed by the secretary of state's counter-terrorist measures.

Despite the tensions of the party conference at the end of 1976, building political structures that would involve both communities in the government of Northern Ireland was still basic SDLP policy. During a debate in London organised by the Young Conservatives in January 1977, Fitt argued: 'Then and only then will the IRA, UDA, UVF, Red Hand Commandos[49] and all the other despicable organisations and their sets of initials which mean so much to the tragedy of Northern

Ireland, fade into insignificance.'⁵⁰ However, the prospects for either the
establishment of a new political dispensation or the withering away of
paramilitarism remained bleak; and were diminished further by personal
tragedy.

In March, Brian Faulkner died in a riding accident. Despite the vitriol
directed against him by anti-power-sharing unionists and the electoral
unpopularity of his moderate Unionist Party of Northern Ireland (UPNI),
Faulkner was the only unionist leader who could perhaps have delivered a
power-sharing government with cross-community support. Fitt was quick
to pay tribute:

> I was a political opponent of his for many years but I found him to be a
> man of absolute honour and integrity in his approach to trying to create
> a power-sharing community in Northern Ireland. Those who still believe
> in power-sharing will sadly miss his influence in this field because he was
> convinced this was the only way ahead for Northern Ireland.⁵¹

Even with Faulkner's considerable political skill, it is highly unlikely that
the concept of power-sharing could have been resurrected in the short
term. His death helped ensure its indefinite suspension.

Meanwhile, Mason continued to pursue his military and socio-economic solution to the problems of Northern Ireland. He told the House of
Commons that the British government had the resolve to win the battle
against the IRA:

> What is required … is for us to point out that this is a battle not only of
> propaganda but of wills, and that we have the will to win. If the people
> will back the RUC in its endeavours they will find out that it is beating the
> terrorists step by step. In 1976, 934 persons were convicted on indictment
> of scheduled offences. It is by giving the RUC encouragement, standing
> by law and order, and being able to process people through the Courts as
> common criminals that we shall beat the terrorists.⁵²

Fitt was certainly no friend of the Provisionals, but he was frustrated by
Mason's lack of endeavour to establish devolved government in Northern
Ireland. He remained loyal to the Labour Party and, along with Maguire,
he voted with the government on 23 March, helping to defeat a Tory
motion of no confidence. This result was 322 to 298 in favour of the gov-

ernment, which by this stage was being propped up by a pact with the Liberal Party.[53]

Despite all Mason's efforts against the Provisionals, Paisley claimed not enough was being done on the security front. He called a strike, demanding tougher counter-terrorist measures and the implementation of the Convention Report with its attendant majoritarian system of government. Fitt declared in the Commons, 'The gauntlet thrown down by the fascists in Northern Ireland should be picked up by this democratic parliament'.[54]

The strike lacked the unity of 1974 and it was launched against the backdrop of relative stability and the resolute administration of Mason rather than the chaos and dithering of the Rees period. On 29 April, shipyard workers voted not to support the stoppage; Official Unionist, Vanguard and Orange Order leaders had already expressed their opposition. Mason refused to be coerced and used army and police to respond to allegations of intimidation. On 1 May, 1,200 extra troops arrived in Northern Ireland. On 3 May, the first day of the strike, many factories remained open. On 6 May, power station workers refused to support the stoppage and it was called off on 13 May, with the UDA largely discredited. Paisley claimed that the strike had been a success (probably because he had promised he would quit political life in Northern Ireland if it was unsuccessful).

The previous day Fitt had made his views on Paisley quite clear at Westminster when he said, 'the hon. Member for Antrim North is in urgent need of psychiatric treatment and ... he is more to be pitied than blamed'.[55] Fitt's concern for the mental stability of Paisley had been a long-term commitment. By contrast, Fitt praised Mason and told the *Irish News*, 'His conduct during the strike leads me to withdraw anything I said when he was appointed. He showed himself to be a person who would not be bullied.'[56] Fitt even gave guarded tribute to the RUC. He said their action during the strike had done much to improve relations between the police and the Catholic community. He also claimed that while there could be no overnight transition in the way Catholics regarded the police, the RUC had done much to 'engender a new trust'.[57] Such sentiments would perhaps have caused some consternation among his 'greener' colleagues in the SDLP, but they provoked outright hostility from Provisional Sinn Féin. A statement described Fitt's comment as 'totally ridiculous' and claimed:

In the two weeks that he refers to, approximately ten cases of torture at the RUC Barracks at Castlereagh[58] have been reported to our offices. It is this performance that symbolises the true role of the Loyalist RUC. As the armed wing of Ulster Unionism, their history has been to smash any opposition to English and Loyalist rule in the six occupied counties, a role seen very clearly in this past nine years. It is very obvious that Mr Fitt is merely doing the British government's work.[59]

The degree to which Fitt's comments may have been detrimental to the SDLP was tested in the local government elections held in the week following the strike. Fitt declared that the election was an opportunity for both communities to make their attitude to the men of violence patently clear.[60] He again contested Belfast Area G, and topped the poll.

The SDLP did well in the election, increasing its vote from just under 14 per cent in 1973 to almost 21 per cent and gaining an extra thirty-one seats. The SDLP could now claim – with some justification – to be the sole representative of the minority community. Fitt was delighted with the result: 'I have been in politics for many years, long before many of the major groups were on the scene and tonight I can say that I have derived greater pleasure and satisfaction from being at this time the leader of one of the most important parties in Northern Ireland.'[61]

This suggested that Fitt was content with the SDLP and comfortable with its direction and policies. Nevertheless, the extent to which the captain was steering the ship is open to conjecture.

The Official Unionists performed badly in the election, securing just under 30 per cent of the vote. The Alliance Party gained 14 per cent and the DUP 12 per cent. Fitt maintained that the strong support for the SDLP and Alliance Party should have encouraged the Unionist Party to sever its links with Paisley and review its policies. He clearly wanted an end to direct rule: 'The only way forward is through reconciliation and a partnership government that can bring back to Northern Ireland most of the powers now held by Ministers seconded here from London'.[62]

On 10 August, the queen began a two-day visit to Northern Ireland as part of her Silver Jubilee celebrations. Since attendance at royal functions by members of the party would have stretched their credibility with many supporters to breaking point, the visit put Fitt and the SDLP in an awkward position. Non-attendance would allow unionists to depict them as 'traditional green nationalists'. The fact that the queen's tour coincided with the anniversary of internment did not make things any easier. Consequently, Fitt and other leading SDLP members declined invitations to attend receptions connected with the visit. Fitt was flippant: 'I have a hazy recollection of getting such a letter, but I have not yet decided what I should do about it. However, I would say that it is not the highest on my list of priorities'.[63]

The queen's presence provoked some rioting in West Belfast. Afterwards Fitt acknowledged that she was likely to be a 'decent human person' but suggested that the violence was a result of 'British royalty and the Union Jack always being identified with one section of the community in Northern Ireland'.[64] This comment is interesting when we consider Fitt's later elevation to the Lords, that other bastion of the hereditary principle. For the time being, the SDLP had managed to tread a fine line between *de facto* and *de jure* recognition of the state.

On most issues, with the exception of the police, they had avoided controversy, but the royal visit posed a special problem. The party had to take a stand and decided to cling to its nationalist principles. Fitt did not stray from this policy. He insisted the loyalist community had adopted an attitude of intransigence and arrogance: 'All our appeals have been rejected and some minority representatives are beginning to feel a little tired when they are being lectured to make further concessions to unionism. We have given so much. We are not prepared to give any more'.[65]

The SDLP had managed to remain united when it had some hope of power, but in the absence of any political initiative, party members became disillusioned. Many of them became more nationalist, and Fitt's militant posturing can be seen as symptomatic of his attempt to retain control of his crew.

While Fitt was prepared to tolerate the overtly nationalist instincts of many within the party for the time being, Paddy Devlin's discomfort was demonstrated when he resigned the chairmanship of the SDLP's constituency representatives council. This move was in response to an SDLP policy committee document, written by Hume, entitled 'Facing Reality', in which he urged the British to reappraise their approach to the conflict and to develop a strategy for partnership government with a greater emphasis on the Irish dimension.[66] Ironically, the content of the document was designed to unite the party; but Devlin castigated the leadership for relinquishing the 'left-of-centre principles' advocated at its formation:

With one or two notable exceptions [probably Fitt and Cooper], none of the leading members has done anything to promote these policies since 1974, and little enough before that. In spite of the fact that we are confronted with the worst figures of unemployment, poverty, housing and general income levels in Western Europe we have rarely heard a cheep of protest from men who a short time ago had ministerial responsibility for those very departments.[67]

Devlin's dissatisfaction with SDLP policy had been widely known for some time. His strong criticism led to his expulsion from the party. Given that both Devlin and Fitt were founder members of the SDLP who shared an urban and labour background, they might have been expected to be natural allies. But this was not the case. Hume claimed, 'They did not get on well at all',[68] a view shared by Austin Currie:

It was an up and down relationship and depended upon how one of them reacted to particular things and to particular personalities at particular times. It was never an easy relationship. Gerry, to a large extent, felt that he had to be careful about Devlin because after all, Devlin was in West Belfast and could have created difficulties there.[69]

Ivan Cooper provided a simple reason for the friction between the two socialists:

There was always a little bit of jealousy between Paddy and Gerry that stemmed from the time they fought an election against each other. Devlin beat him. Gerry did not like anyone beating him. He was that type. He didn't like anyone who opposed him and he didn't like anyone who beat him and Paddy had.[70]

Fitt himself admitted that their relationship was not satisfactory and felt that Devlin resented his success in the latter's bailiwick of West Belfast:

Paddy was from the Falls Road. I was not. I was an import from the other side of the city, coming in. I was like Jesus Christ on the Falls Road and Paddy was bound to resent this. A quite natural feeling and one that I can understand. He always had a bit of a chip on his shoulder. My natural ally in the SDLP was Austin Currie. It should have been Paddy. We were together on most things but there was always the personal thing

... I was never off the television. I was more articulate in a television studio than Paddy could be. Paddy wasn't good television. Paddy was a very good writer but he wasn't good on TV. There used to be some terrible arguments about who would go on television and who wouldn't be on.[71]

Devlin claimed Fitt 'couldn't write and was an awful lightweight in that sense'. He told me that Fitt should have supported him in his resignation stance.[72] And Devlin told Gerard Murray that 'Gerry would have taken the same views as mine, but he didn't fight. He left me do the fighting while he got offside.'[73]

Devlin had a point. He was, like Fitt, less captivated by the Irish dimension and content to find internal accommodation, at least in the short term. More to the point, it was Devlin who provided most of the socialist input into SDLP policy, so, as Fitt always professed that he was a socialist above anything else, would it not have been logical to back Devlin?

While Cooper was 'livid at Devlin's treatment',[74] Fitt proposed the motion to remove the Whip from his socialist colleague.[75] Fitt followed the nationalist swing of the party and a week after Devlin was expelled said:

If the Unionist majority in the North are determined to become more Orange than ever before in pursuit of their own culture, then it is only to be expected that the minority who are part of the majority in this island will want to assert their culture. And that, in short, means the Irish dimension will always be the SDLP policy.[76]

Fitt was quite unequivocal. There was no doubt that on this occasion he subordinated his socialism to nationalism. Interestingly, Mallon suggested that Devlin's resignation was a cynical move, an expression of his anger at not being selected as a candidate for the forthcoming European election. He told me: 'Devlin's resignation happened to coincide with the fact that he did not get the nomination for Europe. The reality was that if he had, he would not have felt it necessary to resign and he would have fought the election on an SDLP ticket'.[77]

As a consequence of Devlin's resignation, Fitt became the only socialist-orientated member of the leadership, and his isolation was reaffirmed. Rather than being a left-of-centre party committed to integrating the

Catholic community into a constitutional framework, the SDLP appeared increasingly like a catch-all pacifist nationalist party.

By not backing Devlin (even though he probably agreed with him at heart), Fitt indicated that he was prepared to submit to this direction. If his nationalist rhetoric reflected party purposes more than personal conviction (as evidence has suggested) he may have felt that relinquishing the leadership would have ended any chance he had of dampening SDLP nationalism. I asked Cooper why Currie was Fitt's 'natural ally' rather than Devlin and he replied 'The common denominator was dislike for John Hume. Currie would not have shown any animosity but he was in politics for a longer time and could not have been terribly comfortable when Hume came along in 1969 and had been elevated relatively quickly and of course Fitt and Currie had been at Stormont together.'[78] What is significant about Cooper's analysis is his provision of further evidence that personality issues played as much a part in Gerry Fitt's political judgement as differences in political outlook, and perhaps had an even greater role in his decision-making.

This is further exemplified by Fitt's relationship with Roy Mason. He detested Mason with a vengeance and was, if his rhetoric was anything to go by, repelled by the secretary of state's agenda. But Fitt certainly underwent something of a transition during Mason's tenure, ending up with a political position not unlike Mason's. There is a case for the view that Fitt was remoulded not only by the power-sharing experience but also by the Mason years, something he was loath to admit because of his antipathy towards the NIO chief. If it is not the case that something of Mason rubbed off on Fitt, some other explanation must be sought for his reorientation during these years.

The Irish Independence Party (IIP) was formed in October 1977.[79] This new party was a direct challenge to the SDLP, its leading figures being the former Unity MP for Fermanagh–South Tyrone, Frank McManus, and Fergus McAteer, son of the Nationalist Party leader and a Derry Councillor. The new party sought British withdrawal and attacked the SDLP for repeated 'sell-outs'. It was felt that because of its more militant profile the new party could be a threat to the SDLP in republican-inclined areas. In essence the Irish Independence Party was a republican electoral manifestation at a time when abstentionism, and a historical distrust of electoral involvement, tied Sinn Féin's hands.

With this new challenge to the SDLP's dominance over the nationalist constituency, it might be expected that a degree of anxiety might have crept into the established party's outlook. But when the SDLP held their seventh annual conference in November, Fitt was surprisingly optimistic: 'For the first time since 1974 and the fall of the Executive there is hope that political progress can be made in governing Northern Ireland through consensus.'[80] He argued that he and his party were eager to reach an accommodation with the unionists, but he again stressed the Irish dimension, claiming that the unionists 'must not ask us to wave Union Jacks or to pay homage to every member of the British royal family who visits these shores. We also have our culture and our cherished ideals.'[81]

Fitt's speech may well have been designed to placate the 'greener' members of the SDLP, as well as being a counter-attack against the IIP. The conference approved the 'Facing Reality' document as party policy, bypassing a full demand for British withdrawal. Three motions in favour of such a move were dropped in the interests of party unity, although Mallon, Cooper, McGrady and Duffy all spoke positively on its behalf.[82] The 'green wing' of the party had been heard nonetheless, and Fitt told Currie 'If the party goes down that road, it will do so without me.'[83]

Fitt's optimism about the conference stemmed from knowledge of Mason's plan to re-open political dialogue and reintroduce a form of devolved power. At the end of November, Mason held talks with the major parties, on the basis of setting up a unicameral assembly with consultative rather than legislative powers. Fitt led the SDLP delegation in the discussions: 'There are no guarantees of success, but at least we must explore the situation.'[84]

However, the hopes for progress were not good, and Mason's approach had to be tentative because both the SDLP and the unionists had, somewhat predictably, taken irreconcilable positions. The unionists were concerned by the intervention of the new Taoiseach, Jack Lynch, who stressed his commitment to eventual unification having been relatively quiet on the northern problem since his re-election in June. The talks failed, but Lynch's rhetoric encouraged those in the SDLP who wanted a policy involving active participation by Dublin and London to resolve the conflict.

Fitt ended the year by consoling himself with the Labour Party's assurance that it was still committed to power-sharing. He reported his meeting with Callaghan and Mason to the *Irish News*:

Jim Callaghan told me that in no circumstances would a Labour government enter into a pact with unionists from Northern Ireland which would lead to the exclusion of the Catholic minority in future government.

These talks confirm the confidence the SDLP has always held in the Labour government, and we now look forward to a series of talks to further cement the relationship which our party has with the Labour Party as members of the socialist movement.[85]

Fitt's optimism was unjustified. He still had blind faith in the Labour Party's capacity and willingness to rectify the problems of Northern Ireland, when in reality the two main parties had adopted an unofficially bi-partisan position. All too often, Fitt was placated by high ministerial dialogue and soothing words.

In early 1978 the SDLP was pushed further in a nationalistic direction by the Conservative Party, which was keen to woo the unionists. When, in February Airey Neave told the Commons that 'power-sharing was no longer practical', Fitt quickly responded to the suggestion of integration. 'Airey Neave is electioneering and is seeking the support of the Unionist MPs at Westminster. He could get their support at the cost of further bloodshed.'[86]

The following day Eddie McGrady warned that the SDLP, 'in the face of new expressions of intolerance, intransigence and insincerity, must immediately re-appraise its approach to constitutional problems'.[87] This meant that an Anglo-Irish strategy should be developed, since working within the Northern Ireland context had proved futile. Fitt supported his colleague:

> This is a natural reaction to what Airey Neave has said. Mr Neave is coming out four-square for a return to majority rule in Northern Ireland, which is fully backing the unionist line on integration. Under no circumstances would we be prepared to accept that, and, by taking up that kind of position, it is naturally going to put us into a situation where we will have to reassess our attitudes. If that is what the Conservatives are doing – and it appears to be a firm lurch to the right, with Mr Neave playing the orange card – then it goes without saying what our reaction would be.[88]

Fitt presumably meant that the SDLP would play the 'green' card. In May, Neave said that if the Conservatives came to power they would carry out major government reforms in Northern Ireland, and if he were made secretary of state he would introduce measures to restore more power to the local electorate. Fitt was alarmed:

> If Maggie Thatcher is ever prime minister – and this is something I doubt very much will ever happen – she would do well to think of someone else to head the representatives of the British government here. We have had our share of trouble and sorrow here but I can't help thinking that it would be a lot worse with Mr Neave in his naivety at the helm.[89]

The following month, Fitt made it quite clear why he had supported the Labour government despite its apathy in finding a political solution. Interviewed on British television, he said that the minority in Northern Ireland would view with suspicion anything that came from a Thatcher government: 'It was different when it was led by Ted Heath because the minority in Northern Ireland felt the Conservatives under Heath were trying to resolve the problems of Northern Ireland. But certainly the Conservatives as we see them now from Belfast are extreme right wing.'[90] Fitt believed a general election might result in a hung parliament, and that if this happened the tories would restore power to the unionist ascendancy as a reward for services rendered. Fitt's dread of the Tories primarily stemmed from nationalist principles rather than from socialist convictions.

The antagonistic relationship between the SDLP and the Conservative Party did not mean that its relationship with the Labour Party was good: indeed, the opposite was true. Fitt was anxious to reaffirm that Callaghan was committed to power-sharing, but this was not enough for some of his colleagues. Mallon, now number four in the party hierarchy, was one of the more vocal critics. Following an SDLP meeting with the Labour Party in February, he said: 'We left the Prime Minister and members of the Labour National Executive in no doubt about our attitude towards them. It is one of quite considerable anger and disgust over their negative position'.[91]

Fitt had also abandoned his new-found admiration for Mason, due to his attitude to the May 1977 strike. When Mason had accused the Republic of allowing its territory to be used by the Provisionals, Fitt responded angrily and suggested that Mason was looking for a scapegoat because he had not achieved military victory against the IRA:

His arrogance and hostile attitude ensured that all the major political parties in Ireland, excluding the Loyalists and unionists, stood together as never before in opposition to the Secretary of State.

Whitelaw, Pym and Rees never united the anti-unionist political parties in this island, but Mason by his arrogance and bombast has achieved this … The days of this type of imperial arrogance have gone even if it does come from a former Yorkshire miner.[92]

Mason's policy had clearly exasperated Fitt, and he had reverted to his initial opinion of the Secretary of State. Fitt may have had reservations about SDLP nationalism, but Mason made him question such feelings and prompted some stinging attacks.

Although Mason had not secured military victory against the Provisionals, he had come close – a point the Provisionals themselves admitted.[93] Mason's record prompted Martin McGuinness to say in 1993: 'The only one who impressed was Roy Mason. He impressed some of the Unionists, because he beat the shit out of us.'[94] Mason's tactics had forced the Provisionals to reorganise, and by early 1978 they had combined a classic cell-like structure (containing three or four members within an active service unit) with confidentiality in leadership, rendering the organisation less penetrable to government agents.

On 17 February 1978, twelve people were killed when the PIRA bombed the La Mon Restaurant outside Belfast. The device exploded prematurely and the Provisionals apologised to the relations of the victims. This, of course, was not enough to prevent condemnation and Fitt, as usual, was one of the first to denounce the atrocity.[95] The tragedy of the La Mon was a setback for the Provisionals, but it proved only temporary. The republican movement had opened up another front that would transform nationalist politics and have a great impact on the political career of Gerry Fitt.

When Rees withdrew Special Category Status in March 1976, it meant that all newly convicted prisoners were to be treated the same – they would have to do penal work and wear prison clothes. The first convicted prisoner under the new policy was Kieran Nugent. He set a precedent by refusing to be treated as an ordinary criminal, claiming political motivation for his actions. He refused to wear prison clothes and was eventually issued a prison blanket. Nugent was the first to go 'on the blanket' at the Maze (Long Kesh) compound near Belfast.[96]

In February 1978, Provisional Sinn Féin joined Peoples' Democracy,

Bernadette McAliskey (formerly Devlin), and others in the Relatives Action Committees to highlight the condition of the prisoners. The following month the inmates intensified their protest for political status by beginning what became known as the 'dirty protest'. They refused to wash or use toilet facilities, instead smearing their own excreta on their cell walls. By the summer the protest involved 250 republican prisoners. This new campaign raised the political stakes, and the situation in the Maze (Long Kesh) Prison became the focal point for outside agitation

In August Archbishop Tomás Ó'Fiaich, the Catholic Church's most prominent figure in Ireland, visited the H Blocks. Ó'Fiaich described the conditions as 'inhuman and degrading' and suggested the authorities should recognise that republican prisoners were different from common criminals.[97] Fitt had little respect for Ó'Fiaich or his place of origin. He said of the archbishop: 'A Crossmaglen man. I have never met any wise man from Crossmaglen in my life. It's the biggest lunatic asylum in the country. All mad. I thought when he was appointed it was the worst thing to happen to Ireland. I thought he will drive the Prods mad and the Provos will think he is one of their own.'[98]

Fitt was correct in at least one respect. Republicans were pleased by such utterances from a leading member of the Catholic establishment: Fitt clearly was not. He later claimed that he seriously contemplated re-signing his Westminster seat because of what he considered to be a pro-Provisional stance by Ó'Fiaich. It was only the intervention of his eldest daughter Joan that persuaded him against this notion.[99] Fitt's opinion that the Provisionals were simply murderers did not alter in the years ahead.

The tenth anniversary of the first civil rights march from Coalisland to Dungannon was commemorated on 24 August by another march. Fitt claimed the demonstration had nothing to do with the ideal behind the Civil Rights Movement in 1968 and explained why he would not attend:

The march that took place on 24 August 1968 was a march which de-manded Civil Rights for everyone in Northern Ireland who had been denied them. They were those who thought they would be denied jobs, homes and votes because of their religion or politics. Tomorrow's march is under completely different auspices and I certainly will not be there. Had the people who are running this march listened to what we had to say in 1968 and took heed of our position on violence, there would not have been 10 tragic years in between and there would be no prisoners.[100]

Currie also said he would not attend. Bernadette McAliskey was candid in her assessment of why the two SDLP men would not participate:

> The frontline in the August '68 march were people who came in from the outside to make their points and be seen. They all went on to do different things. But the people who organised the march and who took part in the rank and file will be there tomorrow, and they won't miss the big wigs from the city.[101]

At its annual conference in November, the SDLP adopted an important shift in party policy. The previous April, Paddy Duffy had argued that loyalist intransigence had made it pointless for the SDLP to continue to strive for power-sharing. From now on, he claimed, the all-Ireland context should be pursued.[102] By the time the conference was held, this attitude was shared by the vast majority of rank and file SDLP delegates. Austin Currie had proposed a motion that declared 'disengagement to be both inevitable and desirable'. Even before the conference began, Fitt felt it necessary to deny that they were returning to old-style nationalism; 'This doesn't mean the SDLP is a green party in the sense that people are trying to project it.'

Currie's motion was passed overwhelmingly by the 400 delegates, with only two votes against and one abstention. It was an intelligent move by Currie, one of many in a long career. The carried motion ended internal disharmony over the issue. Speaking at the end of the conference, Fitt adamantly restated the party's commitment to the reunification of Ireland:

> Let me state it in quite blunt terms ... the SDLP does not believe that the partition of this country was ever justified. The SDLP wants to unite people of all religions and outlooks, not only in Northern Ireland, but the whole of Ireland, so that we can eventually bring about the reunification of this country by consent, not coercion.

Fitt argued that it was inevitable that the British would have to withdraw and it was the task of his party to create the conditions that could make British departure 'come all the more soon' and without the bloodshed that marked colonial disengagement in other parts of the world. If Fitt was less nationalist than his colleagues, he masked it well. His speech contained only one reference to party disunity, which he described as 'a very slight splintering' of the unanimity that had brought all those political parties together to oppose unionism.[103]

External circumstances had forced an evolution in the party's political thinking. Two years before, the SDLP leadership had successfully (though narrowly) fought off such a motion. In 1977, it had done so again, this time more easily. But by the end of 1978, partly because of the politicisation of the prisons issue among the nationalist constituency and by the political stalemate, the vast majority of the SDLP wanted the party to change its political approach. It was thus decided to concentrate on the Anglo-Irish dimension and to seek support from the British and (especially) Irish governments to create political movement and end the deadlock. Since Fitt remained leader of the party, and considering his rhetoric at the conference, one must conclude that he was again prepared to go along with the majority despite any personal reservations he may have had.

The open enmity between Mason and Fitt continued into 1979. In February the secretary of state had given an interview to Independent Radio in which he suggested that the Official Unionists were the party of moderation and that the SDLP and DUP were extremists. Fitt launched a blistering attack in the Commons.[104] Soon afterwards he made it clear that he would not now support the Labour government in a vote of confidence: 'I can't vote for a government whose Northern Ireland Secretary has antagonised most of the population of Northern Ireland and put himself in the pocket of the unionists.'[105] There was no ambiguity in this statement. Fitt was prepared to suspend his socialist principles and operate within the nationalist creed. In short, he was inviting the scenario he most detested, a Tory government with Neave as a possible secretary of state.

Early in the following month he re-affirmed his position:

They [the Labour government] had given into unionist blackmail ... As a matter of pure political expediency it has done deals with the Unionist MPs, the most notorious being the promise of more seats for Northern Ireland at Westminster in return for unionist votes to keep the Labour government in power.[106]

Fitt had been against a greater representation for Northern Ireland at Westminster since May 1977, when Callaghan had given the go-ahead for a special conference to examine the case,[107] and for the rest of the year he opposed any such move.[108] Fitt's resistance was understandable because any redistribution of parliamentary seats would inevitably increase unionist power and thus strengthen rather than weaken the relationship with Britain.

Despite SDLP objections, Callaghan did in April introduce a bill to increase the number of northern Irish MPs to a minimum of sixteen and a maximum of eighteen. In November, Fitt told the Commons that any increase in the number of seats for Northern Ireland at Westminster would consolidate the British dimension and make it less likely that unionist representatives would seek any accommodation with the minority in creating political structures.[109]

Despite Fitt's protestations, Callaghan persisted, and the second reading of the Re-distribution of Seats (NI) Bill (proposing to increase Northern Ireland representatives to seventeen) was passed in the Commons and welcomed by the Conservative Party. Fitt commented on the result: 'I do not accept that this Bill was brought before the House with the intention of giving fairness and justice to the electorate and the MPs of Northern Ireland'.[110] The bill became law and was implemented in time for the 1983 Westminster election. An editorial in the *Irish News* interpreted the new legislation incisively: 'There is a simple explanation for the Callaghan government's show of generosity towards the North by the decision to increase the number of seats at Westminster – survival. Those extra seats could provide the necessary votes to secure victory in vital and close debates.'[111]

Fitt made the same deduction: little wonder he had become so disgruntled. In March 1979, his dismay with the government was given renewed impetus by the allegations of Dr Robert Irwin, a police surgeon, who claimed on television that he knew of at least 150 people who had been seriously injured by the RUC while in custody.[112] This testimony confirmed the findings of an Amnesty International report in June 1978, which expressed concern about RUC interrogation methods. Fitt attacked both Mason and the chief constable of the RUC:

If Mr Mason or the Chief Constable, Sir Kenneth Newman, claim they are unaware of these practices then they prove themselves guilty of incompetence. If they were aware these practices were taking place then they prove themselves to be liars. In either case there is no longer any room for them in Northern Ireland.[113]

The British government issued the Bennett Report, which accepted that there was *prima facie* evidence of ill-treatment. Mason belittled the findings by promising to act on only two of its thirty-four recommendations to counter RUC 'indiscretions'. Fitt was unimpressed.[114]

While the controversy over police brutality continued, Fitt again made it clear that he would not support the government and might even go as far as to help the Conservatives:

> I have made it clear to all these MPs that under no circumstance will I support the Labour government in a vote of confidence because of the attitude of the Secretary of State and the policies of the government in Northern Ireland. I intend to abstain, but I may even vote for the Tories, if I see Enoch Powell[115] going into the lobbies to support the government.[116]

The minority Labour government was clearly in difficulties. Rising inflation, increased debt and the politically disastrous wave of strikes during the so-called winter of discontent had diluted public confidence and sapped the morale of the Parliamentary Labour Party. Despite agreeing, under unionist pressure, to increase the number of seats for Northern Ireland and having an informal pact with the Liberals, any vote of no confidence was certain to be very close.

Fitt, in an emotional speech to the House of Commons, reiterated why he would no longer support the Labour Party. He told the House that this would be the 'unhappiest' speech he had ever delivered. He maintained that throughout his time at Westminster he had never voted in the Conservative lobby, even when it was 'courageously trying to grapple' with the Northern Ireland problem between 1970 and 1974. He lamented the fall of the power-sharing Executive and blamed the UWC strike on the negligent Labour government:

> That strike terrified the Labour government. Since then, the Labour government has been running away. They have not stood up to unionists and loyalist extremists as they should have done ... In all conscience I would be a liar and a traitor to the people who sent me here if I were to go into the Lobby tonight with the Labour government to express confidence in their handling of the affairs of Northern Ireland ...

The penny had finally dropped. Fitt explained the basis on which he intended to cast his vote:

> I have a loyalty to this government, to my own working-class movement in the United Kingdom and further afield, but I have a greater loyalty to the people of Northern Ireland ... It is their voice saying that because of what the government has done in the past five years – disregarded the minority and appeased the blackmailers of the Northern Ireland unionist majority – I cannot go into the Lobby with them tonight.[117]

Fitt duly abstained and the government was defeated by one vote – 311 to 310. (He confirmed to me that if it had been necessary he would have voted against the government.)[118] Callaghan was forced to call a general election for May. In that election the Labour Party was defeated by an ebullient Conservative Party under Margaret Thatcher. So began eighteen years of uninterrupted Tory government. But this Conservative government was a radical departure from the post-war consensual paternalism and pro-Europeanism of Harold Macmillan and Ted Heath. It represented, as Fitt suspected, a new form of Conservatism, which smashed trade union power and drastically altered the agenda of British politics to the detriment of the socialist interest.

What motivated Fitt to undermine a socialist government, when the Conservative alternative so clearly represented everything that was anathema to him? It was, after all, no secret that Thatcher was a proponent of 'new right' economic principles and that her primary objective was to disable the trade unions, which she saw as the main cause of inflation. There is substance to the charge that Fitt had supported successive Labour governments which had, in the past, shown a lack of interest in Northern Ireland and little political and moral courage in defence of British Acts of Parliament. By 1979, however, Fitt had finally had enough. Two factors influenced his change of heart; the decision of the government to press ahead with legislation for extra parliamentary seats for Northern Ireland (ostensibly to keep the province in line with the rest of the United Kingdom); and his disgust over the attitude of Roy Mason, particularly in relation to the Bennett Report.

In his memoirs, James Callaghan talks of Fitt's abstention:

> Gerry Fitt ... who had consistently supported the government in previous

vital votes, spoke and voted against us despite desperate efforts by a number of Labour members to persuade him otherwise … Gerry was a brave man and a warm hearted impulsive character but he took the wrong turning that night.[119]

Fitt certainly came under intense pressure. He told me:

Jim Callaghan was sending for me – slapping me on the back and saying 'have a drink' which I didn't take. The pressure I was under at that time was immense. All the trade unions were on the phone saying, 'Gerry, we know you are right and Mason is a little bastard and Callaghan is not much cop, but please Gerry'. The pressure I had to withstand was tremendous.[120]

I got the distinct impression that Fitt was particularly angry that Callaghan thought he could be bought with flattery and a few gin and tonics.

Fitt remained unrepentant regarding his decision, although he was glad that he only had to abstain:[121] 'The unionists were dictating policy to the Labour government so it was no longer a Labour government. Any allegiance I had to the Labour Party evaporated. I was keeping the unionists in, and so I decided to abstain. I wanted to bring down that government.' I asked him if, as a socialist and in the light of Thatcherism, he regretted his action. He replied, 'No, at that time there was nothing else I could do. Given the circumstances that prevailed, I don't regret it.'[122] Fitt's view was later given substance by Rees, who said, 'Gerry was always his own man' and was never in the pockets of the Labour Party.[123] Fitt had certainly demonstrated this independence.

Mason himself reflected on Fitt's actions in the vote and asked in his memoirs: 'Did he really expect his constituents to do better under the Thatcherite free market than under Labour?'[124] Mason probably believed his government could get away with making concessions to unionism because Fitt, a socialist, would not dare to inflict this new radical right-wing government on the country and, in particular, on his constituents. Fitt's assertion that he was primarily a socialist hardly stands up to examination when judged against his actions. But Mason underestimated Fitt's personal pride, which would not countenance him suffering a small short-term defeat to his local enemies. Ironically, two Ulster Unionists, Harold McCusker and John Carson, who were considered 'more socially progressive' than some of their colleagues in the UUP, both voted with the government.

Fitt had little strategic understanding of the situation in the UK as a whole. If Labour had to make a short-term concession to butter up the Ulster unionists in order to survive and fight an election in more favourable circumstances, then it was in socialist interests to do so. In truth, the concession made was in no way undemocratic. Neither was it detrimental to the nationalist interest in the longer term: recent elections have witnessed an increased number of seats being won by nationalist candidates.

Furthermore, if Fitt was particularly perturbed about greater Northern Ireland representation at Westminster (and there is considerable evidence that he was), it showed a distinct reversal of the sentiment and content of his maiden speech at the House of Commons in 1966. Then he demanded the same rights and privileges for the people of Northern Ireland that were enjoyed in the rest of the United Kingdom. His opposition to attempts to increase the parliamentary representation for the region adds fuel to the charge that his machinations at parliament in the late 1960s were merely an attempt to disrupt the unionist regime in a way that would be advantageous to the ending of partition rather than for a democratic ideal.

In the 1979 general election campaign Fitt was supremely confident that he would retain his Belfast West seat: 'There are some people saying this constituency is going to change hands, but the people know what I have done for them and I'm going to walk it.'[125] He played on his role in bringing about the election, claiming that intransigent unionists had had enough votes to blackmail the Labour government, 'but on 20 March this year I brought that blackmail to an end.' Paradoxically, he hoped that the British electorate would return a strong Labour government which would be 'able to tell the unionist parties where to go in their demands for a return to the old Stormont ascendency rule – then something positive might be achieved towards partnership rule in Northern Ireland'. A proven performer in elections, Fitt prepared for battle against his opponents, none of whom could possibly win, he claimed, as 'A vote for them is a vote for unionism.'[126]

His optimism was justified; he won the election and was again the only SDLP candidate returned to Westminster. The Conservatives were back in office, but at least the SDLP could comfort itself that there would

be no more horse-trading between unionism and a weak Labour government.[127]

The following month, campaigns began for the European parliamentary
election. Northern Ireland was to be a three-seat single constituency, with
election by proportional representation. The PR scheme, which was not
adopted elsewhere in the UK, benefited the minority community, which
might have seen the unionists carry off all three seats in a simple plurality
vote. Fitt can take credit for the continuation of PR.

In February 1978, Enoch Powell had proposed an amendment
calling for the first-past-the-post system to elect Northern Ireland's first
European MPs. Political commentators suggested that it would be a
close vote.[128] Fitt encouraged his Labour colleagues to support him. He
delivered an impassioned speech in the Commons in which he argued
that the first-past-the-post system should not be used in Ulster because
politics in the state was sectarian, and the exaggerated majority produced
under such a system would merely bolster an 'artificially created' unionist
dominance dating back to partition.[129] Fitt told me that he 'pleaded for
PR everywhere I could, even in the bar. It nearly made me an alcoholic!
I persuaded those Labour men to vote for PR and John Hume [who was
one of those elected] was the beneficiary.'[130]

Fitt did indeed succeed in his task. British MPs rejected Powell's
proposal by 241 votes to 150. Fitt was delighted with the outcome: 'This
result is very good for Northern Ireland. We will take that third seat.'[131]

The SDLP selected John Hume to stand for election to the European
Parliament. He conducted a vigorous pro-European campaign, in contrast
to the anti-European stance of the unionists Paisley, West and Taylor.
Hume, as expected, secured a seat, polling 140,622 votes, 24.6 per cent of
the total. He won more votes than the combined total of the two Official
Unionists, but was marginally short of the quota, being elected on the
third count.[132] Barry White argues that the 'European election confirmed
that Hume was popularly regarded as the real leader of nationalist opinion
in the North.'[133] This is a valid comment: Hume had, after all, pushed the
SDLP's share of the poll to a record high. If anybody threatened Fitt's
leadership it was Hume, a point noted by *Fortnight*:

> The SDLP are also having to face up to some changes in the power balance.
> In the good old days you could point to the Social Democratic and Labour
> parts of the Party without too much difficulty. The Labour men were based

in Belfast, and the rest in the country. Now with Paddy Devlin long since gone, Gerry Fitt is the only Labour man left. And who could blame him for feeling a bit uneasy at the phenomenal performance of John Hume in the European election.

The article also suggested that the orientation of the party was changing: 'The word is that most of the votes came from country areas, and that priests and schoolmasters were working hard at it.'[134] If this speculation was true, Fitt's position as leader was being further weakened.

In the meantime Fitt continued his incessant attacks on the Provisionals. Commenting on an upsurge in sectarian violence after the European election, he called them the most 'desperate cowards in Irish history'.[135] The Provisionals remained oblivious. In one of their most ruthless and dramatic operations, on 27 August they detonated three bombs in two separate incidents on either side of the border. One killed Lord Mountbatten, members of his family and a fifteen-year-old Enniskillen boy on a boat off the County Sligo coast, and the others killed eighteen British soldiers outside Warrenpoint in County Down. Fitt was appalled. He described to me his feelings after the Mountbatten murder: 'I thought, imagine doing that to an old man of eighty-one years of age, who was a hero by his standards and some dirty little guttersnipe does that.'[136] The killings put paid to a planned visit into the north by Pope John Paul II during his visit to Ireland. Fitt claimed, 'Where the Paisleyites failed the PIRA had succeeded.'[137]

At Drogheda in the Republic, the pope addressed a crowd estimated at around 250,000 in October 1979, begging all those engaged in violence to desist. The Provisionals rejected the pope's plea in a statement in which it claimed that only force could remove the British presence.[138] Fitt maintained that the deaths in Sligo and Warrenpoint, combined with the Provisionals' repudiation of the papal appeal, made him severely disillusioned with politics in Northern Ireland. 'I told Ann that too much blood has been spilt in this country for it ever to see any sanity again and some people in our party agree with all this.' He concluded that republicans had simply 'told the Pope to fuck off'.[139] It is not unreasonable to suggest that a wavering in Fitt's allegiance to the concept of nationalism could be attributed to Provisional IRA violence.

Austin Currie's view was that the pope's address had a profound impact on Fitt's thinking in relation to his own party. 'I believe that this experience strengthened Gerry's determination to confront violent Republicanism, and created within him such a strong abhorrence of it that it led him to detest even the constitutional republicanism he found in the SDLP.'[140] Currie was correct. Fitt became almost paranoid. He considered Mallon one of those who were too close to the republican mentality: 'Seamus Mallon always has to pay due reference to the republican element. He has to play ball. He has to be anti-police or anti-army because he needs them to get elected.'[141] Fitt's concerns about the direction of party policy would continue to be a heavy burden around his neck and the greater stridency in SDLP thinking was becoming increasingly difficult for him to tolerate.

At the SDLP party conference that year a new policy document entitled 'Towards a New Ireland' was overwhelmingly passed after a debate on the motion, 'Conference deplores the failure by successive British governments to recognise the real nature of the Northern Irish problem and calls on the British and Irish governments to agree to and promote a joint Anglo-Irish process of political, social and economic development within which the representatives of the two traditions in Northern Ireland would work in partnership towards the creation of peace, stability and lasting unity within Ireland.'

The SDLP realised that the political situation was deadlocked and as a response initiated an Anglo-Irish process in which both governments would deal with their 'joint' problem and negotiate a system of government to which both communities could subscribe. Fitt had been very hopeful about the prospects of power-sharing and had frequently lamented its failure in 1974. Despite his public pronouncements about the Irish dimension it is likely that he would have been distressed at the party's new path. Power-sharing was embedded in the psyche of Gerry Fitt: the Irish dimension was not, despite years of nationalistic rhetoric. This was reflected in a motion critical of Fitt's leadership that called for him to concern himself more 'with projecting the Irish dimension and to let others project the British dimension'.

The most controversial motion at the conference came from the mid-Ulster branches. It suggested that the SDLP open contacts with the leadership of 'all political and paramilitary organisations who belong to the Irish tradition with a view to establishing a common ground for reconciliation with those of the British tradition'. The motion was rejected, but the fact that it was proposed at all would have alarmed Fitt, who had established himself as a most implacable opponent of the Provisionals and was opposed to any form of dialogue with them. The writing was on the wall for the party leader.[142]

Following the SDLP conference, Humphrey Atkins, the new secretary of state for Northern Ireland, launched a political initiative. At the end of November 1979, the government published a document on a proposed conference between the constitutional parties. It stated that the constitutional position of Northern Ireland was not a topic for discussion and there was no mention of an Irish dimension. In other words, Irish unity was off the agenda. This did not please the SDLP. Fitt however, on 20 November, gave the document a guarded welcome:

> At a quick reading I find some of the proposals are very interesting so far as they go out of their way to give protection to the minority in Northern Ireland ... I believe the proposals are worthy of the deepest consideration and that is certainly what my party will be doing at the earliest opportunity.[143]

Fitt's comments were impulsively individualistic, and his views clearly did not reflect the more assertive stance of the leaders-in-waiting. In fact he was breaking an agreement with McGrady, the chief whip, that no comment would be made until the party as a whole had considered the paper.[144] In any case the proposals were ill-judged and clearly too close to the unionist position. Fitt's response to Atkins' suggestion was remarkable. He was after all, leader of the SDLP, a party that had committed itself to the Irish dimension under political pressure from its own rank and file.

The next evening the party Executive and constituency representatives met and unanimously decided not to enter into talks unless they included discussions on the Irish dimension. Fitt was present but on the following day resigned from the SDLP, blaming the party's decision not to participate in talks as the main reason for quitting. He described the ruling as 'completely misguided and disastrous' and in an emotional statement added: 'I can only say that I have a feeling of inutterable sadness to see at this time the party which I helped to create with others, turning so violently on the concepts on which it was founded.'

He claimed that republicans had gained greater influence in the party. 'I have noticed that in the absence of a political initiative being taken, there is a strong republican element emerging in the ranks of the SDLP ...', and he went on to repudiate nationalism. 'Nationalism has been a political concept in Ireland over many, many years but I suggest that it has never brought peace to the people of the six counties. I for one have never been a nationalist to the total exclusion of my socialist ideals.'[145] Perhaps not, but he had consistently peddled nationalistic rhetoric nonetheless, and this had consolidated his reputation in, for example, the United States, where socialist diatribes were unlikely to win much respect.

Fitt's declaration was remarkable. Eight months earlier he had abstained from a crucial vote of confidence in the Labour government. He knew full well that his decision could bring down a socialist government and replace it with an anti-working class Conservative administration. He subordinated his socialism to nationalism. Now, however, he repudiated nationalism having declared in the May 1979 general election that a vote for his opponents was a 'vote for unionism'. This all suggested that Fitt's political thinking had either become thoroughly confused (reinforcing the suggestion that he had never formulated a coherent political ideology), or that it was increasingly based on short-term personal animosities, which made him appear inconsistent.

The fact that Fitt had decided to renounce nationalism shows that his politics had changed. Despite his non-sectarian socialist rhetoric, and some cross-community support, Fitt was in essence a nationalist. The explanation for this dramatic *volte face* lies – to a large degree – with the power-sharing experiment. Fitt's early nationalism became less important than an internal Northern Ireland solution, and he clung tenaciously to the belief that amity between politicians could be established, and that it could lead to the formation of a devolved form of government with power-sharing.

Conversely, an important element in the SDLP drew different conclusions from the failure of the Executive, and this 'green' element would become increasingly influential. It likewise became convinced that a more forceful approach by the British government would have ensured the survival of the Executive. This element lost confidence in the British government (something that Fitt inexplicably did not), especially in the light of Mason's attitude. His disregard for political initiatives drove the SDLP to embark on a policy that gave greater significance both to the Irish dimension and to the withdrawal of British troops. In short, the SDLP reverted to a more nationalistic position. Seamus Mallon explained the situation. He rejects the 'greening' terminology and considers the rural/city divide as something of a political myth. The truth was that Fitt the maverick was out of step, not only with the SDLP mainstream, but with the prevailing attitudes in both London and Dublin. Mallon argues:

> You had a whole process of definition and redefinition going on in the political process post-Sunningdale. Many, not just in the SDLP, but many in both governments were beginning to accept the SDLP line that you can't solve the problem in the Northern Ireland context, that power-sharing alone is not going to survive and that a bigger and wider dimension had to be taken into account. Gerry was at odds with his own party on that issue and was essentially at odds with the thinking of both the British and Irish governments.

The seeds of conflict between the leader and his colleagues were there for all to see. The duality or confusion in Fitt's politics can be explained simply by the fact that he remained leader despite the clear disagreements that he had with other leading figures in the party. In order to maintain party unity, he endorsed SDLP policy regarding the Irish dimension at party conferences and at crucial times (e.g., Devlin's resignation).

But his unease was obvious, and when he resigned no one in the media seemed surprised. It can only be concluded that by November 1979 Fitt's nationalist sentiment had become so negligible that he had become a mere figurehead, an honorary leader of a party that was heading in a different direction. His position in the SDLP was no longer tenable.

Mallon also argued, 'There was an attitude in the North of Ireland that wanted the SDLP but they didn't want a nationalist SDLP. They wanted an SDLP that would fit in. Pressure came from London too. It would be a lot easier if we were the nice quiet sister party of the Labour Party settling for the constitutional position.'[146] It appeared that Fitt was willing to 'fit' in and would have perhaps been comfortable with such a scenario, at least in the short term. Those members of the SDLP who rejected this thesis lacked Fitt's London connections. Fitt's dedication to his Westminster duties may have prevented him identifying the shifting attitudes in northern nationalism. This may be his enduring legacy to the party.

The reaction to Fitt's resignation not only re-confirmed (not that it needed it) the polarised nature of northern Irish politics, but also showed how his profile had changed within the respective communities.

The nationalist community, as represented by Sinn Féin, was predictably critical. A spokesman claimed that the resignation was the 'tantrum of a defeated bullyboy who for so long had enjoyed total domination over those he purported to lead and represent.'[147] Nor were there too many tears in the SDLP at Fitt's departure. There was a general feeling that Fitt had lost touch with grass-roots sentiment. Mallon maintained that he was 'not surprised', and Duffy claimed, 'Gerry is totally and absolutely on his own'.[148] Fitt had become isolated and no longer represented the nationalist aspirations that the SDLP had come to express. Cooper later explained the situation:

> You had many in the party who were unhappy about Gerry's inability to create proper branch structures, to toe the party line on very important issues. When Gerry was under fire he simply headed off to Westminster. That was his favourite trick and when he got to Westminster he wasn't contactable. He was hiding. So you had a lot of people in the party who were not terribly happy and a lot of these people were of the view that they wouldn't be unhappy if he went.[149]

Currie preferred to dwell on Fitt's affability and *bonhomie*. 'There was great affection for Gerry throughout the party, and only a few would have favoured humiliation.'[150] Although the *Irish News* editorial did not deviate from its long-established pro-Fitt orthodoxy, it did make the following crucial point: 'Mr Fitt says there has been a strong republican element in the ranks of the party. His strong repudiation of nationalism will surprise many who will recall that Mr. Fitt was once known as a Socialist Republican.'[151]

The *Belfast News Letter* suggested in its editorial:

> While the resignation of Mr. Fitt from the leadership of the SDLP comes as no surprise, its significance cannot be ignored. Not only is it a reflection of internal dissension within the party but clear confirmation that the SDLP is essentially a republican organisation dedicated first and above all to a policy of Irish unity.[152]

The more moderate *Belfast Telegraph* editorial contained a similar response:

> Mr Gerry Fitt's resignation from membership, as well as leadership, of the SDLP should come as no real surprise to those who have been aware

of his increasing disillusion with its nationalist grass-roots. A point had been reached when the West Belfast pragmatist had to part company with a rural-based party which put nationalist principle before practical politics.[153]

William Craig, who had done more than most to bring down the power-sharing Executive, commented: 'I'm sorry that it has happened but Mr Fitt is unquestionably right in this matter. He would not be a leader worth his salt if he did not back up his convictions in this way. It's a sad day for the SDLP but for politics it is very good to see a man who has the qualities of leadership.'[154]

In the Republic, the *Irish Press* editorial commented:

Mr Fitt, a brave, articulate and diligent representative of his people now goes into the wilderness, possibly to be a lone representative in West Belfast. Whether justly or unjustly his eclipse will be seen as that of yet another of the long line of Irish representatives at Westminster who succumbed to the fatal 'tone of the House' and became isolated from their followers in Northern Ireland.[155]

This opinion was merely a watered-down version of republican sentiment. A year earlier, the *Republican News* headline read simply, 'Fitt – British Apologist'.[156] Supporters of this long-held view had attacked Fitt's home, the worst incident occurring in August 1976. There were, however, other examples of intimidation and violence, which were deemed serious enough to be recorded by the press.[157]

I asked Fitt to reflect on why he had resigned from the SDLP and his response suggested the decision had been a long time in the making. He claimed that as early as 1973, Paddy Wilson (on the day before he was murdered by loyalists) had urged him to resign, since both men felt uncomfortable with and despondent about the direction the party was taking. Fitt went on to reiterate some of the reasons he had given at the time of his resignation.

I was always unhappy in the SDLP. It was a Catholic nationalist party. Every day the SDLP was going more nationalist, more Catholic and more anti-Prod. And they were finding excuses for what the Provos were doing. After the Mountbatten murder I said Jack Lynch should come home from his holiday in Portugal and I got stick from Duffy and Dennis Haughey and I asked at a meeting 'is this Provo Party'?

Fitt also told me that Charlie Haughey, as part of his campaign to wrest the leadership from Lynch, persuaded the Taoiseach that it was unnecessary to cut short his holiday, adding that Lynch was so devastated by the murder he was 'drunk for two days'.

On the issue of Atkins' proposals, Fitt turned his attention to Hume and, in particular, his successor's part in the intrigue within the SDLP:

> John Hume was very shrewd. Every time a big decision had to be taken John would have to go off to Europe. He came to me that day and said 'What you think of that White Paper?'
> 'I agree with it,' I said.
> 'But, Gerry, the nationalist people want to retain their aspiration.'
> I said, 'That's all crap, the people down there don't even want us – they couldn't keep us if they got us, Stormont is gone and we were foolish to let the Executive go over the council of Ireland.'
> John said, 'I have got to go to Europe', but before he went he rang up all the others – Paddy Duffy – all the other nationalists and told them, 'I think Gerry is going to agree with the White Paper that says we can't have an Irish dimension.' So he rang them all up and went off to Europe.[158]

Fitt went on to describe the subsequent SDLP meeting in Dungannon. 'Soon as I walked in Seamus Mallon was glaring at me and two or three others. The rural elements were glaring at me.' (Mallon has no such recollection.)[159] Fitt claims he told the gathering that he denied relinquishing the Irish dimension. He stressed that what he believed was important 'was to try and get something going within Northern Ireland so that we could learn to live together'. Then he seemed to have something of an epiphany:

> Then I sat back. I will never forget it. I looked around and looked at them one by one. I thought he's a Derry Taig. He's not bad and he's not mad but his idea is a united Ireland and he wants to aspire to it even though he is never going to get it and if he got it tomorrow he wouldn't want it. He just doesn't see things the way I see it. And I continued going around them. There was Seamus Mallon, 'sure he is a half Provo'. And I went around them all and I thought there is none of them really bad people

but they are all green nationalists and I am 'like a nigger in a woodpile'. I shouldn't be in this party at all because I don't think I'm a bad bastard either. We are never going to see eye to eye.

After the meeting Fitt returned home to find his wife crying. According to Fitt, Mallon was again the villain of the piece. On television he had criticised Fitt for not representing the party view on the Irish dimension, only his own. 'That's it,' said Fitt. 'I'm not having you crying over what bastards say about me and I am going to resign tomorrow and that's when I made up my mind.'[160]

Fitt's opinion that the SDLP had become too republican was denied by his former colleagues, as was the absurd charge that Mallon was a 'half Provo'. Eddie McGrady said Fitt 'may have thought that but he would have been wrong. I do not recall anyone at the top level having any regard for republicanism at all. In fact many suffered greatly at their hands. Certainly Mallon's reputation was unjustified.'[161] Cooper was adamant: 'Mallon has never been a half Provo, a full Provo or a semi Provo. He was very loyal to the SDLP whether you liked him or disliked him – that was a fact.'[162]

The only thing Mallon is guilty of is consistent conviction and honesty. He unequivocally acknowledges that he is 'more of a republican than a nationalist' and always has done.[163] That republicanism is viewed as synonymous with militancy is indeed a misrepresentation. Fitt's conclusion was therefore unwarranted. The appearance in South Armagh of posters and banners with images of a kneeling, blindfolded Mallon being executed, with the caption 'Seamus Mallon is an informer', confirms that he never pandered to the physical force republicans and that the latter patently did not view him as one of their own.

What is interesting about Fitt's departure is that although neither the media nor Mallon was surprised at his resignation, many in the SDLP were. McGrady considered it a 'mysterious break' because 'he had no reason to leave':

My assumption at the time was that Gerry had made a deal to deliver the SDLP to a new engagement that was an election to a new assembly which we were not interested in and I think Gerry gave an undertaking that the SDLP would be all right on the day. It wasn't; it was unanimous, including his hand. Those two or three days were completely irrational from where I was coming from.[164]

Cooper was 'shocked and stunned'.[165] To Currie it 'came out of the blue'.[166] I asked Mallon why he was not surprised:

> The reality was that I was hearing things that Gerry was saying to others in whom he placed some trust. It was a fundamental error because they were not keeping it confidential. I was also aware that the decision taken in relation to the Atkins talks was not a decision about going into them. It was about going into them with the exclusion of the Irish dimension and the vast majority of the party was not going to wear that. I for one would not have gone along with it. Ultimately Gerry voted with us but I knew what he was saying to others.

Nevertheless Mallon was somewhat bewildered. He told me:

> I was surprised that a party leader should not recognise the depth of feeling in his party. He had little if any support. What I believe was happening was that there were those telling Gerry one thing in the bar and doing the opposite when it came to the crunch. I still can't understand how the leader of a party such as ours was going to go into negotiations leaving aside an absolutely essential plank of its policy.[167]

The rejection of Atkins' proposals and Fitt's embarrassment at not being able to deliver his party to talks may have provided him with the opportunity to jump ship, but Cooper is probably the closest to clearing up the real reason for his resignation: he concluded that 'Gerry had an awful lot of bitterness to John Hume'. Cooper certainly dismissed the 'greening' of the party as valid motivation. 'The SDLP did not become any greener than it was at Sunningdale. Just look at what we committed ourselves to in our policy documents and Fitt was leader of the party. That criticism from him and Devlin before him I totally reject.'[168] It was Fitt who had changed, not the party. This was certainly Mallon's view:

> I could see it happening. I think one of the elements in it was the way Westminster can beguile people. I think there was that and there was a certain media nexus that actually wanted the SDLP to become a non-ideological party. Those things were at play. There was always the requirement that the SDLP should accommodate and this was very prevalent in Westminster

and here for that matter and once Gerry had made his decision he moved more and more to filling that requirement.[169]

What is certain about the whole affair is that the majority of the SDLP maintained a consistent course while Fitt floundered in indecision. If it was the goal of the SDLP to work for an institutionalised Irish dimension alongside power-sharing, it achieved this objective. But it would be accurate to say that if Gerry Fitt was on the bridge, John Hume was operating the rudder and his supporters were in the engine room.

Whatever the explanation for Fitt's resignation, he was still the MP for West Belfast, with its chronic social dysfunction which, to adopt a deprivationist approach, would have been a strong reason for some to buy into the romantic idealism of the IRA. Belfast housing was widely believed to be the worst in Europe,[170] and the jobless total in the city was the highest since 1940.[171] In August 1978 the Child Poverty Action Group published a document asserting that nearly one-third of Northern Irish families were living below the poverty line.[172] This is not to say that Fitt remained inactive on such issues. He often spoke passionately at Westminster in an attempt to highlight and improve the situation.[173]

But the forum at Westminster had become increasingly unimportant to large sections of his constituency. The continued army presence, the reports of unreasonable interrogation methods at Castlereagh, the Diplock Courts and the social poverty within the constituency – exacerbated by Mrs Thatcher's economic austerity – were bound to alienate many working-class nationalists.

While Fitt remained a committed parliamentarian, Provisional Sinn Féin began to develop into a substantial political movement, immersed in community concerns and emphasising employment and housing issues in tandem with its demand for British withdrawal and the abolition of the border. Against this backdrop, Fitt's control of the constituency – now as an independent politician – would be threatened and his position would be undermined further by the explosive impact of the prisons issue, which had been simmering since 1976.

7

From Gerry Fitt
to Gerry Adams

The final chapter of Gerry Fitt's representative political career was inextricably linked to the political evolution of the republican movement and the electoral rise of Sinn Féin. His political standpoint became increasingly focused on both opposition to republicanism and criticism of the SDLP, rather than on the wider social and political issues of his early career. Ultimately Fitt's politics became almost exclusively centred on containing the developing electoral power of Sinn Féin. It was ironic that he was the first major political casualty of this realignment within nationalism.

At the end of the 1970s Fitt was a very isolated figure, and in many respects he was the author of his own misfortune. The Conservative victory in the May election had imperilled his relationship with the British Labour Party, and his resignation from the SDLP left him without political colleagues in Northern Ireland. Then he burned his bridges with important politicians in the Republic.

Towards the end of 1979, pressure had built up on the Taoiseach, Jack Lynch, from within his own party. Many of the politicos in Fianna Fáil argued that he had been too acquiescent towards the British, and in December Lynch was succeeded as party leader and Taoiseach by Charles Haughey. Despite his acquittal in 1970 of supplying guns to the newly formed Provisionals, many politicians, media commentators and citizens of the Republic felt Haughey might be a hard-line republican.

Fitt was unhappy about these developments. He felt the forces opposing Lynch in Fianna Fáil were the same that had opposed him in the SDLP. Lynch had settled on a moderate stance in relation to the problems of Northern Ireland and Fitt unmistakably identified with this attitude.[1] This view showed that Fitt had further shifted ground. In the past he had argued that the Republic's government could have made more strenuous efforts to end partition – now he showed himself to be reasonably content with the *status quo*.

Fitt continued in politics under the label 'independent socialist', clinging to this classification as steadfastly as he had done to the power-sharing concept. His socialist arguments at Westminster retained their familiar characteristics. Ideology was replaced with tangible examples of injustice. In March 1980, he attacked Thatcherite policy in Northern Ireland:

> I am sure that Ministers will accept that not only in this part of the United Kingdom but in Northern Ireland every facet of life has been affected by the new Tory government's doctrinaire and monetaristic – if there is such a word … policies.
>
> There is no doubt that the effects of the doctrinaire approach of this government have been an absolute disaster for Northern Ireland. Children's school meals, the cost of housing, the deterioration in the number of jobs and the diminution of the number of home helps – all the things that made life bearable for the people of Northern Ireland have been disastrously affected by the approach of this government.

Although he had maintained a socialist position at Westminster (notwithstanding his decision to undermine the Callaghan government in 1979), he developed no penchant for political theorising. When asked by a Tory MP how increased expenditure was to be funded, he simplistically replied … 'the way of solving the problem is the issue that divides the two sides of this House'.[2] He characteristically followed this with arguments based on anecdotes. (To be fair to Fitt, he always urged alleviation of the social and economic ills of Northern Ireland and particularly West Belfast. He persisted with these arguments even in the House of Lords.) Despite such activity Fitt was somewhat rootless at this time.

In sharp contrast, Provisional Sinn Féin was in the process of internal re-organisation and re-assessment, leading to its eventual transformation.

In June 1979, a major shift in republican policy was indicated at the annual Wolfe Tone commemoration ceremony in Bodenstown, County Kildare. Gerry Adams, now vice-president of Provisional Sinn Féin, made an important speech on future republican policy. He praised the 'blanket men' for their resistance to the criminalisation process and also predictably criticised the governments of both Britain and the Irish Republic. The innovative aspect of Adams' statement was the denial that severing the British connection was the organisation's only goal. He rejected the idea that British withdrawal was the solution to the problem and promoted a socialist programme:

> As republicans we stand with the have-nots against the haves. We stand with the under-privileged, the young, the unemployed, the workers – the people of no property. We are for the ownership of Ireland by the people of Ireland and we believe that national freedom entails economic and cultural independence and that one without the other is useless.

Adams was, in the tradition of social republicanism, directing an appeal to the disadvantaged. This had been a feature of republicanism in times of economic need. For example, during the 1930s, after the shock of deValera's departure, republicans had set up the Republican Congress; and in the 1960s, after the collapse of the border campaign, Sinn Féin had moved into social agitation and socialist theorising. Now, with the Provisionals' military capacity in decline it was decided to broaden the republican campaign and to fight on another front – left-leaning electoral politics.

In West Belfast Adams was ploughing fertile ground. He was anxious not to alienate conservative republicans and so his socialist rhetoric was fused with traditional republican sentiment: 'We are opposed to big business, to multi-nationalism, to gombeenism, to sectarianism and to the maintenance of a privileged class. We stand opposed to all forms and all manifestations of imperialism and capitalism. We stand for an Ireland, free, united, socialist and gaelic.'

Adams then voiced what he felt was the inadequacy of republican strategy: 'Our most glaring weakness to date lies in our failure to develop revolutionary politics and to build a strong political alternative to so-called constitutional politics.'[3] The importance of Adams' address lies in the fact that Provisional Sinn Féin had decided that a 'Brits Out' policy was no longer enough. Ultimate victory would be achieved only if the muscle of the IRA was reinforced with a political alternative to the 'so-called constitutionalists'. The party's left-wing political programme would threaten Fitt and his former colleagues in the SDLP.

While republicans reappraised their strategy Fitt became increasingly popular with elements in the British establishment, a consequence both of his continued refusal to be 'intimidated' by the IRA and his capacity to make the 'right' noises. However, some of this admiration was unwelcome. In February 1980, he turned down an award from the Ross McWhirter Foundation. (McWhirter was an active right-winger and vigorous opponent of the IRA who was killed by the Provisionals on his doorstep in 1974.) Fitt explained that he declined to accept the award not because he had any opposition to commemorating the memory of McWhirter, but because he was a socialist. He added: 'I have also refused it because the foundation appears to have associations with right wing organisations which take a different political view from myself'.[4] However, the fact that the award was offered at all was in itself significant. The British right-wing press had long sought to use Fitt's abhorrence of the IRA for propaganda purposes. Right-wing elements in the McWhirter Foundation were keen to reward an Irish politician who had in a sense disowned his nationalist past by continually attacking the republican movement.

John Hume had succeeded Fitt as leader of the SDLP and Seamus Mallon was installed as Hume's deputy. Time had not erased Fitt's bitterness: in the late 1980s he still resented Hume. He told me: 'John Hume does not like Protestants. John is an anti-Prod. He is a Derry Catholic. He cannot understand them. That is not to say he is malicious. He just cannot understand them.'[5] Ivan Cooper's earlier assessment that there was little personal rapport between the two was confirmed to me by Austin Currie. Currie maintained that the relationship between the successive leaders of the SDLP 'was always a difficult one' although for long periods they cooperated closely. He suggests that Hume increasingly came to articulate SDLP policy and Fitt consequently could not find his own niche.[6]

It seems clear that personal antagonism may well have aggravated their political disagreements. Both men were certainly different. Fitt had a tendency to think that education negated the working-class instinct. Hume was likely to have been frustrated that for many years Fitt controlled the only available political forum. In any case it was a demanding relationship, so it is surprising that a public break did not occur earlier. Ivan Cooper pointed out what he considered a crucial difference. He told me: 'Hume very successfully cultivated relationships with the Irish government and Irish civil servants. That was his great strength to the party. Gerry was not capable of doing that.'[7] Unionism seemed to warm to the first leader rather than the second, while still noting the essential contrast. Revd Martin Smyth told me:

> I don't know if John Hume had the same gift of friendship or companionship. Fitt had this outgoing personality that was quite remarkable. Gerry would talk to anybody. John would hang back on the fringes. A shy man. John would have the academic and more trained mind. That is not to say Fitt was a fool. Gerry had a good brain but not a disciplined mind.[8]

Despite the contrasts, the two were not totally without similarities. Murray makes a somewhat surprising comparison:

> As to the leadership of the SDLP, Fitt and Hume could be seen to have something in common. Both are individualists and have no interest in Party organisation. On the one hand, Fitt was a street politician; on the other, Hume has tended to take the role of the philosopher, always planning ahead. Hume's lack of interest in Party organisation has led to a disparate Party organisation with no strong central base in Belfast.[9]

Mallon gives the view credence: 'Neither recognised the absolute need to organise a party and organise it on the basis of survival. Neither saw the need or fulfilled it.'[10] Cooper, however, insists that Hume was 'very strong on branch structure', though he felt that he 'failed to groom people early enough' to ensure continuity within the party. He went on to make another interesting comparison:

> Hume did not like people of ability close to him. His relationship with Mallon was very poor, extremely poor and that was a mistake. Mallon was a very valuable public representative. He doesn't like sharing public accolades. That was something Gerry was guilty of too.[11]

That the SDLP was led by charismatic individualists in the style of Joe Devlin was both its greatest asset and its Achilles heel. Hume, no less than Fitt, was the subject of rank and file criticism for pursuing his own strategy at the expense, some have argued, of the party. One thing is certain: Fitt took no one with him when he left the SDLP. His distaste for organisation had militated against the party evolving a strong political network in West Belfast. This lack of structure was critical in later years and contrasted with Provisional Sinn Féin's new-found commitment to establishing a challenging political presence in the area.

Fitt had reverted to his role of 'lone operator', content to rely on personal charisma and Westminster contacts. In the years ahead he attacked not only the Provisionals but also the SDLP, placing himself outside nationalist politics as expressed by its two major proponents. He had become something of a political oddity in urban nationalism.

Ironically, the SDLP reversed its position on the Atkins talks and agreed to attend after some political manoeuvring by the Northern Ireland secretary. Atkins said that all parties would be allowed to submit papers on any topic they chose. Hume was not against the idea of talks, but was adamant that the Irish dimension should be discussed. The conference was doomed to failure when the official unionists reaffirmed their decision not to attend. Atkins' focus was too narrow. He had ruled out both Sunningdale-type and Stormont-type arrangements. The SDLP wanted the former, Paisley and the DUP wanted the latter.

At Westminster Fitt accurately described the talks as a 'charade'.[12] He followed his assessment with an attack on the SDLP, telling the *Belfast Telegraph* that his former party had planned to wreck the talks: 'I know with absolute certainty that if the SDLP had been offered a power-sharing arrangement as before – under the Sunningdale Executive – they would have said thank you very much but we want an institutionalised Irish dimension – a Council of Ireland.'[13] He argued that such a disposition effectively precluded any unionist from finding an agreement. Eddie McGrady countered with a valid point:

> The policies of the SDLP were determined at our last annual conference in November, up to which time Gerry was leader and presumably was in full support of the party. He certainly didn't indicate any contrary opinions at the time. In fact he was the main speaker before the constitutional debate at the party conference.[14]

McGrady had effectively exposed the contradiction in Fitt's political posturing. At his last conference as leader, Fitt had indeed told the party: 'If I were not a Belfast man, if I were not a Catholic, if I were not Irish, if I were not a Socialist, I would be forced to arrive at the same conclusion: that the partition of this country was an absolute disaster'.[15]

In May, away from the spotlight of the party conference, Fitt said he would concede the Irish dimension in exchange for power-sharing:

> What we must do is to go out and find a solution within Northern Ireland on the power-sharing issue. After you have done that and allowed time to build up trust between the communities, then you can begin to think about Irish dimensions. To try to institutionalise them both at the same time is self-defeating.[16]

Six years after the Sunningdale experiment he had finally revealed that he considered power-sharing and the Irish dimension mutually exclusive. The *Irish Times* reported Fitt saying:

> There are no more Brian Faulkners around. There's no unionists that I can see in Northern Ireland who would be prepared to talk to anyone about an Irish dimension, much less Irish unity ... I would not let a demand for an Irish dimension prevent me, or prevent the minority, from participating in governmental structures created at Stormont.[17]

He was now prepared to say almost anything to ease Protestant fears on the Irish dimension, but such pronouncements were unlikely to make the impact they once had. If there were any doubts about Fitt's political preference at this juncture, these emphatic disclosures dispelled them. His attachment to the goal of a united Ireland had been an important component of his political success. Now, however, he had unequivocally relinquished the aim in the medium term, focusing instead on an internal solution, and continuing to lament the failure of the Sunningdale experiment.[18] Fitt accused the SDLP of being merely the northern wing of the Fianna Fáil Party.[19]

It could be argued that Fitt had not abandoned his commitment to a united Ireland as an ultimate target but had merely made power-sharing his main political aspiration as a sort of 'stepping stone'. In other words his tactics rather than his principles were flexible. But there is little evidence to substantiate this notion. In contrast to previous years, he never indulged in nationalist rhetoric and if he had considered power-sharing a 'stepping stone', he would have been guilty of trying to dupe the Protestant community. Of this he was not culpable.

Meanwhile the prison protest, which had begun with Kieran Nugent's refusal to wear prison clothes, had gradually escalated. As a gesture of solidarity with their male colleagues, the women in Armagh gaol began their own dirty protest in February 1980. British efforts to break the deadlock met with no success.

In May, Provisional Sinn Féin held a seminar on prisons. Danny Morrison, at this point, editor of *An Phoblacht/Republican News*, articulated the party's position *vis-à-vis* the protest:

> Republican strategy and the way forward on the POW issue must be based on two basic principles. Firstly, to secure political status for POWs in Ireland and comparable conditions and repatriation for those seeking it in English prisons. Secondly, to articulate, exploit and propagandise on the prison struggle, to show how it constitutes an important part of the overall struggle, and to show that the prison struggle is not merely a manifestation of republican resistance to British policy but also a manifestation of the British government's attitude to Ireland.[20]

The prison protest had given Provisional Sinn Féin its best propaganda vehicle since internment and Bloody Sunday. Morrison felt the issue could and should be used to build up anti-British feeling and create a wider base amongst the Catholic community. This, it was hoped, would be converted into support for Sinn Féin itself and, by extension, for the Provisional IRA.

On 10 October, in a move designed to increase the impetus of the protest, republican prisoners announced that they would shortly begin a hunger strike. On 23 October, Atkins had offered civilian-type clothing to the prisoners, but after some deliberation the offer was rejected because it failed to meet their central demand – the granting of political status.

On 27 October seven republican prisoners refused food, vowing that they would fast until either their demands were met or they died of starvation. The stakes had been raised dramatically. The repercussions of the hunger strikes would transform nationalist politics, damaging the SDLP's position as the sole voice of the minority community and having a profound impact on Gerry Fitt's career.

On 10 November, Fitt made his most controversial speech yet in the House of Commons – a speech he suspected would be 'political suicide'.[21] Jim Molyneaux, leader of the Official Unionists, set the tone of the debate:

It is important for the world to know and for distinguished churchmen to remember that IRA hunger strikers are not misguided petty thieves or pickpockets in need of correction or spiritual guidance. They are not even men who have been convicted of murder in a fit of rage. They are evil men who have planned and plotted in cold blood to take innocent lives. They are beasts who have gunned down their fellow men and pumped hot lead into their twitching bodies.[22]

Fitt then spoke, recalling having successfully pleaded for political status in 1972:

I have to tell the House that I bitterly regret having made those representations. At that time there were 80 republican prisoners and 40 Loyalist prisoners. I believed that, because of the special circumstances at that time, the granting of political special category status would end the strife. I was terribly wrong.

He then catalogued numerous incidents when both IRA and loyalist violence had caused death throughout the decade. Fitt pledged to support the introduction of humane prison reforms, but urged the British government to stand firm against granting political status:

The government should make it clear to those engaged in the hunger strike that they will not obtain political status. By telling the truth, and telling it in such a way that it cannot be misunderstood ... it is possible that the men on hunger strike will realise the error of their ways and bring the strike to an end. I do not want to see those men dying. I do not want to see anyone dying. The government must show their resolution and not allow themselves to be blackmailed by people giving support to the hunger strike ...

I ask the Secretary of State to be as humane as possible to every prisoner in Northern Ireland, of whatever political or religious belief – but not to make the mistake of granting political status. That mistake was made in 1972. I believe that it led to the taking of many innocent lives in Northern Ireland.[23]

Fitt's views on republicans and republican prisoners had undergone significant revision since the 1950s and 1960s. Then he had considered them 'men of principle', had employed them as bodyguards in preference to the police, and, on occasion, allowed them to attend 'gun lectures' in his party premises. It was as if Fitt could view republicans as 'men of principle' when they were only a few politically powerless people, hopelessly throwing themselves against the might of the unionist state. But now they had metamorphosed into something more sinister, emerging from the working-class areas of Belfast (his traditional constituency), he could only view them with disdain and hostility.

Fitt saw the hunger strikes in simplistic black and white terms, and while many Catholics admired his stand against violence many more felt it gratuitous to call on the Thatcher government not to give in. There was also the routine of communal politics, whereby a victory for one side was perceived to be at the other's expense. In Northern Ireland, there has always been the instinct to stick with 'one's own', however bad the circumstances. To many, then, Fitt was becoming a unionist.

Gerry Adams later commented on what he saw as the mood of the nationalist community after Fitt's speech:

> I think Fitt's stance was seen precisely for what it was, that here was a man who had come from what he alleged was a socialist republican position and was now siding with the British government against men who were in prison and who were quite clearly in the eyes of a large section of the community not criminals and who were left with nothing but to go on hunger strike. To oppose those demands may have been legitimate enough but to give Thatcher succour was seen by many people as perhaps the last straw.[24]

Adams made a valid point. The decade of conflict that had broken out in Northern Ireland was hardly the result of a spontaneous crime wave from the Catholic community. But Fitt's rationale for the stance he took as regards the hunger strike changed little. He told me:

> When the hunger strike started it was a very emotional thing. It was totally tribal. No reason or intellect went into it. When it started I was in the position of recalling all the coffins that I had carried through graveyards and a lot of them were victims of the IRA. Some of them were women and children and I was in the position of being expected to lend my support to the men who actually carried out these murders. There was no way I could do that.[25]

Fitt was correct to say that the hunger strike reduced the conflict to its communal fundamentals. Rosary rallies played a large part in the agitation, as did recourse to Gaelic mythology, and all the traditional shibboleths of Catholic nationalism. At this stage it was not the sort of ground Fitt wanted to be on.

Reaction to Fitt's 'political suicide' speech was at the time predictably mixed and revealed how his profile had altered. The SDLP had stayed aloof from the controversy, intent to await the outcome of a Thatcher–Haughey summit in December. Provisional Sinn Féin however, was quick to respond, a spokesman claiming, 'We believe that Fitt has lost touch with the nationalist working-class and are confident that provided with an alternative choice, our people will positively reject Gerry Fitt's unionism.'[26] Bernadette Devlin McAliskey described the speech as 'murderous' and called Fitt 'a shadow of a man'.[27]

Moderate unionism, as expressed by the editorial of the *Belfast Telegraph* was, on the other hand, impressed, claiming that Fitt had shown 'considerable political and moral courage' by disregarding 'tribal loyalties'.[28]

This contrasted sharply with the views of newspapers in the Republic. The *Irish Press* was particularly forthright. An editorial by Tim Pat Coogan reprimanded Fitt for 'attacking his own people' and claimed he was nothing but a 'stage Irishman' duped by the British.[29] Conversely, while the pro-Fianna Fáil *Irish Press* castigated Fitt, leading members of the Orange Order praised him (which did him no favours electorally). Revd Martin Smyth described Fitt's speech as 'courageous'.[30]

There were calls from nationalist quarters for Fitt to resign his West-minster seat and contest a by-election on the hunger strike issue. Fitt retorted that he had received over two hundred letters from all over the country supporting his position, with only four dissenting. He claimed that most of them came from deprived areas of Belfast, and from all sections of the community. He also reported having received a telegram from thirty-three employees of the *Irish Press* who (despite what Coogan had written) applauded his stand: 'This is the authentic voice of the people, and shows that I am on the right path.'[31] The future would tell if Fitt's views were representative of those of his constituents. But by that stage, the political landscape had changed dramatically.

The Conservative government was unmoved by the strike. Throughout November, the administration insisted that political status was a concession that would never be met. The prisoners decided to intensify their protest still further and on 15 December twenty-three prisoners joined the original seven. Four days later the protest was suddenly called off.

On 17 December, the Northern Ireland Office had made a tentative bid to resolve the dispute. The prisoners were told that a paper containing some sort of trade-off was being prepared. As it turned out, the hunger strike was called off before the details of what appeared to be an offer were known. One of the original seven fasters had deteriorated more rapidly than the rest. By 27 December Seán McKenna was almost totally blind and lapsing into a coma. The other six strikers and Bobby Sands (the recently appointed leader of the Provisional prisoners), were now in a dilemma. They had to decide whether to await the British proposal, and allow McKenna to die, or to end the strike in the hope that the British proposals would meet their demands. They chose the latter.

The first hunger strike ended in confusion, but there was naturally a general feeling of relief. Initially, Provisional Sinn Féin claimed victory, but the British claimed that they had granted nothing and had not changed their position since the start of the protest. In the event, the prisoners were far from satisfied with what had been offered.[32] Ending the strike did restore calm over the Christmas period, but this was to be short-lived.

Early in the New Year Fitt argued, somewhat extravagantly, that 1981 could be as significant a turning point as the Battle of the Boyne or the Easter Rising – if the British and Irish governments acted quickly and decisively. His reasoning was prompted by the Thatcher–Haughey summit, which had taken place ten days before the end of the hunger strike. (The post-summit communiqué pledged that special consideration would be given to 'the totality of relationships' within the islands.) Fitt optimistically thought there was some hope that the 'terrible agony' of Northern Ireland was finally drawing to a close. He considered the Provisionals a spent force: 'The Provisional IRA staked everything on their trump card, the recent failed hunger strike for political status. By its failure they have shown they have nothing else to offer but mindless violence.'[33]

Fitt was wrong on both counts. Despite all the media hype, the communiqué after the summit represented little more than empty rhetoric. Thatcher and Haughey placed different emphases on the statement, and the Provisionals were far from finished. Mallon appealed to them to lay down their arms and adopt purely political means. Provisional Sinn Féin responded:

If Mr Mallon and his colleagues wish to see the creation of a society free from the spectre of death and suffering, then it is about time they climbed off the fence and set themselves the task of unequivocally demanding the withdrawal of that destructive and divisive influence. Playing politics and kowtowing to the British is what has us in the present situation. It is time the SDLP learned that lesson.[34]

Clearly, the Provisionals were not yet ready to enter the political arena, but their capacity for destruction and death remained undiminished. In January alone, seven people were killed and thirteen injured as a result of IRA activity.

On 27 January, there was violence in the H blocks over the prisoners' refusal to conform to prison regulations. The following day it was announced that a second hunger strike would begin on 1 March. For the second protest, the prisoners changed their tactics. Instead of simply demanding 'political status', they made five specific demands: the right to wear their own clothing instead of prison uniforms; exemption from all forms of penal labour; free association with one another at all times; the right to organise their own recreational and educational programmes; and a full restoration of the sentence remission to which they would be entitled by conforming to prison rules. Bobby Sands was the first to refuse food; the others were to follow at fortnightly intervals.

Soon after the strike began, Frank Maguire, the independent nationalist MP for Fermanagh–South Tyrone, died. His death and the subsequent by-election would have important ramifications for minority politics in Northern Ireland.

Fitt continued to criticise the SDLP, again arguing that his former colleagues were too close to Fianna Fáil:

On leaving the party, I stated that I thought it was becoming too closely aligned with Fianna Fáil and more particularly with a certain militant wing within that party.

My priorities have always been the safety and welfare, not only of my own constituents, but everyone in Northern Ireland and the fortunes of political parties in the South are not of the same importance to me.[35]

Fitt's traditional aspiration to Irish unity does not sit comfortably with his later concentration on internal northern issues. Hume responded by saying that Fitt sounded very much like a 'cracked record' and the rift between the two former colleagues would widen further.[36] However, the feud between the chieftains of the SDLP past and present was merely a sub-plot in the unfolding drama.

There was increasing speculation about the choice of anti-unionist candidate to contest the Fermanagh–South Tyrone by-election. The first to put his name forward was Noel Maguire, brother of the dead MP. It was also suggested that Bernadette McAliskey contest the seat, in the belief that she would obtain a strong personal vote, having recently been the victim of an unsuccessful murder attempt by loyalist gunmen. In the event she stood down, having reached an agreement with Provisional Sinn Féin that Bobby Sands be put forward as a candidate to highlight the hunger strike and British intransigence. The SDLP selected Austin Currie as its prospective MP.[37]

There were thus three proposed anti-unionist candidates – Sands, Maguire and Currie – facing one high-profile unionist, Harry West, in a constituency with a small nationalist majority. If all stood, the unionists would win easily. The decision now facing the SDLP was whether to participate or withdraw, and in the end it was the arguments against contesting the election that carried the day. This can be construed as an intensification of the nationalist sentiment in the party. The decision became even more significant when Maguire withdrew his candidature on the day of nominations after a personal appeal by the Sands family.

Predictably, Fitt criticised the SDLP resolution, saying that the party could no longer claim to be a labour party, nor one of reconciliation: 'It is a shame, an outrage and a gross betrayal of non-unionist voters in this constituency who have been put into a position where they have no candidate for which they can vote in conformity with their opposition to violence.'[38]

In the 1960s Fitt's politics were largely based on denigration, with the Unionist Party as the target. In the 1980s, disparagement was still his main political weapon, but now the SDLP was on the receiving end. There was an element of spite in Fitt's slighting language. Nevertheless, this particular attack was partly justified. The SDLP had always contested elections as constitutional nationalists, but they had made a concession to tribalism by allowing a convicted IRA man a free run. The judgement was that a critical split in the nationalist vote, followed by the death of Bobby Sands, would damage the SDLP's credibility among the nationalist voters. It was a no-win situation for the party, which had to consider, among other things, the personal safety of whoever was going to fight the election. Adams understandably welcomed the concept of a two-horse race and was confident of the result: 'The election of Bobby Sands will serve as an acid test for those who reject British attempts to criminalise opposition to their presence in this country.'[39]

As the election drew closer, Fitt claimed that there was serious dissension in the ranks of the SDLP because of its failure to contest the seat.[40] His advice to SDLP voters was to abstain.[41] Fitt was correct: there was conflict within the party, but this was partially patched up when it was agreed to contest all seats, including West Belfast, at the next general election. Fitt was defiant: 'I was representing West Belfast before the SDLP was in existence and I will be representing the area long after the SDLP has ceased to be a force in Belfast.'[42]

Sands' election campaign was aided by Provisional Sinn Féin's political organisation, with Adams and Morrison campaigning throughout the area. Sands did not stand as a Sinn Féin representative: instead his platform was based on an anti-H Block/political prisoner stand. This attracted a broad spectrum of nationalist support. Frank McManus (former Unity MP for the area), Bernadette Devlin McAliskey and Noel Maguire all lent their support to the campaign. The nationalist population was asked to vote in support of the prisoners' five demands, not for the fact that Sands was a republican who believed in the armed struggle.

Election day was set for 9 April, and Fermanagh–South Tyrone became the focus for the world's media. In line with tradition, and because of the high stakes involved, the constituency achieved a high turnout of 86.8 per cent. Sands was victorious, polling 30,492 votes to West's 29,046.[43] The result showed that all shades of nationalism had come together in support of the prisoners. After forty-one days on hunger strike, during which he had reportedly lost twenty-eight pounds in weight, Bobby Sands became a Member of Parliament. Danny Morrison commented on the outcome: 'This result has finally proved through the ballot box, how deep the support is for republican prisoners. The people of Fermanagh and South Tyrone have spoken on behalf of the Irish nation. He (Sands) will not resign the seat. The hunger strike will take its course.'[44]

Fitt was alarmed. He claimed the result was a 'mandate for the Provisional IRA', and feared the consequences:

There will certainly be untold repercussions for a long time to come, and it will lead to greater polarisation and alienation between the two communities, especially in Fermanagh and South Tyrone where the Protestant population will believe that their Catholic neighbours are giving overt support to the IRA.[45]

Fitt over-estimated the extent to which a vote for Sands was a vote for the IRA. Many Catholics voted for Sands to highlight the H Block campaign and to save him from dying. Fitt's hatred for the Provisionals had induced an inflexible attitude. Adams used the result as an opportunity to attack Fitt:

> The result of the by-election had proved many things – not least that Mr Gerry Fitt's call to the electorate was totally ignored by the nationalist people of the area. Fitt placed his political reputation against the lives of the hunger-strikers and suffered the consequences of his despicable treachery.

He challenged Fitt to resign his seat and claimed the people of West Belfast would give him the same answer as did the people of Fermanagh and South Tyrone.[46]

The essence of Sands' electoral triumph was that he could no longer simply be described as a terrorist – he was now a democratically elected MP with a mandate from the people of Fermanagh–South Tyrone, and this brought enormous international attention.

However, the election victory had no effect on the British government. Thatcher remained steadfast in her refusal to meet the prisoners' demands. Sands died on 5 May, and two days later 100,000 people attended his funeral. A week after Sands' death, Francis Hughes, the second hunger striker, died, and was followed within two weeks by Raymond McCreesh and Patsy O'Hara. In Dublin, there was serious rioting outside the British embassy.

On 20 May, the day before McCreesh and O'Hara died, polling took place for the local government elections. In an extremely tense atmosphere, Provisional Sinn Féin persisted with its policy of abstention. Fitt again contested the election for Belfast Area G. He did not prepare a manifesto or an election address, preferring to rely on his past record as a public representative. He defined what he considered the issues involved:

> So far as I am concerned those who are opposed to me in this election have

made it quite clear that their opposition is based on my stand in relation to terrorism and its supporters. I therefore fully accept that a vote for me is a vote against the gunman, and I leave this decision to the electorate of Belfast.[47]

If Fitt was correct in saying that a vote for him was a vote against the gunmen, the results were grave for constitutionalism. He polled only 541 first-preference votes – only 5.4 per cent of the votes cast and 900 below the quota required for election.

The result showed how polarised the community had become. Sam Ashby of the DUP and Fergus O'Hare of the PD were both elected on the first count. (By this point the People's Democracy profile had been resurrected somewhat by its identification with the hunger strikers, and it had also defended the Provisionals against the British.) Sammy Millar, a member of the UDA, was also elected. The Alliance candidate fared badly but for Fitt the result was a disaster, as the SDLP candidate, Brian Feeney, gained more first-preference votes. After twenty-three years, Fitt's career as a Belfast city councillor was over.

His capacity to campaign in the customary way was severely hindered by open hostility. Feeney subsequently claimed, 'Fitt could not canvass in hard-line republican areas, in fact he even needed a police bodyguard to go to mass. He was totally remote by that stage.'[48]

After his elimination Fitt claimed, 'I put in my nomination papers in the full knowledge that I was going to be defeated', adding 'I hope the electors haven't made as big a mistake as I think they have.'[49] He told me this defeat wounded him deeply because it had occurred in his home constituency.[50] It must have been particularly galling that it was the 'nincompoops' of the PD who had taken the lion's share of the Catholic/nationalist vote.

Seán MacStíofáin, PIRA chief of staff from 1970 to 1972, made an interesting observation that can be applied to this election. 'It has always been a feature of Irish attitudes that while backing for the revolutionary movement may ebb and flow at different times, people's sympathy for republican prisoners and their families is constant.'[51] Fitt refused to accept that, despite their conduct, the militant members of the republican movement remain an integral part of their community.[52] This helps explain why the 'nationally minded' people had abandoned Fitt. Fergus O'Hare interpreted his triumph:

It shows that the people in the area support the prisoners' five demands, not the programme put forward by any other anti-unionist candidate. My vote trebled that of other anti-unionist candidates and quadrupled that of Gerry Fitt's. It was a total rejection of Mr Fitt's stance in the election and his attacks on the prisoners. We call on him to step down from his Westminster seat and put his present views to the electorate.[53]

There can be no doubt that Fitt's stance on the hunger strike had been rejected by a majority of nationalists or that it sent a strong signal of rejection and betrayal. Ivan Cooper suggested that Fitt could not reconcile himself with the voters' decision after everything that he had done for them over many years, and concluded that 'he was deeply hurt'.[54] This analysis was confirmed a week after the results had been declared when Fitt said, with some resentment:

I have no intention of leaving my home. However, I certainly do not feel as committed to this area as I once did. After last week's election in which I lost my City Council seat, it would be more than human for me to open my door to people with the same enthusiasm I once did. I expect that within two or three weeks people who did not vote for me will come back to my advice centre at home with their giro, electricity bill, housing Executive and other problems.[55]

With the first four hunger strikers now dead and their replacements in the early stages of their protest, interest in the prison issue might have diminished. This was not the case. On 11 June, the Irish Republic went to the polls, with nine prisoners – four of whom were on hunger strike – nominated as candidates for the Dáil. The southern election was markedly affected by the strike. Two prisoners were elected – Kieran Docherty in Cavan–Monaghan and Patrick Agnew, a blanket protestor, in Louth, so the impetus of the protest continued. Haughey was ousted and Fine Gael and the Labour Party formed a coalition government, with Dr Garret Fitzgerald taking office as Taoiseach at the beginning of July.

In the north, after four deaths, both the prisoners and the British government took up entrenched positions. On 8 July Joe McDonnell died and on 13 July Martin Hurson became the sixth hunger striker to perish.

Throughout July, further efforts were made to break the deadlock. Fitzgerald's government formally appealed to the United States to intervene, but President Reagan was disinclined to become involved in the Irish problem. The deaths continued, and at the beginning of August both Kevin Lynch of the INLA and Kieran Docherty TD had died.

Despite the continuing deaths, attention again became focused on the political arena. Welsh Nationalist MP Dafydd Elis-Thomas had managed to get the writ for the by-election (caused by Sands' death) passed through the House of Commons. Fitt was totally opposed to the motion and asked the speaker:

> Have you taken into account, Mr Speaker, that the emaciated dead or dying body of an IRA hunger striker is a more lethal weapon than an Armalite rifle in the arms of the men of violence? By accepting the motion now, the House may be condemning hunger strikers and others to death.[56]

Despite Fitt's arguments, the date for the Fermanagh–South Tyrone by-election was set for 20 August.

After Sands' death, the House of Commons passed a bill preventing convicted felons standing for election to a seat at Westminster. This measure was intended to pre-empt a second hunger striker contesting Fermanagh–South Tyrone. Owen Carron, who had acted as Sands' election agent, was selected as a proxy political prisoner.

The by-election again placed the SDLP in a predicament. They were well aware that Carron was a member of Sinn Féin, although he was not standing on that platform. There was division in the party, but the decision not to contest was again taken. The danger of a split in the nationalist vote that would enable a unionist to win had been a significant factor. Fitt quickly condemned the ruling and accused the party of 'political cowardice'.[57]

During Carron's election campaign, the ninth hunger striker, Thomas McElwee, died. On the actual day of the poll the tenth and final hunger striker, Michael Devine (of the INLA) died. In a return of 88.2 per cent Carron actually managed to improve on Sands' vote by 786, polling 31,278. The official unionist candidate and former UDR major Ken Maginnis polled 29,048 votes – almost exactly the same as West had managed against Sands.[58] The vote showed two things: the nationalist community's concern for the plight of the prisoners and its disapproval of Britain's stance; and the deep sectarian division in the constituency. Fitt later claimed, 'That election convinced the Prods that all that talk about the IRA not having any support was not true. It was the greatest propaganda coup for the Provos.'[59]

The hunger strike finally came to an end in October. Ten prisoners had died and the families of those still fasting pledged to intervene to prevent further deaths. On 3 October 1981, the six remaining hunger strikers ended the protest.

The election victories of Sands and Carron and of the two TDs in June convinced many in the republican movement of the usefulness of the political approach, particularly in the context of the IRA's diminishing military capabilities. They would soon decide to give the electorate a further alternative.

During the hunger strikes, Fitt's home was repeatedly attacked with petrol bombs by nationalists angered by his attitude. Crowds often gathered, chanting 'Fitt the Brit', while at other times a single drum was beaten at five-second intervals. Understandably, his wife and family were petrified.[60]

Fitt was clearly becoming identified as an agent of British government policy in Northern Ireland. This idea was reinforced by the approval for him expressed by the British media. For example, in September 1981 *The Times* ran an article entitled 'Fitt – an MP under Siege', praising him for his bravery.[61]

To be fair to Fitt, there is no doubt that he and his family displayed a degree of courage that won admiration from all kinds of people. He was a shrewd politician and could have chosen to bend with the wind in order to survive. However, he never modified his view: 'I have done nothing wrong that would have brought harm or injury to anyone. I've condemned bloodshed and violence. I condemned the hunger strike. It was a tragic loss of life. Since then very nasty things have happened but I've learned to live with it'.[62]

Despite the increasingly polarised state of politics in Northern Ireland, Fitt remained convinced of the merit of power-sharing. In an interview with the *Belfast Telegraph* the previous August he had said with some foresight, 'It will come again, some structure to get Protestants and Catholics to work together.' He clearly felt isolated and spoke with sincerity and accuracy. 'There is a safe feeling of security if you are in one tribe in Northern Ireland. But once you detribalise and stand in the middle it is a cold and lonely place. Your own lot disown you, and the other lot distrust you.' He expressed his suspicions of nationalism: 'Nationalism as a cult is a curse. It only makes people hate each other.

I do want to see the end of the border, but it can only be removed by consent.' He continued, in language reminiscent of James Connolly, 'The nationalism that consists of flags, songs and the beating of drums has nothing to do with jobs or housing. Therefore I became an anti-nationalist.'[63]

Despite Fitt's candour, the man in the street must have been left scratching his head, wondering when Fitt had made this switch. It was certainly hard to pinpoint. Whenever the moment, he was now permanently guarded by detectives wherever he went.[64]

As Gerry Fitt's political fortunes began to wane, the realignment in nationalist politics became clearer when, at the Provisional Sinn Féin Ard Fheis in November 1981, republicans endorsed a proposal to contest elections in the north. Danny Morrison explained the strategy. 'Who here really believes we can win the war through the ballot box? But will anyone here object if, with a ballot paper in this hand, and an Armalite in this hand, we take power in Ireland?'[65] In December the party issued this statement:

> The deaths of our comrades on hunger strike must mark a watershed in this struggle. People looking back on this era in 10 years time must say, yes, it was the selfless idealism of ten young men in 1981 which turned the course of Irish history and led to the reunification of this country. But events do not just happen. They are made to happen. It is up to us to make them happen.[66]

Fitt was unimpressed with Provisional Sinn Féin's debate and their decision to contest elections. He claimed that the IRA meant to create 'anarchy' and said the situation at the close of 1981 was as tense as the period of the UWC strike in 1974.[67]

The 1980s had so far been extremely difficult for Fitt: and the future looked no brighter. He now had a formidable and resurgent republican movement to contend with, whose ballot box/Armalite strategy would threaten his Westminster seat.

In comparison to 1981, the atmosphere in 1982 was less fraught. In its new year message, Provisional Sinn Féin repeated that it would be contesting local and Westminster elections. A statement from Richard McAuley, vice chairman of the Ulster Executive of the party, suggested that the new year held many challenges for republicanism:

I have no doubt that, with the experiences gained in 1981 and given our political development, we can rise to the occasion and provide the nationalist population with the positive leadership they demand. The indomitable spirit of Irish resistance to British aggression was courageously demonstrated in the principled stand taken by our imprisoned comrades and the deaths of our 10 H-Block martyrs. 1981 saw Sinn Féin commit itself to challenge the electoral monopoly of the bankrupt and collaborationist SDLP and if, in the coming year, such an opportunity arises, the republican movement will not be found wanting.[68]

While Provisional Sinn Féin greeted 1982 with some aplomb, Fitt's position was somewhat precarious. He was no longer leader, nor even a member, of the SDLP and had been heavily defeated in the local government elections. Many people, particularly in nationalist circles, felt that Fitt now spoke for no one but himself.

This situation was reflected in newspaper coverage in Northern Ireland – the *Irish News* being the clearest example. In the 1960s and 1970s and indeed until his local government defeat in 1981, the *Irish News* quoted Fitt's views extensively. However, after the hunger strike period, much less attention was devoted to him. There were two reasons for this. First, Fitt was perceived as becoming increasingly irrelevant, even though he was still the MP for West Belfast. Second, he no longer expressed a traditional nationalist/Catholic attitude. In other words, he did not represent the views of his constituents.

In September 1981, James Prior had replaced Atkins as Northern Ireland secretary of state. In his first statement in the post he said he was prepared to lay his political reputation 'on the line' in an effort to secure a political settlement. His 'rolling devolution' plan envisaged a seventy-eight-member elected assembly that would initially have only a consultative role. However, its powers would later be extended to include the devolution of local government departments, on the condition that it achieved sufficient cross-community support.[69]

The SDLP and Taoiseach Haughey were unenthusiastic and dismissed the plan as unworkable.[70] They still wanted to see more progress in the Anglo-Irish context, not in an internal solution. It was evident that the Irish dimension was not going to be facilitated: in fact the proposals seemed to be more like a sop to the unionists. Despite this, even the Official Unionist Party was against the plan, considering it simply a revival of power-sharing.

At Westminster in April, Fitt pointed out that three main elements had expressed opposition and that if they maintained their attitude and received a mandate, it would be impossible to form an Executive.[71] By the end of the month, Fitt's realism had been converted to hope: 'I believe we have to take this chance. We should tell the people of Northern Ireland we are now giving you the opportunity to take into your own hands the success or failure of your destiny.'[72] It is little wonder that Prior found Fitt 'a constant source of inspiration'.[73] However, by this stage Fitt had been reduced to a commentator on political matters and not an influential player.

Paisley's view of the Prior plan laid bare the stark realities of the situation: 'The White Paper must have some good since it has raised the hackles of Mr. Haughey and the SDLP.'[74] He was well aware that a lack of emphasis on the Irish dimension would not please the constitutional nationalists.

While the argument continued over Prior's proposals, Britain and Argentina had gone to war over the Falkland Islands (Las Malvinas). Fitt and nationalist Ireland were again on different sides of the fence; and Fitt again identified with British policy rather than nationalist sentiment. Haughey was opposed to Britain's Falklands (Las Malvinas) operation, reflected in his refusal to back British sanctions against Argentina. Public statements also made it quite apparent where his sympathies lay; and the cordial relationship between the Taoiseach and Thatcher cooled considerably. This was a blow to the SDLP, as it seemed to end any hope for future Anglo-Irish developments.

Fitt took a very different view from the Irish premier. His declaration to the defence secretary at Westminster in May shows how pro-British he had become: 'Will he ... accept that the bellicose and belligerent statements emanating from the extremely anti-British government in Dublin are not representative of the Irish people, who do not see Britain as the aggressor in this conflict?'[75] Fitt's assertion can only really have been made on the basis of intuition and not empirical observation. This does seem to suggest that he was increasingly looking at Ireland from the distant Westminster perspective. Irish people living in England may well have been influenced by the message of the British press, but it is highly improbable that Nationalist Ireland would have endorsed British action and its accompanying jingoism.

Yet was Fitt's stance really that surprising? By his own admission, he had 'done his bit' in the 1939–45 war and had lost a brother on the Normandy beaches. The political milieu at Westminster seemed increasingly to expose the latent imperial influences of his youth, when many young men from nationalist areas had served in the armed forces. In a sense, his life had come full circle, with the republican socialism that dominated his years of political activism diminishing as his political experience took him further from the centre of his early triumphs.

For its part, Sinn Féin castigated the British attitude to the Falklands / Malvinas in *An Phoblacht/Republican News*.[76] The paper quoted Thatcher: 'You have to be prepared to defend the things in which you believe and be prepared to use force if that is the only way to secure the future of liberty and self-determination', and criticised what they considered outright hypocrisy:

It has been said before and we repeat: it is no crime and there is no moral wrong in lifting a stone, raising the muzzle of a rifle or planting a bomb against those who oppress our country, against those who terrorise our people. And that is one lesson well learnt from the hypocrisy of British guns in the South Atlantic.[77]

Ironically, both Fitt and Sinn Féin called for the proposed election to Prior's assembly to be contested. Sinn Féin was ready to seek support at the polls for the first time in the north during the Troubles, albeit on an abstentionist ticket. Fitt recommended that the SDLP contest the election: 'I advise the SDLP to fight the election. I know that it will fight, because, if it does not, it will hand the seats over to abstainers and to Provisional Sinn Féin. A conglomerate of loonies and head cases will win seats in those circumstances.'[78]

As the prospect of an autumn poll became increasingly likely, there were signs of dissent within the SDLP over what its attitude to an election should be. Fitt was well aware of this. At the end of July he asked Prior at Westminster:

Will he take it from me, as a founder member and former leader of the SDLP, that not all its members are opposed to fighting elections, that a small contingent is taking orders from the Taoiseach, whose advice is not to take part in the elections, and that the SDLP as a party will, unless the moon or the sun falls from the sky, be fighting the elections?[79]

Adams also argued against a boycott:

> We call for all republican supporters to mobilise behind Sinn Féin's campaign to smash the new Stormont and British rule in Ireland.
>
> The SDLP are intent once again on masquerading as the sole representatives of the nationalist people, and on the earliest pretext will give Prior the respectability which he needs. We have their past record on this. The time has come to confront them, to break their monopoly and offer the nationalist people a new leadership.[80]

Fitt's analysis proved correct. The SDLP did decide to contest the election but, like Sinn Féin, on an abstentionist ticket. The Official Unionist Party, despite its continued opposition to Prior's plan, also decided to contest seats.

Despite his urging of the SDLP to fight the election, Fitt himself did not take part. His reason was that he saw no hope or future for the assembly, as the 'desperate' needs of the people had been pushed aside by 'protagonists in pursuit of total nationalism and unionism'. He was again critical of the SDLP: 'They are all about domination, not reconciliation.' Fitt must have been fearful of losing votes to the SDLP and Sinn Féin. This may also have influenced his decision not to contest.

He denied, however, that his political career was over: 'I believe that I have proved consistent in my political ideals on which I fought in my first and my last election campaigns. It may be that these policies may no longer be acceptable. If so, it can only be shown in the next Westminster elections'.[81] He accused Sinn Féin of seeking a 'mandate for murder'.[82] The Sinn Féin manifesto countered: 'For far too long the British government has been able to rely upon politicians from the nationalist community going to Stormont Castle, queuing for talks and picking up cheques'.[83]

The result of a general election held in the Republic in February 1982 had been a disappointment to Sinn Féin. They had hoped that the anti-British feeling that existed during the hunger strikes would still be strong, and that it would be converted into political support. But their seven candidates managed to hold only half the H Block vote of June 1981 and they did not gain any seats. Despite this, the party entered the assembly elections with a high degree of confidence. The electorate contained a new generation of disillusioned Catholics who had endured a decade of social deprivation, violence and political deadlock. The hunger strikes had politicised many, previously abstentionist, voters.

The results of the election justified Sinn Féin's optimism. They took five of the seventy-eight seats with more than ten per cent of the first preference votes, a gain of 2.5 per cent over the aggregate pro-H Block vote in the 1981 local government elections. This performance was even more impressive considering they put up candidates in only seven of the twelve constituencies and managed to top the poll in two; Carron in Fermanagh–South Tyrone and – ominously for Fitt – Adams in West Belfast.[84]

Adams called on Fitt to 'resign or donate his salary to the people living in atrocious conditions in Divis flats and Moyard'.[85] Joe Hendron, the defeated SDLP candidate, explained why Adams had won: 'I think Sinn Féin benefited from the votes of young people in the 18–25 age group who used the party to register a vote against the harassment they have suffered from the security forces over the past ten years'.[86] Whatever the reason, the result of the assembly elections was quite simply a vindication of Sinn Féin's electoral strategy.

In its 1983 new year message, Sinn Féin vowed to consolidate its success at the assembly elections and renewed its pledge to overthrow British rule by promising to expose 'weak-kneed nationalist parties'.[87] An editorial in the *Irish News* suggested that Sinn Féin's claim had some validity: 'If the SDLP are to arrest the slide to Sinn Féin they must reorganise and redouble their efforts in places like West Belfast where the Sinn Féin star is rising.'[88]

This year would also witness a Westminster election, as the Thatcher government attempted to cash in on its successful war to expel Argentina from the Falklands / Malvinas. In February, the first clashes took place between the likely candidates: Fitt, Adams and SDLP assemblyman Hendron. During a debate at Oxford University, Fitt launched a scathing attack on Sinn Féin and the PIRA: 'A vote for Sinn Féin is a vote for the gun in politics. All Sinn Féin candidates had been told at their Ard Fheis that they had to unanimously support the armed struggle, which means the shooting of defenceless people'.[89]

Reacting to Fitt's attack, Adams said that it was significant it had been issued from England, 'where he feels more at home than in the ghettos of Moyard or Divis flats, where Sinn Féin is attempting to represent the people in their everyday social and economic problems'. He accused Fitt of 'supporting the British presence in Ireland with the inevitable violence which emanates from the barrels of British army and RUC guns'.[90] Hendron also attacked Fitt, describing him as 'the absentee MP'. He claimed: 'This is an SDLP seat. Stand aside and let the seat be won by the SDLP, which is opposed to all forms of violence, and is prepared to represent the people of West Belfast.'[91]

While Fitt was receiving this criticism from politicians representing the nationalist community, the British press continued to heap praise on him. The *Daily Telegraph* said in a leader article that the IRA hated Fitt with a unique passion as the man from their community who 'sees them for what they are'.[92] Other British newspapers devoted considerable space to the continued attacks on Fitt's home. The *Daily Express* carried a full page headlined 'Fitt's Fortress'.[93] It is hardly surprising that Fitt was increasingly depicted in nationalist circles as a creature of the British.[94]

As the 9 June election drew closer, Fitt renewed his attacks on Sinn Féin: 'Sinn Féin have said they will take control in Ireland with a ballot in one hand and an Armalite in the other. Ah yes, the ballot for those who are with them – the bullet for those who aren't.'[95] He continued to castigate the SDLP: 'Some people may have been mesmerised by the assembly election results last year. Let me remind them that Sinn Féin owes such success as it had last time to the decisions of a cowardly SDLP policy, which twice gave the Provisionals a free run in Fermanagh/South Tyrone.'[96]

The Sinn Féin manifesto insisted that the party would campaign vigorously for a united Ireland, a democratic socialist republic free from foreign occupation and sectarian rule. The manifesto, entitled 'The Voice of Principled Leadership', stated that Sinn Féin welcomed the opportunity to again demonstrate the 'growing support for our principled stand against the British government and Loyalism, and our unapologetic stand in support of national reunification and in defence of the right of Irish people to resist British occupation'.[97]

Fitt argued that the electorate had a stark choice: 'They must choose between the fascist tactics of the Provisionals and the democratic standards I have sought to cherish and uphold for decades.'[98] By 30 May he was showing some confidence: 'A week ago I would have said that Adams was going to win. I'd be second and Joe Hendron third. Now I'm saying that Adams and I are going to fight like hell's gates and Hendron will still come third.' Pressed further about his chances, he replied:

If I lost this election I wouldn't feel bitter with myself, but I'd feel the people of West Belfast were voting for violence, and I wouldn't want to live in a constituency or a country where people were deliberately casting their votes for a continuation of the tragedy we have had down all those years.[99]

To Hendron, Fitt was 'only splitting the moderate vote', while the candidacy of Mary McMahon of the Workers Party complicated the picture further.[100]

The *Irish News* claimed that in 1983 there were about 16,000 unionist voters in the West Belfast constituency.[101] The impact of that vote was reduced by the failure of the official unionists and the DUP to agree on a 'unity' candidate. As a result, Tommy Passmore represented the official unionists and George Haffey the DUP. There was considerable speculation that unionists would cast their vote for Fitt in an attempt to defeat Adams. The *Orange Standard*, in an article entitled 'Fitt the Brit's Great Grit', gave some credence to this suggestion:

Today West Belfast is a very different place, politically. With the very extensive movement of population in the past 12 years, the Official Unionist position has been seriously undermined, and the battle is no longer between unionism and nationalism, but between Gerry Fitt's independent stance and the republicanism of the most extreme form, and, of course, the SDLP.

It may well be that if the Unionist Parties discover that the balance of probability is that the West Belfast seat is not winnable by them, then they will be faced with the option of making a choice between Mr Fitt and those who oppose him.

Should this prove to be the case, then wouldn't it be a magnanimous gesture for the anti-republican, anti-nationalist and anti-SDLP sectors of the electorate in this constituency to throw their weight behind the present occupant, who, one is given to understand, already receives the support of individual unionists.[102]

Fitt's politics had been transformed so much that he was now deemed anti-nationalist enough to allow unionists to vote for him. Hendron considered himself the main threat to Adams: 'Gerry Fitt is a total rank outsider, he just does not count. Any vote for him is ensuring a victory for Sinn Féin. I am the only one who can beat Gerry Adams'.[103]

On 7 June, Fitt took out a full-page advertisement in the *Irish News* listing his achievements during the previous sixteen years.[104] In conversation with a journalist just before the election, he again talked of what he considered were the trials of being 'outside a tribe': 'There is a great deal of comfort and security to belong to one tribe or another in Northern Ireland. If you don't belong to one of those tribes you are regarded as something of an eccentric, a bit of a looney or a traitor'. He pictured the scenario if Sinn Féin polled a substantial vote:

> If any significant section of the Northern Irish Catholic people votes for Sinn Féin candidates, whether they win seats or not, it points a very dark scenario. Because it will be seen then by the Protestants that the Catholics are voting for violence.
>
> My seat is nothing compared to what the outcome of that could be. It would be bad, very bad, it would be frightening. All the Catholic population would be maligned. Maybe it is fortuitous that the Catholic population is being given this choice at this time, before the situation gets really out of hand. It may be hopeful that they are being given this chance to reject violent men and their violent gospels. If this rejection of violence comes from the ballot box – people will start to breathe.[105]

Fitt's hopes were dashed – Sinn Féin achieved a 13.4 per cent poll, 3 per cent up on the assembly election. Adams was elected MP for West Belfast, with Fitt coming third, just behind Hendron.

Fitt's defeat on 9 June 1983 marked an end of an era, and he commented:

> It is a victory which will appear, and which will certainly be interpreted by the outside world, that the Catholic population are endorsing candidates who are openly associated with, and political apologists for the men of violence. I think that holds a very dark future for Northern Ireland and the whole of Ireland.[106]

Adams' victory was on a minority vote, while Fitt's vote represented a considerable improvement from the 1981 local government election when he only managed to poll 541 as against 3,006 in 1977. Passmore and Haffey achieved a combined total of only 4,834, so Fitt claimed that he had secured Protestant support: 'Half my votes came from Protestant working-class in the Shankill Road and half came from the working-class in the Falls Road. I have striven all my political life to unite the Catholic and Protestant working-classes in this tragically divided city, and that is what I did yesterday.'[107] He told the *Belfast News Letter*, in not the most politically correct language, 'It made me feel like a nigger in Alabama who had been voted in by the Ku Klux Klan.'[108] Revd Martin Smyth provides substance to Fitt's claim of unionist support. He told me that when Protestants went to seek advice and help from UUP candidate Passmore after the election he tersely told them 'to go and see those you voted for'.[109]

Republicans did not deny that Protestants had voted for Fitt, but their reasoning was different from his:

In view of his unpopularity amongst nationalists, it is clear that a large section of Fitt's 10,326 votes came from Loyalists. Contrary to his claim that he had succeeded in uniting the Protestant and Catholic working-class, the vote merely demonstrates that even a Catholic can win Loyalist support if he is sufficiently pro-British.[110]

The 1981 local government election results showed that many voters had come to see Fitt as something of a political parasite. However, Fitt did make a considerable comeback in the 1983 Westminster election. Evidence does indeed suggest that there was some tactical voting against Sinn Féin by Protestant voters. The *Ulster* acknowledged that 'in the absence of a candidate of stature who would swing the vote away from the IRA's Sinn Féin, Gerry Fitt secured a big percentage of their votes.'[111]

The tactical voting theory is supported by the 1987 Westminster election. On the basis of the combined Hendron/Fitt vote in 1983, Adams should not have won in 1987, but he did. Although unionists may have felt they could vote for Fitt (who after all had now renounced the concept of nationalism) in 1983, they perhaps could not bring themselves to vote for Hendron and the SDLP given that party's endorsement of the Anglo-Irish Agreement, a deal that was repugnant to the vast majority of Protestants.[112]

Although there is evidence that Protestant voting in West Belfast in 1983 was influenced by tactical considerations, it would be disingenuous not to acknowledge that many Catholics – and some Protestants – voted for Fitt because of sentiment and a sense of loyalty. Fitt had worked extremely hard for his constituents over the years. Few could deny that he helped or at least tried to help people who sought his assistance. Yet the plight of Fitt's constituents had become increasingly desperate during the Thatcher era and Fitt's brand of welfare politics was no longer adequate.[113] Many young and disgruntled nationalist voters demanded radical change and felt Sinn Féin could provide it.

Reaction in Britain was summed up by James Prior, who considered Fitt's defeat 'disastrous' and by the British authorities, which were understandably alarmed by Sinn Féin's success.[114]

In the Republic, the media in general lamented Fitt's defeat. The *Cork Examiner*'s comments were typical:

> Gerry Adams gained their [Sinn Féin's] sole seat and this was at the expense of the 17 year old career of the former SDLP leader and parliamentarian of great moral courage, Gerry Fitt. This outcome, in a constituency in which Mr Fitt could not conduct a normal canvass because of violent conditions, will sadden many admirers of his steadfastness over the lengthy years of northern strife.[115]

Even the *Irish Press*, which had been so critical of Fitt during the hunger strikes, was saddened by the result:

> Perhaps the most impressive result of the day – and in some ways the saddest – was that of Gerry Fitt whose long parliamentary career ended with his defeat in West Belfast. But Mr Fitt, whose political courage and social commitment were always beyond question, said farewell in the most impressive manner possible notching up a very creditable 10,000 votes when his opponents had been predicting that he would be lucky to get even a third of that vote. West Belfast, Protestant and Catholic, ignored the pundits and remembered the hard work Mr Fitt had put in on their behalf for almost 20 years.[116]

With Fitt unlikely to accept the end of his political career, predictions were made that an elevation to the House of Lords was a possibility, and after his election defeat his wife commented: 'If Mrs. Thatcher knows what this man has done for the people of West Belfast, she'll promote him to the House of Lords – but I doubt if he would accept it.'[117] The idea of a promotion to the upper house suggested a degree of deference that Fitt would not have acknowledged at the start of his political life.

On 19 June, the *Sunday Times* reported, 'Many MPs of all parties also hope to see Gerry Fitt, defeated Independent Socialist MP for West Belfast, continue his parliamentary service in the Upper House.'[118] On 22 July 1983, it was announced that Fitt had been offered and had accepted a life peerage. He said:

> I do not think I have done anything to be honoured about. What I have done in politics I have felt to be right. I took decisions which were not supported by everyone. I have over the past 11 years been under serious attack by Provisional IRA supporters and other republican elements. Prior to that, I was viciously attacked by Loyalist supporters. I have always and always will, make my feelings known against IRA violence and Loyalist violence.[119]

The announcement was predictably criticised by Adams:

> This peerage exposes absolutely the anti-democratic nature of the British system of government when a failed politician who has been rejected by the people of North Belfast in a Council election and by the people of West Belfast in a Westminster election, is then installed in a position of making and influencing foreign law for use against these people.[120]

With either a hint of irony or a lack of appreciation of the extent of Fitt's political journey, an official unionist spokesman said, 'I don't think unionists are greatly excited about it. We are not going to celebrate the elevation of a republican to the House of Lords.'[121]

Just over two weeks before the peerage declaration, Fitt's home had been badly damaged in an arson attack. The perpetrators had broken into the house, removed the furniture and burned it in the back yard before setting fire to the house itself. Fitt was adamant that the Provisionals had carried out the raid and admitted defeat. 'They have succeeded after 11 years to drive me out of this house.'[122]

Sinn Féin condemned the burning of 'Fortress Fitt'. Joe Austin, chairman of North Belfast Sinn Féin, declared the burning 'a wanton and mindless act of destruction'.[123]

Fitt told me that it was that attack on his home and, in particular, the

destruction of his wedding photographs that made him accept the peerage as a form of retaliation. 'I felt sick. "Fuck them," I said. 'I'm going
to the Lords. If they offer me a seat I will go to the Lords. It will drive
them (The IRA) fucking mad."That's when I made my mind up to go to
the House of Lords.' The adulation by the British media, the continuing
favour of the British establishment and the violence to which his family
were subjected all perhaps made Fitt's decision inevitable. He also claimed
that Hume had categorised him as an 'irrelevance' after the election and
this may have provided further motivation.[124]

Nevertheless, Fitt's political integrity must be questioned. A disciple
of James Connolly would not become a peer of the realm, with all the
pomp and ceremony that involves. Unsurprisingly, his decision to go to
the Lords was in Britain welcomed by politicians and the media alike.
In the Republic there was little, if any, condemnation from the press.
The *Irish Independent* editorial claimed: 'Fitt was selected and rightly
so.'[125] This sentiment was very different from that of the editorial in the
Irish News (which for so many years had given an almost sycophantic
endorsement of Fitt):

> Gerry Fitt's acceptance of a peerage from Britain can only be regarded by
> the nationalist population of the North as a sort of betrayal. In spite of
> the carefully orchestrated publicity of the past weeks, it had been hoped
> even to the last moment, that this brave, but misguided former idol of
> the nationalist community, would stop short of giving total credibility to
> institutions that are so directly opposed to every principle he once repre-
> sented.[126]

His old colleagues in the SDLP were kinder – at least in retrospect. Cooper
maintained, 'Fitt couldn't live without some involvement in politics. What
else could he do? He wasn't trained for anything. They gave him an office
and that kept his hand in. I wasn't bitter.'[127] Eddie McGrady concurred.
'He was in the House of Lords because he had nowhere else to go.'[128]
Mallon was slightly more critical, but accurate: 'I am not going to make
a judgement but I don't think such a move is compatible with the type of
political philosophies that he and I were pursuing.'[129]

On 26 October 1983, having taken the oath of allegiance to the queen,
Gerry Fitt was ennobled as Baron Fitt of Bell's Hill.[130] Fitt chose this title
because Bell's Hill near Downpatrick in County Down is where the Fitt

family was evacuated to during the Second World War, and also where he and his wife resided for a short time when they were first married. Fitt was proud of the fact that both Thatcher and Michael Foot, the leader of the Labour Party, had nominated him. Fitt had originally been proposed on Foot's list, but Thatcher's respect for him was so great that she told the Labour chief that he could have another peer for his list so Fitt's name could be included on her own.[131] *The Irish News* commented: 'It was a strange day for the one time socialist docker.'[132]

Graffiti that appeared on the walls of the city cemetery on the Whiterock Road neatly summed up what many of his former constituents thought of their one-time MP: 'Lord Flitt of the Dock'.

8

LORD FITT OF BELL'S HILL

Lord Fitt was a member of the Upper House for over two decades. The wavering that had characterised much of his political thinking was not as apparent during these years. In fact, the political conviction he had developed after resigning from the SDLP became more strident. He spoke trenchantly against violence, urging peace and reconciliation and remaining an implacable opponent of Sinn Féin and the IRA. In short, the brand of politics enunciated by Fitt in the House of Lords reflected, and at times amplified, the rhetoric he had produced from 1979. However, the consistency of his days in the Upper Chamber cannot obscure the contradictions that characterised his political career as a whole.

Fitt, a self-confessed disciple of James Connolly, must have realised that the House of Lords represented an unusual destination for an Irish Catholic from West Belfast, particularly a 'Connolly Socialist'. This was, after all, the same chamber that blocked Home Rule in 1893 and whose members threatened to 'die in the last ditch' rather than give up the power to obstruct even a small measure of local government for John Redmond's supporters in 1912. Despite the changes to the composition of the Lords with the introduction of life peerages in 1958, the incongruity of Fitt's position was obvious. In those days, when some Labour politicians still looked with displeasure at the second chamber (rather than rewarding its 'socialist' benefactors with peerages), eyebrows were raised at Fitt's desire to join the aristocratic benches.

Roy Hattersley's opinion reflected what many people on the left of British politics must have felt at the time.[1] Hattersley had considered Fitt's role in bringing down the Labour government in 1979 unforgivable, but he confirmed that Michael Foot was adamant that Fitt should not lose the peerage he had been promised. 'He deserves it,' Michael said, slapping his thigh in the gesture which still characterises his invariably high spirits.

Then he added, with the touch of malice that occasionally shines through the benevolence, "Good luck to him – if he likes that sort of thing."[2]

Fitt was an isolated and lonely figure in the Upper House. Imperfect as his position was, he used the Lords as a platform to express his distinctive political views. These included: condemnation of republican violence; an antipathy towards his former SDLP colleagues and the line the party was taking; a growing affinity with the unionist tradition; and a rejection of the nationalist stance that had defined his early politics. Fitt had once again revised his political colouring to suit the latest backdrop, a trait that had manifested itself at different stages during his political career.

Fitt's abhorrence and condemnation of violence, from whatever source, was one feature. In the 1950s and 1960s, when republicans were virtually non-existent in Belfast and essentially consisted of a small band of southern diehards throwing themselves recklessly at the apparatus of the state, Fitt viewed them as deluded and misguided idealists. From the early 1970s, however, when republicanism began to become more significant, he became repelled by its ideological implications and denounced the IRA as murdering psychopaths.

Gerry Adams considered Fitt "the Conservatives' favourite Irishman".[3] This perception is hardly surprising: Fitt told me he had gone to the Lords to 'keep at the [IRA] bastards'.[4] From his platform in the Lords, Fitt willingly fulfilled his role as the London media's favourite source of condemnation of IRA atrocities, albeit from a safe distance, where he could not influence West Belfast.

On 20 November 1983, three members of the Mountain Lodge Pentecostal Church in Darkley, County Armagh, were shot dead in an attack that was claimed by the Catholic Reaction Force (CRF). The CRF was believed to be a cover name used by the INLA. Fitt correctly said, 'it was deliberately and overtly, without any ambiguity or qualification, designed to be a sectarian murder'.[5] In the following month UUP assembly member Edgar Graham, touted as a potential future party leader, was shot dead by the IRA at Queen's University in Belfast where he was a lecturer in the faculty of law. Fitt claimed the IRA was 'trying to bring about civil war'.[6]

At the end of July 1985, in the period following the bombing of the Conservative Party conference at Brighton on 12 October 1984, the Lords debated whether the British government should recognise that the IRA should have a legitimate role to play in any future resolution. Fitt was robust in his response and clearly was not ready for inclusive dialogue:

My Lords, would the noble Lord accept that the IRA is a murderous terrorist organisation that is illegal in both Northern Ireland and in the Republic? Would he also agree that it has no significant support in the whole island of Ireland, and less than 12 months ago the activists of the IRA tried to murder an entire British Cabinet? I repeat that that was less than a year ago. They have also carried out the most indiscriminate, ruthless and barbaric killings at Harrods and in Regent's Park – and I am not counting all the murders that they have committed in Northern Ireland.

Would the noble Lord agree that if anyone with any claim to responsibility were to ask this House to legalise such an organisation he can only be charged with deliberately giving succour and support to the murderous elements that have so ravaged the name of Ireland and of this country as well?[7]

Fitt's position had become so staunch that he precluded any opening of links with the IRA, even though this had been a frequent objective of British political thinking and subsequently the rock on which the peace process was built.

After the signing of the Anglo-Irish Agreement in November 1985, Fitt warned the British government that nationalists would not withdraw their support for the IRA and Sinn Féin because they had got that support 'at the point of a gun'.[8] He described the Enniskillen bombing of 8 November 1987, which killed eleven people and wounded sixty-three, as a 'vicious, ruthless, heartless attack on the Protestant people'.[9] This comment implicitly condemned those who had given political credibility to the IRA.

A series of incidents in March 1988 illustrated the political significance of Fitt's stance. The SAS assassinated three members of the IRA on 'active service' in Gibraltar (Mairead Farrell, Seán Savage and Daniel McCann). Tensions rose in Northern Ireland as the bodies were returned to their homes in West Belfast for burial. The SDLP publicly urged the RUC to keep a low profile at the funerals. Michael Stone, a maverick loyalist, attacked the joint funeral in Milltown Cemetery, killing three mourners. One of those killed at Milltown Cemetery was Kevin Brady, a member of the PIRA. During his funeral a few days later, two undercover British soldiers driving close to the cortège on the Andersonstown Road were apprehended by a crowd of mourners who believed this was another loyalist attack. The soldiers were beaten by the crowd and subsequently shot by the IRA, the whole sickening incident being relayed on television across the world.

Fitt told the *Sunday Times*, 'There is a degree of savagery which has now entered this conflict that one has never experienced before. I cannot see it going away'.[10] Fitt's view was that of a distant observer. The incidents of March 1988 were certainly shocking but were explicable by such an unusual sequence of events, which Fitt, detached from his former base in West Belfast, seemed unable to appreciate. West Belfast had seen comparable acts of violence, and for a much more sustained period during the mid-1970s, when Fitt had been the constituency's MP.

Fitt's view can be contrasted with that of his successor as leader of the SDLP, John Hume. Hume was also shocked by what had happened, but he felt the vitriol aimed at republicans for what happened in Andersonstown could be used to promote peace. He reasoned that republicans would experience political isolation and be worried enough about their electoral fortunes to make them receptive to overtures from outside their normal circle of allies. He began to use this brief vulnerability in Sinn Féin's leadership to encourage a dialogue that might ultimately lead to the end of the IRA campaign.

Hume's initiative at first brought him considerable criticism, even though it contained the origins of the peace process. Unionists began talking of 'a pan-nationalist front' and there was even disquiet within the SDLP itself about the course Hume was taking. Some felt electoral success was more important than bringing republicans in from the cold. But Hume was a man of huge political stature, with an influence far exceeding the confines of his party. He went the extra mile to pursue his long-term objective to bring republican violence to an end and calculated that his colleagues and enemies could not touch him without risking their own demise.

This was real leadership when it really counted – the type of leadership that Gerry Fitt would have been neither predisposed to nor capable of providing in the circumstances. From his vantage point in the House of Lords he fulminated against republican atrocities while Hume got on with the hard graft on the long and often lonely road that was to lead to a positive result a few years later. Austin Currie, whose personal relationship with Hume was at best lukewarm, was honest enough to put any bitterness aside and tell it as it was: 'Whatever else may be said about John Hume, one thing is incontrovertible: he was the prime mover in bringing peace to Ireland, and in so doing he displayed considerable moral, physical and political courage. There are people alive today who would be in their grave save for John Hume.'[11]

From January to August 1988 a series of talks was held between Hume and Gerry Adams. Hume was keen to integrate the republican movement into mainstream politics. Adams wanted to end the armed struggle. Thus the 'peace process' was born. The road was long and difficult, but by May 1997 the Sinn Féin of the late 1980s was unrecognisable.

On Wednesday 31 August 1994, the IRA issued a statement announcing a complete cessation of military activities. Rumours of this development had not impressed Fitt. He argued two weeks before their ceasefire that anyone who thought the IRA would accept the Downing Street Declaration[12] and call off the violence 'does not understand that the killing is only part of it. Robberies, protection rackets and intimidation are now a way of life. Anyone born after 1969 knows nothing else.'[13]

He went on to criticise what he saw as the fawning of the British authorities and media and dismissed any republican input to peace prospects: 'The IRA and Gerry Adams have been running circles round the British media since December. The British government has made concession after concession. The IRA and Sinn Féin cannot bring peace.'[14]

Fitt was annoyed even further by the enthusiastic reception Adams received in the United States after a successful visit in September. He told the Lords what made him 'cringe':

It was when Edward Kennedy put his arms around Gerry Adams and welcomed him to America. What that man did in an attempt to save his own electoral fortunes was bitterly resented, not only by the Unionist people in Northern Ireland, but by many members of the Catholic minority. Gerry Adams perambulated through America and Canada. He claimed – and every time I heard it I cringed – to speak on behalf of the Irish people, underlining the 'Irish people' or the 'nationalist people'. The reality is that the only credibility Gerry Adams has is with about five per cent in the whole island of Ireland. The only reason he had for going to America or being involved in politics was that he had an army of gunmen behind him.[15]

Fitt's argument was somewhat weakened by the fact that by this stage he represented no one, at least in an electoral sense. Rightly or wrongly, he was perceived by many from the nationalist community as a parrot of the British establishment, perched on the aristocratic benches.

On Friday 9 February 1996, the IRA exploded a large bomb at South Quay in the Docklands area of London. The Army Council of the IRA had been concerned that John Major's government, with its precarious majority, and open to unionist pressure, had begun to dither over the peace process.[16] A number of obstacles, including a demand for the IRA to surrender its arms as a precondition for Sinn Féin's admission to all-party talks, had been introduced by the Conservative government. The IRA decided to concentrate British minds on the issue – did they want peace or more attacks on the British state? The ceasefire was over.

The following November Fitt addressed the House of Lords on the question of the 'peace process'. On the same evening, Thursday 21 November 1996, the Continuity Irish Republican Army (CIRA) left a bomb in Derry, which failed to explode.[17] Fitt's cynicism was plain:

Sinn Féin will say they want talks. The Secretary of State, using coded language, may say that he wants talks, too. But the fact that there was a 600lb bomb there is indicative of what Sinn Féin is about. They want to intimidate, to force their views on Northern Ireland. There must be talk in Belfast and Derry tonight that they were trying to bring about what they call 'a spectacular'. Fortunately, tonight the bomb did not go off and did not kill people. But had it gone off, they would have said, 'We are people of peace. If you don't want this to happen again you had better talk to us.'[18]

Fitt's hatred of the republican movement was understandable. His political adversaries were prepared to burn him and his family out of their home: no wonder if he felt bitterness and hatred. What also followed, however, was political rhetoric designed to condemn rather than to communicate. Fitt's implacable hatred of republicanism had blinded him to the fact that a peace process could only be achieved with its co-operation. History will record that the motivation of republicans was better understood by the British and Irish governments and the SDLP. Fitt's claims to know the people of West Belfast and the nationalist constituency in general were exposed as somewhat fake.

Although lacking the intensity and ferocity of his attacks on Sinn Féin and the IRA, Lord Fitt continued to disparage his former colleagues in the SDLP as he had since leaving the party in 1979. The SDLP emphasis on an Anglo-Irish process had signalled, according to Fitt, a 'greening' of the party and a dilution of its socialism, and Fitt continued to bemoan this development. In November 1985 he explained to the Lords – not a receptive audience for lectures on socialism – that:

> ... after the failure of the [1975–6] convention to find agreement, the SDLP because of its frustrations – frustrations which I can understand because I, too, was part of them – began to take an increasingly nationalistic view of the problem of Ireland. They no longer talked about housing, jobs or the standard of living. All they thought of was the nationalist day, the final reunion of the country, the beating of the Unionists, the symbolisms of victory and defeat.[19]

It was perhaps unfair to attack the SDLP for concentrating on the Irish dimension when the unionists had shown little inclination to share power during this period.

Fitt saw the SDLP under Hume's leadership as being reduced to merely proposing Irish unity by a route other than the one espoused by the republican movement. He appeared to suggest some ambiguity in the party's relationship with republicans, with some sort of 'pan-nationalist front' lurking behind the respectable image of the SDLP. After the Darkley shootings he suggested, 'There are many Northern Ireland politicians on the minority side who talk of the alienation that now exists between the minority community in Northern Ireland and this Government. Such sentiments expressed can only but give succour and support to the murderous thugs of the IRA and INLA.'[20]

Republicans had frequently argued, with some justification, that SDLP influence depended on the muscle of the IRA and that the 'constitutional nationalists' had always been willing to accept the concessions that the 'armed struggle' had forced from the British. Fitt had come to feel that some prominent members of the SDLP had a 'sneaking regard' for the IRA and it seems that he felt this ambivalence remained a characteristic of the party.[21] In November 1996, in another debate on the 'peace process', he concluded his speech with the following words:

> I end with a note of warning to some of my former colleagues in the SDLP. There is talk now that at the forthcoming election,[22] whenever it may be, the SDLP and Sinn Féin will do a deal on seats in Mid Ulster,

Fermanagh and South Tyrone, and the newly created seat of West Belfast. If there is any electoral pact or deal by Sinn Féin and the SDLP, it will do nothing but further divide the communities. I advise the party which I formerly led not to engage in that exercise. If we want to bring about reconciliation in Northern Ireland, let the moderates – Unionists and Nationalists – take a stand against the extremists.[23]

Fitt's concern about the new allegiances in the nationalist community was vindicated in the general election of May 1997, when Sinn Féin increased its share of the vote to 16.1 per cent to become the third largest party in Northern Ireland. The threat to the SDLP was clear. Fitt predicted that his former party was 'heading for the wilderness' and he blamed the Hume/Adams dialogue as the main reason. He claimed that 'to even the most innocent observer, it has become clear that John Hume's alliance with Sinn Féin would have a disastrous effect on the political fortunes of the SDLP', adding that his leaving the party had been shown to be justified by Sinn Féin's gain at the SDLP's expense:

I have to say, after reading the recent election results and being aware of the events since 1988 (when John Hume began talking to Gerry Adams) which led to the present election disaster for the SDLP, that I have been witnessing the funeral of an old friend.

However, I feel vindicated in that the formation of the party – as the Social Democratic and Labour Party – no longer applies to it as it now stands.

Paddy Devlin and myself very early on realised that we were very much a minority, a socialist voice with a conscience in a nationalist party.

He also argued that his attempt to deal with industrial tribunal issues, welfare matters and other 'social evils' counted for nothing when taken alongside the demands of nationalism and republicanism espoused by his party colleagues. Fitt could not resist another jibe at Hume, revealing his resentment at the loss of his West Belfast seat in 1983, and declaring the party had no real future:

John Hume, the leader of the party, I understand, took great satisfaction in having me opposed in West Belfast in 1983. That led to a split vote and the first election of Gerry Adams to the political arena. Since then, it is quite evident that there has been a steady diminishing in the socialist principles on which the party was founded. I say this with no satisfaction but it is apparent to me that the SDLP cannot recover from the defeat they sustained at the recent local council elections and the general election.[24]

Yet despite the criticism and election setbacks Fitt was convinced that Hume was 'not for turning'. In July 1999 he told the Lords:

> I predict – and I am a former SDLP member – that John Hume, the leader of the SDLP, will in no circumstances desert Sinn Féin. John Hume drove Sinn Féin from the political gutter and gave it credibility in Northern Ireland. I cannot foresee any circumstances in which the SDLP will desert Sinn Féin.
>
> There are other people in the SDLP. The SDLP is not unanimous in its support of Sinn Féin. There could be a split in Sinn Féin. There could be a split in the SDLP over its attitude to Sinn Féin. I know many SDLP members who detest Sinn Féin. Some of them have actually spoken in this House. But having brought Sinn Féin from the political gutter to political credibility, I cannot see that John Hume will ever desert it.[25]

Fitt clearly wanted Sinn Féin to remain in the political gutter and it can be assumed that had he still been leader of the SDLP he would not have pursued Hume's strategy, and the 'peace process' as we know it might not have come to pass.

We can only guess what the SDLP would have achieved if Fitt had remained party leader at this time – if the IRA had gone into a slow and chaotic defeat during the late 1990s instead of the orderly retreat that secured maximum political advantage for nationalism through the peace process. What would have been the chances of SDLP persuasion budging a triumphant ulster unionism and an uninterested British government in such circumstances? Alternatively, if a peace process had emerged without John Hume and the SDLP it would possibly have manifested itself as a secret IRA/British government deal followed by Sinn Féin/British dialogue. In such circumstances the SDLP would have been at best marginalised and at worst deemed an irrelevance. It was clear from the course of events that Britain would have sacrificed the SDLP for a deal to secure the end of the IRA threat to the financial heartland of Britain.

A third feature of Fitt's final political incarnation, as a life peer in the House of Lords, was his apparent reorientation towards a position normally occupied by unionists, which gives Adams' taunt that Fitt was the 'Conservatives' favourite Irishman' an element of truth. In the Lords, Fitt did display a tendency to empathise with unionist thinking at the expense of the nationalist ideology. Much of this was done to encourage compromise, but his later views contrasted so markedly with his earlier position that they deserve some scrutiny.

Much of what Fitt said in his time in the Lords can be interpreted as eminently reasonable and sensible, though not consistent with previous rhetoric. His political journey since the 1960s had seen him jettison much of his early stridency. While Fitt was not alone in undergoing changes in his political philosophy, his apparent catharsis was, in Northern Ireland terms, quite remarkable. Back in February 1967, Fitt had told the *Irish Democrat* Conference in London:

> Most of you know about this man Ian Paisley. Paisley has been charged with being an extreme Unionist. He is an embarrassment to the established Unionist Party in Northern Ireland. But I know, because I was born and reared in Northern Ireland, that Paisley is not an extreme Unionist. Paisley is the fundamental expression of Unionism. What Paisley says in public other Unionists say and think in private (Applause). So let us not be taken in by this story going around that Terence O'Neill is a Liberal. Some people may say that they are prepared to let Terry O'Neill walk over them in bedroom slippers because Paisley would wear hob-nailed boots. I am not prepared to let anybody walk over me or my constituents …
>
> The Unionist in Northern Ireland has a siege mentality. He realises that he is there by no right. He is not there by right of being an Irishman, because he disclaims Irish nationality. He is not there because he is an Englishman, because he doesn't like an Englishman and refuses to accept British standards. He is there because he wants to maintain this little oasis of Fascism in Northern Ireland.[26]

It is ironic that, at the time of writing, this same Ian Paisley is now leader of the largest political party in Northern Ireland and is certainly the 'fundamental' as well as the 'fundamentalist' face of unionism. Fitt's view about unionism's public and private face has been shown to have some truth. Time will tell whether Ian Paisley's political legacy will deviate from Fitt's 1967 description of Paisleyism.

Fitt expressed all the prejudices of traditional nationalism when he went on to criticise the unionist working-class in a deplorably patronising manner, which said something about the make-up of the audience as well as himself. He asked his listeners to:

> Put yourself in the position of the Protestant worker in Northern Ireland. It's no good trying to get away from this. Put yourself in the position of the Protestant worker ... After all he is only a human being. He wants the best standard of life which is possible under the prevailing circumstances, and if he joins the Orange Order, he knows it will open up the door to a good job.[27]

To Fitt, unionism was rotten to the core, but statements such as these appear somewhat incongruous when placed next to some of his anti-nationalist rhetoric in the Lords. Either the unionists had changed or Gerry Fitt had.

Fitt's political realignment is best seen in his position on the New Ireland Forum and its recommendations on how to achieve the nationalist vision.

The New Ireland Forum was established in May 1983. The SDLP had been increasingly looking to Dublin to help reinvigorate the Anglo-Irish process. Hume was keen to reinvent the ideology of constitutional nationalism and to discuss what shape Irish unity should take in a new and agreed Ireland. Taoiseach Garrett Fitzgerald hoped to reduce the growing support for the republican movement by working more closely with the British government. Attendance at the forum was limited to Ireland's constitutional nationalist parties, so Sinn Féin was excluded. The unionist parties were invited but, apart from a few individuals, did not attend; and the unionist community subsequently dismissed the forum's discussions.

The forum's report, published in May 1984, showed the way nationalist thinking had changed. The Irish nation was no longer defined as a Catholic nation; furthermore, constitutional nationalism officially recognised the right of unionists to their British identity. The report also posed a direct challenge over the British guarantee to the unionists, refusing to allow it to undermine the nationalists' goal of an agreed united Ireland.

The forum offered three possible solutions. The preferred option was a united Ireland achieved by agreement and consent. The next alternative was a federal or confederal arrangement, while the third option was joint authority. Not surprisingly, the unionists rejected the report outright. The attempt to present a radical new brand of nationalism was damaged by the emphasis on the unity option – which was the only option, according to Charles Haughey, leader of Fianna Fáil and the face of 'traditional nationalism'. Margaret Thatcher also curtly rejected the proposals. The British attitude to the forum report seemed to demonstrate its support of the unionist veto, making the prospect for political progress bleak. Constitutional nationalism was left disappointed and alienated. There was little sympathy from Lord Fitt, whose response to the forum's deliberations signified a clear shift in his political thinking. Fitt spoke in the Lords in June 1984 before Thatcher's official rejection the following November. As was customary, he lamented the conflict, blaming intransigence on both sides, before going on to defend the unionist position:

> Throughout this document [the forum's report] the words that one sees repeated time and time again are 'agreement' and 'consent'. It must be settled by agreement and consent; but what happens if that agreement and consent are not forthcoming? What happens if the Unionist Party said that in no circumstances will it agree with the three proposals which are put forward in this document?
>
> So far as the unionist is concerned, be he elected or otherwise, he sees three issues in that proposal He sees, first, the recommendation of the leader of the largest political party in the republic, Fianna Fáil, and its leader Charles Haughey, that there must be a unitary state. Nothing else was to be considered. Then we have the more accommodating view put forward by Garret Fitzgerald that there could be a confederal or a federal solution to the problem. Then there is the last one, which nobody seems to talk very much about, the joint authority proposal. None of those proposals is in any way acceptable to the unionist majority in Northern Ireland.

He lambasted the consent principle, the acceptance of which in 1974 had signalled a significant shift in the nationalist attitude: 'We hear repeatedly, "Consent, consent." If that consent is not forthcoming, can the Unionists be coerced into consenting? And who does the coercing? Are the British Government expected to coerce the Unionists into consenting?'[28]

The forum report criticised the policies pursued by the British government since the late 1960s. Paragraph 3.15 reads:

The British army was initially welcomed by the nationalist population as providing protection from sectarian attacks. However, the relationship between the nationalist population and the British army deteriorated shortly afterwards. This was due to insensitive implementation of security measures in nationalist areas and a series of incidents in which the British army was no longer perceived by nationalists to be acting as an impartial force. 1970 was thus a critical turning point and the experience of nationalists then and subsequently has profoundly influenced their attitudes, especially in regard to security. Among the major incidents which contributed to this alienation were the three-day curfew imposed on the Falls Road in June 1970; the internment without trial in August, 1971 of hundreds of nationalists; the subsequent revelation that some of those taken into custody on that occasion were subjected to treatment later characterised by the Strasbourg Court of Human Rights as 'inhuman and degrading'; the shooting dead of 13 people in Derry by British paratroopers in January, 1972; and the beatings and ill-treatment of detainees in Castlereagh Barracks and Gough Barracks in 1977/78, subsequently condemned in the official British Bennett Report.[29]

Fitt was somewhat dismissive, especially when one considers how close he was to the events described and what he actually said at the time. He argued:

> ... I think the report has been very unfair in paragraph 3.15 ... It gives a whole list of all the incidents and developments which alienated the Catholic community. I would not disagree with them: all these incidents as they are listed certainly did bring about alienation within the Catholic community. But the report completely disregards all the incidents that brought about the alienation within the Protestant community as well ... The Protestant population has suffered grievously in this conflict as well.[30]

Fitt made a number of valid points, but his sympathies were linked with the unionist position, for which he had acquired a growing empathy. As for the constitutional nationalists, Fitt argued that the 'document should be treated with the seriousness it deserves'.[31] After all, 'at least they did put a lot of work and heart searching into the problem, as they see it, affecting Ireland'.[32] In effect, they had to be content with patronising platitudes.

Anglo-Irish relations in the aftermath of the report were poor. However, within a year the Anglo-Irish Agreement was signed, giving the Irish government an advisory role in Northern Ireland's government while confirming that Northern Ireland would remain part of the UK unless a majority of its citizens agreed otherwise. It also set out conditions for establishing a devolved consensus government in the region. Both premiers feared that Sinn Féin would eclipse the SDLP as the leading nationalist party in the north, so the agreement was an attempt to throw a political lifebelt to the SDLP. Thatcher's main reason for signing was based on security and the hope of persuading the Irish government to extradite IRA suspects. Fitzgerald wanted to undermine the Catholic minority's toleration of the IRA and to bolster support for the SDLP by demonstrating that the agreement was a triumph for peaceful negotiation, in contrast to the lack of progress made by republicans in seeking Irish unity through the 'armed struggle'.

All the main British parties supported the agreement. Unionists, however, were outraged and politically traumatised. They felt abandoned and betrayed by the impression that the agreement would eventually lead to a united Ireland. They found it particularly galling to have been sidelined during negotiations while the SDLP seemed to have had a consultative role. Ironically, Sinn Féin condemned the agreement as copper-fastening partition, but did not try to destroy it, reasoning that it would not achieve much after the hype surrounding it had died down. Fianna Fáil was not enthusiastic about the agreement either, though Haughey said he would not oppose developments that were of benefit to nationalists living in Northern Ireland: and, when Taoiseach, he worked within the terms of the accord.

The SDLP was the real winner. Constitutional nationalism appeared to have delivered progress by calling the unionists' bluff. An external framework had been established, and the Irish dimension recognised and institutionalised. Both governments were committed to the principle of power-sharing and it looked as though the republican movement might become marginalised. Most important, perhaps, the unionist veto was confronted and, according to constitutional nationalism, removed.

The SDLP did not have had much sympathy for the plight of unionism, but Gerry Fitt did. Fitt begged the British not to shut the unionists out: 'Do not cast aside that unionist majority in Northern Ireland. Do not believe that they are all hysterical bigots. They are not. Many thousands of people in Northern Ireland in the unionist community want only to live their lives in peace. Do not force them into taking any action which we could all regret.'[33] He bemoaned the fact that the unionists would not even have an observer to represent their interests in the Anglo-Irish conference:

> The conference will meet and there will be people from the Republic giving their views. There will be British Ministers and the Minister of State from this House. But there will be no Unionist there, there will be no Protestant there. And the Protestants are the majority of people in Northern Ireland. If only they even had but one observer who would allay their fears and suspicions. I am talking as a Catholic, as one who knew the jackboot of oppression under Unionism. I do not want to see the Unionist population in Northern Ireland being treated in the same way as they once treated their political opponents. The Unionist also says 'Why has this agreement been brought about?' The Government will say, 'Because of the violence we have had in Northern Ireland.' That is what they will say. The Unionist will reply, 'But I was at the receiving end of most of that violence.'[34]

Fitt compared the agreement to the Council of Ireland that, according to him, brought down the Executive in 1974:

> The agreement says to the Unionist party, 'You did not like the Council of Ireland proposals. You brought the power sharing Executive to an end. Thus we now have the Council of Ireland in another form, we now have it in this agreement. It will be known as the Conference whether or not you like it, we will ram it down your throats'. That is how the Unionist party see it. They are ramming down their throats that very part of the Sunningdale agreement which was so unacceptable to the majority.[35]

It was almost as if Fitt regretted the perceived loss of the unionist veto. Nevertheless, despite his empathy with and sympathy for the beleaguered unionists, Lord Fitt backed the agreement while simultaneously indicating his admiration for Thatcher and Fitzgerald (the acceptable moderate face of southern nationalism). He was also convinced that the agreement would achieve little:

I believe that this agreement is well intentioned. I believe that this Prime Minister is very concerned about the ongoing situation in Northern Ireland. I believe that in the implementation of this agreement she will show tremendous resolution. I believe that the government of the Irish Republic under Garret Fitzgerald were equally well intentioned to enter this agreement. But let us not kid ourselves into believing that this is the be-all and end-all.[36]

There was no recognition and certainly no admiration from Fitt for what the SDLP had brought to the table. Historically, Fitt would have welcomed some advance in the constitutional nationalist position. If he did so in 1985, he was silent on the subject.

Another indication of Fitt's fear for the fate of unionism was his tendency to support the RUC. The RUC's actions in Derry in 1968, during which Fitt was famously injured, brought him worldwide publicity. But the 'black bastards' and 'Gestapo' of the 1960s had been rehabilitated by Fitt since he became a peer. Just when Westminster was getting around to reforming the police after years of nationalist criticism, Fitt took to defending them. He did not have this view in the mid-1970s, however.

In 2005, the *Irish News* reported that confidential cabinet files released under the thirty years rule revealed that Fitt had raised fears of collusion between the RUC in north Belfast and loyalist paramilitaries just days after two Catholics were murdered in the area in 1974. The files revealed that Fitt had expressed concerns to the British government about the RUC's 'ineffectiveness' in quelling anti-Catholic intimidation in the Rathcoole estate. He also claimed the local police station contained 'UDA sympathisers' and that harassment of Catholics had not been stopped because of the risk of antagonising the loyalist majority.[37]

Twelve years later, however, when allegations of collusion were far more clearly substantiated, Fitt was able to say with confidence, 'I see the RUC as acting in full support of the whole community in Northern Ireland, both the majority and the minority.'[38] Fitt's assertion was perhaps prompted by the fact that the RUC had 'faced down the loyalists' after the Anglo-Irish Agreement and also by a certain degree of empathy. Loyalist anger at the agreement had been intense. By the time Fitt made his claim there had been 138 attacks on off-duty members of the RUC and police reserve. Before anger subsided, over 500 police homes had been attacked and 150 RUC families were forced to move as a result of the intimidation. Fitt clearly appreciated the effects of such intimidation: 'As one who suffered in much the same way as at present the RUC is suffering, having for 11 years been stoned and petrol bombed in my home, I fully understand and sympathise with the awful position in which they find themselves.'[39]

The Stalker affair gave Fitt another opportunity to show where his allegiance lay. In 1986 John Stalker, then Deputy Chief Constable of the Greater Manchester Police, was removed from an official British enquiry into the circumstances surrounding the death of six unarmed Catholics at police checkpoints. There was a suspicion that the RUC had employed a 'shoot-to-kill' policy rather than arresting suspected members of the IRA. Stalker had been stonewalled and was then removed from the investigation on 30 June 1986, but not before he had recommended the prosecution of a number of RUC officers. Stalker was replaced by Colin Sampson, then Chief Constable of West Yorkshire. Allegations had been made about Stalker's association with 'known criminals', but he was cleared of these suspicions and reinstated on 22 August 1986. Fitt admitted later that 'unfortunately', Stalker 'was badly treated by certain sections of those in authority', before asserting that 'in carrying out his investigations he seemed to rely upon opinions that were hostile to the RUC from the outset'. He went on:

> Let us not forget in all the furore that exists throughout Ireland that the clear perception now is that Mr Stalker was on the nationalist side and Mr Stalker was on the Republican side ... Why was it that Mr Stalker received an absolute folk hero's welcome on the streets of Dublin last weekend? It was because he was perceived to be on their side and against the other side.[40]

The perception among nationalists and republicans was that Fitt no longer supported their interests. They were correct in this analysis. Fitt was particularly angered by Stalker's use of the testimony of Father Raymond Murray. According to Fitt, Murray was 'one of the most pro-republican, and anti-British priests that ever donned a clerical uniform in Ireland ... If Father Murray is neutral, I fail to understand what one would recognise to be a bigot in both a political and nationalistic sense.'[41]

In the light of this evidence, it can be established (and confirmed by Paddy Devlin)[42] that Fitt had long been developing a more amenable view of the RUC than some of his former colleagues in the SDLP. This again underlines the fact that his political outlook had altered considerably since the days when he made a name for himself as a vocal critic of the *status quo*. In the 1990s and later, his support for the RUC became even more pronounced and verged on the gratuitous.

The corollary of Fitt's empathy with unionism and unionists was the evolution of the anti-nationalism that became evident once he was released from the SDLP's yoke. This trend represents the fourth feature of Fitt's political existence in the latter years. Again, a rejection of his early thinking can be discerned.

In an interview he gave to *The Times* in August 1994 Fitt suggested that Britain was 'the most tolerant country on the face of God's earth', before adding, 'I only wish to God that we in Northern Ireland could be as tolerant of people's views.'[43] Paradoxically, he was at home in political exile. It is also not unreasonable to assume that he continued to be seduced by the 'tone of the House' and that much of his rhetoric in the Lords was prompted by distance from his former constituents, not only in a physical sense but also politically.

It is worth reviewing just how much of a nationalist Gerry Fitt had been in the formative stages of his political career. In August 1970, just after the formation of the SDLP, he gave an interview to John Murdoch of the Dublin-based *Sunday Press*, in which he spoke in terms consistent with his republican socialist rhetoric of the 1960s. The new party would have no time for sectarianism and he suggested that 'there is a strong probability that the Unionist party will disintegrate within the next two months'. He envisaged the duped Protestant workers joining their Catholic comrades to stand against the interests of bourgeois unionism, creating a genuine 'polarisation' characterised by Right and Left, as opposed to what he would have seen as the false dichotomy created by the sectarian nature of the Northern Ireland state.

The Protestant working-class had nothing to fear: 'Their future will be safe in my hands. If we get their support it will spell the death knell for the Unionists in Northern Ireland. This will eventually lead to a united Ireland Republic where the working-class interests will be paramount.' Despite the Labourite rhetoric, Fitt stressed the nationalist aspiration, arguing that he had the support of Labour MPs: 'They are men who have recognised that partition was wrong in the first place and that it should be abolished as quickly as possible. Partition has never been a success in any country. Unfortunately, Ireland has been the guinea-pig. Ireland was the most atrocious partition on any country.' Fitt dismissed the use of violence as futile and counter-productive before stressing 'Ireland must and will be united and there can be no query on that point.' He concluded, 'I have made it perfectly clear that it is my intention of bringing about a united Ireland with a Labour Government.'[44]

His overt nationalism at this juncture was quite unambiguous, which makes his subsequent retreat from this stance all the more remarkable. Fitt's personal road to Damascus was disrupted by partisan in-fighting, political rivalry and tragic personal circumstances, and these no doubt shaped his ultimate conversion.

Fitt's distaste for nationalism was evident in the Lords debate on the New Ireland Forum. He maintained, 'nationalism is one of the most potent factors that can affect mankind. It can make people do the most irrational and bloodthirsty things.'[45] In the same debate his aversion for 'Irish' nationalism manifested itself in a scathing attack on Charles Haughey:

> I do not trust the man. And I would not expect any Unionist to trust the man. How can the people in Northern Ireland, Protestant representatives, sit down and have any meaningful discussion with a person such as the Leader of Fianna Fáil who has told the Unionist, 'whether you like it or not, you do not have the right to keep partition in this country and you are to be forced into a republic?'[46]

Haughey had his faults, but in this instance he was simply articulating a traditional and widely held nationalist view, which emphasised the territorial integrity of the island and rejected the unionist veto. That view was an imperative of the Irish constitution – the official policy of the state for half a century. Fitt had expressed this traditional view for many years, in 1968 going as far as to chastise the southern government for not being forceful enough in demanding its right to the 'six-county territory'.

Fitt's speech in the Lords debate on the New Ireland Forum also suggested that the economic situation would not help reunification. 'The people in the Republic have got very, very serious economic problems of their own. And in the North it is exactly the same.'[47] His assessment was realistic. Things were dire on both sides of the border. Even so, there was no evidence that Fitt clamoured for the south to subsume the north after the emergence of the 'Celtic Tiger' in the early 1990s.

During the Anglo-Irish Agreement debates, the same anti-nationalist stance prevailed. Fitt wanted the agreement to work but he visualised an internal settlement. He asked, 'Are there any circumstances which could bring them (the two cultures) together to accept the boundaries of the Northern Ireland state and to accept each culture as a legitimate expression?'[48] In what was tantamount to a rejection of nationalist orthodoxy, Fitt appeared to discount the Irish government as a legitimate player in the attempts to forge a solution to the northern problem:

> What the Unionist population are so incensed about at the moment is the fact that there will be people from the Irish Government, from the Republic of Ireland, who will be sitting in this conference which will be virtually the government of Northern Ireland. That is what this conference will be. It will be virtually the government of Northern Ireland because this agreement makes it quite clear that the Irish government will be able to pass opinions on every issue under the sun.[49]

Leaving aside the exaggerated impact Fitt attached to the possible fallout from the agreement, it is difficult not to conclude that he had come full circle. He now denied the propriety of Dublin's involvement in the affairs of the north, just when his former party had helped achieve its institutionalisation. He even went as far as to exonerate the same unionist mismanagement of Northern Ireland that he had attacked – and on which he had built his political career – decades earlier. He argued, 'It was inevitable, given the circumstances of the creation of the Northern Ireland state, that there had to be discrimination. I am not blaming the Unionists for it. They were part of the problem. There had to be discrimination if the Northern Ireland state was to be kept in being.[50] While there is indeed some truth in this view (the devolved partition arrangement imposed by Lloyd George, Churchill *et al.* in 1920 placed the burden of policing a permanently discontented Catholic minority on the Protestant majority in a semi-detached outpost of the UK), Fitt need not have expressed it, with its implicit justification of unionist hegemony. His growing empathy for unionism from his new home in the House of Lords and, *ipso facto*, the dilution of his nationalism would remain the dominant characteristics of his public utterances. Eddie McGrady's explanation for Fitt's stance was simple. 'I thought a lot of his anti-nationalism comments were predicated on his resentment of the SDLP. He played to the gallery. He appeared to be carrying a grudge. His constant accusations that we had become more and more green were primarily driven by bitterness against Hume'.[51]

POLITICAL ENDGAME

The Anglo-Irish Agreement changed the framework of the Northern Ireland problem and how it was viewed by the British government, but it failed to bring an end to the violence. The IRA campaign intensified between 1986 and 1994, particularly in County Tyrone, with the help of Libyan arms and imported Semtex.

The agreement also failed to reconcile the two communities, so the devolved power-sharing government envisaged in it never became a reality. Speaking in March 1991, Fitt argued, 'The existence of the Anglo-Irish Agreement over these past five years has made it impossible for the Protestant unionist community to speak in any way to the Catholic community.'[52] This is not to say that there had been no dialogue: there had been plenty. However, it was the nationalists that were doing the talking and, more importantly, they were talking to each other.

John Hume was harshly criticised for engaging in talks with Gerry Adams. Fitt considered this 'disastrous' for the political fortunes of the SDLP. He was not alone: many party members, some of them very senior, feared Sinn Féin would prosper to the detriment of the SDLP. Unionists glibly and inaccurately claimed there was no difference between SDLP and Sinn Féin policy. Hume tried to persuade Adams that the British had taken up a neutral position on Northern Ireland's continuance in the union. He argued that Sinn Féin should end the military campaign and embrace democracy, but Adams was not easily persuaded. There was some common ground on ultimate aims but little agreement on methodology. Sinn Féin was not convinced that the British were neutral on the issue of their presence in Northern Ireland. The talks failed.

Hume consistently opposed violence throughout his political career, viewing the use of force as morally repugnant. Yet by engaging in these talks he recognised the legitimacy of republican ideology and accepted that republicans were politically motivated, even if he disagreed with their *modus operandi*. In effect, he considered them deluded men of principle – a position held and then abandoned by Fitt decades earlier.

From April 1991 to November 1992 a series of negotiations took place in an attempt to end the stalemate. The Brooke/Mayhew talks, as they became known, involved the British and Irish governments as well as representatives from four of Northern Ireland's main political parties. By July 1991, however, the talks were in difficulty. Peter Brooke, who had become Secretary of State for Northern Ireland in July 1989, was forced to pull the plug when unionists insisted they could not continue if the Anglo-Irish Agreement was re-activated (The talks had taken place during a gap in the operation of the Anglo-Irish Conference meetings.) Fitt was quick to explain why the talks had failed and showed where his sympathies lay:

> These talks began because the representatives of the Protestant Unionist community so detested every single sentence in the Anglo-Irish Agreement that they were prepared to enter into talks which would do away with the agreement, and whip it off the statute book. On the other hand, the SDLP, the nationalists and the Irish Government, entered into those talks with the intention of consolidating and reinforcing the Anglo-Irish Agreement. So there you have the irresistible force and the immovable object. There was no way that a meeting of minds could take place. One wanted to continue the Anglo-Irish Agreement and one wanted to make certain it was dead. I have read every single Irish newspaper every day since these talks began and I must say that from the nationalist point of view there was a great deal of truimphalism – 'we have got the Unionists with their backs to the wall'.[53]

Fitt was convinced the Anglo-Irish Agreement was an obstacle to political progress and 'while that is there, and while Articles 2 and 3 of the Irish Constitution are in existence, there will be no talk of bringing together the two communities in Northern Ireland'.[54]

Further evidence of Fitt's move away from a nationalistic stance came in November 1992 when the unionists withdrew from further talks under the auspices of Brooke's successor, Patrick Mayhew, for essentially the same reasons as they had had in July 1991. Fitt's arguments were likewise essentially the same: 'There will be no agreement if it is insisted that the Irish Government have a role to play in the affairs of Northern Ireland.'[55]

The Anglo-Irish Agreement and the Brooke/Mayhew talks had at least improved co-operation between the British and Irish governments, which was crucial to the 1998 Good Friday Agreement. However, such prospects were not immediately apparent at the beginning of 1993. In April the disclosure that Hume and Adams had resumed talks incensed the unionists. On 24 April 1993, the two men issued a first joint statement saying that an internal settlement was not an option and that the Irish people had a right to national self-determination. In the following September the pair issued a second joint statement outlining the 'Hume/Adams initiative', which 'aimed at the creation of a peace process'.

Meanwhile the British and Irish governments tried to create conditions that might coax ceasefires from the various paramilitaries. In November 1993 it was confirmed that there had been a series of secret talks between the British and Sinn Féin. Fitt was not against establishing and maintaining contacts with the IRA to dissuade them from the use of force: 'I would certainly give my support. I would have absolutely no objection to what has been happening under the present Government for trying to maintain those contacts to see whether it is possible to bring violence to an end.'[56] He was, however, against any form of concession: 'I believe that in all the discussions which … the Government have with the IRA, they must relate only to one thing: that the IRA must call off their campaign of violence and that no concessions should be made for doing so.'[57] He was not convinced that there had been a significant shift in republican thinking: 'They have bombed their way into the media of this country. I believe that the IRA have not changed one single iota from the days when they attacked and harassed me in Northern Ireland'.[58]

The momentum created by the political chemistry between John Major and Albert Reynolds in both London and Dublin led to the Downing Street Declaration of December 1993, when the two governments agreed an outline of their mutual position on the future of Northern Ireland.[59] It affirmed the right of the people of Northern Ireland to self-determination and said the state would be transferred to the republic from the UK only if a majority of its population favoured such a move. We have already seen that Fitt was not convinced that the declaration would civilise the IRA or be capable of bringing peace. He simply equated the Provisionals with the 'Mafia'.[60] Nevertheless, there was enough in the statement for the IRA to announce a ceasefire on 31 August 1994, which was followed by a similar announcement from the Combined Loyalist Military Command (an umbrella for loyalist paramilitaries) on 13 October.

Despite these developments, Fitt was pessimistic, believing that peace was a long way off: 'We have a million miles to go before we can achieve that.'[61] He lamented the political credibility bestowed on representatives of the paramilitaries who had 'left behind scores, hundreds, indeed thousands of grieving relatives who will bitterly resent any attempt to let Loyalist or Republican murder gangs come to the conference table to speak on their behalf.'[62] He was also worried that they would go back to the old habits of murder and mayhem, asking if they were 'prepared to abide by any resolutions which come back from such a forum or will both sides go back and resort to violence', before declaring that under 'no circumstances should those people take part who have committed ferocious murders on the loyalist side or the republican side. They have no mandate from the Irish people to take any part in any solutions to the Irish problem.'[63]

Fitt was not convinced by the nationalist goodwill coming from Dublin. He regarded Articles 2 and 3 as the sacred cows of nationalism, adding 'I cannot see any Irish government, particularly Fianna Fáil, recommending that those two articles be removed.'[64] He also took the opportunity to support the RUC: 'I spent many years of my political life in Belfast and the RUC was the only legitimate force that they had (the Catholic community) and they accepted it'. He also expressed his opposition to the idea that the 'Royal' should be taken out of the title to make the force more acceptable to nationalists, considering any such proposal 'very insensitive at this time'.[65]

Early in 1995 the British government announced that the ban on ministers engaging in contacts with Sinn Féin, the Ulster Democratic Party[66] and the Progressive Unionist Party[67] would end. The following year opened with the publication of the Mitchell report on arms decommissioning.[68]

It had been an eventful twelve months, with British/Sinn Féin contacts proving durable, if somewhat delicate. London and Dublin had co-operated and launched two framework documents, 'A New Framework for Agreement' and 'A Framework for Accountable Government in Northern Ireland'. Nationalists of all shades moved closer together, culminating in a joint call for all-party talks as well as an excellent photo-opportunity in Dublin. Hume was convinced IRA weapons would be decommissioned if Sinn Féin were included in talks. Sinn Féin shared and enjoyed the political limelight, as evidenced by Adams' attendance at the St Patrick's Day reception hosted by President Clinton (which annoyed Fitt).

Paramilitary violence continued, however. Nationalists clashed with the RUC during the summer marching season, prompting the Irish government to accuse the RUC of bias in favour of the Orange Order and to issue an official complaint through the Anglo-Irish secretariat at Maryfield. Perhaps the most significant development was the joint communiqué issued by the British and Irish governments, which stated, 'The two governments have agreed to launch a 'twin-track' process to make progress in parallel on the decommissioning issue and on all-party negotiations.' George Mitchell, a former US senator, was asked to lead an international, independent body to monitor the decommissioning issue.

Two weeks after the publication of the Mitchell report the IRA exploded a huge bomb in London. Two people were killed, dozens injured, and £150 million of damage caused in the commercial heart of the city. The IRA had ended its ceasefire in spectacular fashion with a forceful signal to Whitehall of its intentions.

The six Mitchell principles, ground rules for talks agreed by the British and Irish governments and the political parties, made it clear that a rejection of violence was a condition of participation in the democratic process. Fitt reminded everyone in the Lords of this before declaring, 'the massive wave of revulsion which has swept these islands since last Friday must surely indicate to the IRA that however many bombs it lets off here or in Ireland, or however many people it kills, at the end of the day it cannot succeed in bludgeoning a democratic people to accept its demands'.[69]

Yet Fitt had not given up hope of peace. 'I freely support all those who say that the peace process has not ended. It will take a Herculean effort by all concerned to bring it back from the death throes in which it has been placed. But I believe that we can succeed in replacing it again.'[70]

But events took a distinct turn for the worse in the summer of 1996. During the previous summer an Orange Order parade to and from Drumcree parish church in Portadown, County Armagh had become the catalyst for serious sectarian unrest between Protestants and the local nationalists. The 1995 stand-off at Drumcree was caused when the RUC prevented an Orange Order parade from returning from the church to Portadown along the Garvaghy Road, a mainly nationalist area.

The ruling provoked considerable anger in the loyalist community and civil disturbance followed. A compromise was concluded and a modified parade was allowed to proceed. Loyalists considered this a victory, and this was reinforced by the swagger jig of Paisley and David Trimble (leader of the Ulster Unionist Party) as they entered the centre of town. Fitt was well aware of the symbolism of marching in Northern Ireland. 'People don't march as an alternative to jogging,' he said in 1994, 'they do it to assert their supremacy.'[71] The unionist truimphalism was a pyrrhic victory. Nationalists would not be as acquiescent in the future and the dispute would rumble on for years.

In 1996 Drumcree II, as it was termed, had the same explosive ingredients as the original. After the loyalist community caused havoc across Northern Ireland in support of the Orange Order the RUC reversed its decision to prevent the parade. The threat of physical force meant the Orangemen were allowed down the Garvaghy Road. Nationalist residents, not content to adopt the quiet protest of the previous summer, were beaten out of the way by the RUC. As a consequence nationalist rioting erupted and inter-community relations reached a nadir. Fitt was alarmed:

> I may say that 1996 was the most dangerous year in Northern Ireland that I have seen in my political lifetime. This year, after Drumcree, we were on the verge of a civil war. It was far worse than 1974, when loyalist mobs brought about the downfall of the Sunningdale Executive which we had so laboriously created.[72]

Fitt consistently opposed the IRA and supported the RUC, taking the side of the police in the aftermath of the force's controversial conduct during the removal of protestors from the Garvaghy Road. His support for law and order was again exhibited in this debate, as was as his contempt for loyalist paramilitaries. He had no truck with people of violence from either community and he was clearly appalled at their apparent 'rehabilitation':

> In Drumcree the Unionist mobs once again took control of the streets, as they did in 1974. The RUC were placed in the impossible position of trying to assert the rule of law. What happened? Protestant policemen living in Protestant areas of Northern Ireland were subject to violent attacks from the Orange mobs. The chief constable of Northern Ireland had to leave his own home because of attacks by Protestant mobs. So let us not put all the blame on the IRA.
>
> … I said then, and I say now; I repeat and will continue to repeat – the last elections that were held in Northern Ireland were deliberately designed to bring murderers into the election process. I said that in this House at the time. The Government should never have engaged in an exercise to bring murderers into the democratic process. Those people have been guilty of the most atrocious murders. Now, it makes everyone sick to see them walking into 10 Downing Street with their briefcases and pinstripe suits.

I have been an opponent of the IRA all my life, and will continue to be an opponent of the IRA. But if John White,[73] the murderer of my close friend, is welcomed into Downing Street, I have to agree, although it goes against my every instinct, that Gerry Adams may be entitled to go there. At least he has 116,000 votes behind him. John White does not have that support. The Government should never have designed an electoral process that would bring murderers to the conference table.

Attacks have been made here on the IRA, with which I agree. But let us not forget that we talk about decommissioning, taking arms from the IRA, but there is also an arsenal of arms within the Loyalist community. We should take the arms from them and decommission across the board, including all the so-called Loyalist paramilitaries.[74]

In May 1997 Fitt blamed Hume for Sinn Féin's electoral success. He felt Hume was one of those responsible for allowing the British to entertain republicans in Downing Street. The *Irish News* justifiably adopted a defensive position towards Hume and the SDLP, adding curtly, 'It is ironic that Lord Fitt, who first made his mark as a member of the Republican Labour Party, should now be such a virulent critic of what he perceives as a trend towards republicanism in others.' The paper went on to criticise its former hero for a lack of political *nous* in the 1985 council elections. 'Lord Fitt's own political judgment is very much open to question. Less than a decade ago, he was urging West Belfast voters to back the Workers' Party. Since his endorsement, the Workers' Party has suffered so many splits and electoral setbacks that it has practically disappeared as a political force. Perhaps the SDLP should be relieved that Lord Fitt has transferred his allegiances elsewhere.'[75]

Fitt was not discouraged by the rebuke. As moves towards agreement continued, albeit slowly, he complained that 'Awful nationalistic pressures will be applied to force the Northern Ireland people into constructing some sort of agreement between north and south which will be entirely un-acceptable to them.'[76] It can be argued that Fitt himself applied 'nationalistic pressures' on Northern Ireland for years, but his underwriting of the *status quo* during his later political life represented a considerable move away from the nationalist politics for which he had become so well known.

Like many others, Fitt could not stomach the presence of the leaders of paramilitaries at peace talks. He argued:

Because of a construed or misconstrued policy under the Conservative Government, people who had been killing and murdering over many years were brought in and are now going into the Stormont talks. They have been seen walking in and out of No. 10 Downing Street under both governments. I urge the present Government and those who have initiated tonight's debate to take into account the vast majority of people in Northern Ireland – that is, both Catholics and Protestants – who feel sickened to the stomach at seeing people who have been guilty of murder now going into talks, allegedly to instil confidence into the political process of Northern Ireland. I hope that the Government will take that fact into consideration.[77]

Despite Fitt's misgivings, on 10 April 1998 – Good Friday – Mitchell announced that the two governments and the parties in Northern Ireland had reached agreement on a new political dispensation. Given the integral part played in the negotiations by Sinn Féin and parties in which loyalist paramilitaries were involved, one might have expected a critical response from Fitt. This was not the case. He was cautious but supportive:

I believe that it may be a little premature to refer to this agreement as a settlement. It is not. One can only hope daily that it will become a settlement ... I have no hesitation in saying that I fully support the agreement. I call on anyone in Northern Ireland who has listened to my voice over the years to vote 'yes' in the referendum. It is the only possible way; there is no alternative.[78]

Fitt's career may have been littered with contradictions and U turns, but it must be acknowledged that he always sought reconciliation. This is not true of all Irish politicians. Fitt may not have liked many of the players in the Good Friday negotiations but he had always accepted the will of the Northern Ireland electorate. He later explained why he supported the agreement. 'Although the environment is still far from ideal, I cautiously accept that rigid sectarianism is beginning to dissipate and that the reconcilers and pragmatists already on the march will be emboldened by the creation of new locally sensitive and accountable political institutions to support and promote their good work.'[79]

Fitt took the announcement of the agreement as an opportunity to express his support for the RUC, an institution that would have a radically different future under the terms of the Belfast Agreement. His now habitual endorsement of the police would have antagonised many in the nationalist community, for whom policing reform was a desirable and necessary part of any deal:

> I should like to place firmly on record – perhaps to the total disagreement of some of my former colleagues – my support for the RUC. Had it not been for the RUC over the past 30 years Northern Ireland would have descended into absolute anarchy. It is only by the dedicated service of those policemen that there has been a civilised outcome to the events of the past few years.[80]

Can we conclude from this declaration that Fitt felt the RUC had been acceptable since 1968? Even in the light of the warm relationships that Fitt had developed with individual policemen this seems a quite remarkable statement, bearing in mind that 1968 was the year he was attacked by the RUC in Derry and that he was supportive of many of the accusations levelled at the force. Nationalists would have been dismayed, mystified and exasperated in equal measure by such a statement. Three months later he argued:

> No longer can members of the nationalist community condemn the RUC as a sectarian force. No longer can members of they [sic] say that it is acting in a biased way against the minority nationalist community. The RUC will have to overcome some hurdles, perhaps in days, perhaps in weeks, in order again to assure the people of Northern Ireland that it is the impartial force that I know it to be.[81]

Fitt had developed his early political career advocating southern influence in northern affairs and by hostility to the RUC. Now, just when his former party had achieved his earlier demands by securing southern influence in the affairs of the province and the fundamental reform of the RUC, he decided his earlier oppositional stance had been a bad idea after all.

When the Lords discussed the form of oath that a reformed police force might have to make, Fitt's opinion again showed how far he had travelled away from his nationalist roots. 'The only oath that may be necessary is for the RUC men to swear their allegiance, if that is necessary, to the people of the state of Northern Ireland.'[82] Clearly Fitt no longer considered the 'six counties' the manipulatively composed artifice that he had in the 1960s.

On Monday 29 November 1999, power-sharing returned to Northern Ireland after a gap of twenty-five years. As the new assembly met, Fitt was excited and optimistic, telling the *Sunday Times*:

> I have been privileged to watch the triggering of a political process that, I am now convinced, will ultimately succeed ... Now I share the widespread hopes that, with the threat of coercion having been replaced by the right of consent, we have indeed reached a turning point, that is genuinely historic, and that the failures of the past will soon give way to a brighter future.[83]

Three years later Fitt's optimism about political progress had turned to pessimism and despair. He claimed, 'The Government should find the means not to cling tenaciously to an agreement that has so often failed and is doomed to failure; they must try to resurrect some other constitutional means. This one has gone. I believe that it has gone forever.'[84]

The vague wording of some of the provisions of the Good Friday Agreement, which had helped ensure acceptance of it at the time, served only to postpone debate on some of the more contentious clauses – most notably paramilitary decommissioning, police reform and the construction of north–south bodies. Ongoing paramilitary activity further reduced confidence, making the implementation of the agreement problematic. Fitt's solution to these problems was likely to include a dilution of the all-Ireland dimension, a less radical re-organisation of the police service and a review of Sinn Féin's suitability for government. He had again come full circle, promoting a set of ideas that was more suggestive of a unionist agenda than anything remotely connected to his political origins in the republican socialist tradition.

CONCLUSION

I believe that political opportunists, although they may win short term successes, generally fail in the long run, because in due course people find them out. One cannot forever be a republican in Belfast and a socialist in London, a nationalist at Stormont and a British subject at Westminster. Nor can one build an enduring political career upon a great heap of irresponsible criticism and denigration.

(Terence O'Neill, *Irish News*, 25 May, 1968)

The above quotation has already featured in the main body of this work, but this repetition is justified as O'Neill's statement neatly encapsulates Gerry Fitt's political dilemma. Fitt endeavoured to defy the dictum that you cannot please all of the people all of the time. In the 1960s, he strove to be all things to all men. Therefore, the remarkable *volte face*, from Republican Socialist to Peer of the Realm is in reality not remarkable as Fitt was neither a republican nor a socialist in the commonly accepted sense. He was, however, a nationalist who became disillusioned with the ideology he espoused earlier in his life. When he saw extreme nationalist instincts put into practice by the IRA, he felt justified in accepting a place in the British House of Lords, almost in reaction to what the Provisionals were doing. A consideration of each of Fitt's political labels will demonstrate just how perceptive O'Neill was.

In the early part of his political career Fitt was sympathetic to, and on occasions supportive of, republican tradition. In 1962 he demanded the release of republican political prisoners considering them 'men of principle' and 'political opponents' of unionism. He even helped them in a practical way, facilitating arms training for republican volunteers in his party premises in the mid 1950s. Later, in 1972 he called for the granting of political status for republican prisoners, therefore tacitly agreeing that this was a political struggle with the character of a war. By 1980, however, he denounced republicans on hunger strike and asked the British government to deny their political demands. This stance suggests that Fitt had radically altered his views on republicans. He either came to betray his original ideals or alternatively saw his faith in the imperatives of his ideology shattered. This appraisal, however, does not tell the whole story. It does not appreciate that Fitt's republicanism, when exhibited, was mostly of a tactical nature. Furthermore it fails to recognise that he operated in shifting historical circumstances. The IRA of the 1950s and 1960s was of a very different nature than that which emerged in the 1970s and beyond.

The IRA campaign of 1956 – 1962 was little more than a series of border incidents impinging to a minimal degree on the life of the citizens in either the north or south. It demonstrated that the republican movement did not reflect the practical demands of nationalists and that the policy of physical force was not viable at this time. Fitt's apparent republicanism in the 1950s and 1960s must be placed in this context. He was astute enough to understand that republican laurels would be helpful, if not absolutely necessary, to an aspiring Catholic politician. Fitt was nothing, if not versatile in this period, being supportive of the republican prisoners and making sure he was seen at the annual Easter parades designed to show deference to the republican dead. In essence, in the early 1960s, Fitt's republicanism was a mixture of tactical opportunism and sentimental idealism based on a consideration that practical republicanism was a spent force and the preserve of a small minority. Likewise, when Fitt and Harry Diamond joined forces in 1964, the 'Republican Labour Party' was a mere label based on tactical considerations. In time, Fitt was able to jettison this republican tag with little difficulty. Furthermore, in his maiden speech at Westminster, he freely acknowledged that he was not a republican in the true sense and posed instead as a working-class British subject with working-class grievances. Although he appeared to have republican sympathies in Belfast, he showed no such inclination in London.

Although Fitt occasionally flirted with rhetoric that suggested 'unconstitutional' methods of political agitation, he was, like all politicians, totally unprepared for the re-emergence of the IRA. In the 1970s his republican posturing seemed inappropriate and he began to condemn the new manifestation of republicanism, the Provisional IRA. Although Fitt was never a true republican, he had played the role sufficiently well to convince many in Belfast of his sincerity. Thus his condemnation of the IRA seemed strangely inconsistent in the light of previous public pronouncements. This apparent transfiguration left Fitt open to charges of gross betrayal, particularly in relation to his final elevation to the House of Lords – the last great repudiation of his former years and the community he came from. Yet when the nature of Fitt's republicanism (in the ideological sense of the word) is considered, his peerage was not so paradoxical.

Like his republicanism, Fitt's socialism was largely tactical in the electoral sphere. It was also extremely vague and based on intuition and sentiment rather than on political theory. His socialism was a product of his environment and based on the politics of the British welfare state. Nevertheless, it must be stressed that Fitt was extremely conscientious in his endeavours for the working-class, albeit on a clientelist basis. Indeed, it would be more appropriate to label Fitt as a 'fixer' rather than a socialist, his brand of socialism being more akin to populism. In this he was similar to Joe Devlin, the acknowledged leader of nationalists in Northern Ireland until his death in 1934. There are further grounds for comparison. Both Devlin and Fitt were from humble working-class Belfast families and both left school after only an elementary education to become archetypal self made politicians. Devlin like Fitt was a colourful figure who championed the underdog and both West Belfast MPs went on to be 'Kings of the Falls Road' for decades. There were however some major differences between Fitt and Devlin. Devlin was the consummate political organiser and was primarily concerned with the Catholic interest. Neither of these traits, one admirable the other rather narrow, could be found in Fitt.

James Connolly was the political inspiration for Gerry Fitt. Early in his career, Fitt had articulated the socialist rhetoric of Connolly and played on it when necessary. This strategy was instrumental in winning election after election in the 1960s. Yet Fitt was not in the same tradition as Connolly, as the latter sought change through the militancy of the working-class, and not by parliamentary means. Despite some of his language Fitt was a moderate reformer while Connolly was a revolutionary socialist. This was no more evident than when the northern state's existence was threatened and Fitt decided to distance himself from elements intent on realising something akin to Connolly's ideals. Fitt's later argument that Connolly committed a mistake by his involvement in the 1916 Easter rebellion was an admission that his allegiance to Connolly's legacy had become qualified. In short, Fitt's politics had little to do with the Connolly brand of socialism, although the emotional attachment to populist and proletarian politics provided him with some sort of thread to that tradition, although he stopped short of revolutionary planning. But then, the world had moved on and the examples of socialism in practice were arguably not worth emulating.

If there is another Irish historical figure from that period that can be likened to Fitt, it is John Redmond. Like Fitt, Redmond exhibited a tremendous faith that the British parliament could right Ireland's wrongs. F.S.L. Lyons said of Redmond: 'He seems to have found it difficult to hate Englishmen and things English'.[1] The same could be said of Fitt.

According to Eddie McGrady, two of Fitt's declared adversaries, Cardinal O'Fiaich and Seamus Mallon, 'were very Irish'.[2] Perhaps Fitt, without ever realising it, was not of the same ilk and therein lay his paradoxical position. He undoubtedly felt that unionists 'trusted him more than other nationalists' because of his exploits during the war[3] and the Reverend Martin Smyth certainly seemed to think that Fitt was a different type of nationalist: 'I still believe that underneath he was not just a 'little Irelander' because as a merchant seaman travelling the world and also knowing of his time at Westminster he came to realise that there was a bigger world out there and he got acclimatised to that'.[4]

By the 1970s, Fitt's references to Connolly had virtually stopped. He was the leader of the SDLP which, despite his early protestations to the contrary, was not a socialist party. It became the voice of Catholics opposed to the Provisionals' campaign and was mildly left-reformist in social policy. Fitt was adamant that he was a socialist in a socialist party but on two crucial issues he demonstrated that this was not the case. First, when Paddy Devlin resigned from the SDLP on socialist principles, Fitt did not support him. Secondly, Fitt was instrumental in bringing down the Labour government in Britain in 1979, an action he did not regret, despite the subsequent policies orchestrated by Margaret Thatcher which proved injurious to the interests of the working-class. Furthermore, Fitt's peerage undoubtedly allowed his critics to mock his socialist principles. Seamus Mallon felt that the socialism of both Fitt and Paddy Devlin was somewhat superficial. He told me:

It was rumoured that Gerry had a letter from Paddy seeking Gerry's good offices to help him get a Lordship. Gerry boasted about this quite often at Westminster almost as a means of a threat. In fact maybe more cynically as a means of saying 'what a fool that man is. I am going to get it – not him'. So you had a situation where the two socialists left our party seeking advantage: vying with one another to be appointed a Lord.[5]

In retrospect it is also clear that Fitt did not or could not differentiate between revolutionary socialism and the social democratic tradition of the British Labour Party. A feature of Fitt's career was his belief that the incrementalist approach to social injustice would solve the problems of Northern Ireland. He was confident the British Labour Party could deliver an end to sectarianism and discrimination. However, it became obvious that the Labour Party lacked the will to put the necessary pressure on the unionist majority or indeed to fully engage in Northern Ireland affairs. Fitt never grasped the fact that British politicians tended to regard Ireland as a political graveyard. An example of this fear was provided by Tony Benn, who as Minister of Technology recorded in his diary on 19 August 1969, a cabinet meeting held to discuss the situation in Northern Ireland. He noted:

Denis (Healey, Minister of Defence) said he thought it was better to get Chichester-Clark, or another Ulsterman to carry the can … Jim (Callaghan) said he thought Chichester-Clark was anxious to help because he was a frightened man.

Jim then considered the possibility of a broadly based government, although it was agreed that this should not be done unless it was acceptable. But if all else fails what do we do? Denis stressed again. Let's keep Chichester-Clark carrying the can. Jim agreed. Yes I too want to avoid responsibility.[6]

It is hardly surprising then that in the 1960s the Labour government did not help Fitt address the iniquities of unionism or seek to transform the politics of Northern Ireland. Despite this, in the 1970s he clung to the belief that his 'socialist colleagues' would make the unionists toe the line. They did not. They failed to underwrite power-sharing when the process began to unravel. Rees' promise that Sunningdale would be ratified did not materialise and Orme's pledge to the SDLP that the NIO would act strongly against UWC strikers and that internment would end did not come to pass. Furthermore, Wilson's speech to the Loyalist strikers was counter-productive and to add insult to injury, Rees went on to placate the

Provisional IRA, belittling the importance and political credibility of the SDLP. When he finally ended internment it was too little too late. When Fitt helped to bring down the Labour government in 1979, it was hardly surprising that it was as much to do with pique as anything else. In short, it can be said that Fitt's attachment to socialism had limits and his faith in the progressive social democracy of the Labour Party was misplaced.

Although Fitt's socialist credentials do not stand up to purist examination, it cannot be denied that he had a deep affinity with the working-class. He was in many respects rather typical of many British Labour MPs of his time, articulating a 'them and us' attitude and providing a voice for the marginalised: or, as he put it 'to help lame dogs over stiles'.[7] His populist appeal proved enduring: Fitt's electoral success should not be sneered at, fighting twenty-two campaigns and losing only three. Furthermore, Fitt secured some Protestant support at elections (particularly in the 1960s) which stemmed, from his stance as a champion of the working-class. Considering the sectarian nature of northern Irish society, this was an admirable feat. In the 1960s Protestants as well as Catholics brought their problems to his clinic, and a growing reputation for assiduity as a public representative for the working-class enabled him to partly cross the religious divide in northern Irish politics. This was reflected both in his ability to retain the Dock seat, which no one had managed to do before and also in his success in securing the West Belfast seat in 1966. However, although Fitt may have had some Protestant admirers when in the SDLP, the party itself was unable to attract the support of the broader Protestant community, despite the fact that he became increasingly eager to respect unionist fears. In 1983, when his political credibility amongst nationalists was on the wane, the question of cross-community support for Fitt was re-opened. It would not be unreasonable to conclude that although many Protestants voted for Fitt as an anti-IRA move, some cast their vote out of a sense of loyalty for past favours, recognising the diligence with which he approached constituency work. Indeed, some Catholics also did so.

Although it can be argued that the political labels republican and socialist cannot be applied to Fitt with total precision, there is no doubt that in his early career he was a nationalistic politician with very strong views on the unification of Ireland. Despite this, Fitt had always prided himself on his socialism. He claimed in 1967 that 'I am only a nationalist because I am a socialist'. His reasoning was predicated on the argument that Catholics were oppressed in Northern Ireland, and since socialists always support the oppressed, he became a nationalist in pursuit of an objective that would free Catholics from their oppression and unite them with their Protestant comrades against the unionist grandees. But Fitt was a Catholic before he was a socialist (something that he can hardly be blamed for) and therefore in the political context of Northern Ireland a Catholic is by default, a nationalist. If Fitt had been a Protestant who became a socialist and then, in turn, became a nationalist, he could have, in all sincerity, said that he came to nationalism through socialism. The fact of his birth and upbringing amidst the communal politics of Catholic/ nationalism made him a nationalist first and there is evidence that Fitt was at times very comfortable with this state of affairs:

However, in essence the relationship between Fitt's nationalism and socialism was really symbiotic. Nationalism and socialism were complementary to Fitt, existing in tandem, blended in differing measures to suit the occasion and environment. This was particularly the case in the 1960s when the combination flourished. But in the mid 1970s Fitt's nationalism started to wither concurrently with his socialism, and by the time he had joined the House of Lords his commitment to the principles that he had previously advanced had long since died.

Fitt's retrospective assertion that he was not interested in nationalism is simply an attempt to rewrite history. His maiden speech at Stormont in 1962 (when he strongly articulated his desire to see a united Ireland) and his public speech after the West Belfast triumph of 1966 (when he declared that he would never renounce the ideal of national unity) clearly establish that Fitt was indeed a nationalist. But whilst Fitt was fundamentally a nationalist in his early career Ulster unionists were his principal political opponents rather than the British state itself.

And so Fitt's nationalism was much more pronounced outside Westminster, which he treated with great respect. In the United States, for example, he was openly nationalist, playing to the republican gallery. Furthermore, he was not averse to criticising the government of the Irish Republic for not doing enough to end partition.

Clearly whilst Fitt was a nationalist there is therefore a contradiction between his later anti-nationalist position as a peer of the realm and the former political position upon which he built his support and which helped him win so many electoral contests.

Fitt's political antenna shifted at some point. The watershed came when Fitt became convinced of the merit of power-sharing. Peter McLachlan, who was one of Brian Faulkner's closest advisers, particularly during the Sunningdale Conference, recalled the aftermath of the first meeting of the assembly after the Power-Sharing Executive took office:

> There was Fitt, myself and three or four others. Fitt's coat was across on a stand just on the other side of the corridor and Faulkner fetched the coat and he held it for Fitt to put on and Fitt's eyes filled with tears and he said 'this is a moment in history with the Unionist Chief Executive holding the coat for an SDLP Deputy Chief Executive, this is a great moment'. And he was very moved, you could see that he was very moved by that symbolic gesture.[8]

Fitt's retrospective assertion that he wanted nothing from the north-south dynamic agreed at Sunningdale because a cross community Executive had already been agreed, negated years of his nationalist rhetoric. After the fall of the Executive Fitt spoke of power-sharing as a golden age and made its restoration his main political aim. His position, therefore, had changed from wanting to initiate the demise of the northern state to one where he was satisfied with its reform and then finally to one of co-operation in its continued existence. It would be naïve in the extreme to suggest that politicians do not change their policies when circumstances alter. Fitt, however, felt unable to acknowledge that his politics changed, thus leaving himself open to charges of betrayal.

The notion of power-sharing as a watershed in Fitt's career is not, however, a neat concept. Although he endorsed power-sharing, he led a party that was not content to work only in a British context. The SDLP became increasingly nationalist orientated. Fitt supported this 'green' position in public but evidence suggests that in private he did not. He played a duplicitous game that was reflected in two political manoeuvres that were completely contradictory.

In 1979 Fitt brought down the Labour government on principles of nationalism, arguing against a greater Northern Ireland representation at Westminster, which he viewed as a dispensation of favours to Ulster unionist MPs in return for their support of the administration. This was a complete reversal of his position as articulated in his maiden Westminster speech which demanded parity of democracy. Eight months later he resigned his leadership of the SDLP because the party had become, in his opinion, too stridently nationalist. He had now crossed the political divide and repudiated nationalism. His joining of the House of Lords was tantamount to giving unconditional support to British policy on Northern Ireland and endorsing the continuation of partition. In the build up to the 1992 general election, he argued: 'I believe a united Ireland is not possible, then (1974 – 5) or now. The realities, social, economic and political, just do not bear thinking about. I think that many of those who call for it are just making a tribal call, an anti-unionist gesture.[9] Was the political rhetoric of Gerry Fitt in the 1960s and beyond in reality empty anti-unionist jargon? The answer is probably no. Fitt was a committed anti-partitionist in those days but latterly he had in effect become a unionist, not by ideological association, but in terms of *realpolitik*. He had been driven to this position by bitterness, directed at and derived from the republican movement, John Hume's SDLP and the Dublin government.

Ivan Cooper, however, is adamant that Fitt until his death 'in private conversation subscribed to the view that Ireland should be united by consent'. Cooper had maintained contact with Fitt and the veracity of his statement cannot be questioned. He also acknowledged that Fitt did not articulate any nationalistic views while in London, stating that 'Fitt was not flogging it publicly. In the House of Lords he was not saying it but that was where his sympathies lay.'[10] But why was he not saying it? If Fitt was precluding himself from advocating such a view because he did not wish to upset the genteel conservatism of the Upper House, it reflects none too well on his attachment to principle. The retention of his core values in private is one thing, but the public persona of any politician forms the basis of historical reputation and Fitt was increasingly seen as a defender of unionism and the unionist interest. He told the Lords in April 1996 that:

The Protestants in Northern Ireland – the loyalists – do not vote for gunmen. The whole history of Northern Ireland shows that the loyalist population does not vote for murderers or convicted criminals. I am sorry to have to say this, but it is not the same of the nationalist population. Time and time again, the nationalist population has voted for released terrorists, whether or not they have been murderers. It votes for people who have been sentenced for terrorist or criminal acts. The Protestant population does not do that.[11]

Fitt had intimated such feelings for the duration of the hunger strike period and during and after his election defeat to Adams. By this point however he felt no compulsion to be furtive. The implication of his analysis was that there is an ambivalent attitude towards violence within the nationalist community, with unionists displaying a degree of moral superiority.

It is as absurd to suggest that all unionists who vote for the DUP and UUP have no regard for loyalist paramilitaries as it is to suggest that no sectarian bigots vote for Sinn Féin. It is equally absurd not to acknowledge that many nationalists vote for Sinn Féin not because they support the IRA but because they wish to see republicanism take a peaceful path. Fitt was wrong to make a distinction between the voting behaviour of Catholics and Protestants in relation to support for paramilitaries. Circumstances establish communities' reactions towards the use of violence rather than their intrinsic characteristics. In short the nationalist community is no less moral than the unionist one and vice versa – they are both prisoners of their history and the complex set of relationships that exist within these islands.

Furthermore, Fitt ignored the tacit support that unionists have given paramilitarism, in the form of Vanguard, Ulster Resistance (which was initially supported by leadership figures within the DUP), the Third Force and the time when prominent DUP member William McCrea shared a platform with the notorious loyalist Billy Wright. It should be remembered that it is not always necessary to kill to terrorise.

In 1970 Fitt argued, 'It does not require a great deal of academic knowledge to understand the political situation in Northern Ireland. If you are born and reared here and know something of Irish history you can see the whole political picture clearly'.[12] Yet despite this self-belief, Fitt appeared to have no understanding of the historical complexity of the situation - or perhaps the clear picture he saw in 1970 had become clouded due to his political evolution. Whatever the case, Fitt's understanding of Northern Ireland's political development was weak and this ultimately led him to lose his political bearings.

During the 1960s Fitt blamed the unionist regime as the source of all political ills. His efforts in this regard took him close to Desmond Greaves and the Connolly Association. When the repressive forces of the unionist regime attacked Fitt's community in August 1969 one would have expected him to have viewed this as a confirmation of his analysis. But Fitt, having called for direct rule and opposing Greaves' strategy for a reformed

Stormont held in check by a Bill of Rights, changed tack and supported the continuation of the devolved assembly, albeit in revised form. Why did he do this? The only explanation that seems logical is that he put his faith in the British Labour leaders who were intent on continuing the policy of keeping the state and its political life at arms length as a semi detached part of the UK with 'Ulstermen carrying the can'. This, of course was the fateful decision that led to British support for internment (to save the Stormont regime) and the drastic escalation of the conflict on all sides.

At the same time as Fitt saw the future in a reformed power-sharing devolved government, the Provisionals were keen to blast Stormont out of existence so that Britain would be forced to take direct responsibility for what was, indeed, Westminster's responsibility.

When Stormont finally fell Britain found itself in direct confrontation with the Provos. Fitt began to increasingly believe, from here on, that the problem was not the unionist regime but the Provos and his political will began to be directed against the Republicans. He began to see the IRA as the problem rather than merely a symptom of the problem, as he had in the 1960s.

Fitt just could not ever seem to contemplate that the British government's policy toward Northern Ireland might be the root cause of the conflict. So whilst in the 1960s and early 1970s he caricatured the unionists and pilloried them as the problem, in the late 1970s and 1980s he swung to defining the problem as the militant republicans and engaging in extravagant diatribes against them.

It is a seeming paradox that an Irish Republican Socialist should end up a peer of the British realm. But the key to understanding this paradox – so that it ceases to be paradoxical and becomes understandable – is in comprehending of the nature of Gerry Fitt's nationalism. Fitt's formative environment was the northern Catholic working-class. The force that moulded the character of Fitt's environment more than any other was Joe Devlin. A fundamental characteristic of the northern Catholic working-class is its anti-unionist anti-partitionism. It was defined in relation to its antagonism to the alien substance in its midst – the unionist community of north-east Ulster – and it had continued within the influence of the British system when the rest of the nation and its nationalism went off on an independent course under DeValera's guiding hand.

Fitt was therefore a product of a nationalism that was primarily anti-unionist in character rather than anti-British. What was most intolerable to the northern nationalist in Belfast was the unionist regime that governed them and which cut them off from the rest of the nation and its national development. The British system had some positives for northern Catholics (e.g. the welfare state) and Fitt was fundamentally a product of it, for good or ill.

There are not many bad words about Britain in Fitt's nationalistic anti-unionist tirades of the 1960s. He was a socialist of the British type, with British labourist instincts, and Westminster had a gravitational pull on him. On the other hand, the south had little appeal to him; he was largely ignorant of southern politics, and often hostile to the interference of southern politicians in his backyard. Only in the supreme moment of crisis, in August 1969, did he go south for help. And yet he turned to the British Labour leaders first and foremost for military aid and as soon as they got a grip on the situation he was back in the British ambit again.

What is consistent in Gerry Fitt's political career is his fundamental Britishness. His Irish nationalism is a characteristic within the British framework rather than an opposition to it – as James Connolly's was. He is a product of the Redmondite/Devlinite innovation in Irish nationalism that conceived a future where nationalism could achieve expression within the imperial framework as long as it was not subservient to Protestant unionist government.

That innovative form of Irish nationalism was largely wiped out on the island in 1918 with the electoral victory of Sinn Fein. But the cutting off of the six counties from the rest of the nation in 1921 led to its persistence and development in Northern Ireland. And even the stresses of a 35-year Republican campaign have not eradicated it.

So Gerry Fitt was able to transform himself from an Irish Republican Socialist into a British Lord because his Irish nationalism was, all the time, a product of his Britishness. He made the transition from anti-unionist to pro-unionist along the British road under the impact of the Provisionals' campaign and the auspices of his natural mentors in the ranks of the British Labour movement.

A primary example of Fitt's transition to pro-unionist and anti-nationalist rhetoric was his support for the RUC, particularly in his later years. The Reverend Martin Smyth provided an explanation:

Fitt came to understand that by and large that the RUC performed its duties with a greater degree of commitment to society than police forces in

England and an awareness that any organisation can have corrupt people. And I think he realised that when he saw so many killed and some of them were his own friends that they were people as well as police.[13]

It is totally understandable that the years of bloodshed would have had a dramatic and indeed a traumatic effect on Fitt that led to a softening in his attitude towards the police. Nevertheless, to many of his former constituents the RUC was the embodiment of sectarianism. Throughout its history, the force faced constant and serious allegations of improper behaviour and political and religious bias. These are charges that Fitt subscribed to himself, particularly in the late 1960s when he resorted to having the republican Kelly brothers act as bodyguards because he did not trust the intentions of the RUC. Furthermore, the RUC was condemned by human rights groups including Amnesty International, while the Stevens inquiry[14] report talked of 'institutionalised collusion' between the police and the UDA and 'gross unprofessionalism and irresponsibility',[15] leading to the loyalist murders of many innocent people in the 1970s and 1980s. Fitt managed to divorce himself from these and other revelations which served only to bemuse and infuriate the nationalists.

Ivan Cooper provided another explanation of Fitt's later position. 'His nationalism was much more fervent in the early days. In the latter days he was looking over his shoulder. At one stage he was the biggest target the IRA had. And who was keeping him alive? Policemen. So he diluted his nationalism'[16]. Fitt had, as was his wont, come full circle. In the late 1960s he was wary of the RUC but as the years progressed he came to rely on it. Conversely in the late 1960s he relied on republicans to protect him but later he had every right to be wary of them.

The most intriguing personal aspect of Gerry Fitt's career is how such a political animal could traverse such a strange political path? The answer lies in his individuality and his instinct to survive politically. Although the political labels of republican, socialist and nationalist never stuck, he was always a 'survivor'. The political transferences from Dock Irish Labour to Republican Labour to SDLP to Independent to House of Lords were all made with the minimum of fuss. It was not really that a one time Republican Socialist entered the Upper House but rather a 'political chameleon', who refused to be denied a political forum even though he knew it would stretch if not ruin his political credibility. Of course Fitt's stance on the hunger strikes does not fit into this pattern of longevity based on opportunism. In this instance, it can only be assumed that Fitt took his position on this life and death issue on moral grounds in keeping with his tendency to view things in black and white.

Fitt's instincts for political survival were complemented by his individuality. He never doubted his own political intuition. His 1966 election victory was not symptomatic of the change in Catholic politics that occurred from the late 1950s to the mid – 1960s. Although he may have been aided by the increased desire amongst Catholics for representation and attendance at Westminster, he was essentially a political loner, populist but uninterested in large parties with their attendant bureaucracies. Nevertheless, although Fitt was not a member of the northern Irish Catholic middle-class that emerged in the 1960s he became its political leader. The incongruity of this is shown by Fitt's severe clashes with the middle class National Democratic Party and his acceptance of the leadership of the SDLP which incorporated and was greatly influenced by that same body.

Fitt was correct to hold on to his independence for he was never cut out to be a party politician, as his spell with the SDLP proved. He was not always comfortable within the party, which was in many respects the organised intelligentsia that emerged from the education reforms of the 1940s, and remarked on one occasion 'I'm up to my arse in fucking teachers'.[17] Fitt's propensity to see educated colleagues as being 'too clever by half' removed him from their circle and to an extent from the wider electorate, that which lay beyond West Belfast. In reality he was only the titular head of 'the countrymen'. In his diary of 18 January 1974, the publishing magnate Cecil King noted that Ian Paisley 'has no opinion of Fitt, but regards Hume as the effective leader of the SDLP'.[18] In this estimation Paisley showed sound judgement.

Fitt's long political shelf life was in part explained by an endearing personality that transcended politics. His humour was a great attraction and there is no doubt that he was a tremendous raconteur. But he could be a devious and ruthless politician. Cooper who considered Fitt 'a true friend' nonetheless recognised that he had a spiteful streak. He provided an example from the period of the Executive: 'I was offered the health ministry by Gerry. It would have been totally inappropriate for me to take health because Paddy Devlin was the spokesman for health. He was older and more senior than me but it was an example of the old friction between himself and Devlin.[19] Fitt also had the capacity to make his contempt for people very clear. Yet he was also a sensitive man who was easily hurt, and this affected his political judgement. His attitude to Hume, Mallon, Logue and Mason was predicated as much on insecurity and perceived slights as differences in political outlook.

Fitt's figurehead position in the SDLP should not detract from the fact that he made a mark in both British and Irish history. His maiden speech at Westminster in 1966 stands as a landmark, as does his direct and dramatic involvement in the Derry Civil Rights march in 1968. Both ensured that he played a major role in destabilising the Stormont government and, in consequence, the northern state. In addition, he was instrumental in bringing British troops to Belfast, which created a political dilemma for him that he could never resolve. It should also be remembered that for a day he was acting chief Executive for Northern Ireland in the period of power-sharing. Furthermore, many on the British Left will also remember him for his part in bringing Margaret Thatcher to power.

Fitt's last twenty years or so in public life saw him more honoured and respected in London than Ireland, following his estrangement from all sections of nationalism. He was an Irish Quisling to republicans, a source of some embarrassment to the SDLP and 'Lord Courage'[20] to the tabloid press in Britain.

Even the *Irish News* placed him on the road to rehabilitation only a few years after castigating him for accepting a peerage. In an editorial marking twenty years of the 'troubles' the paper stated: The historical record for every objective observer and researcher will show that Fitt was one of the outstanding public figures of the Northern Ireland scene who, from the outset, did not compromise with violence. He revealed a political and moral courage that was truly remarkable.[21]

One thing is certain about Gerry Fitt; he was one of the most distinctive figures in Irish politics. When defeated by Adams in June 1983 admirers and critics alike would have agreed that it was the end of an era. But he failed to transform the substance of Northern Irish political life even to the limited degree that others of his time managed to do, while his latter years in the Lords were in the opinion of many, an unfortunate and unnecessary sequel to his colourful career.

EPILOGUE

Lord Fitt had watched the Northern Ireland assembly and Executive established under the Good Friday Agreement operate on a stop-start basis with repeated disagreements over IRA decommissioning. During his last few years in the Lords he continued to urge that no concessions be made to the republican movement. He summed up the 'Sinn Féin/ IRA' attitude as 'If we do not get another concession from you, we will give you another Canary Wharf.'[1] He was also critical of the changes to policing, telling the Lords in the committee stage of the Police (Northern Ireland) Bill, 'the change of name has been brought about by people who are determined to humiliate and condemn the RUC'. Referring to Chris Patten's report on policing, which proposed a name change and removal of symbols, he said:

> When Patten was given this undertaking he was told to try to find a resolution to the divisions which were taking place within the RUC. In one part of his report he said that his job was to take the RUC out of politics. He has done exactly the reverse. He has brought the Royal Ulster Constabulary to the forefront of political divisions in Northern Ireland. If these are his conclusions, they do not augur well for sanity in Northern Ireland.
>
> At the beginning of my remarks I said that you will get unionists, Protestants, maybe lapsed Catholics, who will speak out in support of the RUC. I am a Catholic; I have a Catholic education and a Catholic belief in the present and the hereafter, and I speak with a conscience in regard to this clause. I support the retention of the name of the RUC.[2]

Fitt, the other Northern Ireland peers and the Conservatives were to be disappointed. The Lords overwhelmingly backed the government by 198 to 99, and the RUC name and badge was voted out of existence, paving the way for the advent of the Police Service of Northern Ireland (PSNI).

Inevitably nationalists of all shades were not pleased with Fitt's intervention. Alex Attwood, SDLP assembly member for West Belfast, made the pertinent point that, 'Members of the House of Lords tend to represent their individual opinions; government should hear the common view of very large numbers in the north.'[3] Republicans also questioned Fitt's motives. John Kelly, by now a Sinn Féin assembly member for Mid-Ulster, opined that 'Gerry Fitt's espousal of the RUC position has more to do with his antipathy to the republican movement than it has to do with the politics surrounding the RUC.'[4] Alex Maskey, who within two years, would be the first member of Sinn Féin to serve as Belfast's lord mayor, claimed that Fitt 'allows himself to be used as a smokescreen by those who are anti-agreement.'[5]

Nationalists would have found it difficult to understand Fitt's attitude, particularly if they remembered that he was angered by the name 'Ulster Defence Regiment' (given to the force that replaced the B Specials), considering it offensive. Is the word 'Royal' any less offensive to the nationalist community than the term 'Ulster', when the latter is equated with Northern Ireland? The answer is probably not. The transition in Fitt's position is pointed up by William Whitelaw's comment in his memoirs that he 'finally persuaded' Fitt and Hume at the time the Executive was created that the name RUC had to be retained.[6]

In any event it is very unlikely that Fitt would have been perturbed by criticism from nationalists of whatever hue. In November 2000 he had been congratulated by the right-wing *Daily Telegraph* for voting with Conservative peers against Clause 1 of the Disqualifications Bill, which would have allowed members of Dáil Éireann to be elected to the House of Commons and the Northern Ireland assembly.[7] The Conservatives felt that 'IRA/Sinn Féin' would have been the beneficiaries of such a proposal, and Lord Cope argued, 'It would be a huge step towards a united Ireland by stealth.'[8]

By this stage it appeared that Fitt did not want a united Ireland – by stealth or any other means. In 1994 he had claimed that for economic reasons, 'At least 30 per cent of Catholics living in Northern Ireland do not want to see a united Ireland; they do not want to live in the Republic under any circumstances.'[9]

Peers voted by 165 to 152 to delete the key first clause of the Dis-qualifications Bill. Interestingly, the other Labour peer to support the Conservatives was none other than Lord Mason of Barnsley, Fitt's former adversary who had riled the then MP for West Belfast so much, such was the difference in their political philosophy. Joint authority was still too much for Fitt to tolerate. He advised the Lords in 2002 that such an outcome 'will never be the answer to Northern Ireland's problems'.[10]

Lord Fitt died, aged 79, on 26 August 2005. His passing brought tributes and criticism across the political divide, the tone ranging from genuine affection to outright hostility. For some, Fitt's journey was a courageous acknowledgement of the political landscape and an acceptance of politics as the art of the possible. For others, he had fallen for a false epiphany, wrapped in the trappings of pomp and patronage, that had led him to betray his roots and reject the orthodoxies of Irish nationalism.

If there were animosities in later life between Fitt and some of his former colleagues in the SDLP they were forgotten. The SDLP was generous to its former leader. John Hume said, 'Gerry was a great human being; he was a very humorous man, but also a very committed man',[11] while Seamus Mallon argued, 'History will show that the way in which he brought the problems of Northern Ireland to the immediate attention of parliament and a worldwide television audience had a fundamental effect on what happened since.'[12]

There was a sense, though, that Fitt's best work was done in the 1960s; his departure from the SDLP was glossed over, as was the evolution of his later career. Even his great friend Austin Currie suggested that Fitt's 'outstanding and crucial achievement' was placing the issue of sectarian discrimination in 'John Bull's political slum' at the heart of British politics.[13] The same sentiment was heard from the Republic: Taoiseach Bertie Ahern said that Fitt had made a very significant contribution to constitutional politics and civil rights in Northern Ireland, adding, 'history will record that he played his part by word, by deed and by example'.[14]

Warm and sincere tributes were also paid by Fitt's journalist and writer friends. Chris Ryder called Fitt 'The unrivalled champion of nationalism,'[15] adding, 'He set a compass to the great values of social justice, tolerance and reconciliation, and his course never veered ... He felt betrayed by those who did not share his unambiguous and unequivocal opposition to violence and terrorism.'[16] Ryder rightly appreciated Fitt's humane nature and personal courage, and in his heyday he may well have been the leading voice of constitutional nationalism, but to suggest that he was the embodiment of these principles and had not veered off course would be very difficult to demonstrate.

It is too simplistic to see Fitt's journey into political isolation as the consequence of divisive communal politics: this has been the fundamental characteristic of the state since its foundation and it was the very environment in which Fitt prospered for a decade. Fitt may have felt betrayed, but equally many of his former constituents may have felt betrayed by the radical changes in his views as he grew older.

Conservative opinion in Britain made the same mistaken assumption. Lord Glentoran, Conservative spokesman on Northern Ireland in the Lords, said Lord Fitt was a 'giant of nationalist politics'.[17] Fitt would not have welcomed and did not deserve a 'tribute' from *Conservative Future*, the youth movement of the British Conservative Party, entitled 'The Passing of a Gent':

> Unlike most nationalists he [Fitt] held a special regard for British rule and the need for Northern Ireland to unify under it. His time spent in the navy [*sic*] during the Second World War, probably entrenching his royalist beliefs ... The sadness of his forced departure from the Province at the hands of the IRA led him to accept a place in the House of Lords where he served admirably and with good humour for many years. Seldom would Gerry be seen without a drink in his hand and for what he had tried for so long to achieve, he probably deserved every last drop.[18]

The terms 'Royalist beliefs' and 'regard for British rule' do not equate with nationalism let alone with the description of Fitt as a 'giant of nationalism'. The accolade, for want of a better word, showed that some of the up and coming Tory faithful saw Fitt as little more than a stage Irishman with the inevitable weakness for a pint – or, in Fitt's case, a gin and tonic. No wonder Fitt appeared such a forlorn figure in the Upper House. He was perhaps as misunderstood there as he was in other political environments.

There is an element of pathos in Fitt's final political incarnation as a peer of the realm. Seamus Mallon, by no means a political accomplice by this time, met Fitt regularly at Westminster and later offered a compassionate description of his erstwhile colleague:

> I think there is a great sadness in Gerry's position in the latter years. He was a man of Belfast more than anybody I ever met and yet he felt he could no longer live there because of the experiences he had. He

was also very much the Westminster person and yet over the last ten years the people he had known there, his colleagues and contemporaries, they had either all gone or maybe were in the same position as himself – looking around wondering if anybody would recognise them and wondering if anybody would talk to them. The sadness was that he was removed from his roots in Belfast and he was left with a very lonely type of existence.[19]

Fitt's former unionist adversaries were kind in their assessment, though their tributes reflected how far Fitt had moved towards their position. Lord Maginnis, the former Ulster Unionist MP and UDR major, said, 'Gerry was somebody who, like most of us over the past 30 years, travelled the whole gamut of political emotions in Northern Ireland. Gerry was a genuine socialist – a man who believed even more strongly in later years in fair play for everybody.' In other words, Maginnis thought Fitt had shifted ground and come to take more of a unionist position. The Revd Ian Paisley reflected on his last meeting with Fitt:

When I last saw Gerry, it was in the library at the House of Commons. He wasn't well. He told me he couldn't do research any more, but that he loved talking in the debates in the House of Lords. Gerry said to me 'I always pray the debates have passed through the House of Commons before hand so I can get a copy of your speech and add my own tinges to it'. I replied 'You don't only add your tinges to it; you add your green as well.'[20]

So Fitt had resorted to using the speeches of Paisley to inform his understanding of what went on in the north. Perhaps he found them increasingly convincing: there is little evidence to suggest that he added any 'green tinges'. I asked Revd Martin Smyth if he felt it was fair to say that Fitt had come to defend the unionist position. This was his honest and candid reply:

I think that he did because he saw that position helped his own people over the years, and I think he went in that direction because he knew what his own people suffered at the hands of the IRA. He would have also discovered the high percentage of Irish people who had no problem living under British law.[21]

Republicans' reaction to Fitt's death was initially circumspect, though this changed once it was evident that the canonisation of their old political foe was under way. Bitter reminiscing was the main characteristic. Danny Morrison said Fitt had taken Margaret Thatcher's side against the hunger strikers. 'He was pro-British and was guilty of hypocrisy … He was a cheerleader for the British and he deserted his roots. He took the queen's shilling.'[22] Gerry Adams claimed, 'The differences between Gerry Fitt and Republicans were many and profound.'[23]

The zenith of Fitt's career was power-sharing and his political rhetoric after 1974 is peppered with references to the wasted opportunity, as he saw it, that the short-lived Executive symbolised (this is particularly the case during his tenure in the House of Lords). In the light of the Good Friday Agreement, are there grounds for a reappraisal of Fitt, particularly from a republican perspective?

Seamus Mallon described the Good Friday Agreement as 'Sunningdale for slow learners', and from a constitutional viewpoint this argument has some validity. To highlight this point, Vincent Browne of the *Irish Times* asked, 'Had Gerry Fitt's politics been given time to mobilise, might not thousands of lives been saved?'[24] Fitt himself considered it 'bizarre and tragic' that it had taken twenty-five years of violence to get to the point they had reached in January 1974, before pointing out, 'There is nothing new that was not implicit in Sunningdale.'[25] There can be little doubt that many of the features of the Good Friday Agreement bore more than a passing resemblance to the Sunningdale proposals. Austin Currie went as far as to suggest that Sunningdale was a superior arrangement for nationalists. He told the Dáil:

> In comparison with the Good Friday Agreement, I believe that from the point of view of Nationalist Ireland, Sunningdale was a better deal. It not only had power sharing but a Council of Ireland which had an elected tier so politicians from the Dail and Stormont would meet in regular session. Articles 2 and 3 also remained in the Constitution.[26]

Mark Durkan, leader of the SDLP, highlighted the irony of Northern Ireland's political evolution: 'The tragedy for him (Fitt) and everyone else was that Sunningdale was opposed and brought down by intransigent unionism and violent republicanism – the same people who now claim they are for the principles that were at its core.'[27]

In 1974 republicans had viewed any deal short of a British withdrawal and a commitment to Irish reunification as not enough to call a halt to their military campaign. The 'partition parliament' of Stormont was anathema to them. By 1994, however, Sinn Féin had become enthusiastic supporters of devolved power-sharing government at Stormont and, according to their republican critics, were administering British rule in an internal settlement. Before the 1990s republicans had never recognised the right of any minority on the island to resist being part of the Irish nation. But under the terms of the Belfast Agreement, the consent principle had been at least implicitly, if not explicitly, recognised and, in effect, so had British sovereignty. Also, republicans were clearly moving towards an acceptance of the Police Service of Northern Ireland, despite the claim that Patten has not been fully implemented.

Sinn Féin had abandoned much of its own republican ideology and in formal respects at least, they were supporting a political position not at all distinguishable from Fitt's in 1973–4. As Murray and Tonge concluded:

> Traditional Republican demands for an end to partition and the ending of British sovereignty over Northern Ireland had been downgraded to long-term aspirations, to be preceded by participation in political institutions linking Northern Ireland, the Irish Republic and the British and Irish governments.[28]

Was Fitt correct in 1974? Was his political thinking more progressive and imaginative than the republican movement's? Was he ahead of his time, or simply bowing to the historical pressures that promote pragmatism in the same way as Michael Collins and, currently, Gerry Adams have had to do?

Clearly, mainstream republicans would disagree: they have a different interpretation of the agreement and the context within which it was framed. Caoimhghín Ó Caoláin, parliamentary leader of Sinn Féin in the Dáil, stated his party position two days after the Executive was appointed:

> Sinn Féin's view of the Good Friday Agreement is clear. We see it as a major step forward, a vehicle for progressive change. We are totally committed to the full implementation of the Agreement. That in no way negates our republican beliefs and goals. On the contrary, we see the Agreement and the new political dispensation it brings with it as a secure foundation for building a better society here and now and as a bridge to a new future for

all our people. We will be working to ensure that it hastens the day when we will see a united Ireland, sovereign and independent. That is our central aim.[29]

Sunningdale was an attempt to marginalise republicans; the Good Friday Agreement was an attempt to co-opt them into a permanent settlement. It is obvious that Ó Caoláin and his Sinn Féin colleagues did not see the Good Friday Agreement as a permanent settlement and were clearly keen to stress its transitional nature.

Sinn Féin would also point to the different political contexts of the two agreements. In 1973 and 1974 the political power of unionism was immense, as demonstrated in the ultimate demise of the power-sharing agreement and British reluctance to pursue any other political initiatives afterwards. By 1994 a process of political, social and economic attrition had worn down the unionist community and the very durability and persistence of the republican campaign in both its military and political manifestations seemed to lift that community to a far greater level of confidence than the generation growing up during the Stormont era had had. Coupled with this were other factors making for wider nationalist confidence and unionist demoralisation. These included: the decline of Protestant working-class power with the destruction of Northern Ireland's manufacturing base; the withdrawal of the Protestant middle-class from political and social life with the trauma of the troubles; the series of political defeats suffered by unionism from the time of the Anglo-Irish Agreement as the political agenda began to be set by John Hume's philosophy and Seamus Mallon's resolve; and the rise in the Catholic proportion of the population.

In a situation where the conflict is being translated from a military to a political one, the relative strengths of the political forces involved (in relation to any comparisons with 1973–4) is a very important consideration, as well as the formal terms of the agreement itself.

Something that should also be considered in any comparison of the two 'agreements' is that Sunningdale died after a short, traumatic life; while, though possibly terminally ill, the Good Friday Agreement is still managing to cling to life and has been reformulated by the blueprint devised at St Andrew's in October 2006.

However, not everyone in the republican movement is happy with the direction of Sinn Féin. John Kelly was a supporter of the Good Friday Agreement and he also spoke out against dissident republican violence.

But in 2003 he withdrew from the party, explaining his reasons the following year: 'Sinn Féin is a very controlled organisation. Some of my republican colleagues referred to them as a benign dictatorship. That's their cynical view of it. It is a 'control dictatorship' with all the elite at the top. Everything has to be filtered through that and no one else is to be given space to express an opinion.'[30] His own cynicism was clear when I asked him to comment on Fitt's elevation to the peerage: 'Yes, Gerry Fitt joined the House of Lords – so might Gerry Adams.'[31]

What of the SDLP? Does it now have to accept that Fitt was correct in his analysis of the potential political demise of the party? Its contribution to the agreement cannot be denied, but its reward has been to witness the electoral advance of Sinn Féin. As Murray and Tonge put it, 'The SDLP was respected as the producer of the constitutional architecture, but it was Sinn Féin that was increasingly trusted with the furnishing.'[32] To criticise Hume and, by extension, the SDLP for their attempts to achieve peace is preposterous. Nonetheless, the SDLP's aim to re-establish itself as the main nationalist party in Northern Ireland is a formidable if not impossible task.

On hearing of Fitt's death, Currie suggested that 'The history books will be kind to him.'[33] Perhaps they will – but surely history should not strive to be kind or disparage, only to explain.

This book has tried to explain how Gerry Fitt, a fundamentally decent and sincere man, evolved from a constitutional nationalist with republican and socialist trappings to a defender of the unionist position. Such *voltes faces* are not uncommon in history. Winston Churchill moved from the Liberals to the Conservatives; Mussolini was a revolutionary socialist who became a fascist; and Ian Paisley and the DUP seem likely to cut a deal with Sinn Féin. There is perhaps a degree of inevitability about politicians reappraising their political outlook when faced by the intractability of the Northern Ireland problem. Fitt's career was a political journey and, perhaps, the education he never had. But he also became detached from his roots, and the breaking of this relationship between a public representative and his constituents was something that left a legacy of bitterness in West Belfast.

It was predictable and somehow appropriate that Fitt's final words in the House of Lords, on 22 February 2005, were a condemnation of the IRA. The previous month, Robert McCartney was brutally murdered by some of its members after an argument in a bar in Belfast city centre. Fitt said that McCartney was another innocent victim of the IRA campaign.[34] Six months later and one month before the death of Lord Fitt the IRA made a public statement ordering an end to its armed campaign and instructing its members to dump its weapons and to pursue purely political methods.

Notes

Introduction

1 There was nothing inevitable about this course. The republicanism of the United Irishmen is a complex issue. In Enlightenment terms, a republican form of government was one that could be said to exude virtue and rationality. Republicanism in this sense is entirely compatible with enlightened monarchy, for example.

2 Budge and O'Leary, *Belfast: Approach to Crisis*.

3 For a detailed account of Gerry Fitt's parentage, see C. Ryder, *Fighting Fitt* (Belfast, 2006), pp. 11–15.

4 Lord Fitt, interview by author, 19 December 1988, House of Lords.

1: Catholic Politics in Transition

1 G. Adams, 'Twenty Turbulent Years', *Irish Times*, 3 October 1988.

2 Longford and McHardy, *Ulster*, p. 74.

3 Farrell, *Northern Ireland: The Orange State*, pp. 327–8.

4 *Hibernia*, November 1965.

5 Bew and Patterson, *The British State and the Ulster Crisis*, p. 10.

6 Bowyer Bell, *The Secret Army*, p. 445.

7 Coogan, *The IRA*, pp. 369–70.

8 Farrell, *op. cit.*, p. 218.

9 Coogan, *op. cit.*, p. 385.

10 Farrell, *op. cit.*, p. 210.

11 Kelley, *The Longest War*, p. 74.

12 Coogan, *op. cit.*, p. 385.

13 IRA statement quoted in Farrell, *op. cit.*, p. 221.

14 *Ibid.*

15 *Irish News*, 28 February 1962.

16 *New York Times*, quoted in Kelley, *op. cit.*, p. 74.

17 *New Nation*, January 1964.

18 Bowyer Bell, *op. cit.*, p. 349.

19 McAllister, *The Northern Ireland Social Democratic and Labour Party*, pp. 13–14.

20 White, *John Hume: Statesman of the Troubles*, p. 55.

21 B. Devlin, *The Price of My Soul* (London, Andre Deutsch, 1969), p. 161.

22 *Sunday Independent*, 21 June 1964.

23 *Hibernia*, July 1961.

24 *Ibid.*, February 1963.

25 *Ibid.*, December 1962.

26 *Irish Times*, 18 May 1964.

27 Buckland, *A History of Northern Ireland*, p. 109.

28 *Irish News*, 3 February 1965.

29 For a reproduction of National Unity's strategy statement see *Irish News*, 28 December 1959.
30 *Hibernia*, March 1961.
31 I. McAllister, 'The National Democratic Party 1965–1970', *Economic and Social Review*, vol. 1 (1975), p. 358.
32 *The Nation* was the weekly journal of the Young Ireland Movement. The journal was intended to make Irish people more conscious of their nationality and history. Young Ireland inspired the failed rebellion of 1848.
33 *New Nation*, April 1964.
34 *Irish News*, 20 April 1964.
35 *Ibid.*, 21 April 1964.
36 McAllister, *op. cit.*, p. 359.
37 *Irish News*, 9 September 1964.
38 McAllister, *op. cit.*, p. 363.
39 Revd Ian Paisley is an almost exact contemporary of Gerry Fitt. Fitt was born on 9 April 1926, Paisley on 6 April 1926. The two became political opponents. Paisley has since the early 1960s been the most vocal and controversial loyalist politician. At the time of writing he would claim, with considerable justification, that he represents mainstream unionism.
40 Moloney and Pollack, *Paisley*, p. 92.
41 *Ibid.*, p. 93.
42 *Irish News*, 3 June 1965.
43 *Ibid.*, 18 January 1964.
44 See Ditch, *Social Policy in Northern Ireland, 1939–50*.
45 Farrell, *op. cit.*, pp. 328–9.
46 Murphy, *Ireland in the Twentieth Century*, p. 162.
47 Kelley, *op. cit.*, pp. 82–3.
48 Bew and Patterson, *Seán Lemass and the Making of Modern Ireland*, p.9
49 *Irish News*, 22 July 1959.
50 *Ibid.*, 11 November 1959.
51 O'Neill, *Autobiography*, p. 72.
52 *Ibid.*, p. 75.
53 *Hibernia*, February 1965.
54 *New Nation*, February 1965.
55 *Irish News*, 15 January 1965.

2: FROM DOCK TO WESTMINSTER: GERRY FITT 1958 – 66

1 *Hibernia*, May 1966.
2 Hibernianism was the fusion of activist Catholicism, social politics and nationalism most effectively developed by Joe Devlin in Ulster and beyond in the first two decades of the twentieth century. Devlin combined the social activism of the Ancient Order of Hibernians, the economic influence of the Lloyd George social insurance provisions and the political power of the Irish Parliamentary Party in an effective political machine that was ranged against various opponents across the country.
3 Lord Fitt, interview by author, 19 December 1988, House of Lords.
4 C. O'Leary, 'Belfast West', in D. E. Butler and A. King (eds), *The British General Election of 1966* (London, Macmillan, 1967), p. 254.
5 Rumpf and Hepburn, *Nationalism and Socialism in Twentieth-Century Ireland*, p. 188.
6 *Sunday Press*, 30 August 1970.
7 McCann, *War and an Irish Town*, p. 13.
8 Rumpf and Hepburn, *op. cit.*, p. 191.
9 *Belfast News Letter*, 19 March 1958.

10 *Belfast Telegraph*, 18 March 1958.

11 *Belfast News Letter*, 19 March 1958.

12 *Irish News*, 12 March 1958.

13 The headquarters of the Unionist Party was at this time situated in Glengall Street, Belfast.

14 *Belfast Telegraph*, 11 March 1958.

15 *Irish News*, 17 March 1958.

16 *Belfast Telegraph*, 12 March 1958.

17 *Irish News*, 12 March 1958.

18 *Ibid.*, 17 March 1958.

19 *Ibid.*, 20 March 1958.

20 *Belfast News Letter*, 19 March 1958

21 *Ibid.*, 20 March 1958.

22 In the election for councillors to Belfast Corporation electors could vote for up to three candidates.

23 *Irish News*, 20 May 1958.

24 *Ibid.*, 21 May 1958.

25 Lord Fitt, interview by author, 19 December 1988, House of Lords.

26 *Irish News*, 23 May 1958.

27 Northern Ireland *Parliamentary Debates* (Commons), vol. 42 (1958), cols. 1072–3.

28 Lord Fitt, interview by author, 19 December 1988, House of Lords.

29 See *Irish News*, 3 June 1958.

30 *Ibid.*, 14 August 1958.

31 *Ibid.*, 5 August 1959.

32 Lord Fitt, interview by author, 19 December 1988, House of Lords.

33 *Irish News*, 3 May, 4 October, 2 December 1960

34 See *Irish News*, 16 December 1960.

35 *Ibid.*, 8 April 1961.

36 *Ibid.*, 4 May 1961.

37 *Ibid.*, 10 May 1961.

38 *Ibid.*, 16 May 1961.

39 *Ibid.*, 20 May 1961.

40 *Ibid.*, 2 August 1961.

41 *Ibid.*, 7 October 1961.

42 *Ibid.*, 15 March 1962.

43 Moloney and Pollack, *Paisley*, p. 101.

44 *Irish News*, 15 May 1962.

45 *Belfast Telegraph*, 17 May 1962.

46 *Ibid.*, 25 May 1962.

47 *Irish News*, 29 May 1962.

48 G. Fitt, *Election Manifesto*, 23 May 1962.

49 *Belfast Telegraph*, 30 May 1962.

50 *Ibid.*, 30 May 1962.

51 *Belfast News Letter*, 31 May 1962.

52 *Ibid.*

53 Lord Fitt, interview by author, 19 December 1988, House of Lords.

54 Paddy Devlin, interview by author, 25 March 1989, Belfast.

55 *Hibernia*, July 1962.

56 *Belfast News Letter*, 18 June 1962.

57 *Irish News*, 19 June 1962.

58 *Northern Ireland Parliamentary Debates* (Commons), vol. 52 (1962), cols. 138–40.

59 See *Irish News*, 18 April 1960.

60 *Northern Ireland Parliamentary Debates* (Commons), vol. 52 (1962), col. 146.

61 John Kelly, interview with the author, 21 September 2006.

62 Ryder, p. 69.

63 *Irish News*, 5 December 1962.

64 *Ibid.*, 19 December 1962.

65 Lord Fitt, interview by author, 19 December 1988, House of Lords.

66 The Orange Order is the largest Protestant organisation in Northern Ireland. It was founded in 1795 to commemorate the victory of William of Orange over the Catholic King James II in July 1690. The group is often charged with promoting discrimination against Catholics.

67 *Irish Times*, 3 October 1988.

68 Lord Fitt, interview by author, 19 December 1988, House of Lords.

69 Paddy Devlin, interview by author, 25 March 1989, Belfast.

70 *New Nation*, January 1964.

71 *Hibernia*, March 1964.

72 *Irish News*, 22 April 1964.

73 *Ibid.*, 12 May 1964.

74 *Ibid.*, 15 May 1964.

75 *Belfast News Letter*, 16 May 1964.

76 *Irish News*, 2 October 1964.

77 *Northern Ireland Parliamentary Debates* (Commons), vol. 57 (1964), cols. 2873–4.

78 *New Nation*, October 1964.

79 There were twelve seats at Westminster for representatives from Northern Ireland.

80 *Hibernia*, November 1964.

81 *Irish News*, 7 December 1964.

82 *Ibid.*

83 *New Nation*, December 1964.

84 *Irish News*, 20 January 1965.

85 *Northern Ireland Parliamentary Debates* (Commons), vol. 58 (1965), cols 295–6.

86 *Irish News*, 5 February 1965.

87 *Ibid.*, 7 July 1965.

88 *Ibid.*, 8 July 1965.

89 The new bridge spanning the Lagan was initially named Carson Bridge, after Edward Carson (1854–1935), leader of the opposition to Home Rule for Ireland. To the Catholic population he epitomised the unionist ascendancy. The row eventually led to the bridge being named after Queen Elizabeth II.

90 Lennon was Nationalist opposition leader in the Northern Ireland Senate, 1965–71.

91 *Belfast News Letter*, August 1965, quoted in *Hibernia*, October 1965.

92 *Belfast Telegraph*, 16 August 1965, quoted in *Hibernia*, October 1965.

93 *Irish News*, 24 November 1965.

94 *Ibid.*

95 *Belfast Telegraph*, 25 November 1965.

96 *Belfast News Letter*, 26 November 1965.

97 *Hibernia*, December 1965.

98 *Irish News*, 8 December 1965.

99 *Ibid.*, 15 December 1965.

100 Lord Fitt, interview by author, 19 December 1988, House of Lords.

101 Currie, *All Hell Will Break Loose*, p. 65.

102 See I. McAllister, 'The National Democratic Party 1965–1976', *Economic and Social Review*, vol. 1 (1975), p. 301

103 Lord Fitt, interview by author, 19 December 1988, House of Lords.

104 *Ibid.*

105 *Irish News*, 3 March 1966.

106 *Ibid.*

107 *Ibid.*, 7 March 1966.

108 *Ibid.*, 10 March 1966.

109 *Ibid.*

110 *Ibid.*, 11 March 1966.

111 *Ibid.*

112 *Ibid.*

113 Joseph Lavery, interview with the author, 23 June 2006, Belfast.

114 *Belfast News Letter*, 29 March 1966.

115 *Belfast Telegraph*, 30 March 1966.

116 See O'Leary, *op. cit.*, p. 257.

117 *Belfast Telegraph*, 29 March 1966.

118 Lord Fitt, interview by author, 19 December 1988, House of Lords.

119 *Belfast Telegraph*, 29 March 1966.

120 *Irish News*, 1 April 1966.

121 *Belfast News Letter*, 2 April 1966.

122 See O'Leary, *op cit.*

3: CIVIL RIGHTS OR NATIONAL RIGHTS

1 O'Neill, *Autobiography*, p. 74.

2 Bew and Patterson, *The British State and the Ulster Crisis*, p. 12.

3 Frontline online 1998: www.pbs.org/wgbh/pages/frontline/shows/ira/inside/kelly.html.

4 *Irish News,* 18 April 1966

5 *Belfast News Letter,* 18 April 1966.

6 Lord Fitt, interview by author, 19 December 1988, House of Lords.

7 Brendan Clifford first drew attention to Connolly's pro-Germanism in *Connolly Cut Outs* (Belfast, Athol Books, 1984). In *Workers' Republic* Connolly described the First World War as 'the war on the German nation'. In February 1916 he ran articles from Frederic Howe's book *Socialised Germany* agreeing with his view that 'German state socialism' was the secret behind its commercial and military success. This view is given further credence in *James Connolly Re-assessed* by Manus O'Riordan, Aubane Historical Society, Millstreet, Co Cork, 2006. The thrust of O'Riordan's pamphlet is that James Connolly's journalism during the First World War shows him to have favoured a German victory

8 Bishop and Mallie, *The Provisional IRA*, p. 61.

9 John Kelly, interview with the author, 21 September 2006.

10 Frontline online, *op. cit.*

11 Bowyer Bell, *The Secret Army*, p. 346.

12 *Irish News*, 6 April 1966.

13 British Parliamentary Debates (Lords), vol. 640 (2002), col. 731.

14 *Sunday Times*, 11 September 1994.

15 *Irish News*, 6 April 1966.

16 British Parliamentary Debates (Commons), vol. 727 (1966), cols. 437–40.

17 *Irish Independent*, 27 April 1966.

18 *Belfast Telegraph*, 29 April 1966.

19 *Hibernia*, June 1966.

20 British Parliamentary Debates (Commons), vol. 728 (1966), cols. 721–2.

21 For a list of the twenty amendments/grievances, see *Irish News*, 31 May 1966.

22 *Ibid.*

23 *Belfast News Letter*, 24 June 1966.

24 See *Sunday Telegraph* editorial, 5 June 1966.

25 British Parliamentary Debates (Commons), vol. 733 (1966), col. 1586.

26 *Irish News*, 4 August 1966.

27 O'Neill, *op. cit.*, p. 83

28 British Parliamentary Debates (Commons), vol. 733 (1966), cols. 1277–89.

29 *Irish News*, 11 August 1966.

30 'The Irish Question – Challenge to Democratic Britain', Conference Report, 25 February 1967, p. 7

31 C Ryder *Fighting Fitt* (Brehon Press Belfast 2006 p. 106)

32 *Ibid* , p. 391

33 'The Irish Question – Challenge to Democratic Britain', Conference Report, 25 February 1967, p. 8

34 *Ibid.*, p. 17.

35 Fitt's closing statement is not reported in the official conference report, but it does appear in the *Irish Democrat*, March 1967.

36 *Irish Democrat*, September 2005.

37 Anthony Coughlan, correspondence with author, December 2006.

38 *Protestant Telegraph*, 1 April 1967.

39 See *Belfast Telegraph*, 28 April 1967.

40 Tony Benn, a politician very much on the left of the Labour Party.

41 Keith Joseph, Conservative politician who served as a cabinet minister under three different ministries.

42 Arthur Scargill was the leader of the National Union of Mineworkers from 1981 to 2000.

43 Enoch Powell was a right-wing Conservative Party MP between 1950 and February 1974, and an Ulster Unionist MP for South Down between October 1974 and 1987.

44 Lord Fitt, interview by author, 27 July 1989, House of Lords.

45 *Irish News*, 14 April 1967.

46 Austin Currie, interview by author, 6 April 1989, Dungannon.

47 *Irish News*, 17 April 1967.

48 See *Belfast Telegraph*, 6 May 1967.

49 *Ibid.*, 18 May 1967.

50 *Irish News*, 19 May 1967.

51 *Belfast Telegraph* 29 May 1967.

52 *Ibid.*, 30 May 1967.

53 *Ibid.*, 31 May 1967.

54 *Ibid.*, 3 June 1967.

55 *Ibid.*, 5 July 1967.

56 *Ibid.*, 4 November 1967.

57 *Irish News*, 2 January 1998.

58 *Belfast Telegraph*, 8 August 1967.

59 *Irish Times*, 3 July 1967.

60 Eric Mercer showed that Catholics provided 27 per cent of Belfast's recruits in 1914–15, despite making up only 23 per cent of the population of the city. See 'For king, country and a shilling a day – Belfast recruiting patterns in the *Great War*', *History Ireland*, Winter 2003.

61 British Parliamentary Debates (Commons), vol. 751 (1967), cols. 1662–74.

62 Callaghan, *A House Divided*, p. 1.

63 *Irish News*, 1 January 1968.

64 *Ibid.*, 26 January 1968.

65 *Ibid.*, 9 October 1968.

66 *Ibid.*, 29 January 1968.

67 *Ibid.*

68 *Ibid.*, 25 May 1968.

69 *Ibid.*, 6 June 1968.

70 The Wolfe Tone Society's aim was to nurture republicanism by educating Catholics and Protestants in the cultural and political heritage as exemplified by Tone.

71 *Irish Times*, 3 October 1988.

72 See *Irish News*, 21 June 1968.

73 *Ibid.*, 24 June 1968.

74 British Parliamentary Debates (Commons), vol. 768 (1968), Cols. 732–3.

75 *Belfast News Letter*, 22 July 1968.

76 *Irish News*, 24 July 1968.

77 McAteer was rather off the mark in his appraisal, but still somewhat prophetic. Connolly was no friend of the Nationalist Party but he certainly would have 'turned in his grave' at Fitt's elevation to the House of Lords, that bastion of aristocratic and unionist privilege.

78 *Irish News*, 24 July 1968.

79 *Ibid.*, 24 August 1968.

80 *Ibid.*, 26 August 1968.

81 Bernadette Devlin (McAliskey), interview by author, 7 June 1989, Belfast.

82 Bernadette Devlin, *The Price of My Soul* (London, Andre Deutsch, 1969), p. 93.

83 Lord Fitt, interview by author, 27 July 1989, House of Lords.

84 *Belfast Telegraph*, 28 August 1968.

85 *Irish News*, 3 October 1968.

86 The Apprentice Boys of Derry is one of the Protestant Loyal Orders, named after the thirteen apprentice boys who closed the gates of Derry against the army of James II in December 1688, before the 1689 siege.

87 *Irish News*, 4 October 1968.

88 *Ibid.*, 28 October 1968.

89 Bernadette Devlin (McAliskey), interview by author, 7 June 1989, Belfast.

90 *Irish Times*, 3 October 1988.

91 British Parliamentary Debates (Commons), vol. 770 (1968), cols. 1088–9.

92 *Ibid.*, vol. 772 (1969), col. 503.

93 *Irish News*, 9 November 1968.

94 *Ibid.*, 11 November 1968.

95 Bew and Patterson, *op. cit.*, p. 16.

96 For the full text of O'Neill's television address see *Irish News*, 10 December 1968.

97 *Ibid.*

98 *Belfast News Letter*, 23 December 1968.

99 *Irish Times*, 3 October 1988.

100 McCann, *War and an Irish Town*, p. 53.

101 Eamonn McCann, telephone conversation with author, 26 June 2006.

102 *Irish News*, 6 January 1969.

103 *Ibid.*, 8 January 1969.

104 *Ibid.*, 6 January 1969.

105 *Ibid.*, 8 January 1969.

106 Ryder, *op. cit.*, p.132

107 *Irish Press*, 27 January 1969.

108 G. Fitt, Election Manifesto, February 1969.

119 *Belfast Telegraph*, 20 February 1969.

110 *Belfast News Letter*, 21 February 1969.

111 Lord Fitt, interview by author, 27 July 1989, House of Lords.

112 *Belfast News Letter*, 1 January 1969.

113 *Irish Press*, 13 March 1969.

114 *Belfast Telegraph*, 18 March 1969.

115 *Ibid.*, 27 March 1969.

116 *Irish Times*, 2 April 1969.

117 *Ibid.*, 9 April 1969.

118 *Belfast News Letter*, 9 April 1969.

119 *Belfast Telegraph*, 11 April 1969.

120 *Ibid.*, 9 April 1969.

121 Ryder, *op. cit.*, p.135

122 *Irish News*, 29 March 1969.

123 *Ibid.*, 11 April 1969.

124 Lord Fitt, interview by author, 27 July 1989, House of Lords.

125 Callaghan, *op. cit.*, p. 47.

126 Louden Seth had acted as Devlin's election agent.

127 Eamonn McCann had been Devlin's press officer.

128 Lord Fitt, interview by author, 27 July 1989, House of Lords.

129 Bernadette Devlin (McAliskey), interview by author, 7 June 1989, Belfast.

130 Bloody Sunday is the term used to describe an incident in Derry on 30 January 1972 in which thirteen Civil Rights protestors were shot dead by members of the 1st Battalion of the British Parachute Regiment during a march in the Bogside area of the city.

131 Lord Fitt, interview by author, 27 July 1989, House of Lords.

132 *Ibid.*

133 Bernadette Devlin (McAliskey), interview by author, 7 June 1989, Belfast.

134 *Irish News*, 19 April 1969.

135 *Belfast News Letter*, 16 April 1969.

136 *Irish News*, 29 April 1969.

137 *Ibid.*, 2 May 1969.

138 Northern Ireland Parliamentary Debates (Commons), 1969, cols. 2132 – 3.

139 *Belfast Telegraph*, 6 August 1969.

140 *Belfast News Letter*, 7 August 1969.

141 *Irish News*, 30 July 1969.

142 Farrell, *Northern Ireland: The Orange State*, p. 261.

143 Callaghan, *op. cit.*, p. 49.

144 *Belfast Telegraph*, 19 August 1969.

145 *Ibid.*, 22 August 1969.

146 Roy Johnston, *Century of Endeavour* (Tyndall/Lilliput, 2006), p. 264.

147 *Ibid.*

148 Roy Johnston, correspondence with author, December 2006.

149 *Belfast Telegraph*, 26 August 1969.

150 P. Devlin, *Straight Left*, p. 110.

151 *Belfast Telegraph*, 5 September 1969.

152 *Ibid.*, 12 September 1969.

153 Disturbances in Northern Ireland: Report of the Commission appointed by the Government of Northern Ireland (Cameron Report, HMSO Belfast, September 1969), para. 46.

154 *Irish News*, 13 September 1969.

155 *Belfast Telegraph*, 15 September 1969.

156 J. O'Brien, *The Arms Crisis*, p. 59.

157 J. Kelly, *The Thimbleriggers*, p. 12.

158 Quoted in O'Brien, *op. cit.*, p. 59.

159 John Kelly, interview with author, 21 September 2006.

160 *Ibid.*

161 Captain Kelly later made contact with a Hamburg-based arms dealer with a view to importing arms to Northern Ireland. Two attempts failed and the Garda Special Branch became aware of the plans. These developments led Jack Lynch to reverse his policy and sack two of his ministers, Neil Blaney and Charlie Haughey, after the British put pressure on him to desist from attempting to influence the political direction of the North. In May 1970 the 'Arms Trial' began. James and John Kelly were charged in relation to the attempted importation of arms, as were Haughey and Belgian-born, Dublin-based businessman Albert Luykz. All four were acquitted. Before this a separate trial for Blaney had been thrown out of court.

162 John Kelly, interview with author, 21 September 2006

163 Lord Fitt, interview by author, 27 July 1989, House of Lords.

164 *Belfast Telegraph*, 18 October 1969.

165 Extract from journal of Desmond Greaves, 20 October 1969, provided by Anthony Coughlan.

166 Tom is Seán Redmond's younger brother, a Communist Party activist, but primarily a Connolly Association supporter when in Britain in the 1960s. By 1969 he had returned to Dublin and was active in attempting to build the Communist Party of Ireland.

167 Seán Redmond, interview with author, 10 December 2006.

168 Extract from journal of Desmond Greaves, 21 October 1969, provided by Anthony Coughlan.

169 Seán Redmond, interview with author, 10 December 2006.

170 *Irish News*, 2 March 1970.

171 Anthony Coughlan, correspondence with author, December 2006.

172 Bew and Patterson, *op. cit.*, p. 227

173 *Belfast Telegraph*, 10 October 1969.

174 *Irish News*, 13 November 1969.

4: THE SOCIAL DEMOCRATIC AND LABOUR PARTY

1 See *Belfast Telegraph*, 29 June 1973.

2 *Ibid.*, 19 February 1973.

3 *Irish News*, 4 February 1970.

4 *Belfast Telegraph*, 5 February 1970.

5 J. Kelly, *The Thimbleriggers*, p. 12.

6 *British Parliamentary Debates* (Commons), vol. 797 (1970), col. 162.

7 *Irish News*, 4 February 1970.

8 *Belfast Telegraph*, 3 April 1970.

9 *Ibid.*, 6 April 1970.

10 *British Parliamentary Debates* (Commons), vol. 799 (1970), col. 280.

11 *Irish News*, 18 May 1970.

12 *Ibid.*, 29 May 1970.

13 *Ibid.*, 6 June 1970.

14 *Ibid.*, 12 June 1970.

15 *Ibid.*, 15 June 1970.

16 *Ibid.*, 18 June 1970.

17 *Ibid.*, 23 June 1970.

18 *Belfast Telegraph*, 4 July 1970.

19 *Irish News*, 6 July 1970.

20 *Belfast Telegraph*, 6 July 1970.

21 *Irish News*, 8 July 1970.

22 P. Devlin, *Straight Left*, p. 134.

23 Frontline online 1998: www.pbs.org/wgbh/pages/frontline/shows/ira/inside/kelly.html.

24 *Irish Times*, 20 June 1988.

25 *Belfast Telegraph*, 12 August 1970.

26 Bishop and Mallie, *The Provisional IRA*, pp. 56 and 145.

27 *Belfast Telegraph*, 13 August 1970.

28 An organisation for Catholic men, founded in 1915.

29 Lord Fitt, interview by author, 27 July 1989, House of Lords.

30 Rumpf and Hepburn, *Nationalism and Socialism in Twentieth-Century Ireland*, p. 141.

31 Paddy Devlin, interview by author, 25 March 1989, Belfast; and Lord Fitt, interview by author, 27 July 1989, House of Lords.

32 Lord Fitt, interview by author, 27 July 1989, House of Lords.

33 *Belfast Telegraph*, 18 August 1970.
34 *Irish News*, 18 August 1970.
35 *Belfast Telegraph*, 18 August 1970.
36 For a list of aims of the new party see *Irish Times*, 22 August 1970.
37 *Ibid.*
38 P. Devlin, *op. cit.*, p. 143.
39 Ivan Cooper, interview by author, 31 July 2006, Belfast.
40 Lord Fitt, interview by author, 27 July 1989, House of Lords.
41 *Irish Times*, 3 October 1988.
42 Austin Currie, interview by author, 6 April 1989, Dungannon.
43 Lord Fitt, interview by author, 27 July 1989, House of Lords.
44 Murray, *John Hume and the SDLP*, p. 87.
45 Paddy Devlin, interview by author, 25 March 1989, Belfast.
46 John Hume, interview by author, 17 April 1989, Derry.
47 *Ibid.*
48 Seamus Mallon was to become an MP for Newry and Armagh in 1986.
49 Teachers were disproportionately highly represented in the SDLP membership. See P. Devlin, *op. cit.*, p. 189.
50 Ivan Cooper, interview by author, 31 July 2006, Belfast.
51 Eddie McGrady, interview by author, 26 June 2006, Downpatrick.
52 Conor Cruise O'Brien was, at the time of the formation of the SDLP, a Labour Party member of Dáil Éireann representing the Dublin North East constituency. In 1973 he was appointed Minister for Posts and Telegraphs in the coalition Cosgrave government.
53 Currie, *All Hell Will Break Loose*, p. 206.
54 Ivan Cooper, interview by author, 31 July 2006, Belfast.
55 Eddie McGrady, interview by author, 26 June 2006, Downpatrick.
56 Lord Fitt, interview by author, 27 July 1989, House of Lords; and Paddy Devlin, interview by author, 25 March 1989, Belfast.
57 Fitt's prediction was wrong. In 1992 Joe Hendron won the West Belfast seat from Gerry Adams. However, Adams regained the seat for Sinn Féin in 1997 and has retained it ever since.
58 Lord Fitt, interview by author, 27 July 1989, House of Lords.
59 John Hume, interview by author, 17 April 1989, Derry.
60 *Belfast News Letter*, 24 August 1970.
61 *Irish Times*, 22 August 1970.
62 Lord Fitt, interview by author, 27 July 1989, House of Lords.
63 Currie, *op. cit.*, pp. 154–5.
64 P. Devlin, *op. cit.*, p. 138.
65 Lord Fitt, interview by author, 27 July 1989, House of Lords.
66 John Kelly, interview by author, 21 September 2006.
67 *Belfast Telegraph*, 23 October 1970.
68 Farrell, *Northern Ireland: The Orange State*, p. 275.
69 I. McAllister, 'The National Democratic Party 1965–70', *Economic and Social Review*, vol. 1 (1975), 365.
70 *Belfast Telegraph*, 6 November 1970.
71 *Ibid.*, 15 January 1971.
72 *Ibid.*, 20 January 1971.
73 *Northern Ireland Parliamentary Debates* (Commons), vol.78 (1971), col.1459.
74 *The Times*, 5 August 1994.
75 *Belfast Telegraph*, 6 February 1971.
76 *Irish Press*, 8 February 1971.
77 Callaghan, *A House Divided*, p. 138.
78 *Northern Ireland Parliamentary Debates* (Commons), vol. 78 (1971), cols. 30–1.

79 *Irish News*, 19 March 1971.

80 *Northern Ireland Parliamentary Debates* (Commons), vol. 78 (1971), col. 742.

81 *Belfast Telegraph*, 24 March 1971.

82 *Irish News*, 22 June 1971.

83 *Ibid.*, 12 July 1971.

84 *An Phoblacht*, September 1971.

85 Lord Fitt, interview by author, 27 July 1989, House of Lords.

86 Currie, *op. cit.*, p. 170.

87 *Ibid.*, p. 171.

88 P. Devlin, *op. cit.*, p. 155.

89 Lord Fitt, interview by author, 27 July 1989, House of Lords.

90 Currie, *op. cit.*, p. 171.

91 *Irish News*, 13 July 1971.

92 *Belfast Telegraph*, 13 July 1971.

93 P. Devlin, *op. cit.*, p. 156.

94 Ivan Cooper, interview by author, 31 July 2006, Belfast.

95 *Irish News*, 17 July 1971.

96 *The Times*, 4 August 1971.

97 Coogan, *The IRA*, p. 382.

98 Frontline online, *op. cit.*

99 Lord Fitt, interview by author, 27 July 1989, House of Lords.

100 Ivan Cooper, interview by author, 31 July 2006, Belfast.

101 *Irish News*, 11 August 1971.

102 *Ibid.*, 14 August 1971.

103 *Belfast Telegraph*, 16 August 1971.

104 *Ibid.*, 24 August 1971.

105 *Ibid.*, 26 August 1971.

106 *Ibid.*, 27 August 1971.

107 *Ibid.*, 30 August 1971.

108 Farrell, *op. cit.*, p. 284.

109 *Irish Independent*, 9 September 1971.

110 *Belfast Telegraph*, 9 September 1971.

111 *British Parliamentary Debates* (Commons), vol. 823 (1971).

112 *Belfast Telegraph*, 15 September 1971.

113 *Ibid.*, 25 October 1971.

114 *Irish News*, 27 October 1971.

115 *Belfast Telegraph*, 26 October 1971.

116 John Duffy would become General Secretary of the SDLP in 1973.

117 P. Devlin, *op. cit.*, p. 164.

118 Bew and Patterson, *The British State and the Ulster Crisis*, p. 55.

119 *Belfast Telegraph*, 6 December 1971.

120 *Belfast News Letter*, 3 January 1972.

121 *Irish News*, 31 January 1972.

122 *British Parliamentary Debates* (Commons), vol. 830 (1972), col. 310–13.

123 Lord Fitt, interview by author, 27 July 1989, House of Lords.

124 *Irish News*, 7 February 1972.

125 *Belfast Telegraph*, 7 February 1972.

126 *Ibid.*, 6 March 1972.

127 *Irish News*, 26 February 1972.

128 *Ibid.*, 28 February 1972.

129 *Ibid.*, 8 March 1972.

130 *Belfast Telegraph*, 14 March 1972.

131 *Irish News*, 24 March 1972.

132 *Belfast News Letter*, 25 March 1972.

133 Lord Fitt, interview by author, 27 July 1989, House of Lords.

134 The Parliament building at Stormont was actually opened in 1932. Fitt may have meant to say 1920 and have been referring to the Government of Ireland Act of that year.

135 *Belfast Telegraph*, 24 March 1972.

136 *British Parliamentary Debates* (Commons), vol. 834 (1972), col. 295.

137 Farrell, *op. cit.*, p. 293.

138 *Belfast Telegraph*, 10 April 1972.

139 *Irish News*, 19 April 1972.

140 *Irish Times*, 25 May 1972.

141 *Irish News*, 30 May 1972.

142 *Ibid.*, 14 June 1972.

143 *Ibid.*

144 *Ibid.*, 15 June 1972.

145 Paddy Devlin, interview by author, 25 March 1989, Belfast.

146 *Belfast Telegraph*, 10 July 1972.

147 *Ibid.*, 14 July 1972.

148 *Irish News*, 28 July 1972.

149 Ivan Cooper, interview by author, 31 July 2006, Belfast.

150 *Irish News*, 8 August 1972.

151 *Free Citizen Unfree Citizen*, 21 August 1972.

152 It should be noted, however, that in the 1980s PD held two seats on Belfast City Council (including the one Fitt had held for twenty-three years) during a period when Sinn Féin were boycotting electoral contests.

153 *Irish News*, 22 September 1972

154 Quoted in Farrell, *op. cit.*, p. 300.

155 *Irish News*, 27 November 1972.

156 *Ibid.*, 27 January 1973.

157 *Belfast Telegraph*, 10 March 1973.

158 *Irish News*, 23 March 1973.

159 *Belfast Telegraph*, 30 March 1973.

160 The DUP began life as an extreme right-wing loyalist party. It was formed by Ian Paisley in September 1971. It is now the largest unionist party in Northern Ireland

161 *Belfast Telegraph*, 17 April 1973.

162 *Sunday Independent*, 6 May 1973.

163 *Irish News*, 30 May 1973.

164 *Belfast Telegraph*, 27 June 1973.

165 *Irish News*, 30 June 1973.

166 Bew and Patterson, *op. cit.*, pp. 56–7.

167 *Sunday Independent*, 6 May 1973.

168 *Irish Times*, 3 July 1973.

169 *Irish News*, 14 July 1973.

170 *Belfast News Letter*, 18 September 1973.

171 *Belfast Telegraph*, 9 October 1973.

172 Currie, *op. cit.*, p. 213.

173 *Ibid.*, pp. 215, 218–19.

174 *Irish News*, 22 November 1973.

175 *Irish Times*, 11 November 1973.

176 *Belfast Telegraph*, 23 November 1973.

177 *British Parliamentary Debates* (Commons), vol. 864 (1973), col. 1653.

178 *Irish News*, 26 November 1973.

179 *Belfast Telegraph*, 22 November 1973.

180 *Ibid.*, 11 October 1972.

181 Lord Fitt, interview by author, 27 July 1989, House of Lords.

182 The Diplock Courts were non-jury trials introduced for a wide range of terrorist offences.

183 For a review of Fitt's opposition to the Diplock Courts see *Belfast Telegraph*, 21 December 1972, 8 May 1973; *Irish News*, 4 April 1973, 9 May 1973.

5: THE EXECUTIVE AND AFTER

1 *Belfast Telegraph*, 1 December 1973.

2 *Irish News*, 3 December 1973.

3 Fortnight, 14 December 1973.

4 Ivan Cooper, interview by author, 31 July 2006, Belfast.

5 *Belfast Telegraph*, 3 December 1973.

6 P. Devlin, *Straight Left*, p. 203.

7 Lord Fitt, interview by author, 27 July 1989, House of Lords.

8 P. Devlin, *The Fall of the Northern Ireland Executive*, p. 32.

9 Lord Fitt, interview by author, 27 July 1989, House of Lords. See also White, John Hume: Statesman of the Troubles, p. 150.

10 A Currie, *All Hell Will Break Loose*, p. 233.

11 Ivan Cooper, interview by author, 31 July 2006, Belfast.

12 *Ibid.*

13 *Belfast News Letter*, 10 December 1973.

14 *Irish News*, 10 December 1973.

15 Currie, *op. cit.*, p. 240.

16 See Faulkner, Memoirs of a Statesman, pp. 226–38; and White, *op. cit.*, pp. 140–56.

17 Farrell, *Northern Ireland: The Orange State*, p. 311.

18 *Belfast Telegraph*, 31 December 1973.

19 Lord Fitt, interview by author, 27 July 1989, House of Lords.

20 *Belfast Telegraph*, 31 December 1973.

21 *Irish News*, 1 January 1974.

22 *Belfast Telegraph*, 5 January 1974.

23 See Faulkner, *op. cit.*, pp. 245–6.

24 *Irish News*, 5 January 1974.

25 Minutes of the Northern Ireland Executive, 8 January 1974.

26 *Ibid.*, 17 January 1974.

27 Before 1999, Articles 2 and 3 of the Irish Republic's constitution made the claim that the whole island formed one 'national territory'.

28 *Ibid.*, 22 January 1974.

29 Northern Ireland Assembly Debates, vol. 2 (1974), col. 704.

30 Faulkner, *op. cit.*, p. 241.

31. Devlin, *op. cit.*, p. 9.

32 *Irish News*, 16 February 1974.

33 *Belfast Telegraph*, 18 February 1974.

34 Lord Fitt, interview by author, 27 July 1989, House of Lords.

35 *Belfast Telegraph*, 26 February 1974.

36 P. Devlin, *Straight Left*, p. 227.

37 *Irish News*, 28 February 1974.

38 *Ibid.*

39 Minutes of the Northern Ireland Executive, 5 March 1974.

40 *Ibid.*

41 *Belfast News Letter*, 2 March 1974.

42 P. Devlin, *op. cit.*, p. 228.

43 *Irish News*, 5 March 1974.

44 *Ibid.*, 6 March 1974.

45 Eamonn McCann, telephone conversation with author, 26 June 2006.

46 Ivan Cooper, interview by author, 31 July 2006, Belfast.

47 Lord Fitt, interview by author, 27 July 1989, House of Lords.

48 Extracts from speech by Deputy Chief Minister Mr Gerard Fitt for the Lord Mayor of Nottingham, 1 March 1974 (Northern Ireland Executive Office of Information Services).

49 Three days before the Executive's installation, the SDLP had called on the strikers to withdraw from the rent and rates strike as an indication of its support for the new institution.

50 P. Devlin, *op. cit.*, p. 248.

51 Currie, *op. cit.*, pp. 257–8.

52 Paddy Devlin, interview by author, 25 March 1989, Belfast.

53 Lord Fitt, interview by author, 27 July 1989, House of Lords.

54 Faulkner, *op. cit.*, p. 253.

55 Minutes of the Northern Ireland Executive, 7 May 1974.

56 *Ibid.*, 20 May 1974.

57 *Ibid.*, 21 May 1974.

58 Currie, *op. cit.*, pp. 271–2.

59 Faulkner, *op. cit.*, p. 272.

60 P. Devlin, *op. cit.*, p. 248.

61 Faulkner, *op. cit.*, p. 272.

62 Currie, *op. cit.*, p. 272.

63 *Ibid.*, pp. 272–3.

64 Seamus Mallon, interview by author, 28 August 2006, Armagh.

65 Minutes of the Northern Ireland Executive, 23 May 1974.

66 *Ibid.*, 24 May 1974.

67 Faulkner, *op. cit.*, p. 263.

68 Rees, *Northern Ireland: A Personal Perspective*, p. 74

69 British Parliamentary Debates (Commons), vol. 874 (1974), cols. 631–8.

70 Minutes of the Northern Ireland Executive, 27 May 1974.

71 *Ibid.*, 28 May 1974.

72 For an account of the strike see *Fisk, The Point of No Return.*

73 See Faulkner, *op. cit.*, p. 6.

74 Lord Fitt, interview by author, 27 July 1989, House of Lords.

75 Minutes of the Northern Ireland Executive, 28 May 1974.

76 The Good Friday Agreement was signed in Belfast on 10 April 1998 by both governments and endorsed by most Northern Ireland political parties. It was the apogee of Northern Ireland's peace process.

77 British Parliamentary Debates (Lords), vol. 593 (1998), col. 1461.

78 *Irish News*, 11 October 1997.

79 Lord Fitt, interview by author, 27 July 1989, House of Lords.

80 John Hume, interview by author, 17 April 1989, Derry.

81 Eddie McGrady, interview by author, 26 June 2006, Downpatrick.

82 *Irish News*, 11 October 1997.

83 Faulkner, *op. cit*, p. 287.

84 *Irish Times*, 3 October 1988.

85 Ivan Cooper, interview by author, 31 July 2006, Belfast.

86 P. Devlin, *op. cit.*, p. 242.

87 *Belfast Telegraph.* 29 May 1974.

88 *Ibid.*, 31 May 1974.

89 *Ibid.*, 1 July 1974.

90 *Irish News*, 5 July 1974.

91 White, *op. cit.*, p. 175.
92 British Parliamentary Debates (Commons), vol. 877 (1974), col. 66.
93 See *Irish News*, 7 June 1974.
94 See *Irish News*, 20 July 1974.
95 *Ibid.*, 24 July 1974.
96 *Ibid.*, 3 August 1974.
97 *Ibid.*, 9 August 1974.
98 *Ibid.*, 20 August 1974.
99 *Belfast Telegraph*, 23 August 1974.
100 *Irish Times*, 14 June 1974.
101 *Irish News*, 10 September 1974.
102 *Ibid.*, 11 September 1974.
103 *Belfast News Letter*, 3 October 1974.
104 *Irish News*, 1 October 1974.
105 Lord Fitt, interview by author, 27 July 1989, House of Lords.
106 *Belfast Telegraph*, 12 October 1974.
107 *Irish News*, 15 October 1974.
108 *Ibid.*
109 See White, *op. cit.*, p. 176.
110 *Irish News*, 30 October 1974.
111 *Ibid.*, 31 October 1974.
112 *Ibid.*, 4 November 1974.
113 British Parliamentary Debates (Commons), vol. 883 (1974), cols. 2012–20.
114 Rees, op.cit., p. 188
115 British Parliamentary Debates (Commons), vol. 883 (1974), cols. 2012–20.
116 Ivan Cooper, interview by author, 31 July 2006, Belfast.
117 On 1 December 1974, the IRA denied that any of those arrested for the Birmingham blast were members of their organisation. On 14 March 1991, the 'Birmingham Six' were released when their convictions were found to be unsafe.
118 *Belfast Telegraph*, 20 December 1974.
119 *Irish News*, 3 January 1975.
120 British Parliamentary Debates (Commons), vol. 885 (1975), cols. 1383–95.
121 Rees, *op cit.*, p. 172
122 P. Devlin, *op. cit.*, p. 253.
123 Murray, John Hume and the SDLP, p. 32.
124 *Irish News*, 14 January 1975.
125 British Parliamentary Debates (Commons), vol. 886 (1974), col. 581.
126 *Belfast Telegraph*, 14 February 1975.
127 *Ibid.*, 20 January 1975.
128 *Ibid.*, 15 April 1975 .
129 *Ibid.*
130 *Ibid.*, 16 April 1975.
131 Ten days after this expression of assurance, the *Irish News* reported that Gerry Adams, who would eventually contest Fitt's West Belfast seat, was given a three-year sentence for attempting to escape from Long Kesh in July 1974.
132 *Belfast Telegraph*, 23 April 1975.
133 *Irish News*, 24 April 1975.
134 *Belfast Telegraph*, 3 May 1975.
135 Northern Ireland Constitutional Convention Debates (1975), 5.
136 *Irish News*, 29 December 2005.
137 British Parliamentary Debates (Commons), vol. 896 (1975), col. 754.
138 *Belfast Telegraph*, 9 September 1975.
139 *Ibid.*, 8 November 1975.

140 British Parliamentary Debates (Commons), vol. 899 (1975), cols. 233–41.
141 *Ibid.*, vol. 900, col. 240.
142 *Irish News*, 1 December 1975.
143 *Ibid.*, 6 December 1975.
144 *Belfast Telegraph*, 5 December 1975.
145 *Ibid.*, 6 January 1976.
146 *Irish News*, 13 January 1976.
147 British Parliamentary Debates (Commons), vol. 906 (1975), col. 1720.
148 *Irish News*, 24 November 1975.
149 *Belfast Telegraph*, 8 May 1975.
150 C. McKeown, 'The New Europa Style SDLP' quoted in O'Malley, *The Uncivil Wars*, pp. 98–9.

6: Isolation and Resignation

1 *Belfast Telegraph*, 28 October 1975.
2 *Ibid.*, 3 March 1979.
3 Margaret Thatcher had become leader of the Conservative Party in 1975.
4 *Belfast Telegraph*, 11 March 1976.
5 *Ibid.*, 31 March 1976.
6 *Ibid.*, 30 April 1976.
7 *Ibid.*, 5 May 1976.
8 *Sunday News*, 6 June 1976.
9 *Belfast Telegraph*, 14 June 1976.
10 P. Devlin, *Straight Left*, p. 261.
11 See *British Parliamentary Debates* (Commons), vol. 913 (1976), cols. 37–100.
12 *Irish News*, 10 August 1976.
13 *Ibid.*
14 *Belfast Telegraph*, 10 August 1976.
15 *Ulster*, August 1976.
16 *Orange Standard*, September 1976.
17 *Daily Mirror*, 10 August 1976.
18 *Sun*, 10 August 1976.
19 *Guardian*, 10 August 1976.
20 *Daily Mail*, 10 August 1976.
21 Revd Martin Smyth, interview by author, 21 August 2006, Belfast; and Gerry Adams, interview by author, 20 February 1990, Belfast.
22 Lord Fitt, interview by author, 27 July 1989, House of Lords.
23 *Irish News*, 31 August 1976.
24 Ivan Cooper, interview by author, 31 July 2006, Belfast
25 Kelley, *The Longest War*, p. 257.
26 *Irish News*, 11 November 1976.
27 Lord Fitt, interview by author, 27 July 1989, House of Lords.
28 Longford and McHardy, *Ulster*, p. 181.
29 *Belfast Telegraph*, 20 September 1976.
30 *The View from the Castle* (Bridge Television, BBC Northern Ireland, October 1988).
31 *Belfast Telegraph*, 11 September 1976.
32 *Irish News*, 17 September 1976.
33 *Ibid.*, 23 September 1976.
34 *Belfast Telegraph*, 6 October 1976.
35 *Ibid.*, 5 November 1976.
36 *Irish News*, 9 November 1976.
37 *Belfast Telegraph*, 4 December 1976.

38 White, *John Hume: Statesman of the Troubles*, p. 197.
39 *Irish News*, 6 December 1976.
40 *Belfast Telegraph*, 6 December 1976.
41 *Irish News*, 6 December 1976.
42 *Belfast Telegraph*, 6 December 1976.
43 *Ibid*.
44 White, *op. cit.*, 197.
45 Currie, *All Hell Will Break Loose*, p. 303.
46 *Belfast Telegraph*, 6 December 1976.
47 *British Parliamentary Debates* (Commons), vol. 923 (1977), vols. 1623–4.
48 *Irish News*, 1 February 1977.
49 A loyalist paramilitary group launched in 1972.
50 *Irish News*, 18 January 1977.
51 *Ibid.*, 4 March 1977.
52 *British Parliamentary Debates* (Commons), vol. 927 (1977), col. 1623.
53 *Irish News*, 24 March 1977.
54 *Belfast Telegraph*, 27 April 1977.
55 *British Parliamentary Debates* (Commons), vol. 931 (1977), col. 1528.
56 *Irish News*, 16 May 1977.
57 *Ibid*
58 The main interrogation centre in Belfast.
59 *Irish News*, 17 May 1977.
60 *Ibid.*, 18 May 1977.
61 *Ibid*
62 *Ibid.*, 23 May 1977.
63 *Belfast Telegraph*, 8 August 1977.
64 *Irish News*, 12 August 1977.
65 *Belfast Telegraph*, 22 August 1977.
66 *Irish Times*, 12–15 August 1977.
67 *Irish News*, 26 August 1977.
68 John Hume, interview by author, 17 April 1989, Derry.
69 Austin Currie, interview by author, 17 April 1989, Derry.
70 Ivan Cooper, interview by author, 31 July 2006, Belfast.
71 Lord Fitt, interview by author, 27 July 1989, House of Lords.
72 Paddy Devlin, interview by author, 25 March 1989, Belfast.
73 Paddy Devlin quoted in Murray, *John Hume and the SDLP*, p. 67.
74 Ivan Cooper, interview by author, 31 July 2006, Belfast.
75 Currie, *op. cit.*, p. 315.
76 *Irish News*, 3 September 1977.
77 Seamus Mallon, interview by author, 28 August 2006, Armagh.
78 Ivan Cooper, interview by author, 31 July 2006, Belfast.
79 *Irish Times* and *Irish News* (Belfast), 8 October 1977.
80 *Belfast Telegraph*, 4 November 1977.
81 *Ibid.*, 5 November 1977.
82 *Ibid.*, 7 November 1977.
83 Currie, *op. cit.*, 306.
84 *Belfast Telegraph*, 21 November 1977.
85 *Irish News*, 21 December 1977.
86 *Ibid.*, 2 February 1978.
87 *Belfast Telegraph*, 3 February 1978.
88 *Ibid*.
89 *Irish News* (Belfast), 31 May 1978.
90 *Ibid.*, 21 June 1978.

91 *Belfast Telegraph*, 18 February 1978.

92 *Irish News*, 20 March 1978.

93 Kelley, *op. cit.*, p. 259.

94 *Irish News*, 27 September 1999.

95 *Belfast Telegraph*, 18 February 1978.

96 Bishop and Mallie, *The Provisional IRA*, pp. 349–50.

97 *Irish News*, 2 August 1978.

98 Lord Fitt, interview by author, 27 July 1989, House of Lords.

99 *Ibid.*

100 *Belfast Telegraph*, 26 August 1978.

101 *Ibid.*

102 *Irish News*, 6 April 1978.

103 *Irish Times*, 6 November 1978.

104 *British Parliamentary Debates* (Commons), vol. 962 (1979), cols. 397–8.

105 *Irish News*, 8 February 1979.

106 *Ibid.*, 5 March 1979.

107 *Belfast Telegraph*, 25 May 1977.

108 *Belfast Telegraph*, 28 June 1977, 29 June 1977, 20 July 1977; and *Irish News*, 1 December 1977.

109 *British Parliamentary Debates* (Commons), vol. 957 (1978), cols. 107–15.

110 *Irish News*, 29 November 1978.

111 *Ibid.*, 30 November 1978.

112 *Irish News*, 10 March 1979.

113 *Ibid.*, 12 March 1979.

114 Longford and McHardy, *Ulster*, p. 281.

115 Enoch Powell had used tactics – including supporting the Labour government – to gain as much advantage as possible from the narrowly balanced parliament.

116 *Belfast Telegraph*, 23 March 1979.

117 *British Parliamentary Debates* (Commons), vol. 965 (1979), cols. 515–22.

118 Lord Fitt, interview by author, 27 July 1989, House of Lords.

119 Callaghan, *Time and Chance*, p. 562.

120 Lord Fitt, interview by author, 27 July 1989, House of Lords.

121 *Ibid.*

122 *Ibid.*

123 Rees, *Northern Ireland: A Personal Perspective*, p. 287.

124 Mason, *Paying the Price*, p. 224.

125 *Belfast Telegraph*, 28 April 1979.

126 *Irish News*, 30 April 1979.

127 In some respects, from the position of the Hume-led SDLP, the return of a strong Tory government could be defended, if only in hindsight. Only a strong right-wing leader could have achieved the Anglo-Irish Agreement of 1985 against the unionists; a weaker Labour administration would never have had the steel to face them down. But from Gerry Fitt's labour perspective it is harder to defend – particularly since by the time of the agreement Fitt was heading in a unionist direction.

128 *Belfast Telegraph*, 2 February 1978.

129 *British Parliamentary Debates* (Commons), vol. 943 (1978), col. 726.

130 Lord Fitt, interview by author, 27 July 1989, House of Lords.

131 *Belfast Telegraph*, 3 February 1978.

132 Flackes, *Northern Ireland: A Political Directory 1968–1983*, pp. 282–3.

133 White, *op. cit.*, p. 204.

134 *Fortnight*, October 1979.

135 *Belfast Telegraph*, 25 June 1979.

136 *Irish News*, 28 August 1979; Lord Fitt, interview by author, 27 July 1989, House of Lords.

137 *Belfast Telegraph*, 1 September 1979.

138 *Irish News* , 3 October 1979.

139 Lord Fitt, interview by author, 27 July 1989, House of Lords.

140 Currie, *op. cit.*, p. 316.

141 Lord Fitt, interview by author, 27 July 1989, House of Lords.

142 For a full report of the ninth annual SDLP conference see *Irish Times* , 5 November 1979.

143 *Belfast Telegraph*, 20 November 1979.

144 Currie, *op. cit.*, p. 315.

145 *Belfast Telegraph*, 22 November 1979.

146 Seamus Mallon, interview by author, 28 August 2006, Armagh.

147 *An Phoblacht/Republican News*, 24 November 1979.

148 *Belfast Telegraph*, 22 November 1979.

149 Ivan Cooper, interview by author, 31 July 2006, Belfast.

150 Currie, *op. cit.*, p. 315.

151 *Irish News*, 23 November 1979.

152 *Belfast News Letter*, 23 November 1979.

153 *Belfast Telegraph*, 22 November 1979.

154 *Ibid.*, 22 November 1979.

155 *Irish Press*, 23 November 1979.

156 *Republican News*, 25 November 1978.

157 *Irish News* , 8 March 1977, 2 May 1977, 13 May 1978; and *Belfast Telegraph*, 9 August 1978, 12 May 1979, 17 September 1979.

158 Lord Fitt, interview by author, 27 July 1989, House of Lords.

159 Seamus Mallon, interview by author, 28 August 2006, Armagh.

160 Lord Fitt, interview by author, 27 July 1989, House of Lords.

161 Eddie McGrady, interview by author, 26 June 2006, Downpatrick.

162 Ivan Cooper, interview by author, 31 July 2006, Belfast.

163 Seamus Mallon, interview by author, 28 August 2006, Armagh.

164 Eddie McGrady, interview by author, 26 June 2006, Downpatrick.

165 Ivan Cooper, interview by author, 31 July 2006, Belfast.

166 Currie, op.cit., p. 314.

167 Seamus Mallon, interview by author, 28 August 2006, Armagh.

168 Ivan Cooper, interview by author, 31 July 2006, Belfast.

169 Seamus Mallon, interview by author, 28 August 2006, Armagh.

170 *Belfast Telegraph*, 3 December 1976.

171 *Irish News*, 25 January 1978.

172 *Irish News*, 17 August 1978.

173 See for example, *British Parliamentary Debates* (Commons), vol. 947 (1978), col. 214; vol. 949 (1978), col. 1392–3; *Written Questions*, vol. 949 (1978), cols. 95, 280, 281, 285, 286, 287, 288, 297–8; vol. 950 (1978), cols. 1954–69. For other examples of Fitt's work to help the unemployed see *Irish News*, 12 May 1978, 23 August 1978, 4 April 1979, 26 June 1979, 9 July 1979.

7: FROM GERRY FITT TO GERRY ADAMS

1 *Belfast Telegraph*, 5 December 1979.

2 *British Parliamentary Debates* (Commons), vol. 980 (1980), cols. 1703–4.

3 *An Phoblacht/Republican News*, 23 June 1979.

4 *Belfast Telegraph*, 28 February 1980.

5 Lord Fitt, interview by author, 27 July 1989, House of Lords.

6 Austin Currie, interview by author, 6 April 1989, Dungannon.

7 Ivan Cooper, interview by author, 31 July 2006, Belfast.

8 Revd Martin Smyth, interview by author, 21 August 2006, Belfast.

9 Murray, *John Hume and the SDLP*, p. 257.

10 Seamus Mallon, interview by author, 28 August 2006, Armagh.

11 Ivan Cooper, interview by author, 31 July 2006, Belfast.

12 *British Parliamentary Debates* (Commons), vol. 980 (1980), vol. 637.

13 *Belfast Telegraph*, 21 March 1980.

14 *Ibid.*

15 *Irish Times*, 29 November 1979.

16 *Fortnight*, July/August 1980.

17 *Irish Times*, 12 August 1980.

18 *British Parliamentary Debates* (Commons), vol. 988 (1980), cols. 591–603.

19 *Belfast Telegraph*, 6 October 1980.

20 *An Phoblacht/Republican News*, 3 May 1980.

21 Lord Fitt, interview by author, 27 July 1989, House of Lords.

22 *British Parliamentary Debates* (Commons), vol. 992 (1980), col. 134.

23 For the full text of Fitt's speech, see *British Parliamentary Debates* (Commons), vol. 992
      (1980), cols. 135–45.

24 Gerry Adams, interview by author, 20 February 1990, Belfast.

25 Lord Fitt, interview by author, 27 July 1989, House of Lords.

26 *Irish News*, 12 November 1980.

27 *Ibid.*

28 *Belfast Telegraph*, 11 November 1980.

29 *Irish Press*, 12 November 1980.

30 *Belfast Telegraph*, 13 November 1980.

31 *Irish News*, 14 November 1980. See also *Irish Times*, 14 November 1980.

32 The British proposal sent to the prisoners was never made public. It seems that the docu-
      ment was largely ambiguous and came nowhere near recognition of political status.

33 *Irish Independent*, 12 January 1981.

34 *Irish News*, 15 January 1981.

35 *Irish News*, 16 March 1981.

36 *Ibid.*

37 *Irish Times*, 27 March 1981.

38 *Belfast Telegraph*, 31March 1981.

39 *Ibid.*

40 *Irish News*, 4 April 1981.

41 *Ibid.*, 6 April 1981.

42 *Irish Press*, 6 April 1981.

43 Flackes, *Northern Ireland: A Political Directory 1968–1983*, p. 285.

44 *Irish News*, 11 April 1981.

45 *Ibid.*

46 *Ibid.*

47 *Ibid.*

48 *Five Seven Live*, RTÉ Radio 1, 26 August 2005.

49 *Irish Times*, 23 May 1981.

50 Lord Fitt, interview by author, 27 July 1989, House of Lords.

51 MacStíofáin, *Memoirs of a Revolutionary*, p. 86.

52 Burton, *The Politics of Legitimacy: Struggles in a Belfast Community*.

53 *Irish News*, 23 May 1981.

54 Ivan Cooper, interview by author, 31 July 2006, Belfast.

55 *Belfast Telegraph*, 26 May 1981.

56 *British Parliamentary Debates* (Commons), vol. 9 (1981), col. 966.

57 *Belfast Telegraph*, 5 August 1981.

58 Flackes, *op. cit.*, p. 285.

59 Lord Fitt, interview by author, 27 July 1989, House of Lords.

60 *Ibid.*

61 *The Times*, 22 September 1981.

62 *Belfast Telegraph*, 23 October 1981.

63 *Ibid.*, 19 August 1981.

64 Lord Fitt, interview by author, 27 July 1989, House of Lords.

65 *An Phoblacht/Republican News*, 5 November 1981.

66 *Irish News*, 2 January 1982.

67 *Irish Independent*, 20 November 1981.

68 *Irish News*, 2 January 1982.

69 This was to be measured as seventy per cent of those elected.

70 In February 1982 Haughey was re-elected Taoiseach after Fitzgerald had called a snap election in a failed attempt to increase support for his seven-month-old administration.

71 *British Parliamentary Debates* (Commons), vol. 21 (1982), col. 698.

72 *Irish News*, 29 April 1982.

73 Prior, *A Balance of Power*, p. 199.

74 *Irish News*, 29 April 1982.

75 *British Parliamentary Debates* (Commons), vol. 24 (1982), col. 651.

76 In April 1982 the Workers' Party became the official name of what had previously been Republican Clubs in Northern Ireland and Official Sinn Féin in the Republic. From this point on in the book, therefore, Provisional Sinn Féin will be referred to as Sinn Féin.

77 *An Phoblacht/Republican News*, 29 April 1982.

78 *British Parliamentary Debates* (Commons), vol. 22 (1982), col. 913.

79 *Ibid.*, vol. 28 (1982), col. 1215.

80 *Irish News*, 28 September 1982.

81 *Ibid.*, 29 September 1982.

82 *Ibid.*

83 *Ibid.*, 2 October 1982.

84 See Flackes, *op. cit.*, p. 287.

85 *Irish News*, 22 October 1982.

86 *Ibid.*

87 *Ibid.*, 3 January 1983.

88 *Ibid.*, 29 January 1983.

89 *Ibid.*, 25 February 1983.

90 *Ibid.*

91 *Ibid.*

92 *Daily Telegraph*, 21 April 1983.

93 *Daily Express*, 21 April 1983.

94 See also L. Curtis, *Ireland: The Propaganda War* (London, Pluto Press, 1984), pp. 185–6.

95 *Irish News*, 20 May 1983.

96 *Belfast Telegraph*, 21 May 1983.

97 *Irish News*, 21 May 1983.

98 *Ibid.*, 28 May 1983.

99 *Ibid.*, 30 May 1983.

100 *Ibid.*

101 *Ibid.*

102 *Orange Standard*, May 1983.

103 *Irish News*, 11 June 1983.

104 *Ibid.*, 7 June 1983.

105 *Ibid.*

106 *Belfast Telegraph*, 10 June 1983.

107 *Irish News*, 11 June 1983.

108 *Belfast News Letter*, 11 June 1983.
109 Revd Martin Smyth, interview by author, 21 August 2006, Belfast.
110 *An Phoblacht/Republican News*, 10 June 1983.
111 *Ulster*, August 1983.
112 The Anglo-Irish Agreement was an agreement between the United Kingdom and the Republic of Ireland signed on 15 November 1985. It gave the Irish government an advisory role in the government of Northern Ireland, while confirming that the state would remain part of the UK unless a majority of its citizens agreed to join the Republic. It also set out conditions for the establishment of a devolved consensus government in the region.
113 By 25 February 1981, unemployment had reached a record level.
114 *The Times*, 11 June 1983.
115 *Cork Examiner*, 11 June 1983.
116 *Irish Press*, 11 June 1983.
117 *Belfast News Letter*, 11 June 1983.
118 *Sunday Times*, 19 June 1983.
119 *Irish News* , 22nd July 1983.
120 *Ibid.*
121 *Ibid.*
122 *Ibid.*, 5 July 1983.
123 *Ibid.*
124 Lord Fitt, interview by author, 27 July 1989, House of Lords.
125 *Irish Independent*, 22 July 1983.
126 *Irish News*, 22 July 1983.
127 Ivan Cooper, interview by author, 31 July 2006, Belfast.
128 Eddie McGrady, interview by author, 26 June 2006, Downpatrick.
129 Seamus Mallon, interview by author, 28 August 2006, Armagh.
130 *British Parliamentary Debates* (Lords), vol. 444 (1983), col. 245.
131 Lord Fitt, interview by author, 27 July 1989, House of Lords.
132 *Irish News*, 27 October 1983.

8: LORD FITT OF BELL'S HILL

1 Roy Hattersley served as deputy leader of the Labour Party from 1983 to 1992.
2 Observer, 13 July 2003.
3 G. Adams, *Before the Dawning* (Kerry, Brandon Books, 1996), p. 299.
4 Lord Fitt, interview by author, 27 July 1989, House of Lords.
5 British Parliamentary Debates (Lords), vol. 445 (1983), col. 24.
6 *Ibid.*, col. 1118.
7 *Ibid.*, vol. 467 (1985), col. 160–1.
8 *Ibid.*, vol. 468 (1985), col. 818.
9 *Ibid.*, vol. 489 (1987), col. 1221.
10 *Sunday Times*, 20 March 1988.
11 Currie, *All Hell Will Break Loose*, p. 417.
12 The Downing Street Declaration was a joint declaration issued on 15 December 1993 by the two governments. It affirmed the right of the people of Northern Ireland to self-determination. It also pledged the governments to seek a peaceful constitutional settlement, and promised that parties linked with paramilitaries could take part in a settlement as long as they abandoned violence.
13 *The Times*, 5 August 1994.
14 *Ibid.*
15 British Parliamentary Debates (Lords), vol. 558 (1994), col. 52.
16 John Major became leader of the Conservative Party on 27 November 1990. The next day

he was appointed prime minister.

17 A republican paramilitary group composed of disaffected members of the IRA.

18 British Parliamentary Debates (Lords), vol. 575 (1996), col. 1437.

19 *Ibid.*, vol. 468 (1985), col. 814.

20 *Ibid.*, vol. 445 (1983), col. 24.

21 Currie *op cit.*, p.314

22 This general election took place in May 1997.

23 British Parliamentary Debates (Lords), vol. 575 (1996), col. 1439.

24 *Belfast Telegraph*, 28 May 1997.

25 British Parliamentary Debates (Lords), vol. 604 (1999), col. 352.

26 'The Irish Question – Challenge to Democratic Britain', Conference Report, 25 February 1967. p12 – 13

27 Fitt's closing statement to this speech is not reported in the official record but it is in the March edition of the *Irish Democrat*.

28 British Parliamentary Debates (Lords), vol. 453 (1984), col. 405–6.

29 New Ireland Forum Report, para. 3.15 (Dublin, Stationery Office, May 1984).

30 British Parliamentary Debates (Lords), vol. 453 (1984), col. 407.

31 *Ibid.*, col. 410.

32 *Ibid.*, col. 409.

33 *Ibid.*, vol. 558 (1985), col. 819.

34 *Ibid.*, col. 818.

35 *Ibid.*, col. 816.

36 *Ibid.*, col. 818.

37 *Irish News* , 29 December 2005.

38 British Parliamentary Debates (Lords), vol. 437 (1986), col. 96.

39 *Ibid.*

40 *Ibid.*, vol. 439 (1988), col. 674–5.

41 *Ibid.*, col. 674.

42 P. Devlin, *Straight Left*, p. 279.

43 *The Times*, 5 August 1994.

44 *Sunday Press*, 30 August 1970.

45 British Parliamentary Debates (Lords), vol. 437 (1984), col. 405.

46 *Ibid.*, col. 406.

47 *Ibid.*, col. 409.

48 *Ibid.*, vol. 468 (1985), col. 813.

49 *Ibid.*, col. 817.

50 *Ibid.*, col. 812.

51 Eddie McGrady, interview by author, 26 June 2006, Downpatrick.

52 British Parliamentary Debates (Lords), vol. 530 (1991), col. 1005.

53 *Ibid.*

54 *Ibid.*, vol. 530 (1991), col. 1005.

55 *Ibid.*, vol. 540 (1992), col. 226.

56 *Ibid.*, vol. 550 (1993), col. 449.

57 *Ibid.*, col. 450.

58 *Ibid.*

59 Albert Reynolds was Taoiseach of the Republic from 1992 to 1994.

60 *The Times*, 5 August 1994.

61 British Parliamentary Debates (Lords), vol. 558 (1994), col. 51.

62 *Ibid.*, vol. 558 (1994), col. 52.

63 *Ibid.*, col. 53.

64 *Ibid.*

65 *Ibid.*, col. 54.

66 The Ulster Democratic Party was the political party of the UDA, formed in 1989.

67 The Progressive Unionist Party is linked to the Ulster Volunteer Force. It was formed in 1979.

68 George Mitchell is a former Democratic Party politician and United States senator from the state of Maine. Since 1995 he has been active in the Northern Ireland peace process. He led a commission that established the principles of non-violence to which all parties in Northern Ireland had to adhere and later chaired the all-party peace negotiations that led to the Belfast Peace Agreement signed on Good Friday 1998.

69 British Parliamentary Debates (Lords), vol. 569 (1996), Col. 418.

70 Ibid., col. 419.

71 The Times, 5 August 1994.

72 British Parliamentary Debates (Lords), vol. 575, (1996) col. 1438.

73 John White was responsible for the murders of SDLP senator Paddy Wilson and Irene Andrews, Wilson's Protestant friend, in 1973. White confessed to the murder in 1978 and was sentenced to life imprisonment. On his release in 1992, White joined the Ulster Democratic Party and helped broker a loyalist ceasefire. He was initially a strong supporter of the Good Friday Agreement.

74 British Parliamentary Debates (Lords), vol. 575 (1996), col. 1438.

75 Irish News, 29 May 1997.

76 British Parliamentary Debates (Lords), vol. 575 (1996), col. 789.

77 Ibid.

78 Ibid., vol. 588 (1998), col. 942.

79 Sunday Times, 5 December 1999.

80 British Parliamentary Debates (Lords), vol. 589 (1998), col. 942.

81 Ibid., vol. 592 (1998), col. 981.

82 Ibid., col. 982.

83 Sunday Times, 5 December 1999.

84 British Parliamentary Debates (Lords), vol. 639 (2002), col. 766.

CONCLUSION:

1. F. S. L. Lyons, Ireland since the Famine (London: Fontanna, 1985), 261.

2 Eddie McGrady, interview by author, 26 June 2006, Downpatrick

3 Lord Fitt, interview by author, 19 December 1988, House of Lords, London.

4 Reverend Martin Smyth, interview by author, 21 August 2006, Belfast. Smyth's argument is reminiscent of the Redmondite criticisms of Sinn Fein, who they labelled 'little Irelanders' because their horizons were seen as too narrow in comparison to the British Empire that Redmondism aspired to be an active part of.

5 Seamus Mallon, interview by author, 28 August 2006, Armagh.

6 Independent, 14 December 1987.

7 Belfast Telegraph 19 August 1981.

8 Peter McLachlan, interview by Gordon Gillespie, 14 February, 1991, Belfast.

9 Belfast News Letter, 25 March 1992.

10 Ivan Cooper, interview by author, 31 July 2006, Belfast

11 British Parliamentary Debates (Lords), vol.571, (1996) Col. 1295.

12 Sunday Press 30 August 1970

13 Reverend Martin Smyth, Interview by author, 21 August 2006

14 In September 1989 Sir John Stevens was appointed to enquire into breaches of security by the Security Forces in Northern Ireland. Known as the 'Stevens Inquiry' it resulted in 43 convictions and over 800 years imprisonment for those convicted.

15 Irish Times 14 June 2002.

16 Ivan Cooper, interview by author, 31 July 2006, Belfast

17 F. O'Connor, In Search of a State-Catholics in Northern Ireland (Belfast: Blackstaff Press, 1993), p. 64.

18 C.King, Diary 1970 – 1974 (London: Jonathan Cape Ltd., 1975), p. 341.
19 Ivan Cooper, interview by author, 31 July 2006, Belfast
20 *Sunday Mirror Magazine* (London), 6 May 1990.
21 *Irish News*, 14 August 1989.

Epilogue

1 *British Parliamentary Debates* (Lords), vol.669 (2005), col. 61. Fitt was referring to the IRA's bombing of the South Quay in the Docklands area of London on Friday 9 February 1996.
2 *Ibid.*, vol. 618 (2000), cols. 30–1.
3 *Irish News* (Belfast) 10 November 2000.
4 *Ibid.*
5 *Ibid.*
6 Whitelaw, *The Whitelaw Memoirs*, p. 118.
7 *Daily Telegraph*, 21 November 2000.
8 *British Parliamentary Debates* (Lords), vol. 619 (2000), col. 537.
9 *Ibid.*, vol. 558, (1994), col. 51–6.
10 *Ibid.*, vol. 637 (2002), col. 380.
11 www.sdlp.ie/prdurkanremembersgerryfitt.shtm, August 2005.
12 *Ibid.*
13 *Irish News*, 14 March 2006.
14 *Irish Times*, 27 August 2005.
15 *Sunday Times*, 28 August 2005.
16 *Irish News*, 14 March 2006.
17 *The Scotsman*, 27 August 2005.
18 *Conservative Future*, 31 August 2005.
19 *This Week*, RTÉ Radio, 28 August 2005.
20 *Belfast Telegraph*, 27 August 2005.
21 Revd Martin Smyth, interview with author, 21 August 2006, Belfast.
22 *Sunday Life*, 29 August 2005.
23 *Irish News*, 27 August 2005.
24 *Irish Times*, 31 August 2005.
25 *Sunday Times*, 5 December 1999.
26 *Dáil Éireann Debates*, vol. 512 (1999), col. 34.
27 www.sdlp.ie/prdurkanremembersgerryfitt.shtm, August 2005.
28 Murray and Tonge, *Sinn Féin and the SDLP from Alienation to Participation*, p. 255.
29 *Dáil Éireann Debates*, vol. 512 (1999), col. 40.
30 *Irish News*, 2 March 2004.
31 John Kelly, interview by author, 21 September 2006.
32 Murray and Tonge, op.cit., pp. 208–9.
33 *The Scotsman*, 27 August 2005.
34 *British Parliamentary Debates* (Lords), vol. 669 (2005), col. 1206.

Select Bibliography

Primary Sources:

Interviews:

Gerry Adams, president of Sinn Féin, 20 February 1990.

Ivan Cooper, founder member of the Social Democratic and Labour Party, 31 July 2006.

Austin Currie, founder member of the Social Democratic and Labour Party, 6 April 1989.

Paddy Devlin, founder member of the Social Democratic and Labour Party, 25 March 1989.

Lord Fitt, former leader of the Social Democratic and Labour Party, 19 December 1988 and 27 July 1989.

John Hume, former leader of the Social Democratic and Labour Party, 17 April 1989.

Joseph Lavery, former member of the National Democratic Party, 23 June 2006.

John Kelly, Belfast republican and founding member of the Provisional Irish Republican Army, 21 September 2006.

Seamus Mallon, former deputy leader of the Social Democratic and Labour Party, 28 August 2006.

Bernadette McAliskey (Devlin), former MP and civil rights activist, 7 June 1989.

Eamonn McCann, writer and member of the Socialist Workers Party, 26 June 2006.

Eddie McGrady, MP for South Down, 26 June 2006.

Séan Redmond, former General Secretary of the Connolly Association, 10 December 2006.

Revd Martin Smyth, former grand master of the Orange Order and MP for South Belfast, August 21 2006.

Correspondance:

Anthony Coughlan, Connolly Association activist, December 2006

Roy Johnston, Connolly Association activist, December 2006

Collections

Linenhall Library, Belfast. Files: Northern Ireland Election Manifestos.

Government Reports

Assembly Debates, vols 1–3. Official Report. HMSO, 1973–4.

British Parliamentary Debates (Commons). Official Report. HMSO, 1966–83.

British Parliamentary Debates (Lords). Official Report. HMSO, 1981–2005.

Constitutional Convention. Official Report. HMSO, 1975–6.

Disturbances in Northern Ireland (Cameron Report), Cmd. 532, HMSO Belfast, 1969.

New Ireland Forum Report, Dublin, May 1984.

Northern Ireland Parliamentary Debates (Commons). Official Report. HMSO, 1964–72.

Violence and Civil Disturbances (Scarman Report), Cmd. 566, HMSO Belfast, 1969.

SECONDARY SOURCES:

BOOKS:

Adams, G., *The Politics of Irish Freedom* (Belfast, Brandon Books, 1986).

Arthur, P., *The People's Democracy 1968–73* (Belfast, Blackstaff Press, 1974).

Bardon, J., *A History of Ulster* (Belfast, Blackstaff Press, 1992).

Bell, G., *The Protestants of Ulster* (London, Pluto Press, 1973).

Beresford, D., *Ten Men Dead: The Story of the 1981 Irish Hunger Strike* (London, Grafton Books, 1987).

Bew, P. and Gillespie, G., *Northern Ireland: A Chronology of the Troubles 1968–93* (Dublin, Gill and Macmillan, 1993).

Bew, P., Gibbon, P. and Patterson, H., *The State in Northern Ireland 1921–72* (Manchester, Manchester University Press, 1979).

Bew, P. and Patterson, H., *The British State and the Ulster Crisis: from Wilson to Thatcher* (London, Verso, 1985).

_____. *Seán Lemass and the Making of Modern Ireland* (Dublin, Gill and Macmillan, 1982).

Bishop, P. and Mallie, E., *The Provisional IRA* (London, Corgi Books, 1988).

Bleakley, D., Faulkner: *Conflict and Consent in Irish Politics* (Oxford, A. R. Mowbray, 1974).

Boland, K., *We Won't Stand Idly By* (Dublin, Kelley Kane, 1972).

Boulton, D., *The UVF 1966–73* (Dublin, Gill and Macmillan, 1973).

Bowyer Bell, J., *The Secret Army: The IRA 1916–79* (Dublin, Academy Press, 1979).

Boyd, A., *Holy War in Belfast* (New York, Grove Press, 1969).

_____. *Brian Faulkner and the Crisis of Ulster Unionists* (Tralee, Anvil Books, 1973).

Boyce, D. G., *Irish Nationalism* (London, Croom Helm, 1982).

Boyle, K., Hadden, T. and Hillyard, P., *Ten Years in Northern Ireland* (London, Cobden Trust, 1980).

Bruce, S., *God Save Ulster: The Religion and Politics of Paisleyism* (Oxford, Clarendon Press, 1986).

Buckland, P., *A History of Northern Ireland* (Dublin, Gill and Macmillan, 1981).

Budge, I. and O'Leary, C. *Belfast: Approach to Crisis. A Study of Belfast Politics 1603–1970* (London, Macmillan, 1973).

Burton, F., *The Politics of Legitimacy: Struggles in a Belfast Community* (London, RKP, 1978).

Butler, D. E. and King, A. (eds) *The British General Election of 1966* (London, Macmillan, 1967)

Callaghan, J., *A House Divided* (London, Collins, 1973).

_____. *Time and Chance* (London, Collins, 1987).

Clark, D. J., *Irish Blood* (New York, Kennikat Press, 1977).

Clifford, B. *Connolly Cut Outs* (Belfast: Athol Books, 1984).

Coogan, T. P., *On the Blanket* (Dublin, Ward River, 1980.

_____. *The IRA* (London, Fontana, 1980).

_____. *The Troubles: Ireland's Ordeal 1966–1995 and the Search for Peace* (London, Hutchinson, 1995).

Cronin, S., *Irish Nationalism* (London, Pluto Press, 1984).

Currie, A., *All Hell Will Break Loose* (Dublin, O'Brien Press, 2004).

Darby, J., *Conflict in Northern Ireland* (Dublin, Gill and Macmillan, 1976).

Devlin, P., *The Fall of the Northern Ireland Executive* (Tralee, Kerryman, 1975).

_____. *Straight Left* (Belfast, Blackstaff, 1993).

Dillon, M. and Lehane, D., *Political Murder in Northern Ireland* (London, Penguin Books, 1973).

Ditch, J., *Social Policy in Northern Ireland 1939–1950* (Aldershot, Avebury, 1988).

Edwards, D. D. and Ranson, B. (eds), *James Connolly: Selected Political Writings* (London, Cape, 1973).

Farrell, M., *Northern Ireland: The Orange State* (London, Pluto Press, 1976).

Faulkner, B., *Memoirs of a Statesman* (London, Weidenfield and Nicolson, 1978).

Fisk, R., *The Point of No Return: The Strike which Broke the British in Ulster* (London, Andre Deutsch, 1975).

Flackes, W. D., *Northern Ireland: A Political Directory 1968–1983* (London, BBC, 1983).

Garvin, T., *The Evolution of Irish Nationalist Politics* (Dublin, Gill and Macmillan, 1981).

Gillespie, G., *Albert H McElroy: The Radical Minister 1915–1975* (Belfast, McElroy Memorial Fund, 1985).

Greaves, C. D., *The Life and Times of James Connolly* (London, Lawrence and Wishart, 1961).

Hall, M., *20 Years: A Concise Chronology of Events in Northern Ireland from 1968 to 1988* (Newtownabbey, Island Publications, 1988).

Hamill, D., *Pig in the Middle: The Army in Northern Ireland 1969–1984* (London, Methuen, 1985).

Harbinson, J. F., *The Ulster Unionist Party 1882–1973* (Belfast, Blackstaff Press, 1973).

Hepburn, A. C., *The Conflict of Nationality in Modern Ireland.* (London, Edward Arnold, 1980).

Johnston. R. *Century of Endeavour*, Dublin (Tyndall/Lilliput 2006).

Kee, R., *The Green Flag: A History of Irish Nationalism* (London, Weidenfield and Nicholson, 1972).

Kelley, K., *The Longest War: Northern Ireland and the IRA* (Dingle, Brandon Books, 1982).

Kelly, H., *How Stormont Fell* (London, Gill and Macmillan, Dublin, 1972).

Kelly, J., *The Thimbleriggers* (Dublin, Sarsfield Press, 1999).

Longford, Lord and McHardy, A., *Ulster* (London, Weidenfield and Nicolson, 1981).

Lyons, F. S. L., *Ireland since the Famine* (London, Weidenfield and Nicolson, 1971).

MacStíofáin, S., *Memoirs of a Revolutionary* (Edinburgh, Cremonesi, 1975).

Maguire, M., *To Take Arms* (London, Macmillan, 1973).

Marrinan, P., *Paisley* (Tralee, Anvil Books, 1973).

Mason, R., *Paying the Price* (London, Hale, 1999).

McAllister, I., *The Northern Ireland Social Democratic and Labour Party* (London, Macmillan, 1977).

McCann, E., *War and an Irish Town* (London, Pluto Press, 1981).

McGuffin, J., *Internment* (Tralee: Anvil Books, 1973).

Miller, D., *Queen's Rebels* (Dublin, Gill and Macmillan, 1978).

Moloney, E. and Pollack, A., *Paisley* (Dublin, Poolbeg Press, 1986).

Murphy, J. A., *Ireland in the Twentieth Century* (Dublin, Gill and Macmillan, 1975.)

Murray, G., *John Hume and the SDLP* (Dublin, Irish Academic Press, 1998).

Murray, G. and Tonge, J., *Sinn Féin and the SDLP from Alienation to Participation* (Dublin, O'Brien, 2005).

Nelson, S., *Ulster's Uncertain Defenders* (Belfast, Appletree Press, 1984).

O'Brien, C. C., *States of Ireland* (London, Hutchinson, 1972).

O'Brien, J., *The Arms Crisis* (Dublin, Gill and Macmillan, 2000).

O'Connor, F., *In Search of a State-Catholics in Northern Ireland* (Belfast, Blackstaff Press, 1993).

O'Malley, P., *The Uncivil Wars* (Belfast, Blackstaff Press, 1983).

O'Neill, T., *The Autobiography of Terence O'Neill, Prime Minister of Northern Ireland 1963–1969* (London, Rupert Hart-Davis, 1972).

O'Riordan, M. *James Connolly Re-assessed* (Aubane Historical Society, Millstreet, Co. Cork, 2006).

Patterson, H., *Class Conflict and Sectarianism* (Belfast, Blackstaff Press, 1981).

Peck, J., *Dublin from Downing Street* (London, Gill and Macmillan, 1978).

Phoenix, E. *Northern Nationalism: Nationalist Politics, Partition and the Catholic Minority in Northern Ireland, 1890–1940* (Ulster Historical Foundation, Oct. 1994)

Prior, J., *A Balance of Power* (London, Hamilton, 1986).

Probert, B., *Beyond Orange and Green* (London, Zed Press, 1978).

Rees, M., *Northern Ireland: A Personal Perspective* (London, Methuen, 1985).

Rose, R., *Government without Consensus. An Irish Perspective* (London, Faber and Faber, 1971).

Roth, A., *Heath and the Heathmen* (London, RKP, 1972).

Rumpf, E. and Hepburn, A. D., *Nationalism and Socialism in Twentieth-Century Ireland* (Liverpool: Liverpool University Press, 1977).

Ryder, C. *Fighting Fitt* (Brehon Press, Belfast 2006)

Stewart, A. T. Q., *The Narrow Ground* (Belfast, Pretani Press, 1986).

Sunday Times Insight Team, *Ulster* (London, Penguin, 1972).

Target, G. W., *Bernadette* (London, Hodder and Stoughton, 1975).

Utley, T. E., *Lessons of Ulster* (London, J. M. Dent and Sons, 1975).

White, B. *John Hume: Statesman of the Troubles* (Belfast, Blackstaff Press, 1984).

Whitelaw W. *The Whitelaw Memoirs* (London, Aurum, 1989).

THESES:

Greene, J. T., 'The Comparative Development of the SDLP and Sinn Féin 1972–1985', MSc thesis, Queen's University, Belfast, 1986.

NEWSPAPERS:

NORTHERN IRELAND, 1958–2005:

Andersonstown News. Belfast, weekly.

An Phoblacht/Republican News. Weekly newspaper of Sinn Féin, Belfast Dublin.

Belfast News Letter. Belfast, daily.

Belfast Telegraph. Belfast, evening newspaper.

Combat. Monthly journal of the Ulster Volunteer Force, Belfast.

Fortnight. Belfast, fortnightly or monthly.

Free Citizen Unfree Citizen. Publication of People's Democracy.

Irish News. Belfast, daily.

Loyalist News. Belfast, monthly.

New Nation. Publication of National Unity.

Northern Ireland Civil Rights Association Bulletin. Londonderry, monthly.

Orange Standard. Belfast, weekly.

Protestant Telegraph. Weekly newspaper of Ian Paisley's Free Presbyterian Church, Belfast.

Resistance. Newspaper of the New Lodge, Belfast.

Sunday Life. Belfast, weekly.

Sunday News. Belfast, weekly.

UDA News. Belfast, monthly.

Ulster. Monthly journal of the Ulster Defence Association, Belfast.

Republic of Ireland, 1958–2005:

Cork Examiner. Cork, daily.

Hibernia. Dublin, weekly or fortnightly.

Irish Independent. Dublin, daily.

Irish Press. Dublin, daily.

Irish Times. Dublin, daily.

Sunday Independent. Dublin, weekly.

Sunday Press - Dublin weekly

Britain 1958–2005:

Daily Express. London, daily.

Daily Mail. London, daily.

Daily Mirror. London, daily.

Daily Telegraph. London, daily.

Guardian. London and Manchester, daily.

Irish Democrat. The bi-monthly newspaper of the Connolly Association.

The Scotsman. Edinburgh, daily.

Sun. London, daily.

The Times. London, daily.

Sunday Mirror Magazine. London, weekly.

Sunday Times. London, weekly.

Website:

CAIN web service. Conflict and politics in Northern Ireland (1968 to the present).

INDEX